Malcolm Wright is an Australian maritime artist who is also an internationally-known wargames designer and writer and lecturer. He has spent five decades researching this volume, making notes while interviewing veterans, as well as consulting official sources, photographs and the work of artists of the era. He lives in Adelaide.

British and Commonwealth WARSHIP CAMOUFLAGE of WWII

MALCOLM WRIGHT

Destroyers, Frigates, Escorts, Minesweepers, Coastal Warfare Craft, Submarines & Auxiliaries

DEDICATION

This volume is dedicated to the memory of my late father-in-law, Royal Marine Andrew Wall, of Cobh, Ireland, who served through the Battle of the Atlantic 1939–45. He was present at the sinking of the *Bismarck* and at the Battle of North Cape, with most of his service being on HMS *Belfast*.

Copyright © Malcolm Wright 2014

This paperback edition first published in 2023 by

Seaforth Publishing,
George House,
Units 12 & 13,
Beevor Street,
Barnsley, S71 1HN.

www.seaforthpublishing.com

British Library Cataloguing in Publication Data
A catalogue record for this book is available from the British Library

ISBNs
978 1 3990 2486 0 (Paperback)
978 1 84832 271 4 (Kindle)
978 1 84832 272 1 (Epub)

All rights reserved. No part of this publication may be reproduced or transmitted in any form or by any means, electronic or mechanical, including photocopying, recording, or any information storage and retrieval system, without prior permission in writing of both the copyright owner and the above publisher.

The right of Malcolm Wright to be identified as the author of this work has been asserted by him in accordance with the Copyright, Designs and Patents Act 1988.

Typeset and designed by Stephen Dent.
Printed and bound in India by Replika Press Pvt. Ltd.

CONTENTS

	Introduction	6
	Reference Sources	10
	Abbreviations	11
1	Destroyers Built to WWI Programmes	13
2	Destroyers Built Between the Wars	31
3	Early WWII Destroyers	48
4	War-Built Destroyers	57
5	'Hunt' Class Escort Destroyers	66
6	Sloops	74
7	Frigates	88
8	Corvettes	97
9	Minesweepers	108
10	Trawlers	121
11	Auxiliary AA ships	130
12	Coastal Warfare Craft	135
13	Submarines	144
14	Miscellaneous Vessels	148
	Index	158

INTRODUCTION

This work was inspired by friends and readers of my WWII *Convoy* series of wargame books who felt I should publish the hundreds of colour drawings of ships that I have made over the years as well as my maritime paintings and cover art. They were gathered together over the past fifty years, sometimes from descriptions given by veterans, models in museums, works of art, etc. Where I have remembered the sources, these have been included in the bibliography. Many were taken from a study of war art that I did some decades ago. There are some which, across half a century, I have simply forgotten the origin of. In these cases where mistakes occur in the drawings I have produced, I accept full blame.

One of the first occasions on which I recall realising the importance of paint schemes used in war was when, as a boy, and later as a young man, I spent many hours in the company of various naval veterans of several nations, particularly British and Australian. Of great value was that I was able to meet two men who had served in naval dockyards: one of the two in Sydney, Australia, and the other in three dockyards in the UK from slightly before the war to just after it. It was fortunate that I met these men in the prime of their lives with memories still fresh and not distorted or dulled by age and the years in between.

These hours were many decades ago and the veterans have sadly all passed on. How I wish they were still here so I could clarify some things with them. They were kind enough to help me match colours on various model ships I built and with some of my early art work. There were colours that I found hard to imagine being used in my young days but, of course, since then there have been publications showing the paint schemes for a whole range of ships. Today we know much more about them, but even so many records were destroyed or lost. I remember one ex-sailor laughing that HMAS *Hobart* arrived in Fremantle from the Mediterranean painted pink. In his story, he said he thought it was because they had mixed undercoat into grey because they were short of paint, but as soon as the ship arrived in Sydney they painted it grey again. He had obviously never heard of the famous Mountbatten Pink scheme, and nor had I, so I was unsure if he was just telling a tall tale. In later years, I realised what he had seen was a well-used camouflage scheme in the Mediterranean theatre of war up till late 1942.

An analysis of colour photographs is helpful but the film used in WWII is not necessarily true to shade, with many colours appearing darker or lighter than in real life due to poor-quality film or just tricks of the light. But black and white photographs can be quite helpful if you have access to the shades that were available and which were probably used on the ship in question. With patient research, it is possible to reconstruct schemes.

In this manner, and with a lot of detective work, I have assembled line drawings of the hundreds of ships that appear in this series. If any are wrong, then, again, I accept responsibility, but would point out that in some cases there are no hard references and therefore my deductions are probably as good as any.

In some instances I was able to use the work of earlier authors for reference or to check my own research against theirs. I have not always totally agreed with some and if my drawings vary from other sources it is because that is my opinion based on the research of many decades. Sometimes the difference may be merely the size and shape of a squiggle or triangle or the exact tint of the shade.

This book is intended as a quick reference source for people wanting to paint model ships as a hobby, for wargaming or art. Mostly I show only the starboard side of a ship. This is because I found in research that a remarkable number of starboard-side views were able to be interpreted compared to far fewer port-side views. It must be kept in mind that some ships did have a different layout on each side. Others did not and, of course, many standard schemes had to be identical on either side.

I have not listed them by camouflage scheme, rather by ship type. This should enable the reader to go straight to the ship type wanted and find an appropriate scheme. They are also listed by name and, while not all the ships of each class are always shown, I have nonetheless included a lot of them, so the reader can also often chose by name when painting a model. The classes include ships that were British Commonwealth-built yet manned by other navies in exile. I have occasionally included ships that were captured to show how they looked in enemy hands. There were few of them, but the changes are of great interest.

Overhead views are included with some ships as concealment from aircraft was important for much of WWII. However, where not shown, it was common to paint upper surfaces grey or in the case of Cemtex to leave it in its natural grey. Some camouflage schemes were carried across the deck. But by and large the easiest way was to use grey, even if it meant painting over wooden decks that had been kept holystoned for years by the sweat of sailors.

One of the very important issues for those painting models to remember is that sometimes there is no exact shade. There may well be a recommended shade, and even a paint guide with colour chips to go with it, but you must put yourself in the shoes of the sailors of the day. Imagine you have been at sea with a convoy for a week or two; you arrive back in harbour exhausted, in need of rest. But half the ship is sent off for a few quick days leave and the others remain behind to carry out minor maintenance. This usually meant either touching up the paintwork or preparing it for the half on leave to tackle when they returned. Laid out in front of you is a sort of cook book telling you to add this much of a certain pigment to that much white or grey and the result will be the shade specified for a particular scheme. But you are tired, or perhaps the ship is on standby to leave harbour on yet another mission. So your level of care when told to add a cup of this to a tin of that can be rather less than ideal. The famous 'TLAR' comes into effect. The buffer puts in the pigment, a seaman stirs it, they look at the result and say 'That looks about right'.

Veteran after veteran told me how arduous the task of chipping rust and repainting was. It was hated. This was even more so by tired men waiting for the rest of their shipmates to get back so they could get a few days leave themselves. So up until 1943 we must accept some of the official Admiralty shades with a pinch of salt. Even they accepted that a ship may not have the right amount of paint and recommended a scheme be as near as possible. In some cases this meant the colours might not even be the same, in which instance the recommendation was that they be of similar shade tone. Hence pale blue was often used instead of pale green and vice versa. No ship was going to be held back from her vital role in war just because the paint scheme was not exact.

From 1943 onward this was eased (though never fully overcome). That was because the Admiralty started to issue ready-mixed paint to the ships along with full instructions for specific schemes. Thus in later wartime photography we are more likely to see ships looking much the same shade when wearing various regulation schemes. Also new ships coming from the shipyard would have been painted in the yard using paint delivered for the purpose.

But, to emphasise, it was never <u>fully</u> overcome, because there were often shortages and a ship might have to make do with what was available to the crew to use. There were instances of there being insufficient of a particular shade to cover the amount of area intended so that area was either made smaller than specified, or often the problem was solved by mixing some other spare paint to eke out the shade that was running out. Therefore you should never assume a ship is exactly one shade or another regardless of what official records might state.

The most reliable paint jobs were those provided by the various yards while ships were in for refit or repair. The crew were usually not involved and the work was carried out by workers under the supervision of a foreman painter. But even here many were not familiar with naval requirements and despite written instructions they could easily get things wrong under the pressure to get the job done and on to the next one. Firstly, they had to mark out the areas of the ship to be painted. One of the gentlemen I met who had worked in a naval dockyard said they would take measurements from drawings provided and mark the areas with a large lump of chalk. On each side of those lines they painted a dab of the shade required and moved on to another area. The painters then got to work and filled in the marked-out areas. Sometimes there was an 'oops' moment and a straight line now had a bend in it, or a curve was a bit flatter than originally intended. But in general it would be as marked. But of course the markings depended on the accuracy of the measurements in the first place. Hence one foreman docker might get a few things wrong that another got right. Similarly, from ship to ship supposedly painted in the same pattern these human errors were present. It is very important to remember this. The accuracy of the pattern depended on the human who marked it out in the first place. Inexperienced foreman painters could make some howlers. I have included one ship where the flag superior and pennant has been painted on along with the abbreviations intended only as notes for his reference. I have seen this in photographs on two occasions. Even shipyards ran short of paint and rather than hold a vessel up from entering service it would be sent to sea with whatever was available. This explains why the reader will see ships of exactly the same class, but which, although painted similarly, the colours may not necessarily be the same.

The gentleman I met years ago who had worked in Royal Dockyards told me that, when he started work there a few years before WWII, there were stocks of paint on hand. But they were limited to specific colours only: Primrose, buff, dark grey, light grey, white and black. Sometimes there was a quantity of Brunswick green. And always lots and lots of red lead undercoat. Therefore, when a ship required painting, or for the paint locker to be filled, they were the only ones on offer. It should therefore be no surprise that early schemes, which were worked out by the officers of the ship, would be based around what they had, or what they could mix with those shades.

During research for the 'Insect' class gunboats I was aware that, having been stationed in China, they would have had lots of buff and white as part of the normal stores in the paint locker. In later reading I came across a verbal account of HMS *Ladybird* having been given an emergency coating of 'stone' during the period she spent defending Tobruk harbour and needed to hide close to the shore during the day using an inlet to avoid German aircraft. There are two possibilities. One is that there were still some stores of buff on board and these were combined with white to produce stone. But then again, when on passage from China under tow, the ships of the class were stripped of armament and almost everything else. So when they were rearmed and refitted at Bombay it would have needed the original contents of the paint locker to have been put back aboard after being transported all the way from the Far East. That sounded unlikely. Then it occurred to me that I knew a gentleman who had been a stores officer with the Australian Army and was at Tobruk. In conversation with him it became obvious that they had stores of British army paint in the port and that, if the RN had asked to borrow some, there would have been little dispute about it as daily air raids were destroying so much anyway. Therefore the RN could have 'found it' or were given some stone on asking. As the *Ladybird* was considered of great value to the army, due to her gunnery support, I formed the opinion that it was more likely that the actual stone colour mentioned in writing was in fact army stone as used on vehicles and tanks. I have no proof, but it is a logical deduction. One should not pass up the chance to think these things out.

Other issues affected how a ship looked. The sudden demand for masses of paint was a major problem for all the nations involved. Even the USA, with its vast resources, ran short from time to time. This meant that sometimes the pigments accepted were below standard and faded very quickly. Those who have looked at photographs of US warships in dark navy blue will realise how quickly that faded, often in patches. US shipyards were churning out ships at a prodigious rate and, rather than delay them, new ships could be painted in what was available and the task of providing the correct shades left to the dockyard where the ship had its first refit, or for the crew to alter during the working-up period. Getting the ships completed and at sea was more important than the exact shade of paint.

In addition to poor-quality pigments fading, there were at times great difficulties in supplying particular colours. Green, for example, was in high demand by the Army and the Air Force as part of their camouflage schemes. Many shades of khaki required green pigment too, as did olive drab. For this reason, green was often not available for warships and other colours had to be substituted. Blue was in less demand by the other services and therefore pale blue often stood in for pale green in naval schemes. Indeed there were many shades of blue and blue grey used although the designer of a particular scheme may have specified green of various hues.

Lastly, not only were paint schemes affected by shortage of pigments, the 'TLAR' system, fading and wrong colours being available, there was also the effect of seawater on the paint itself. Ships spending lots of time at sea suffer salt corrosion and become rusty. Paint can bubble up in rust patches and flake off, exposing previous paint colours underneath. For some paint schemes this effect was very bad. White and other pale shades of the famous Western Approaches Scheme became much less effective once they became rusty. For larger ships with more crew available, touching up was much easier. But, for small vessels, keeping up with the effects of rust was very difficult. As mentioned earlier, a ship returning from some arduous mission would return to harbour with a very tired crew and touching up the paintwork was secondary to getting a good rest before heading out again. The smaller ships, with less crew, therefore had much more difficulty in keeping elaborate schemes looking smart.

So where does that leave us? I guess it is up to the person painting a model as to how specific they are. But, when using reference sources, just keep in mind that the very neat-looking ship in a photograph has probably just come from a refit or dockyard job. The ship that looks rather scruffy has probably been worked hard and had little time for the fancy touch-up jobs. I recall years ago seeing a photograph in a book with a caption that referred to a particular destroyer returning to harbour with its paint scheme in a 'disgraceful condition'. A veteran WWII sailor looking at the book was quite derisive of the caption. It was a case, he said, of the person writing it having no consideration or understanding of what that ship must have been through in the weeks preceding the photograph for it to be in that state. No doubt he was quite correct.

So if your model-painting skills are not the best you can always claim your model ships have seen a lot of sea time. If you are a very discerning model painter that strives for total accuracy in shade, spare a thought that perhaps you

INTRODUCTION

may not be producing a realistic model after all, simply one that looks perfect. A more genuine approach would be to deliberately alter shades, change patterns slightly and add a rust streak or two here and there. Then you can truly claim your model is very accurate. There could be an area that has been cleaned of rust and touched up, but the new paint is not exactly the same shade. Close but darker or lighter!

A final point; when working on this book I deliberately made contact with some naval veterans and asked them their opinion of the 'TLAR' attitude. Most responded that it was by far the most common way of mixing paint, especially when in a hurry. Another pointed out, and then just recently yet another, that, even in peacetime, when ships were painted to regulation and with crew who had time to do it, there was nothing at all unusual in seeing a group of sister ships tied up together all resplendent in new paint straight out of the regulation tins, and all still somewhat different. In the case of flotilla craft, this could have even been deliberate to enable individual ships to be recognised while operating together.

SCALE

DRAWINGS ARE NOT TO SCALE. In order to give the reader a good view of the drawings, they have not been produced to a comparative scale, rather they are drawn to the best size for viewing in the format of this book.

PHOTOGRAPHIC ANALYSIS

Black and white film varies in quality and did so even more during WWII. The armed services used vast quantities, which left civilian photographers and even military ones at the mercy of what they could obtain. As a result, true shade is not always present. A scheme can look lighter or darker than it really was. Pale blue can come out quite dark grey and give the wrong impression of the real shade. Similarly, it can fade almost to nothing and look like there is no camouflage at all.

With diligent research, one can sometimes be lucky enough to come up with multiple photographs of the same ship, from different sources. Some may be in sepia and others a variety of faded or under-exposed film. But if one knows what the colour was supposed to be, it is possible to take these, analyse them and come to a fairly reasonable conclusion as to the pattern and the depth of shade. This is helped if the collection includes the ship from different angles and one can work out the depth of shade from the sun etc. It is not perfect, but in some cases where records have been lost, it is our best way of working out what a particular ship looked like.

I have used this technique many times. It is a case of using some detective work to gather a whole range of evidence and, from that, then coming to a reasonable conclusion. It is something that requires great diligence in finding the different sources to compare, but in this day of the internet that has become much easier. With patience, one can look up the memories posted on-line either by a veteran, or his family, along with some Box Brownie photographs these people took, and compare them with more official sources.

I have touched on issues here that I have used for fifty years of my life during research. I have of course referred to official sources too. That is the easiest of all and does produce lots of 'what it should have been' as well as a lot of 'what it actually was'. The archives of the Imperial War Museum in London are excellent. But I am firmly of the belief, based on personal interviews over many decades, that what was supposed to be and what actually was has not been recorded.

As the famous song goes: 'It ain't necessarily so.'

ACKNOWLEDGEMENTS

I wish to thank Dave Schueler, Andy Doty and Ian Thompson for their assistance, corrections and patient proof reading of this volume.

Mal Wright
January 2014

REFERENCE SOURCES

Numerous paintings by war artists. Some were actually 'there' and I place a higher reliance on their work than some who painted later.

Brown, David K, *Atlantic Escorts* (Seaforth Publishing, 2007). Although about the escorts themselves it has some excellent illustrations that are very helpful.

Camera at Sea, 1939-45. Compiled by the staff of *Warship.* (Conway Maritime Press, 1978).

Elliott, Peter, *Allied Escort Ships of World War II* (MacDonald and Jane's, 1977).

Ellis, Chris, *United States Navy Warship Camouflage, 1939-45* (Pique Publications, 1975). A famous name in the modelling world and, although dealing with US ships, there are issues that cross over to the RN.

Gillett, Ross, *Australian and New Zealand Warships 1914-45* (Doubleday Books, 1987).

Gooden, Henrietta, *Camouflage and Art, Design for Deception in World War 2* (Unicorn Press, 2007). Some good technical discussion on the how and why.

Hodges, Peter, *Royal Navy Warship Camouflage, 1939-45* (Almark Publications, 1973). Long out of print but an invaluable work nonetheless.

Hreachmack, Patrick, *The Painter's Guide to World War Two Naval Camouflage* (Clash of Arms, 1996). A useful guide.

Lenton, HT, and College, JJ, *Warships of WWII.* (Ian Allen, 1964)

Raven, Alan, *Warship Perspectives* (WR Press, 2000-2003). Four volumes. I have been a great admirer of this author's work for years going back to early magazine articles. His volumes on Royal Navy warships are highly recommended.

Raven, Alan, and Roberts, John, '*Man O' War*' series. (Arms and Armour Press, 1978-1980).

Warship Profiles, (Profile Publications, 1971-74). A large number of these older booklets are very helpful.

Williams, David, *Naval Camouflage 1914-1945* (Naval Institute Press, 2001). A brilliant book though with relatively few colour illustrations.

There are numerous other books not specifically related to camouflage but which contain colour photographs and illustrations, as well as those that show good quality black and white illustrations.

The champion source of them all are the veterans to whom we owe so much for the sacrifice they made in fighting WWII in which they often lost their health and suffered the pain of friends killed. I deliberately sought many out over the past five decades and am so glad that I did while they were young and vital, able to call on clear memories. They were an inspiration to me and so many were always happy to tell proud stories of their beloved ships. It is sad that nearly all those I consulted over the years have passed on, taking their memories with them.

'At the going down of the sun
And in the morning
We shall remember them.'

ABBREVIATIONS

AA = anti-aircraft
AM = Minesweeper
AM(c) = Coastal minesweeper
ASW = Anti-submarine warfare
ATW = Ahead throwing weapon (Usually Squid but also sometimes used for Hedgehog)
AWED = Admiralty War Emergency Destroyer (Usually WED –War Emergency Destroyer)
BYMS = British Yard Minesweeper (US)
DD = Destroyer
DC = Depth charge
DCT = Depth charge thrower
DCR = Depth charge rack
DCD = Depth charge dropper
DE = Destroyer escort
DP = Dual-purpose (gun mount)
EC = East coast (UK)
FCS = Fighter catapult ship
FDS = Fighter direction ship
FF = Frigate
FFN = Free French Navy
HA = High-angle (gun)
HDML = Harbour defence motor launch
HrMs = Her Netherlands Majesty's Ship
HF/DF = High Frequency / Direction Finding
HH = Hedgehog
HMAS = His Majesty's Australian Ship

HMCS = His Majesty's Canadian Ship
HMIS = His Majesty's Indian Ship
HNoMS = His Norwegian Majesty's Ship
HMNZS = His Majesty's New Zealand Ship
HMS = His Majesty's Ship
HMT = His Majesty's Tug
IFF = Identify friend or foe
IJN = Imperial Japanese Navy
LA = Low-angle (gun)
LCF = Landing craft flak
LCG = Landing craft gun
LCG(M) = Landing craft gun (medium)
LCM = Landing craft mechanised
LCP = Landing craft personnel
LCT = Landing craft tank
LL(V) = Landing lighter (vehicle)
LRE = Long-range escort
LSH = Landing ship headquarters
LSI = Landing ship infantry
LSS = Landing ship stern chute
LST = Landing ship tank
MG = Machine gun
MGB = Motor gun boat
ML = Motor launch
MS = Minesweeping
MMS = Motor minesweeper
MTB = Motor torpedo boat

ORP = Okrêt Rzeczypospolitej Polskiej (Ship of the Republic of Poland)
PCE = Patrol craft (escort) (US)
PG = Patrol gunboat (sloop)
PG(E) = Patrol gunboat (escort)
RAN = Royal Australian Navy
RCN = Royal Canadian Navy
RFA = Royal Fleet Auxiliary
RHN = Royal Hellenic Navy
RINS = Royal Indian Naval Service
RN = (British) Royal Navy
RNZN = Royal New Zealand Navy
RPN = Republic of Poland Navy
SL = Searchlight
Soviet = (Russian) USSR
SRE = Short-range escort
TSDS = Two-speed destroyer sweep
UK = United Kingdom
UP = Unrotated projectile (launcher)
USN = United States Navy
USS = United States Ship
USSR = Union of Soviet Socialist Republics
WA = Western Approaches
WAIR = Old 'V&W' class destroyer converted to AA escort

BRITISH AND COMMONWEALTH WARSHIP PAINTS DURING WWII

Note: Unofficial paint colours were known as 'Local procurement shades'. This was very common in the early years of WWII or on ships in areas where official paints were not available. In these cases it was expected that an attempt would be made to obtain the nearest possible official or appropriate shade. However, through human intervention, official shades were often badly mixed and were not exactly as intended.
Cemtex is not shown because its colour depended on age and wear and tear. It started out as mid to light grey but could fade to a creamy grey.
★ All 'white' referred to in the captions is WS white.

DESTROYERS BUILT TO WWI PROGRAMMES 1

ADMIRALTY 'R' AND 'S' CLASS DESTROYERS

HMS SKATE H39
Admiralty 'R' Class Destroyer 1939

HMS SKATE H39
Admiralty 'R' Class Destroyer 1940–1

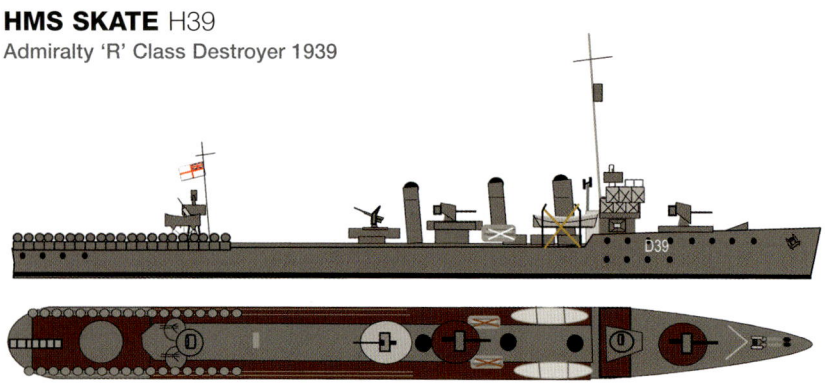
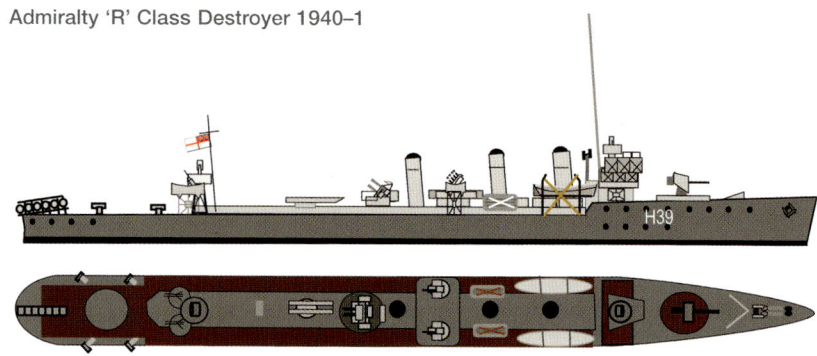

Skate at the start of WWII when a minelayer. This ship had a variety of roles between the wars and during WWII. She was the only three-funnel destroyer still in RN service. Her numerous sisters were scrapped in the 1930s, having been poorly maintained in reserve. Note the effect of dull grey in dull conditions, such as a minelayer would operate under at night or in low light. MG light AA and 12pdr AA. Colour 507b. Deck Corticene brown and 507b.

Skate had a very good top speed and is shown when in service as an influence minesweeper. She used her high speed to avoid the explosions of magnetic mines, but it was still a very dangerous duty steaming up and down mined areas to set off magnetic mines that had been triggered for slow merchant ships. She had adopted the medium hull, light upper works style common to many ships. These duties kept her close to the coast and well in range of the Luftwaffe so she carries a quad 2pdr, quad 0.5in MGs and twin Lewis guns aft. Only one main gun is carried. Colours are MS4a and 507b.

HMS SKATE H39
Admiralty 'R' Class Destroyer 1941–2

HMS SKATE H39
Admiralty 'R' Class Destroyer 1943–5

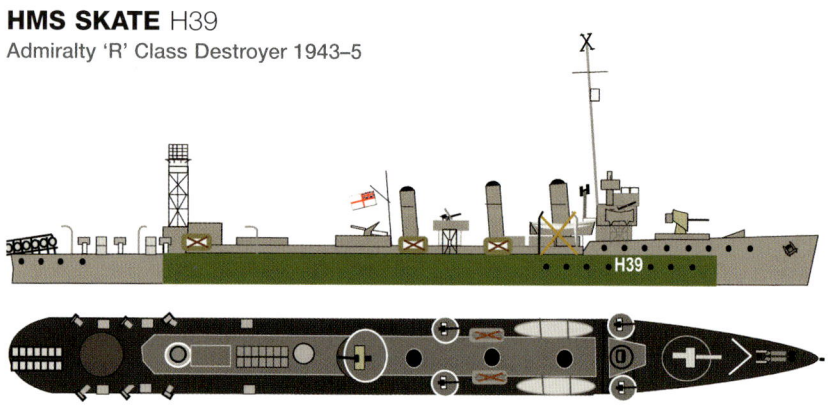

Skate altered as a Short-Range Escort (SRE), for convoy runs from the UK to Iceland, and the UK East Coast convoys. Eight depth-charge (DC) throwers are fitted. Fixed Type 286 radar on foremast. Splinter mats and quad 0.5in MG between the funnels, There is a single 12pdr AA amidships and two 20mm aft. A very heavy depth charge load is provided. She carries an unofficial paint scheme nonetheless influenced by Western Approaches (WA) ideas. Green was often difficult to obtain. Only one LA 4in carried. Colours WA green and white.

Old but still useful! This is *Skate* as she looked at the Normandy landings in 1944. She has a Type 271 radar lantern on a lattice mast aft. The ship finally paid off in 1945 having lasted longer in service than many younger vessels. Note the late war Admiralty standard scheme of B30 dark olive panel camouflage on B55 overall. Her AA armament comprises a 12pdr and four 20mm. Her deck is now dark grey. The single LA 4in was original but the barrel had been changed several times. She carried a powerful load of DCs and could deliver quite a punch in ASW operations. Type 291 radar is at the foretop. Colours B30 and B55.

HMS STURDY H28
Admiralty 'S' Class Destroyer 1942

This shows *Sturdy* as a minelayer but with contrast camouflage of unofficial design and colours. Two LA 4in still carried, and a 12pdr AA aft. Twin Lewis guns in bridge wings. There is a single 2pdr AA on the aft deckhouse. No depth charges. Colours 507c, 507a and B5 edged white on the hull. Corticene brown on decks with MS1.

HMS SARDONYX H26
Admiralty 'S' Class Destroyer 1941–4

Sardonyx shows her appearance during the Battle of the Atlantic as an SRE. She has a 12pdr AA amidships, 2pdr AA aft and 20mm. Twin Lewis guns in bridge wings. Eight DC throwers and a very large number of charges carried. The scheme is typical early WA type but she soon moved to the east coast of the UK as her range was too short for the Atlantic convoys. Colours WA green, WA blue, white.

HMS SCIMITAR H21
Admiralty 'S' Class Destroyer 1941

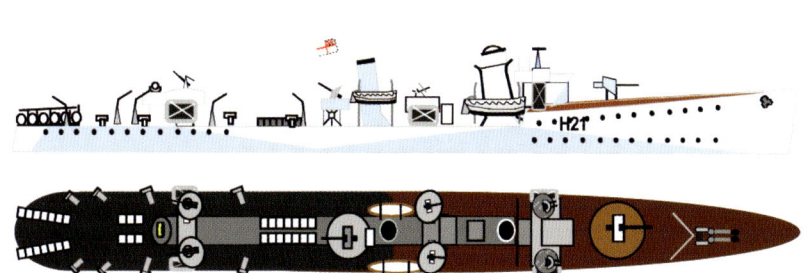

Scimitar is depicted in a WA-style camouflage in very pale blue. Ships in this scheme often used pale green or both. Her ASW capacity is huge and she could deliver heavy attacks. The radar fitted is a fixed early Type 286 at the foremast top. Colours white and WA blue.

HMS SHIKARI I85
Admiralty 'S' Class Destroyer 1941–4

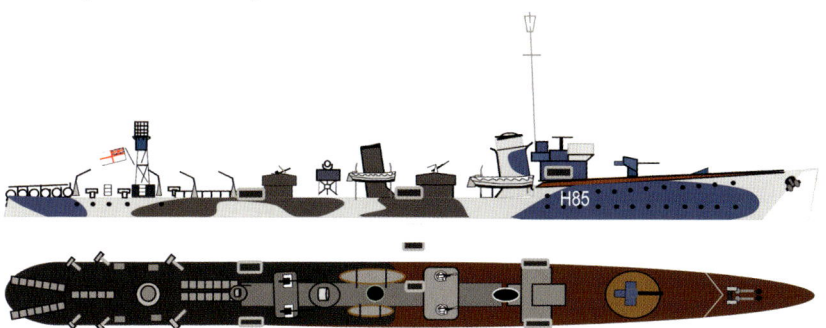

Shikari altered for escort duty in an Admiralty paint scheme. Note the Type 271 radar on a tower aft. Type 286 and later rotating Type 286P on foremast, itself later replaced by Type 291. Colours white, 507a, 507c, PB10. These ships were overcrowded due to new electronics and weapons. They were also very unhealthy in rough conditions as the crew quarters were continually damp.

DESTROYERS BUILT TO WWI PROGRAMMES

Admiralty 'S' class destroyers were built at the end of WWI. Although similar to the 'R' class the bridge was moved further aft as the previous designs had been very wet forward. The hull was given more sheer and in good weather they were very fast ships. Small 14in torpedo tubes for anti-destroyer work were mounted at the break of the hull, but found too wet when at speed, and soon removed. They were good for the North Sea, but very cramped, small and short-ranged for work in the North Atlantic. Units did serve on distant stations, however.

HMS SALADIN H54
Admiralty 'S' Class Destroyer 1942

Saladin in a green and blue WA-style camouflage which probably suited work on the Eastern Approaches as well. As with her sister ships, she has a big ASW capability. Her light AA is twin Lewis guns in the bridge wings, 20mm between the funnels, a 12pdr amidships and two single 2pdr aft. Radar Type 286 on masthead. WA white, WA blue, WA green. Decks Corticene brown and 507b.

HMS SABRE H18
Admiralty 'S' Class Destroyer 1942

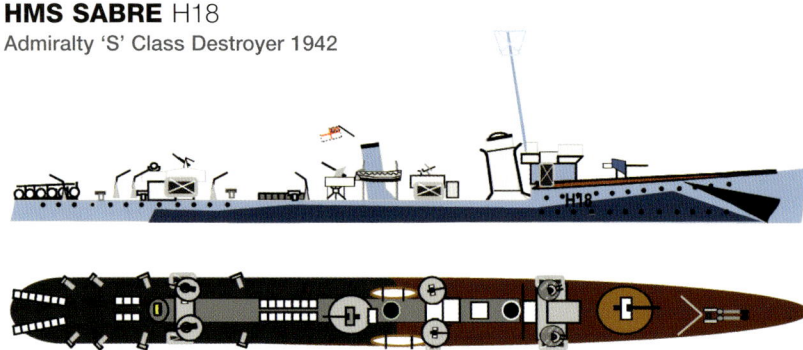

Sabre in a very dark, unofficial or experimental scheme suited for the Icelandic convoy run in poor light conditions. The effect would be to make the ship look shorter or further away. She spent a lot of time with convoys to and from Iceland. Her general appearance and armament is similar to her sister ships in home waters. She has Type 286 radar at the top of the foremast. Colours are PB10 blue, G5/MS1 and mid-blue washed.

HMS TENEDOS H04
Admiralty 'S' Class Destroyer 1942

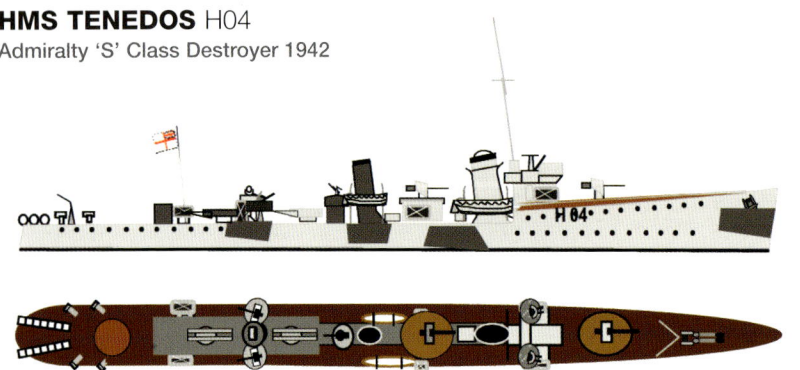

Schemes in the Far East were locally designed with the paint available. This is taken from photographic records and verbal descriptions. Mostly unmodified, she still carries a full Corticene deck covering. Light AA was twin Lewis guns, a single 2pdr and two single 20mm. The aft gun was removed for minelaying but she carries both sets of twin torpedo tubes. No radar fitted. Colours possibly 507a and 507c, but probably mixed locally.

HMS SCOUT H51
Admiralty 'S' Class Destroyer 1942

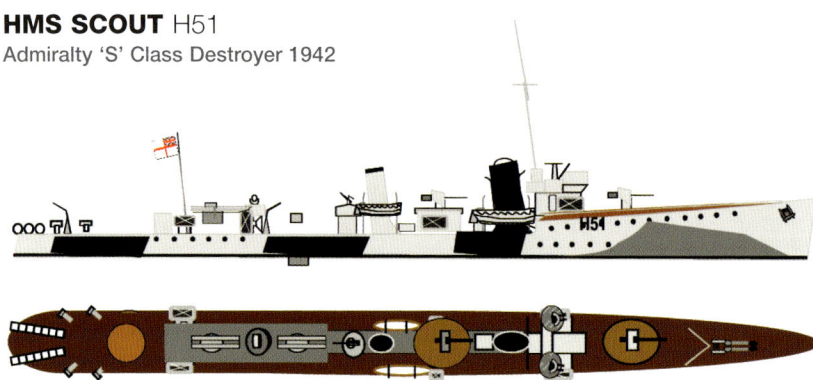

Scout is shown in another unofficial scheme probably designed by the officers based on information from other war zones and paint available. Aft gun removed for minelaying which was a major mission for these ships in the run-up to war with Japan. They were at the bottom of the priority list to get radar and modern AA due to the demand in the Atlantic and Mediterranean. No radar fitted. One single 2pdr pom-pom and Lewis guns make up her only AA armament. Colours black, 507c, B6.

DESTROYERS BUILT TO WWI PROGRAMMES

HMS STRONGHOLD H50
Admiralty 'S' Class Destroyer 1942

HMS THANET H29
Admiralty 'S' Class Destroyer 1942

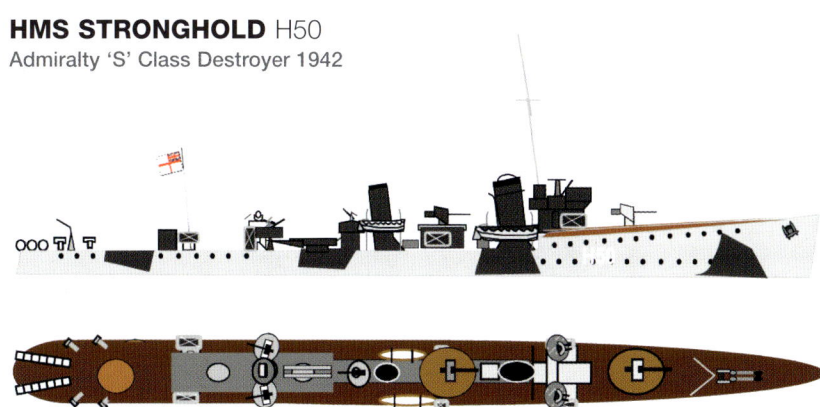
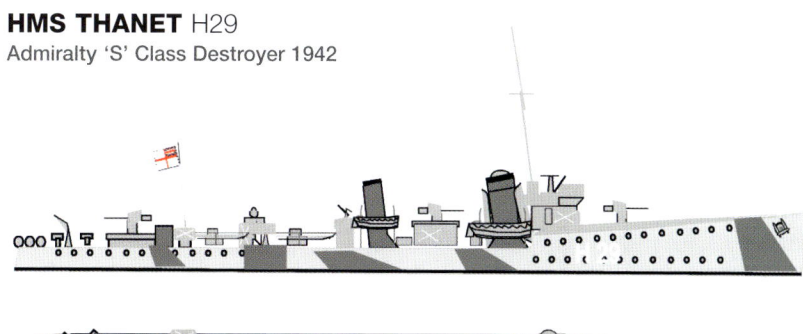

Stronghold is shown as in official records. However, like Thanet, she may have reshipped her aft gun as it was stored on station. The aft tubes had been landed while on minelaying duty. They may also have been re-shipped when the first warning of Japanese attacks came. Note no radar. Camouflage based on MS1 and 507c.

Prior to departing on her last mission, Thanet had re-shipped her full gun and torpedo armament. She had previously reduced her armament to carry out minelaying duties. Confirmation of final fit comes from divers who have visited her wreck and from official action reports that describe her using all three guns and both torpedo mounts. Her light AA is just a 2pdr and some Lewis guns. Colours 507c and 507b.

MOUNTBATTEN PINK

HMS THANET H28
Admiralty 'S' Class Destroyer

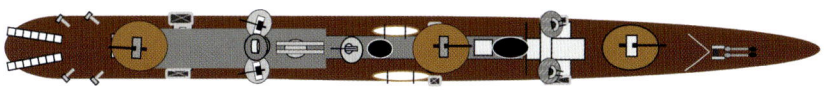
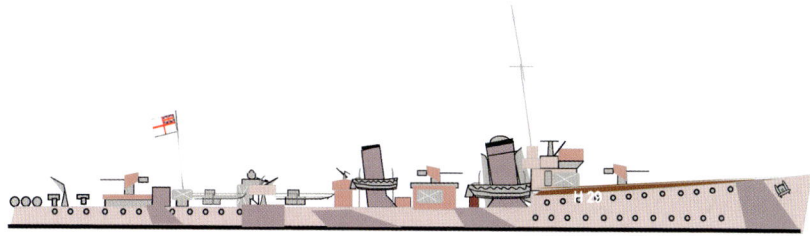
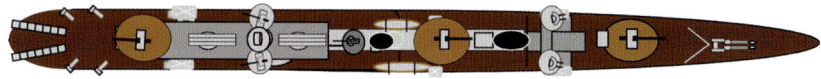

Many years ago I was told by an Australian veteran that some of the British ships on the Far East station adopted Mountbatten Pink late in 1941 due to contact with officers from the Mediterranean Fleet. I have found no written evidence of this at all. However, considering the rapid course of events from December 1941 onward and the loss of some ships I cannot entirely discount it. These drawings of Thanet show how she may have looked if dark and light Mountbatten Pink was applied, instead of the grey seen in black and white photographs. Unofficial schemes were quite common early in WWII. Mountbatten Pink was very popular with crews and thought to have superior qualities. However, research showed that in some conditions it could make the ship more visible, not less. In fading light or at sunset it appeared darker. Its use eventually died out. Colours are Mountbatten Medium and Light.

PB 101
British Admiralty 'S' Class Destroyer 1943

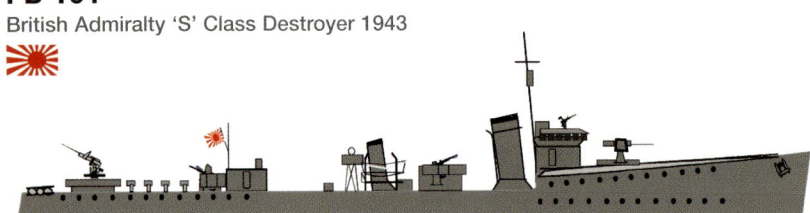

PB 101
British Admiralty 'S' Class Destroyer 1945

HMS *Thracian* ran aground at Hong Kong on Christmas Day 1941 and was scuttled. The RN considered her too damaged for salvage having even removed some parts. The Japanese raised her as Patrol Boat *101*. She is shown here in IJN dull dark grey. There is a 3in AA aft and a 4.7in forward, both of Japanese type. There are triple 25mm guns to port and starboard amidships, another triple behind the aft deck house and twin 13mm on the bridge roof. She has a row of DC throwers and a rack aft. The new bridge is IJN style. The grey is similar to 507b.

Thracian had been so severely damaged when scuttled by the RN that the Japanese found her mechanically unreliable as an ASW patrol boat. She sailed for Japan and was fitted as a radar trials ship with some patrol boat capability. She now has single 4.7in AA fore and aft and has single 25mm added abreast the bridge. Type 22 radar is carried on a platform over the bridge. The large tower aft was for testing new types of radar. ASW ability has been reduced but she retains the triple 25mm mounts. There are some sources that say these were possibly 25mm twins, especially the aft mount.

'V&W' CLASS DESTROYERS IN FLEET AND SRE CONFIGURATION

HMS VORTIGERN I37
SRE Destroyer 1941–2

HMS VETERAN I72
Modified 'W' Class Destroyer 1942

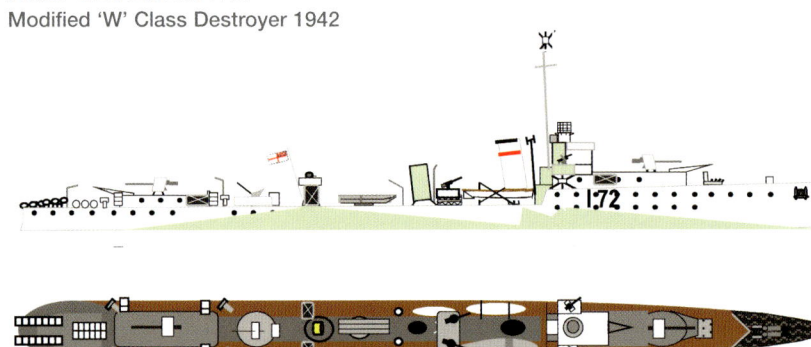

A typical WA scheme using green without blue as originally intended. She has a HF/DF mast aft to enable the interception of U-boat signals. Her AA armament is a 12pdr in place of the aft tubes, single 2pdrs behind the aft funnel and single 20mm in the bridge wings. There is a Type 276 radar at the masthead. Colours are white and WA green.

There were many variations of the WA scheme but a green aft funnel is typical. The modified 'W' class did not have the usual thin fore funnel of most 'V&W' class ships. She is fitted with a Hedgehog forward and her bridge has a Type 271 radar lantern. The masthead Type 276 was soon to be replaced. Most SREs retained some torpedo tubes. The Type X one-ton DC was usually fired from a torpedo tube against very deep U-boats. Colours are WA green on white.

HMS VIVACIOUS I36
Modified 'W' Class Destroyer 1942–3

HMS WIVERN I66
'W' Class Destroyer 1942

Blue was often substituted for green due to wartime shortages and became the most famous image of the WA scheme; however, it was originally intended to have been pale green. All light AA are 20mm. Type 271 and 291 radars are carried. Colours are WA blue and white.

WA schemes were often very simple, as shown here with WA blue and white. Note *Wivern* has a HF/DF mast aft. Her radar lantern is amidships raised on a lattice platform. Type 291 radar at the masthead, replacing Type 276 which was far too noisy and easy for U-boats to detect. She still has single 2pdr AA guns amidships.

HMS VENETIA D53
'V' Class Destroyer 1939–40

HMS WINDSOR I42
Modified 'V&W' Class Destroyer 1941–2

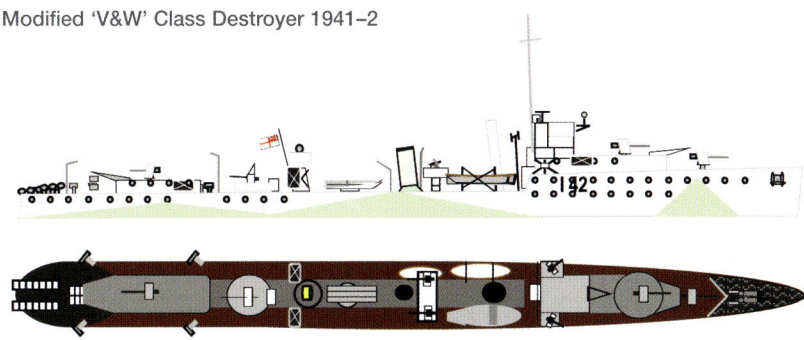

A typical 'V&W' in plain mid-grey 507b. 'Y' gun has been replaced by extra DCs, the only wartime alteration. Corticene decks were retained by most. There is a single old-model 2pdr amidships but she probably had twin Lewis guns in the bridge wings. She has a pre-war pennant number. Black waterline still retained. This was the configuration of most old destroyers used on fleet duty.

Windsor shows some wartime modifications, reduced torpedoes for a 12pdr AA gun etc. But she retains three of her main guns and a set of torpedo tubes which would allow her to be used for a wide range of operations. SREs generally took convoys out part-way into the Atlantic and met others coming in to the UK. Their range was too short to cross the Atlantic. Colours are typical white and WA green.

HMS WILD SWAN I62
'V&W' Class Destroyer 1942–3

HMS WITHERINGTON I76
'V&W' Class Destroyer 1941–3

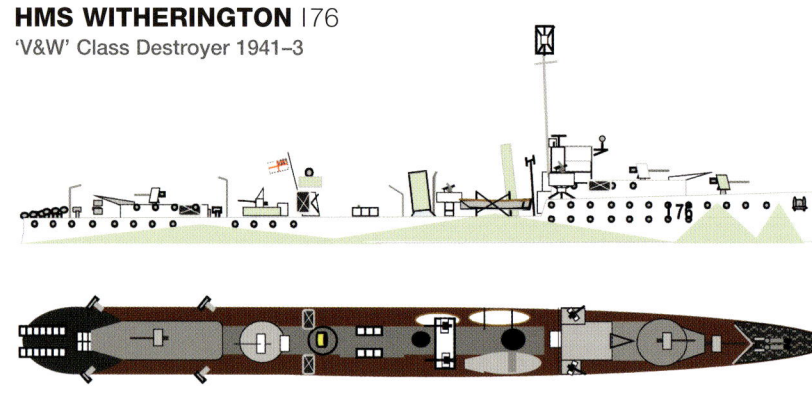

SREs retained most guns as they were more likely to see action against enemy coastal forces. *Wild Swan* has a HF/DF mast aft for detecting U-boat radio transmissions. All 2pdrs have been replaced by 20mm Oerlikons. Her scheme includes WA green, WA blue, on white.

This SRE has had all her torpedo tubes removed and extra DC stowage added. These were often far more important than torpedoes. All her light AA are 20mm Oerlikons. Type 286 radar was later replaced by Type 291 which was harder for U-boats to detect. Her scheme includes irregular patches of WA green on white.

HMS WITCH I89
Modified 'W' Class Destroyer 1943

HMS WESSEX D43
'W' Class Destroyer 1939–40

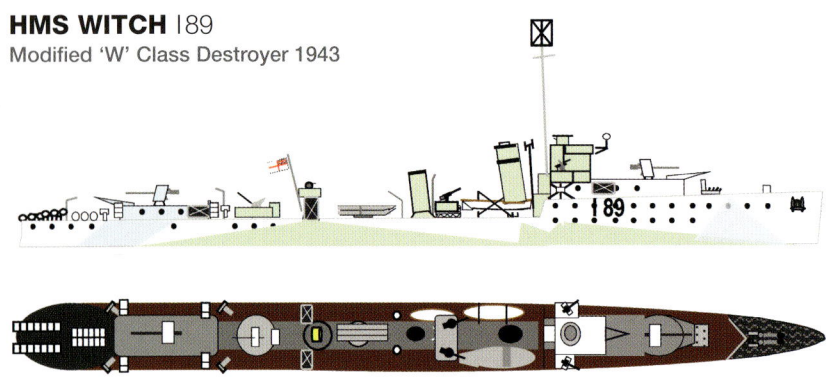
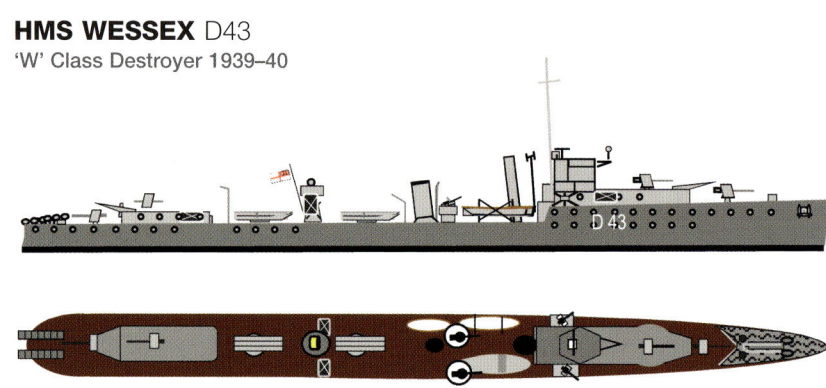

Witch has 'A' gun replaced by a Hedgehog. She carries a blue and green mix WA scheme, which includes rather more green above the hull than usual. Interestingly, she has retained her director on the bridge and only has Type 291 radar. Wartime alterations were far from standard and instead of all 20mm Oerlikons she retains single 2pdrs between the funnels.

Wessex is shown as a fleet destroyer in an early-war paint scheme. Corticene was a lightweight linoleum material that gave grip, but also stopped decks becoming too hot or too cold in various climates. Note that the only light AA comprises two single 2pdrs. She was sunk in 1940 with very few alterations having been made. Colours may be 507b and MS 4a but are possibly also unofficial mixes.

DESTROYERS BUILT TO WWI PROGRAMMES

HMS WOLVERINE I78
'W' Class Destroyer 1942

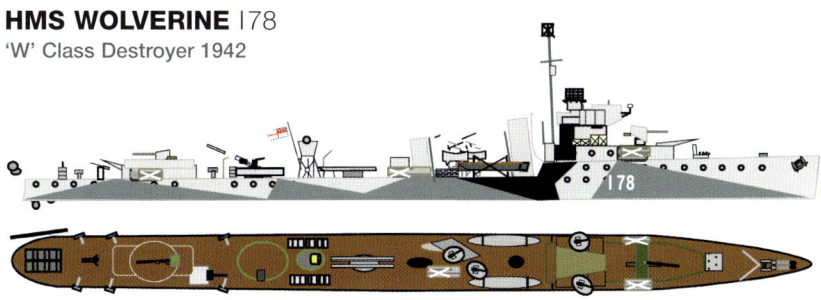

Wolverine was very active escorting convoys in the Eastern Atlantic. This camouflage scheme is based on shades of grey plus black, colours more available than most others. She has four 20mm AA but her ASW equipment is more extensive than most other SRE. These ships had priority to receive radar and *Wolverine* used hers with great success. Colours are 507c, B6 and black.

HMS WALPOLE I41
'W' Class Destroyer 1944

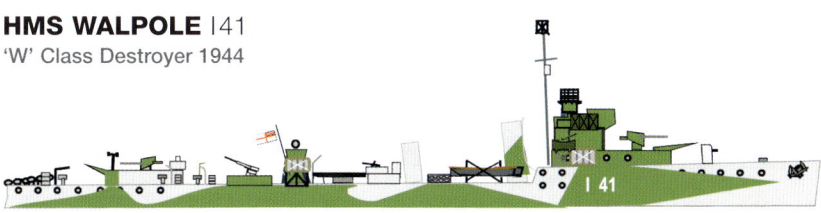

Walpole is shown here wearing a grey and green camouflage that was no doubt intended to be suitable for her role supporting the allied landings in France. These are 507c and 1940 green. She has a twin automatic 6pdr forward for fighting coastal craft. There are rockets on 'B' mount for illumination. The AA fit is pretty standard for her type.

HMAS VOYAGER D31
'V&W' Class Destroyer 1940

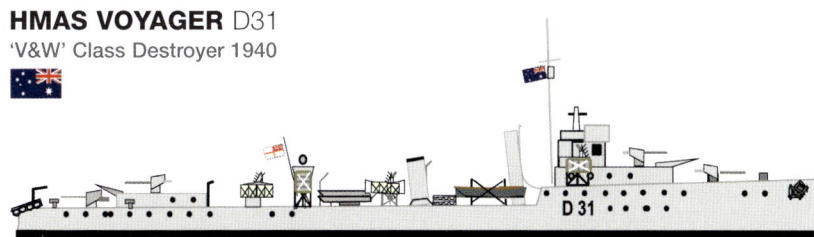

Voyager is shown early in her Mediterranean Fleet service. She still bears the peacetime pennant number D 31. The aft torpedo tubes have been removed and replaced by a quad MG mount while she waits for a 12pdr AA gun for that position. Her light AA comprises four quadruple MG. She still carries her four main guns. DCs not yet increased. Her scheme is 507c overall.

HMAS WATERHEN I22
'V&W' Class Destroyer 1941

Australia received four 'V&W' class destroyers in 1933 and sent them to the Mediterranean when WWII broke out. They gained the nickname 'The Scrap Iron Flotilla' after a derisive Lord Haw-Haw broadcast. As can be seen, *Waterhen* had an Admiralty design camouflage in three colours of 507a and 1941 blue on 507c. Note that she has a single 4in AA gun on the aft shelter deck. Records do not confirm this but the gun with its AA-type shield appears in a photograph of her at Alexandria before leaving on her final voyage and was confirmed by the author's uncle who was a survivor of her sinking. Her AA armament is a 12pdr in place of the aft torpedo tubes quad 0.5in MG mount behind the aft funnel; twin Lewis guns in the bridge wings.

HMAS VAMPIRE I68
'V&W' Class Destroyer 1941

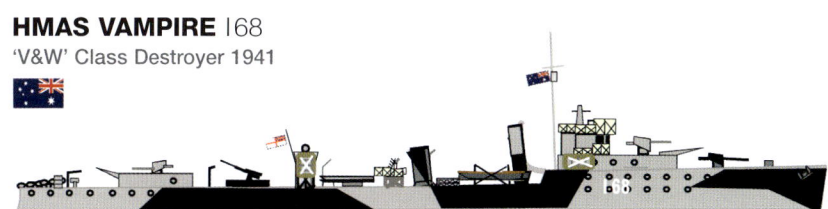

Vampire shows a 1940 Mediterranean scheme in grey and black. These colours provided an easy camouflage and many ships used this style in the Mediterranean theatre. The grey appears to be 507c. Her bridge is protected with splinter mats. She had twin Lewis guns in the bridge wings but many Australian ships had additional unofficial MGs salvaged from sunken ships. Some Italian MGs were even used until captured ammunition supplies ran out.

HMAS VOYAGER I31
'V&W' Class Destroyer 1941

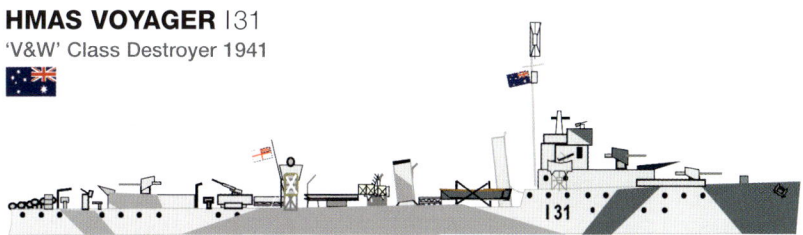

Voyager altered for war service sports a fairly standard camouflage type utilising three shades of grey. 'Y' gun has been removed. She has a 12pdr AA in place of the aft torpedo tubes and 20mm in the bridge wings. There are twin Lewis guns on the bridge and aft in 'Y' position. An early fixed Type 286 radar is at the masthead. Flag superior of her pennant has been changed to 'I'. Her scheme is B6, 507c and 507b.

HMAS VENDETTA D69
'V&W' Class Destroyer 1941 🇦🇺

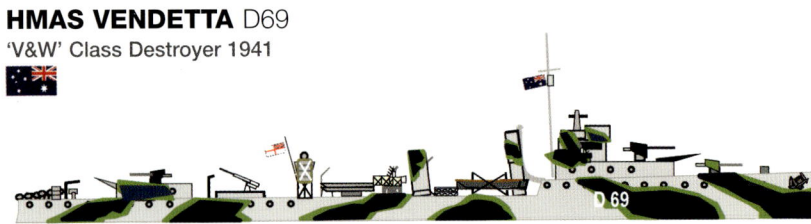

This confusion scheme was worn by *Vendetta* during her service with the Mediterranean Fleet. It was intended to confuse from a distance and, apart from the light green edging, was similar to that used by Italian torpedo boats and destroyers. She has three sets of quad 0.5in MG, one in each bridge wing and one amidships. The Mediterranean Fleet was well known for some of the more lurid camouflage schemes worn by British and Commonwealth warships. Colours are B15 outlined in G45 on 507c. It is possible that these shades were non-standard, acquired locally.

HMAS VENDETTA D69
'V&W' Class Destroyer 1944 🇦🇺

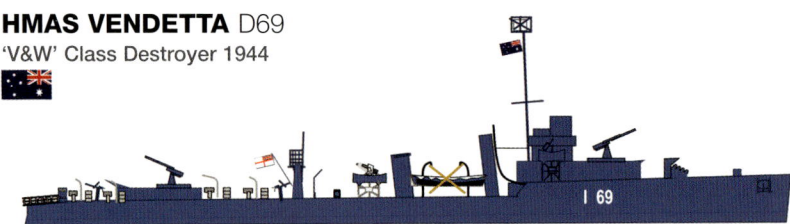

The only ship of the four Australian 'V&W' class to survive the war, *Vendetta* underwent several modifications. In this, her last form, she was converted to an escort destroyer and operated in New Guinea waters, where she sometimes conveyed troops to combat zones. Her guns have been replaced with an HA 4in, four 20mm Oerlikons and two single 2pdrs, plus numerous MGs. The scheme she wears is the American overall blue which was used by several Australian ships. Note the impressive number of DC throwers and USN radar on mast. British Type 271 radar aerial amidships.

'V&W' CLASS DESTROYERS CONVERTED TO AA ESCORTS (WAIR)

HMS VANITY L38
'V&W' Class AA Destroyer 1940

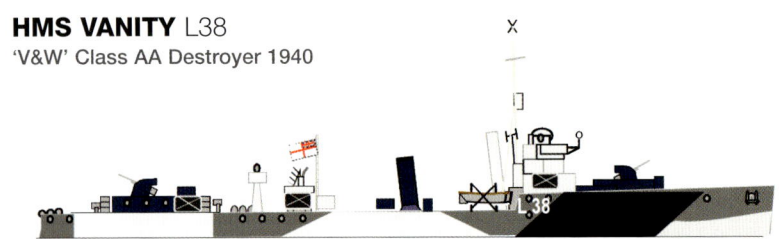

Vanity is shown wearing an early unofficial scheme. Her only light AA is multiple MG mounts amidships. Note the false wave effect of the camouflage. She has early radar at the masthead. Black and grey were of course very easy to obtain and a scheme based around them is hardly surprising. The lack of Type 285 radar on the gun director would have affected her efficiency in the AA role. Scheme is possibly an unofficial mix, appearing to be G5/MS1 and MS4 on a 507c hull. Gun mounts and aft funnel are dark blue.

HMS VICEROY L21
'V&W' Class AA Destroyer 1942

Viceroy is shown in an Admiralty scheme common to ships escorting convoys on the UK East Coast. The colours are PB10, mid-blue washed and 507c hull. There is a lower than usual radar lantern amidships, perhaps indicating a topweight problem as it should have been carried higher. AA defence was very important for the North Sea and coastal convoys and the extra light guns fitted here may be the cause of the weight problem. There is extra DC stowage, and a mix of 20mm and single 2pdr AA guns, with the 2pdrs in front of the radar lantern. Type 285 radar on the gun director.

HMS VANITY L38
'V&W' Class AA Destroyer 1942+

Vanity has an Admiralty light disruptive camouflage scheme. Note radar lantern aft. Four single 20mm guns. She served mostly on the UK East Coast convoys. WAIR ships did not need to carry the large number of DCs other destroyers needed on Atlantic convoys. Colours are mid-blue on white washed with PB10.

HMS VALOROUS L00
'V&W' Class AA Destroyer 1944

Valorous is shown wearing an Admiralty light scheme. She has some extra DC stowage. Light AA four single 20mm. There is Type 285 radar on her gun director and Type 291 at the masthead and this would have been her final war configuration. Note HF/DF mast aft. It was unusual for WAIR ships to carry that equipment. The colours are PB10 and a lightened 1941 blue on a 507c hull.

HMS VEGA L52
'V&W' Class AA Destroyer 1940

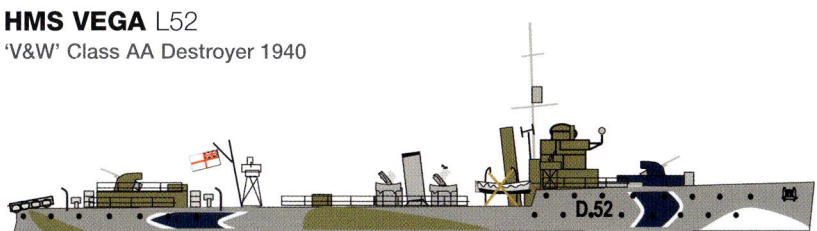

This was a very early unofficial scheme for ships that served near the coast. The main colour is MS4a but the khaki was almost certainly locally mixed. 1941 blue is outlined in white, but even this could have been local procurement. There is a prominent bow wave. Note the ship has no radar fitted. The light AA comprised two quad 0.5in MG mounts and Lewis machine guns in the bridge wings.

HMS VEGA L41
'V&W' Class AA Destroyer 1942

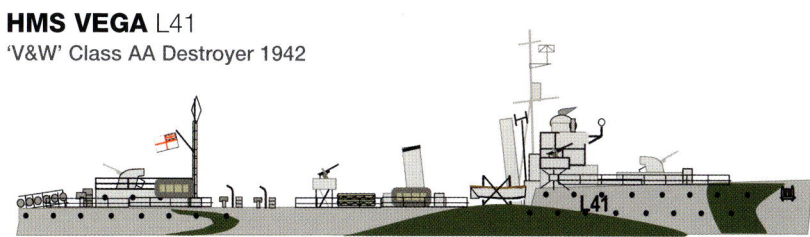

Vega is shown in MS4a Home Fleet grey with areas of MS2 mid olive. There was a radar type 285 on the director and a 286P rotating set on the mast. It was most uncommon for ships on the UK East Coast to have a HF/DF mast but this implies she may also have been used on convoys to Iceland.

HMS WOLFHOUND I56
'V&W' Class AA Destroyer 1941

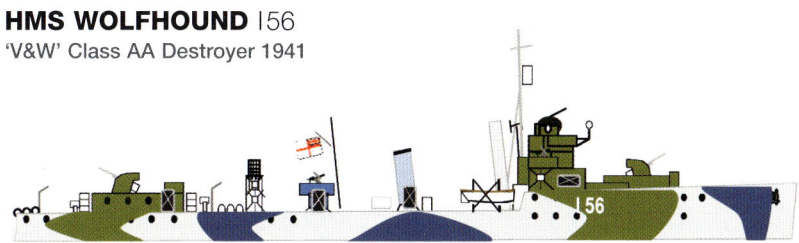

This scheme was intended for coastal convoy work where the WAIRs were mostly employed. It comprises a light grey hull, probably 507c, 1941 blue, and the aft funnel possibly in WA blue. However, this is still in the period when many unofficial or experimental schemes were used and the colours could have been unique to the ship as the green appears non standard. Four 20mm singles was standard for these ships. Type 271 radar amidships and Type 285 on the director.

HMS WINCHESTER L55
'V&W' Class AA Destroyer 1942

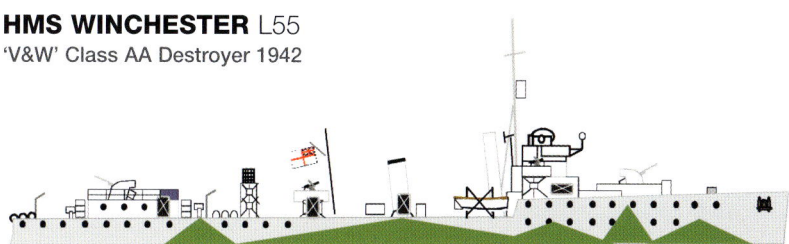

A Type 271 radar lantern sits aft but in 1942 *Winchester* does not yet seem to be fitted with Type 285 on the gunnery director. Although it was a high priority, there was a heavy call on production of this set and refit of the director to use it. Her scheme is of mixed type utilising 507c grey and 1940 green but with white or very pale upper works. This was probably derived from the WA scheme but darkened for the East Coast of the UK.

HMS WOOLSTON L49
'V&W' Class AA Destroyer 1942

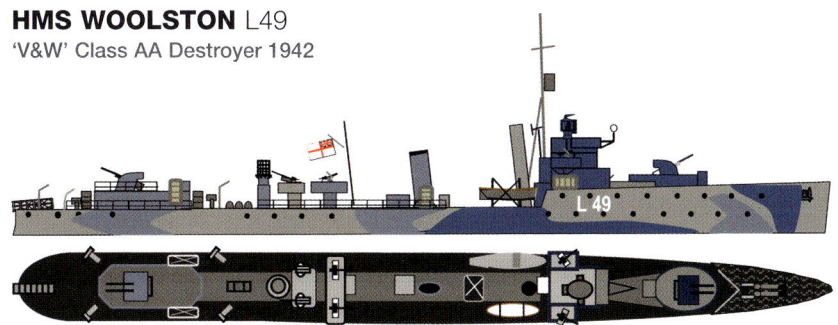

Woolston is shown wearing an Admiralty Intermediate scheme of B6/B30, B5, and 1941 blue. It was intended that at a distance these would blend together to make the ship harder to see. There was a radar lantern for 271 aft but positioned rather lower than normal. As usual the director has type 285 radar fitted. The light AA armament is unusual in that there are four single 20mm Oerlikon guns, as well as two single 2pdr manual mounts.

HMS WALLACE L64
Shakespeare Class AA Destroyer Leader 1939-40

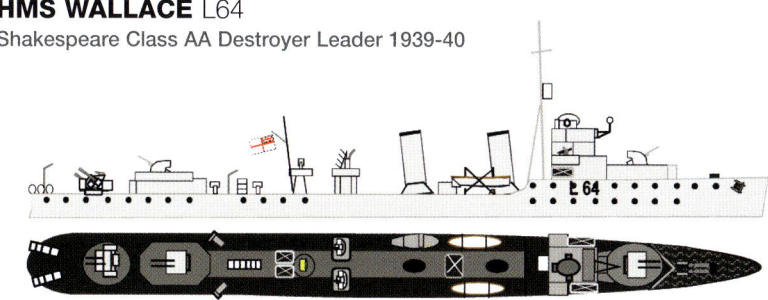

Wallace was larger than the other WAIR ships and carried a quadruple 2pdr AA aft. She has no radar as shown here and has quad 0.5in MGs as part of her AA armament. She was built as a destroyer leader and was intended to act in that role for WAIR ships. Pale grey was a common 1939–40 scheme but without a black boot topping.

HMS WALLACE L64
Shakespeare Class AA Destroyer Leader 1942

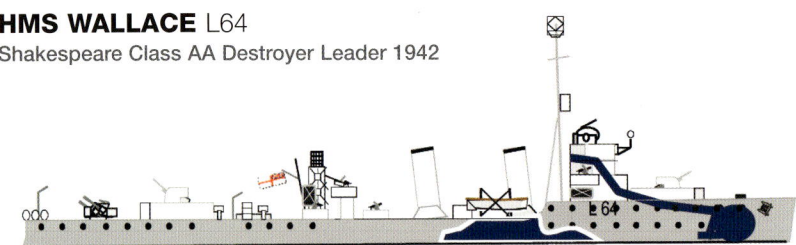

By 1942 *Wallace* had a radar lantern Type 271 in place of her searchlight platform. The 1941 blue with bold outline was distinctive, but a similar area near the bow was not outlined in white. The hull was MS4a grey. The upperworks were much lighter in 507c pale grey. Decks were dark grey. Extra depth charge stowage had been added amidships. Single 2pdr AA guns have replaced the previous quad machine gun mounts and there were four single 20mm as well.

HMS WALLACE L64
Shakespeare Class AA Destroyer Leader 1944-5

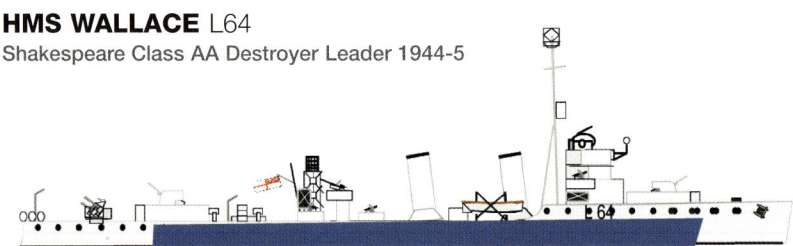

Wallace at the end of WWII. The 1941 blue panel, on 507c light grey, was intended to make the ship look shorter or further away to spoil the aim of a torpedo being fired. A full range of electronics and radar types are fitted, making her very up to date for the period. It is worth remembering that when *Wallace* was first built radar did not exist and no ships were actually designed to carry it until the first wartime designs. Yet by 1945 it was considered indispensable.

'V & W' CLASS CONVERTED TO LONG-RANGE ESCORTS (LRE)

HMS WALKER I27
'W' Class LRE

This is an Admiralty intermediate scheme favoured for ships that might work in several areas rather than just Atlantic convoys. On a WA blue hull, she has B5 forward and PB10 aft. She has extra DC stowage and, of course, the forward funnel removed with its boilers to create more space for fuel tanks. There are single 20mm in the bridge wings and another right aft on the quarterdeck. There are two single 2pdr AA amidships and a Hedgehog forward in place of 'A' gun mount. The Type 271 lantern on the bridge is set low to reduce topweight. These ships had a very long endurance.

HMS VANQUISHER I54
'V' Class LRE

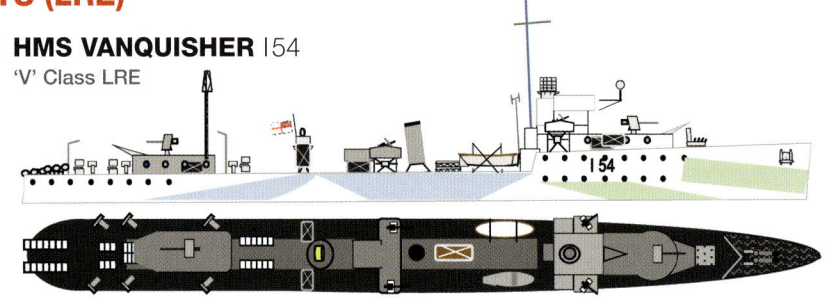

Vanquisher is shown in a non-typical WA scheme including MS4a grey. The remainder is of standard WA blue and WA green. She has a Type 271 radar lantern on the bridge, Type 291 at the masthead, and HF/DF mast aft. There is a Hedgehog forward in 'A' position and four single 20mm AA. All torpedo tubes have been removed and extra DCs are in the aft tube position. The forward boilers and funnel have been removed in order to provide extra fuel tanks to increase range.

HMS VISCOUNT I92
Thornycroft 'V' Class LRE

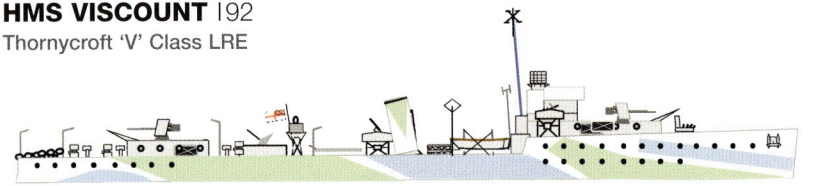

Not all 'V&W' class had a thin aft funnel. *Viscount*'s camouflage scheme is based around the WA style but a bit more elaborate with more WA green and WA blue on white than usual. The forward tubes have been retained and probably carry a single one-ton Mk X DC. There is also a Hedgehog forward. A 12pdr AA has replaced the aft torpedo tubes. Only the 'V&Ws' in best condition were given this refit to extend their lives and range. The light AA is mixed, with single 20mm in the bridge wings and two single 2pdr aft of the funnel.

HMS VANSITTART I64
Modified 'W' Class LRE

Vansittart is displaying a standard WA camouflage scheme of white hull with patches of WA green and WA blue. Type 271 radar on the bridge with Type 291 at masthead. There are 20mm in the bridge wings and aft of the funnel. Weight had been drastically reduced and the forward boiler room removed for extra fuel stowage which enabled these ships to cross the Atlantic without refuelling. All torpedo tubes have been removed to save weight and allow extra DC stowage. These ships not only had a very long range, but were also formidable ASW ships.

DESTROYERS BUILT TO WWI PROGRAMMES

HMS VIMY 133
'V' Class LRE 1942

Vimy wears a dark Admiralty scheme best suited for dull northern waters. The pattern seems to concentrate the eye on the centre of the ship using dark colours yet with a break to make it seem there could be two ships. All ideas to fool a U-boat captain during his quick glimpse through a periscope were considered. It was often necessary to have a dark colour aft to enable other ships to keep station when steaming in line. Here the aft gun shield is black. Note there is no Hedgehog. Colours are black, white, 1941 blue, and a patch of WA blue at the bow.

HMS WHITEHALL 194
Modified 'W' Class LRE 1944

This is an Admiralty intermediate scheme introduced mid-war, intended for use on ships not necessarily on the Atlantic convoy runs, but nonetheless able to be used there if there was no time to repaint. 1941 blue, darkened WA blue and a hull that appears to be MS4a with a greenish tint. The ship is fitted with 20mm AA in the bridge wings and amidships. There is a Hedgehog in place of 'A' gun and no tubes are fitted. A Type 271 radar lantern is on the bridge with Type 244 IFF on top plus Type 291 at the masthead. There are Type 253 hourglass interrogators on the mast.

HMS WATCHMAN 126
'W' Class LRE 1943

Although a LRE and displaying a powerful DC stowage, *Watchman* has a single 2pdr in the eyes of the bow which indicates that, despite carrying a WA paint scheme, the ship must have had to venture into areas were E-boats were likely to be encountered. The HF/DF mast aft is, however, more indicative of an Atlantic convoy escort. The mix of WA green and WA blue on a white ship is what the scheme designer intended but shortages of green did not always make this possible.

HMS VERITY 163
Modified 'W' Class LRE 1943

Verity has a WA blue on white scheme without green. There is a large DC stowage. There are five 20mm AA and two main guns retained. Hedgehog forward and radius of action has been greatly increased for a drop in speed to 25 knots. It was only when newer ships started to come on line that the Admiralty could spare ships for such an extensive refit, hence LREs did not start to appear until mid-war and later.

WWI PROGRAMME SHAKESPEARE CLASS DESTROYER LEADERS

HMS KEPPEL 184
Destroyer Leader 1940

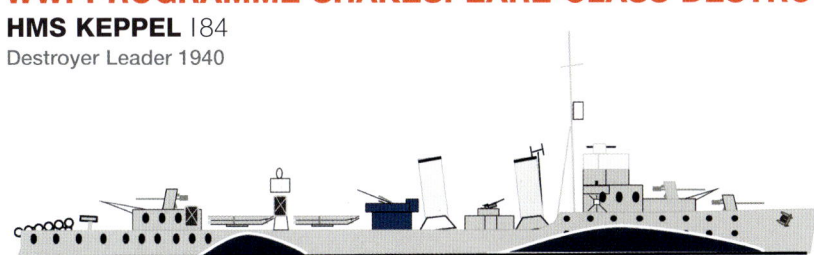

This was a very early camouflage scheme that is almost certainly unofficial, or at the direction of the flotilla commander. Early schemes often favoured blue with outlines in white or black. Note that the funnels, upper bridge and searchlight platform are in a lighter grey. There is no radar fitted as yet. 'Y' gun has been landed for more DCs. There are single 2pdr between the funnels and a 3in AA aft of the rear funnel. All tubes are retained. Twin Lewis guns in the bridge wings.

HMS KEPPEL 184
Destroyer Leader 1942

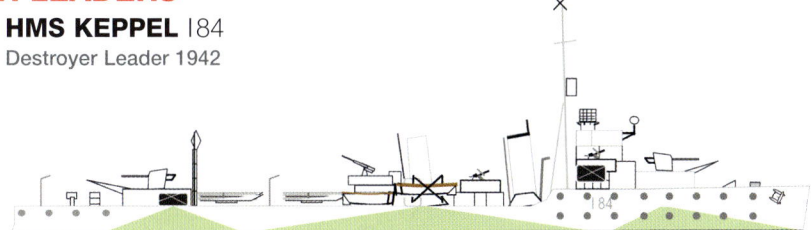

Green on white was preferred for the WA scheme rather than the often used pale blue but, due to wartime shortages, green was not always available due to heavy army and air force demand. Pigment availability and whoever mixed it could result in differences in shade. This ship had not lost any torpedo tubes for a 3in AA gun as she already had one aft of the rear funnel. There are 20mm in the bridge wings and between the funnels. Two main guns have been retained and a Hedgehog fitted forward. Radar fit is typical with Type 291 at the masthead and a Type 271 lantern atop the bridge.

HMS BROKE I83
Destroyer Leader 1940

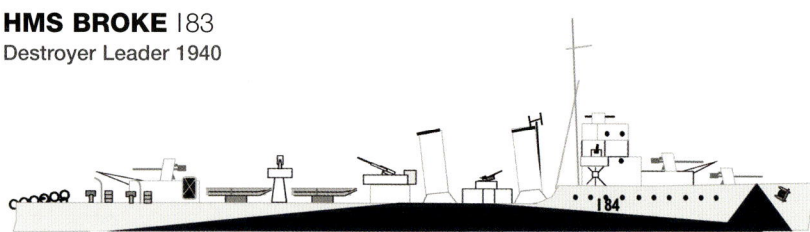

A very early unofficial attempt at camouflage. Very pale upper works of lightened grey, 507c grey hull and black areas. Decks were Corticene with steel areas painted dark grey. This type of scheme was often designed by the officers of each ship. In some cases, Captain (D) may have influenced how the ships of his flotilla were painted. More depth charges fitted at the expense of landing 'Y' gun. No radar fitted.

SCOTT CLASS DESTROYER LEADERS

HMS MALCOLM I19
Destroyer Leader 1942

Malcolm wears a very intense scheme based on the white, blue, green colours of the WA type. Her deck was painted in dark grey. There is a Hedgehog forward and extensive DCs aft including extra stowage replacing her after torpedo tubes. She retains two of her 4.7in guns and a 3in AA behind the aft funnel. She has 20mm in the bridge wings and a single aft in 'Y' position, as well as two 2pdr between the funnels. HF/DF has been added on a mast aft. There are radar Types 286PU (full rotation) on the mast and 271 in a lantern on the bridge.

HMS MONTROSE I01
Destroyer Leader 1940

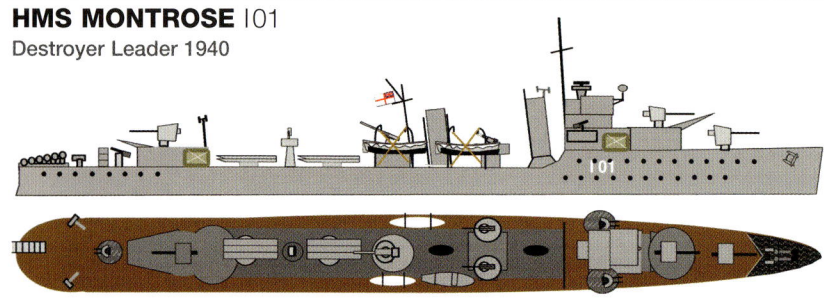

Montrose shortly after the outbreak of war. The aft gun has been landed for more DCs and a twin Lewis gun. The 3in AA is still aft of the rear funnel and the old 2pdrs between the funnels. There are twin Lewis in the bridge wings as well. Deck is Corticene brown. The rest of her scheme is a dulled-down grey overall and the black boot topping at the waterline has been painted out.

HMS BROKE I83
Destroyer Leader 1942

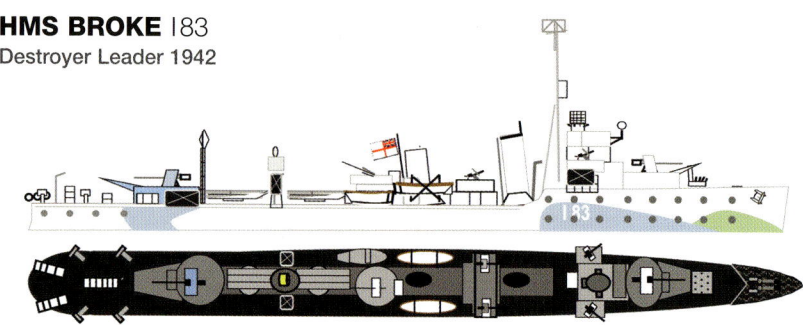

Broke displays a typical WA scheme worn by many convoy escorts, but with WA blue and green concentrated forward and aft, leaving most of the ship white. She now has a Hedgehog forward, four single 20mm AA added and more DCs, but still retains her torpedo tubes. Radar Type 271 fitted with fixed Type 286 on the masthead. There is a HF/DF mast aft to detect the brief signals made by U-boats. If other units with the equipment were present it was possible to triangulate the position of the U-boat and hunt it down or drive it off.

HMS CAMPBELL I60
Destroyer Leader 1939–40

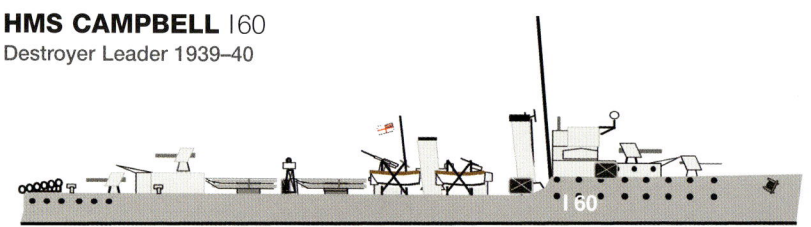

Grey is itself a camouflage colour and *Campbell* is shown in very light and mid-grey soon after the start of WWII. However, she retains a black boot topping for smartness. Ships from destroyer down were later ordered to paint out the black waterline but some retained it. She still has her WWI Corticene decks (see *Montrose*) and around her guns. There are 2pdrs between the funnels and a 3in AA aft of them. There are MGs on the bridge but no other major alterations. No radar is fitted.

HMS MONTROSE I01
Destroyer Leader 1943–4

This leader is an experimental Admiralty scheme intended to make the ship look shorter. It could also make it look like two separate ships. Colours forward are WA blue on white. From the break of the foredeck she has 1941 blue on mid-grey. There is a twin 6pdr automatic mount in 'A' position for fighting E-boats. There are single 20mm AA in each bridge wing, between the funnels and another aft of the second funnel. The 3in AA gun originally from that position has been relocated to the aft deck house. Radar Type 271 is atop the bridge, and Type 291 would be at the masthead.

DESTROYERS BUILT TO WWI PROGRAMMES

HMAS STUART D00
Destroyer Leader 1939–40

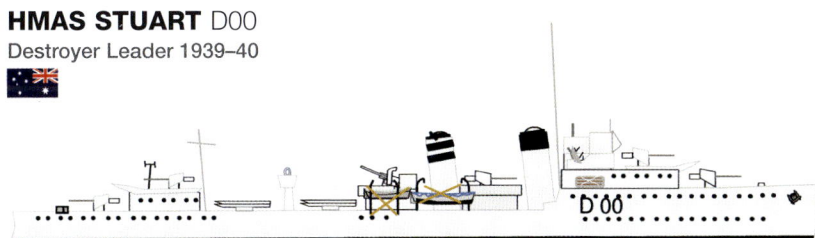

The leader of the Australian 'V&W' class destroyers is shown here in the 507c colour scheme she carried on arrival in the Mediterranean with her flotilla. The armament is as built with the addition of quad MGs in each bridge wing. Her paint style is peacetime with no attempt at camouflage and pennant number is pre-war. The application of camouflage was not necessarily carried out as soon as WWII broke out. The Admiralty issued some guidelines and designs were left up to the officers of the ship, which in many cases became a matter of wardroom ideas settled on. Then it was a matter of what paint was available. Black, white, grey and red lead undercoat were in most ship paint lockers and therefore had to form the basis of designs.

HMAS STUART I00
As Fast Escort 1942–3

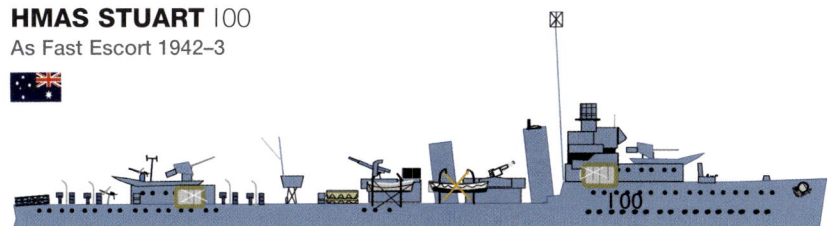

Another year and *Stuart* is now a fast escort back in Australasian waters. She is now shown in overall B6. Her armament is now two 4.7in, one 3in AA, two single 2pdrs between the funnels, and single 20mm in each bridge wing and in the place of 'Y' gun. Her ASW equipment is heavily increased. But she was an old ship and would be converted as to the right with reduced speed.

HMS CAMPBELL I60
Destroyer Leader 1941

An unofficial scheme using white to highlight and possibly suggest white waves from high speed. The design is almost certainly one derived aboard, but influenced by other ships. Edging in white was popular for some time in the early-war period. Note the 3in AA has been moved aft to 'X' position and a 20mm replaces it amidships. There are single 2pdr AA between the funnels and single 20mm in the bridge wings. The forward torpedo tubes have been removed to save weight for more DCs. Type 286 radar at the masthead and a Type 271 lantern has replaced the gun director.

HMAS STUART I00
Destroyer Leader 1940–1

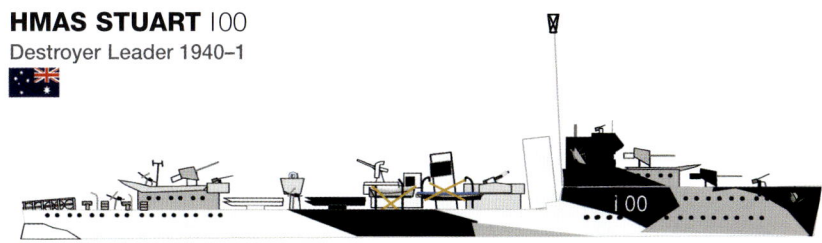

The lessons of war learnt, *Stuart* now wears a three-tone scheme that uses two shades of grey combined with black. This was a very popular mix of colours in the Mediterranean. Many ships mixed their own paint shades in this period. Her pennant has changed to 'I'. The increase in AA is remarkable. She has a single 20mm in place of 'Y' gun, a single 20mm on the aft blast shield and a captured 20mm Italian Breda on the forward end of the aft deck house. Quad MGs in the bridge wings, single 2pdrs between the funnels and a single 20mm Breda abreast the SL platform. There are twin Lewis guns on the bridge and she had a single Vickers 0.303in MG on the foredeck. ASW has also been increased. Fixed early Type 286 at masthead. Aft funnel cut down to save weight. According to a veteran of the ship, she had up to eight Breda 20mm on the deck on one occasion.

HMAS STUART I00
As Fast Transport 1945

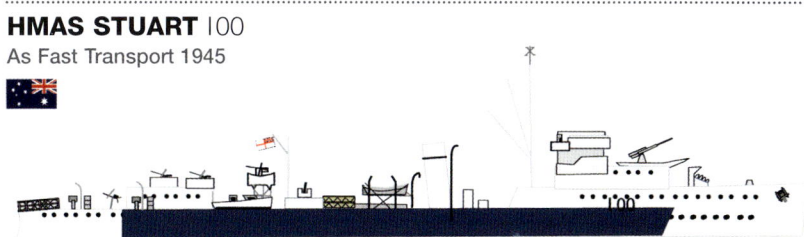

With new ships coming into service *Stuart* was altered to a fast transport. For that role, the vessel is wearing a British-style pale 507c grey with dark blue panel probably of PB10 or US Navy pattern dark blue. The panel was supposed to be from the aft end of the rear shelter deck to the fore end of the forward shelter deck and with a slight tilt forward as shown. However, as with all such things, there were many versions. The armament is now a single 4in AA, seven 20mm and three 2pdrs. She had a refrigerated store hold.

HMS MONTROSE I01
Destroyer Leader 1944-5

Montrose is shown here at the end of the war. She has a dark blue PB10 panel on the hull and 507c grey elsewhere. 'A' gun position still has the twin automatic 6pdr for anti-E-boat work, derived from the Army anti-tank gun of the same calibre. The 3in gun is on the aft deckhouse and six single 20mm are carried. The forward tubes have now been landed to save weight.

EX-US FLUSH-DECK DESTROYERS

HMS STANLEY I73
Converted to LRE

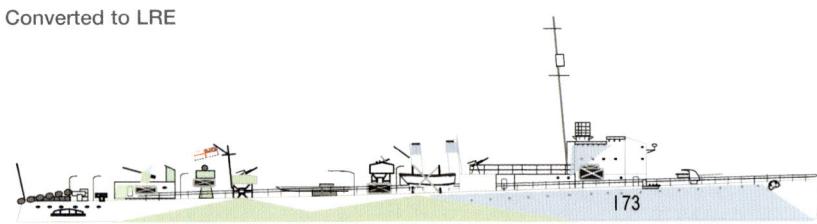

Stanley was rebuilt as an LRE but was lost immediately afterwards while escorting Convoy HG76. When lost, she was wearing a camouflage scheme of WA pale green and WA pale blue on WS white. New bridge and two funnels removed. There is a 4in forward, a 12pdr AA aft, four 2pdrs and two 20mm. Alterations gave the ship a far greater radius of action and more stability.

HMS CLARE I14
Converted to LRE

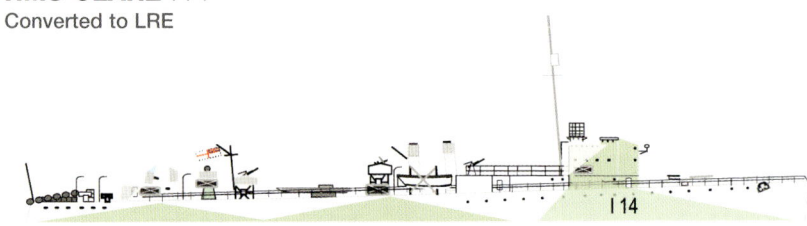

Clare had the same refit as *Stanley* but most of her type were not given this conversion as the ships were too old and worn out. The drawing shows a very pale version of the WA scheme which uses the very pale WA green that was originally intended by the designer. There is a Hedgehog forward and Type 271 radar on the bridge. The AA comprises a 12pdr aft, three 2pdr singles and a single 20mm Oerlikon.

HMS CHESTERFIELD I28
1940

Chesterfield is shown on her first convoy duty under the White Ensign. The camouflage is probably an invention of the wardroom using what was available from her paint locker. See illustration right for later appearance. Her only AA is an old US 3in aft and some MGs.

HMS CHESTERFIELD I28
1942

Chesterfield after extensive wartime alterations. Hedgehog, lots of DCs and only one set of torpedo tubes. She has 2pdr AA amidships, only a single 4in forward, 12pdr AA aft and 20mm AA on SL platform. A typical radar lantern for Type 271 is on the bridge. The scheme is one of the Admiralty patterns experimented with on these ships. The intent is to form a false impression of length and speed. MS4a hull with MS1 over 1941 blue.

DESTROYERS BUILT TO WWI PROGRAMMES

HMS RAMSEY G60
1942

Ramsey demonstrates an Atlantic scheme based on the WA type but with more extensive application of colours. The scheme was intended to have more white areas and only small panels of WA green or blue. Three funnels lowered. She has been modified for escort duty but her AA is limited to a 12pdr aft and two single 20mm Oerlikons amidships. Note that the two US-type 4in guns amidships have been retained. These were uncomfortable ships in the mid-Atlantic and every opportunity to save weight and lower the centre of gravity was taken.

HMS RIPLEY G79
1943

Ripley has an Admiralty-designed paint scheme and standard modifications for her type. The overall colour is MS4a with areas of MS1 forward and 1941 blue aft. Two funnels are also in blue. The intent is to confuse the length of the ship. Note HF/DF mast aft, 2pdrs amidships and 20mm in place of the aft SL tower. Fore funnel has been capped. There is a Hedgehog directly forward of the bridge. One torpedo tube was retained but has been relocated onto the centreline. These alterations are pretty much the ultimate for ships of her kind in RN service.

HMS BUXTON H96
1941

This is a well-thought out official scheme with a MS4a hull, broken up with patches of 1941 blue, but the use of sand or pale stone is unusual if serving on convoys. She has radar, Hedgehog, single 2pdrs and single 20mm. Her only set of tubes have been placed aft. This layout was very typical of her escort type that had received the full modifications. Radar at mast top is Type 286 fixed with Type 271 on the bridge. US-type 3in AA has been replaced by a RN 12pdr on the aft deckhouse.

HMS BRIGHTON I08
1942

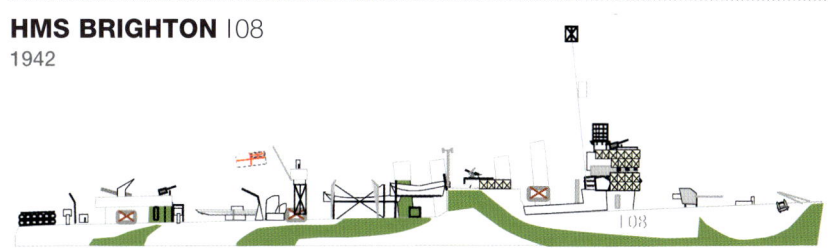

Brighton is shown in a variant of white and 1940 green. She is heavily protected with splinter mats around the bridge. Although she has Type 271 radar in a lantern and Type 291 at the masthead, her AA armament is very poor, being restricted to a 12pdr aft and two single 20mm. Apart from that, she only had MGs on the bridge and aft.

HMS NEWMARKET I47
1941

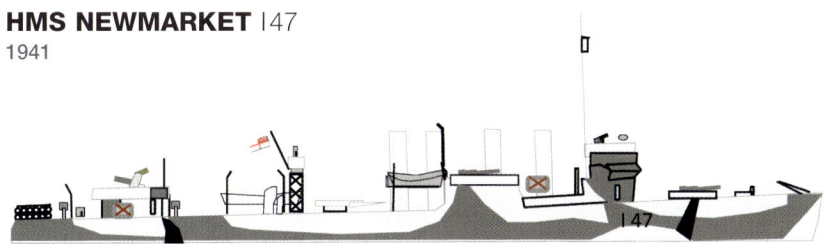

Newmarket is shown not long after transfer and with very basic changes to make her useful for Atlantic convoy duties. Like *Chesterfield*, the scheme is an early unofficial one utilising available paint. She still has 4in guns port and starboard amidships and one forward but the aft one has been replaced by a 12pdr AA. Her only light AA consists of MGs on top of the bridge. She still carries her forward torpedo tubes each side but one was soon removed and the other placed on the centreline.

HMS LEWES G68
1942

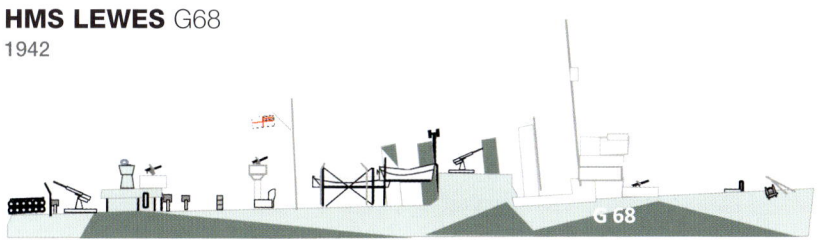

Lewes was unusual in that she had 3in guns port and starboard amidships and one aft. Forward, she had two single 2pdr side by side. Others were on the centreline and SL moved to the rear of the aft deck house. She later had all her 3in removed and more light guns added. She served mostly in the South Atlantic and later as a target ship in Australian waters. Her scheme is very unusual, utilising white for some upper areas. On a pale grey-green hull, she carries panels of MS3.

HMCS GEORGETOWN I40
1942

Georgetown is shown in a design that features a black line to catch attention and draw the eye elsewhere, a trick often used by artists. However, in this instance there seems little to draw the eye to except the black funnel top. Her hull is overall white but the panels are 1941 blue. HF/DF mast fitted, Type 271 on the bridge and one set of tubes. There is a Hedgehog forward and three of the funnels have been lowered to save topweight in an attempt to improve stability

HMCS MONTGOMERY G95
1942

Montgomery wears an interesting camouflage design which visually seems to divide her into two different ships. The 'front' ship is in MS1 and B6 grey while the 'rear' ship is in a WA scheme of green on white. Visually it looks very impressive but, out on the Atlantic, one wonders, because the whole idea of the WA scheme was to make a ship almost invisible. However, as a means of shortening the ship to the observer it is certainly effective.

HMCS ANNAPOLIS I04
1942

This is a reverse application of colours to the WA scheme and features a dark panel amidships. The shades are intended to conceal and the dark area to confuse the eye. *Annapolis* was one of several ships of this type manned by the RCN.

HMCS SALISBURY I52
1942

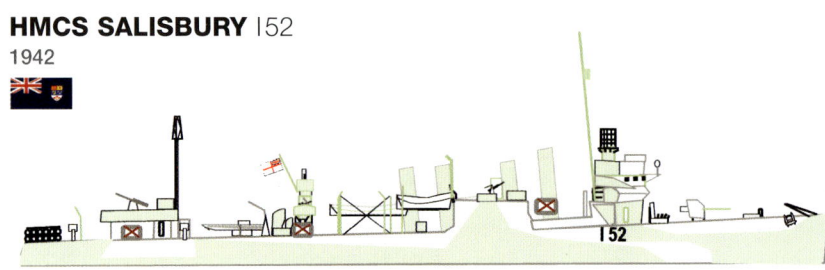

This is a pale and ghostly version of the WA scheme of light green on white. It would certainly provide a lot of concealment from an anxious U-boat captain taking very quick sightings through the periscope while getting into attack position on a convoy. There is a HF/DF mast aft. The US 3in AA gun has been moved

HNoMS ST. ALBANS I15
1943

St. Albans is depicted in an Admiralty light scheme in MS3 grey-green on a lighter shade of the same. There is also pale grey 507c. The ship was manned by the Royal Norwegian Navy from 1941 to 1944 but retained the name given by the RN on transfer. She was transferred to the Soviet Northern Fleet in 1944 as the *Dostoini*.

DEIATELNYI I45
1945

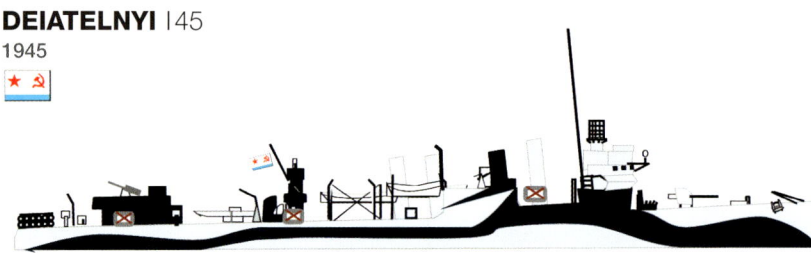

Deiatelnyi was HMS *Churchill* until 1944 when transferred to the Soviet Northern Fleet. The scheme is much the same style as she wore on transfer but repainted with Russian black or a hue called 'black blue'. The hull is in WA blue. Soviet schemes varied considerably. The ship still has British Type 271 radar on the bridge and the armament is unchanged.

DESTROYERS BUILT BETWEEN THE WARS 2

'A' TO 'I' PROTOTYPES

HMS AMBUSCADE D38 Experimental 'A' to 'I' Class 1940

Ambuscade was under refit when war broke out in 1939 and entered the fray in 507c pale grey without any other form of camouflage. As can be seen, grey is itself a camouflage and in misty conditions this would have been quite effective. The black waterline is rather prominent and spoils any chance of the pale grey making it hard to tell how long the ship is. This remained a common feature of fleet destroyers for most of WWII although camouflage instructions recommended it be omitted. The ship carries her pre-war armament with quad 0.5in MGs and no other light AA at all. Some splinter mats have been added in a pale canvas colour and the ASW fittings are very basic.

HMS AMBUSCADE I38
Experimental 'A' to 'I' Class 1942–3

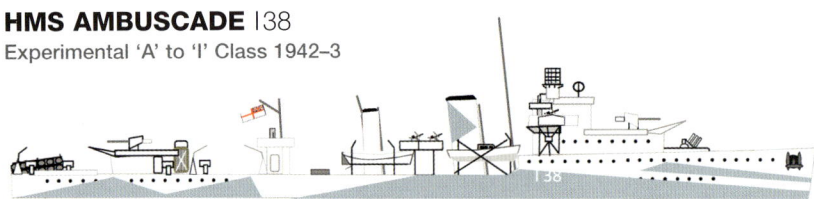

Ambuscade was a trials ship for the new Squid ASW weapon. She is shown here in a late WA scheme of WA white overall with WA blue. The Squid has replaced 'A' gun and because of weight all torpedo tubes and the 12pdr gun have been removed. Note the gun shields were of the 'V&W' class type. A Type 271 radar lantern on the bridge has replaced the gun director. Aft funnel cut down to save weight. There are only four single 20mm carried as light AA. Her duties were mostly training and experimental by 1943.

HMS AMAZON I39
Experimental 'A' to 'I' Class 1942

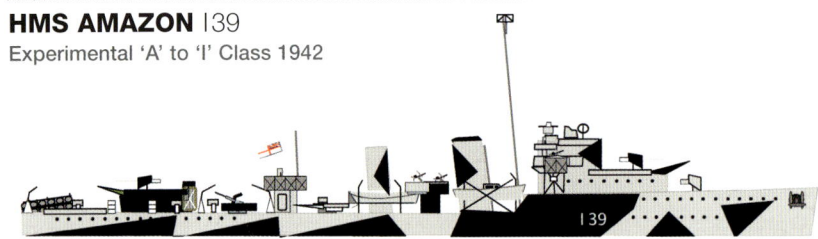

Amazon is shown here in a typical Mediterranean scheme using black on 507c grey. These were colours available in her paint locker. Ships in that region were nearly always camouflaged and many destroyers wore schemes similar to this. She now has a 12pdr AA gun in place of her aft torpedo tubes. There are four single 20mm AA and there is a fixed Type 286 radar aerial at the foretop. Few ships had this before 1941 and it was soon replaced by Type 286PU or a similar fully-rotating type. Type 286 was abandoned in 1943 when it was found U-boats could easily detect it with their Metox sets.

HMS AMBUSCADE I38
Experimental 'A' to 'I' Class 1941

By 1941 the aft tubes had been replaced by a 12pdr AA gun. She landed 'Y' gun to enable more DCs to be carried. She still carries her forward tubes in this illustration but they were removed in 1942 for even more DCs. The black waterline is painted out to enhance the camouflage which is based on WA white overall with patches of WA blue and green. The aft funnel has been cut down to save weight. There are single machineguns on the SL platform, single 20mm in the bridge wings and a pair of quad 0.5in MG between the funnels. The ASW fit aft has been greatly increased to allow her to act as an escort although, at this time, she was still spending a lot of time with the fleet. There is a fixed-aerial Type 286 radar at the foretop.

HMS AMAZON D39
Experimental 'A' to 'I' Class 1940

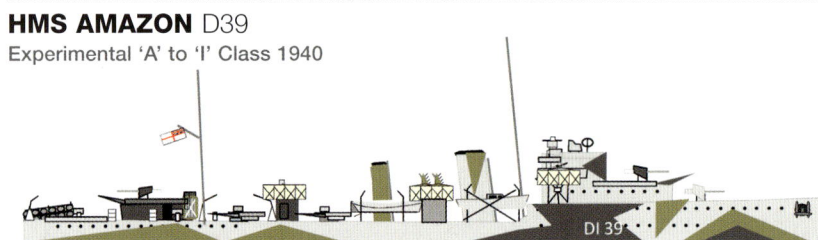

Camouflage schemes that were an advantage in restricted coastal waters were worn by many British ships in 1940. *Amazon* is in an unofficial scheme using khaki brown and B5 patches over MS4a. Her aft gun has been removed to allow more DC stowage and to save weight. Note splinter mats around SL and light AA positions. There are MGs in the bridge wings and the usual quad 0.5in MG amidships. Pre-war flag superior would soon be altered to I 39. No radar fitted.

HMS AMAZON I39
Experimental 'A' to 'I' Class 1943

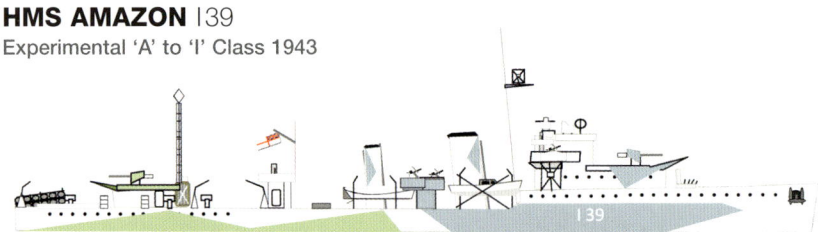

Amazon as a convoy escort. Note she has gained a HF/DF mast and a Hedgehog forward. 3in AA gun and forward tubes have been removed to enable her to carry more DCs and throwers for a larger pattern. She no longer carries splinter mats as they were thought by some as too much topweight for too little protection. Note the aft funnel has been reduced in size to save weight. There is improved rotating Type 286PU radar set on the foremast. Her scheme is now a fairly standard WA green and WA blue on white.

'A' TO 'I' DESTROYER CLASSES

HMS ACHATES H12 'A' Class Destroyer 1940

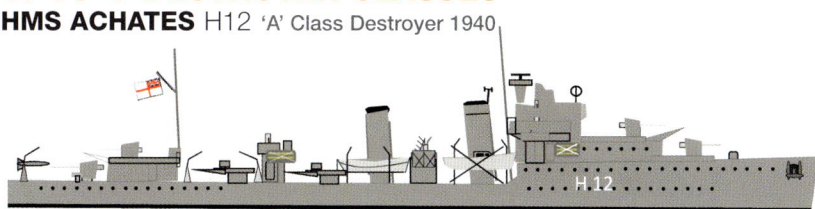

A dull overall grey was adopted on the outbreak of war, usually achieved by adding some black to pre-war pale grey. The fleet loved a smart black waterline and it was difficult to persuade officers to paint it out. Black boot topping could give the length of the ship away to an observer. Grey was a camouflage in itself and preferred by some senior commanders. *Achates* is carrying the two speed destroyer sweep (TSDS) aft and has her full pre-war armament. No extra AA guns added yet. Depth charge armament is very poor and she only has two throwers. The projection on the front of the bridge is the ASDIC cabinet where the ASW crew listened for U-boats.

HMS ACHATES H12
'A' Class Destroyer 1942

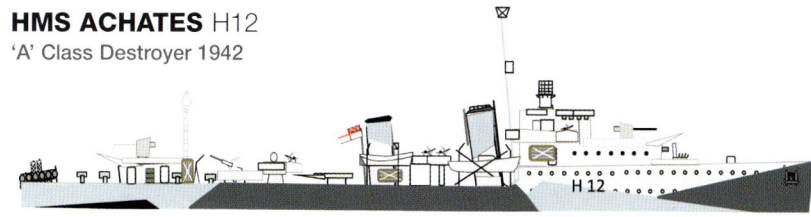

This light-type camouflage was applied from the end of 1940 but was at the instigation of a local commander. It does resemble a type later used as a standard destroyer scheme and could have been an experimental application to see how it went at sea. It is using a 507c overall, with patches of B5 and WA blue. Note there is a Type 271 radar lantern on the bridge. Destroyers had priority to receive the Type 286 fixed radar at the masthead and she was one of the first ships fitted with a HF/DF mast aft. *Achates* was lost soon after this refit.

HMS ANTHONY H40
'A' Class Destroyer 1942

By mid-war *Anthony* has lost the TSDS and a set of torpedo tubes and her aft funnel has been shortened. But she has gained a 3in gun plus four 20mm and a very large DC capacity plus a HF/DF mast aft. The use of 507c pale grey with a WA over white scheme and WA green was very unusual and probably due to a shortage of WA blue when she was last in dock. It appears to be not an entirely poor substitute. Although obviously employed as an escort, she retains most of her fleet destroyer capability.

HMS ANTHONY H40
'A' Class Destroyer 1944

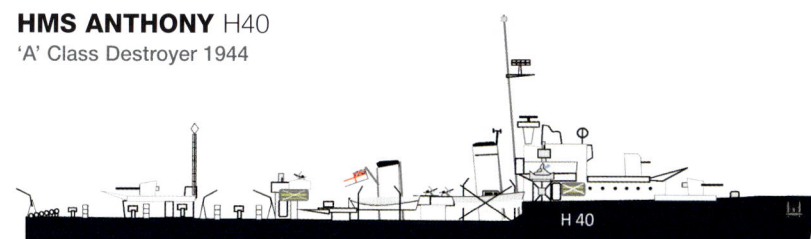

In late-war configuration *Anthony* has a simple PB10 dark blue hull and 507c grey upper works scheme. To save weight, the 3in AA has been landed. The single 20mm have been moved from the bridge to the SL platform and in turn replaced by 20mm mounts. 'B' gun has been replaced by a twin automatic 6pdr mounting for fighting E-boats and late-war Type 291 radar fitted. The ship retains a large DC capacity including extra throwers. The early 14-charge pattern was rarely used by 1944 but perhaps on German Biber midget subs off Normandy.

HMCS SKEENA D59
Saguenay ('A') Class Destroyer 1939

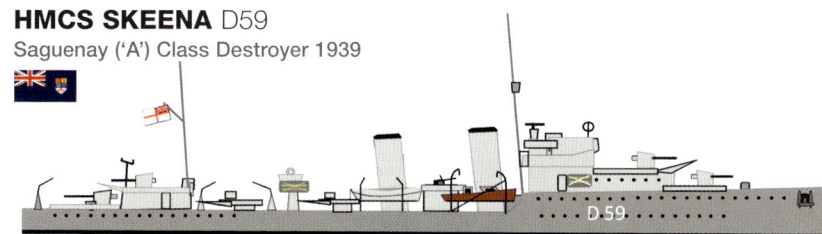

Skeena started the war with a mid-grey B6 hull and the lighter 507c for her upper works. This was fairly common among ships of the Commonwealth and some RN ships. The only light AA guns are old pattern single 2pdr between the funnels. No depth charges can be seen aft and usually only a few were carried in this early period. Her motorboat is in peacetime brown so senior officers can look smart when transferring from ship to ship but would soon be removed to save weight.

HMCS SKEENA I59
Saguenay ('A') class Destroyer 1942

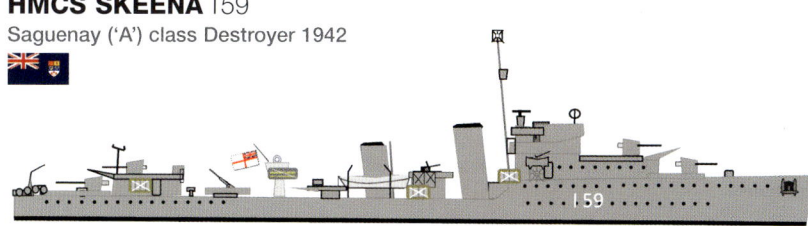

By the end of 1941 *Skeena* had adopted a mid-grey lightened 507b overall, but has a heavy black waterline. The decks would be a similar grey. The rather inefficient Canadian SW1C radar is at the masthead. Aft tubes have been replaced by a 3in AA which was standard for most British and Commonwealth destroyers. Note again how the black waterline is distinctive and spoils any effect from the dull grey.

HMCS SKEENA I59
Saguenay ('A') Class Destroyer 1943

In 1942 *Skeena* received a refit to suit her for escort duty with convoys. She carries a Canadian-style camouflage scheme for convoy duty in the Atlantic. The blue covers more area than the standard WA scheme and is darker. She has a HF/DF mast aft, 'Y' gun removed for more DC stowage and 'A' gun replaced by a Hedgehog. There are now 20mm AA amidships replacing the old-pattern 2pdr guns. There is a British Type 271 radar lantern on the bridge. The radio direction finder (RDF) previously mounted on the bridge is on a forward extension and a smaller design.

HMCS RESTIGOUCHE H00
Fraser ('C') Class Destroyer 1943

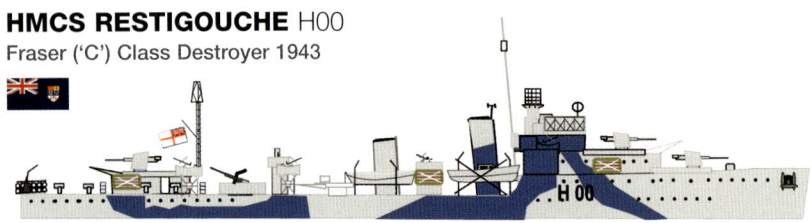

The ships intended to be the 'C' class were reduced to four by the Labour Government for economy reasons during the Depression. As four ships did not fit into the RN flotilla arrangements, they were sold to Canada. *Restigouche* was to have been named *Comet* in the RN. She has most of the usual wartime alterations for destroyers of her era. The aft funnel has been lowered to save weight. It is unusual that she carries eight single 20mm. British Type 271 radar has replaced the gun director and the remaining guns are locally controlled. Colours are MS4a and 1941 blue.

HMS BEAGLE H30
'B' Class Destroyer 1941

Beagle is depicted in a solid 507b grey scheme and the usual fleet destroyer black waterline. The funnel markings are group and flotilla identification. Early in the war 'Y' gun was landed for more DC stowage. Aft tubes replaced by a 12pdr AA gun. But she still has only quad 0.5in MGs and no other light AA. The radar on the foretop would be an early fixed Type 286 and she would be a lucky ship indeed to have that. Radar was much sought after by ship captains but was in very short supply. Once again, although obviously on occasional escort duty, the black waterline is retained which did not help one bit for concealment of the otherwise dull grey vessel. Splinter mats are carried for protection from aerial strafing but were of dubious value and added unwanted weight.

HMCS SKEENA I59
Saguenay ('A') Class Destroyer 1944

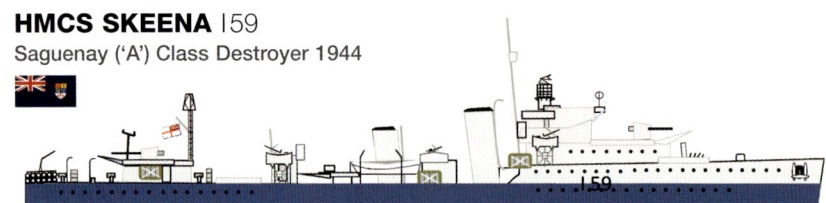

At the time of her loss, *Skeena* has changed to PB10 dark blue lower hull with 507c pale grey upperworks. The aft funnel has been lowered to save weight. She now has single 20mm on the SL platform and carries a large load of depth charges aft. The 3in AA gun has been removed to make way for DC stowage. She probably carried at least one or two Mk X DCs in her torpedo tubes. Unusually, she has another radar aerial on top of the Type 271 lantern, possibly Type 291.

HMCS ASSINIBOINE I18
Kempenfelt ('C') Class Destroyer Leader 1944

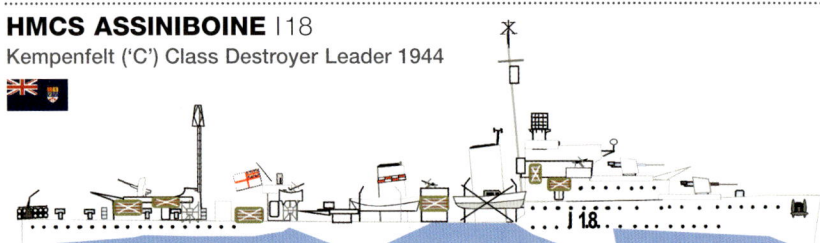

This ship was to be the leader of the 'C' class in the RN but was sold to Canada as well. Instead of a fifth 4.7in gun she originally carried quad 0.5in MG between the funnels. She is shown here late in the war with a typical Atlantic paint scheme of white and WA blue. 'Y' gun has been replaced with DCs. 'X' gun has been removed to save weight and replaced by the 3in AA gun she originally carried behind the aft funnel. There is a HF/DF mast and she has six single 20mm AA. Type 271 radar carried on the bridge in place of the gun director and Type 291 at the masthead. In the late war she carried an unusually large number of Carley floats as shown, but there is no record as to why.

HMS BEAGLE H30
'B' Class Destroyer 1943–4

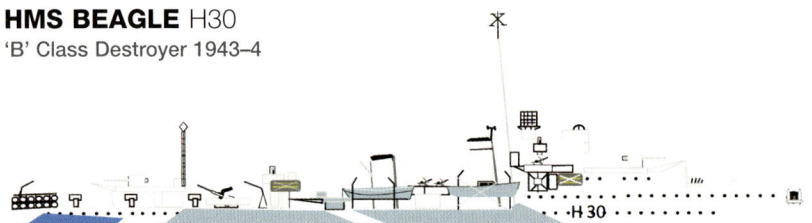

Beagle is shown with a non-typical WA scheme. WA blue is concentrated aft of the bridge and a darker blue aft. This type of scheme was intended to highlight the aft and hide the forward area of the ship to confuse a viewer as to her actual length. She has a Hedgehog in place of 'A' gun and a 12pdr in place of her aft tubes. 'Y' gun was landed to make room on the quarterdeck for DC stowage and handling. HF/DF mast fitted aft. There is Type 271 radar on the bridge top and a later type on the mast. The rear panel of the WA scheme is slightly darker blue to assist ships astern with station-keeping as this scheme was notorious for collisions and near misses through ships following having difficulty seeing the one in front. Waterline painted out as per instructions.

HMS BULLDOG H91
'B' Class Destroyer 1942

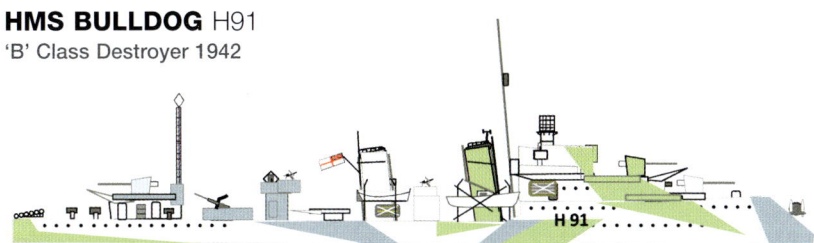

Bulldog is shown in a splinter pattern version of the WA scheme using WA green and WA blue. It uses more colours on the overall white ship than the designer intended. She retains a set of torpedo tubes and probably carried at least one Mk X DC in a tube. It was too heavy to carry like a normal DC and was fired from a torpedo tube against U-boats that were very deep. This is a fairly comprehensive pattern for the WA style and draws on other Admiralty ideas as well. The small cabin that projects from the front of the bridge is where the ASDIC operated searching for U-boat contacts.

HMS BULLDOG H 91
'B' Class Destroyer 1944–5

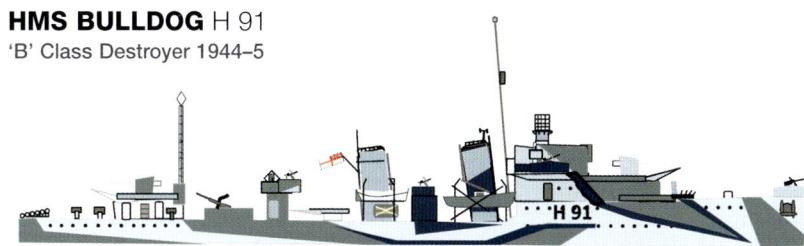

It was not uncommon for already marked-out areas to be retained but changed to another colour. In this case, the overall colour is WA blue, with areas of 507b and PB10, some of which follow previous lines. There is also a single 2pdr gun right forward in the eyes of the ship for E-boat fighting. These changes were made when she operated in confined waters after Normandy. She has probably landed the Mk X DC and carries torpedoes in all tubes on coastal duty. Radar Type 291 at the masthead and Type 271 lantern on the bridge.

HMS KEITH D06
'B' Class Destroyer Leader 1939–40

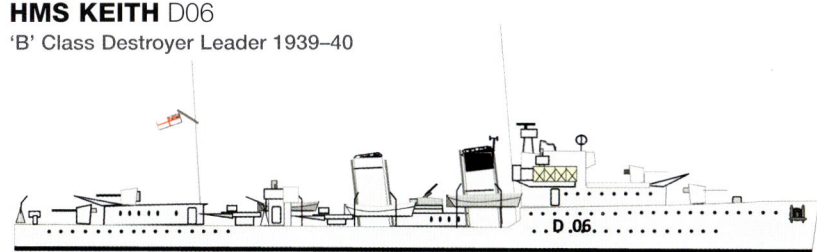

This 'B' class destroyer leader was lost early. She is shown in 507c pale grey. There are pale khaki splinter mats on the bridge. During operations off France in 1940 she may have been painted in a darker grey. Flag superior of her pennant number is still using the prefix 'D'. It changed to the letter 'I' in 1940. Prominent black boot topping stands out. As a leader, the top of the fore funnel is painted black.

HMS BOADICEA H65
'B' Class Destroyer 1942

An Admiralty dark disruptive scheme on *Boadicea*. Overall 507b with areas of MS3 and MS3 slate green. The colours are intended to blend together at a distance and make the ship hard to distinguish from the background in dull conditions. *Boadicea* has Type 286P on the mast and HF/DF aft. Her light AA comprises four 20mm. Aft tubes replaced by a 3in AA. 'Y' gun has been removed for more DCs to be carried.

HMS DEFENDER H07
'D' Class Destroyer Pre-War

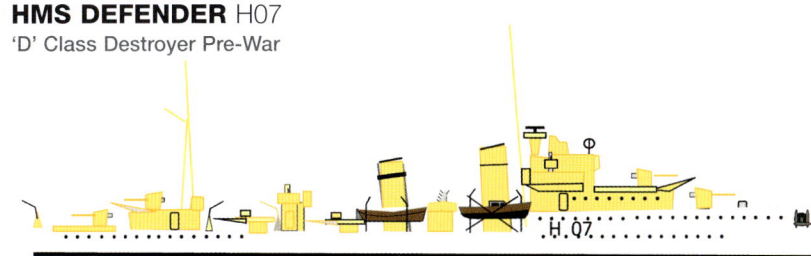

This scheme harked back to the previous century but had been retained during peacetime on the China station and for some other colonial areas. Ships on station in September 1939 retained this scheme until they had an opportunity to repaint, usually at a dockyard as it was an all-over job and required more than just the crew. The colours are primrose and white.

HMS DECOY H75
'B' Class Destroyer 1943

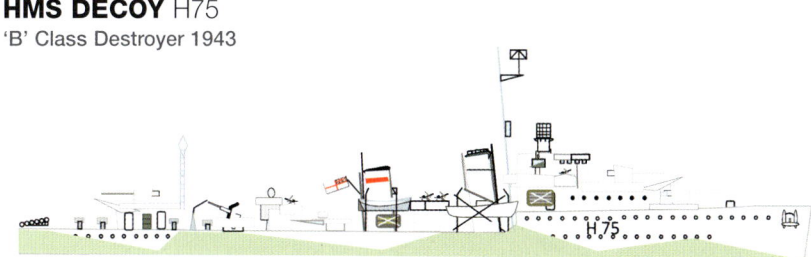

Decoy is shown with a Western Approaches paint scheme in the prescribed WA green on white. The red funnel band is a flotilla marking. Type 286P aerial on the mast but it was soon removed as it was too easy for U-boats to detect on their Metox receivers. A Type 291 was fitted the same year instead.

HMS DUNCAN I99
'D' Class Destroyer Leader 1941

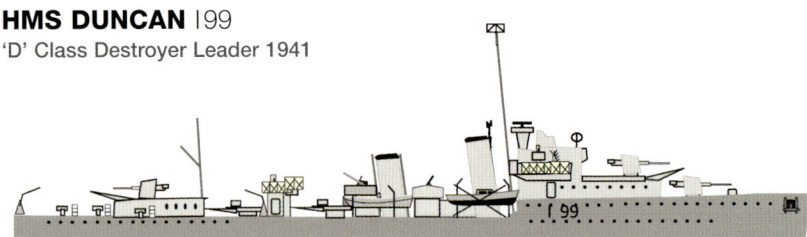

This leader was the same size as the 'D' class ships but had more accommodation. She is shown with a two-tone grey paint scheme of B5 hull and MS4a upperworks prior to her major wartime alterations. She was an important ship on convoy runs and saw considerable action. As shown, she has lost her 'Y' gun for more DCs. She had quad MGs on the signal bridge, 2pdrs between the funnels and a 3in AA behind the aft funnel and has retained all her torpedo tubes. Radar is a fixed Type 286 aerial at the masthead.

HMS ECHO H23
'E' Class Destroyer 1942

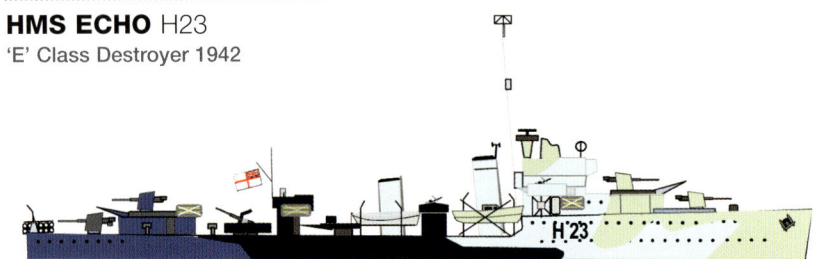

This Admiralty intermediate scheme concentrates the eye on the rear of the destroyer while reducing the bow through the use of dark shades aft and lighter colours moving forward. These are 1941 blue aft, then MS1, followed by WA green and WA blue. There was much experimentation and huge variations in ships within a class, even when serving together in a particular flotilla. There has been no attempt to dull down the pennant number and the wartime censor often removed these from photographs, yet left other more important items visible. Dark colours aft helped station keeping when ships were following others. Radar Type 286 at the masthead.

HMS ESK H15 'E' Class Destroyer 1940

Two of the 'E' class were fitted as minelayers but when operating in that form they had to land their torpedo tubes and two of their main guns. This was a very poor arrangement compared with vessels of other navies and they needed other destroyers to escort and protect them. *Esk* was lost in 1940. Her overall colour is 507b. The white bow wave shown is from a conversation the author had with one of her crew who said she had it for one operation though he could not recall which one.

HMS DUNCAN I99
'D' Class Destroyer Leader 1942+

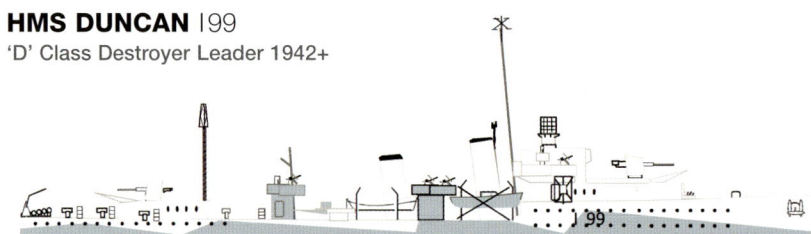

Convoy duty has seen *Duncan* given a WA scheme of WA blue on WS white. The blue panels are to the shape and general idea of the original designer. Her rangefinder and director are replaced by a Type 271 radar lantern. 'A' gun has been replaced by a Hedgehog. The aft tubes and the 3in AA aft of the funnels have gone but she has several 20mm AA added. There is a HF/DF mast but most of the aft part of the ship is given over to a heavy DC armament and six throwers. Type 291 radar on masthead. *Duncan* took part in many of the major convoy battles in the Atlantic but wartime alterations made her stability a serious problem.

RHN NAVARINON H23
'E' Class Destroyer 1944

By the time she was transferred to Greece in 1944 as *Navarinon*, the former *Echo* had landed 'Y' gun for more depth charges but was in most ways still a fleet destroyer rather than an escort. Type 291 radar is at the masthead. The ship flew the RN White Ensign to avoid confusion. Camouflage is typical of the Mediterranean with high contrast between very pale 507c grey and 507a dark grey.

HMS ECLIPSE H08
'E' Class Destroyer 1942

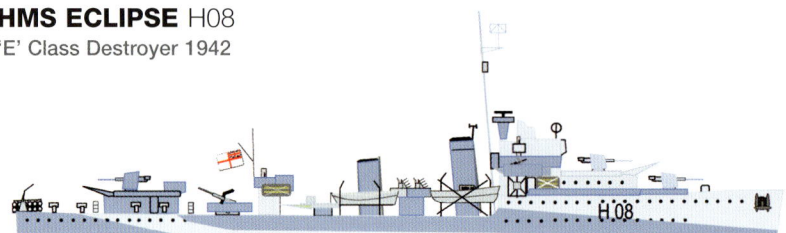

A non-standard blue scheme is carried by *Eclipse* while on convoys to Russia. WA blue overall has areas of lightened 1941 blue. She later adopted a more typical WA style by changing the pale blue to white as well as the funnels and some of the superstructure. Note that at this period she was still carrying her quad 0.5in MGs between the funnels, but does have 20mm Oerlikons in the bridge wings. The fitting of better AA was a matter of when a ship was in dock for a refit and what was available at that time. Some ships carried the quads for a long time and others had them very quickly replaced. Type 286P radar is on the foremast.

HMS ESCAPADE H17
'E' Class Destroyer 1942

Escapade after conversion to a convoy escort. Most of the standard items have been added or removed. Her camouflage pattern is a fairly good WA scheme in the preferred WA green on overall white. Note the Type 286P rotating radar on the mast, Type 271 lantern and HF/DF aft. There is also a Hedgehog forward, making this ship a very serious U-boat hunter.

HMS ESCAPADE H17
'E' Class Destroyer 1945

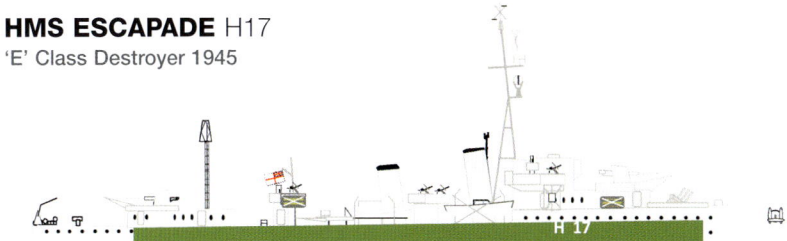

At the end of the war this ship had landed her Hedgehog and shipped twin Squid forward. The aft deckhouse has been enlarged to provide more accommodation. Note the considerable reduction in DC load aft now that Squid has been shipped. Late-war Types 291, 244, 277 radars are carried. The colour scheme is now a typical late-war type for the European theatre with a 1940 green hull panel. This could vary quite a lot, with some ships having a darker one and others a much lighter panel. Sometimes the rest of the ship was painted in a duck egg green.

HMS FAME H78
'F' Class Destroyer 1941

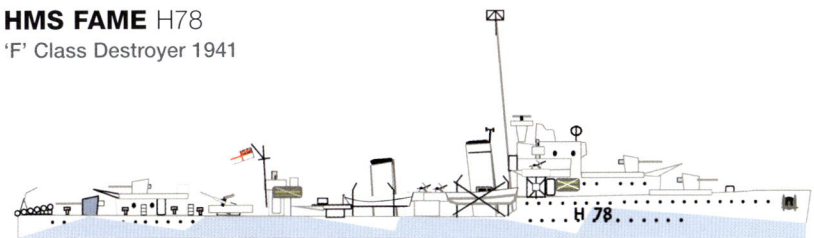

Fame is shown in a WA paint scheme of WA blue on white. She has not yet lost any guns to anti-submarine weapons but her aft tubes have been replaced by a 3in AA gun of dubious value as it was locally controlled and slow to train. There are four 20mm carried as light AA and the older quad MGs removed. Type 286 fixed radar is carried at the head of the mast. She is in all respects still a fleet destroyer despite WA-type camouflage being worn.

HMS FAME H78
'F' Class Destroyer 1942

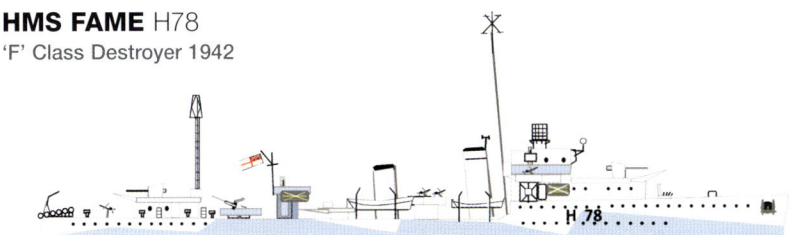

Fame in late 1942. She now has a WA blue panel on the bridge and the SL platform is also blue. These are minor but interesting differences. Was it official or just a dockyard thing? Other changes are structural and quite considerable. She has a single 20mm AA on the quarterdeck in place of 'X' gun, a Type 271 radar lantern has replaced the director and rangefinder. Type 291 radar is carried at the mast head. 'A' gun has been replaced by a Hedgehog. Removal of 'Y' gun enabled more DCs to be carried. This is the ultimate escort conversion.

HMS FAULKNOR H62
'F' Class Destroyer Leader 1941

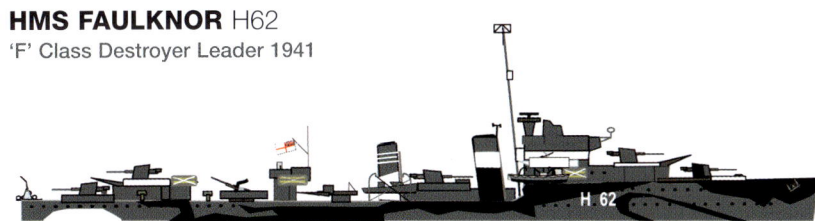

This is an Admiralty dark camouflage scheme introduced in early 1942. It has MS2 overall, with areas of black and white. The white patch aft at water level is to give an impression of the ship at speed. *Faulknor* is still a fleet unit and carries all her guns. Only a set of torpedo tubes has been removed to allow for the fitting of a 3in AA gun. This was common practice after Norway and the fall of France when the full fury of air attack had been experienced. These pre-war destroyers had little to fight back with against intensive air attack as their main guns were LA weapons. There are 20mm in the bridge wings but they are the only light AA carried. No anti-submarine changes have been made yet. The lack of alteration suggests that, as a leader, the ship has been too busy for anything but the most cursory dockyard visits.

HMS FAULKNOR H62
'F' Class Destroyer Leader 1942

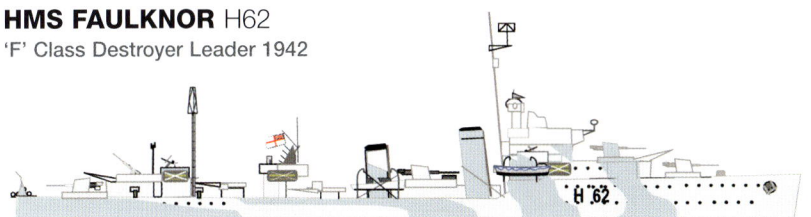

Faulknor is shown in a very pale WA variation of 507c grey instead of white and WA blue. Apart from the 'Tribal' class, it seems to have been unique to this ship. Note she has Type 285 radar on the bridge-top AA director instead of the original rangefinder. Main radar is now the fully rotating Type 286P. She has a HF/DF mast aft. Her 3in AA gun has replaced 'X' gun and four 20mm are carried. Her torpedo tubes are restored but she may carry a reduced number of torpedoes to save topweight which was critical on Atlantic convoy work. Aft funnel cut down. Quad 0.5in MGs were replaced by 20mm in 1943. In 1945 the amidships gun was replaced by a quad 2pdr AA.

HMS GRENADE H86
'G' Class Destroyer 1940

Grenade is shown in a very early style of camouflage that was probably unofficial and used paint that was available. It is very close to 507c, MS 1 and khaki. It was up to the captain how to camouflage his ship as there were no official guidelines at this time. However, the Captain 'D' of the flotilla may have also had a say in what was done in his flotilla. This style was common in the Mediterranean where the fleet took to camouflage with more enthusiasm than in Home waters. *Grenade* was wearing this scheme at the time of her loss during the Dunkirk evacuation.

HMS GRIFFIN H31
'G' Class Destroyer 1940

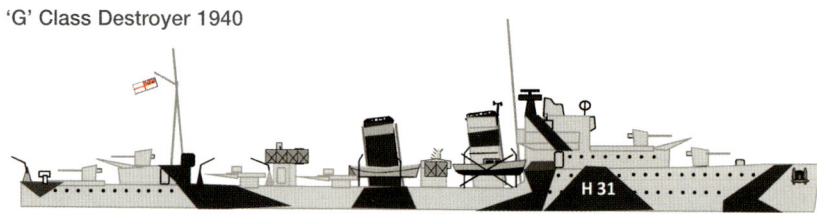

Griffin shows a move toward a more regular style of camouflage that was typical of destroyers in the Mediterranean. It is a rather simple system probably using available black or MS1 paint over 507c grey. It is rather along the lines of a disruptive scheme. There is no radar fitted at this time and her light AA is merely quad 0.5in MGs between the funnels.

HMS GARLAND H37
'G' Class Destroyer 1939

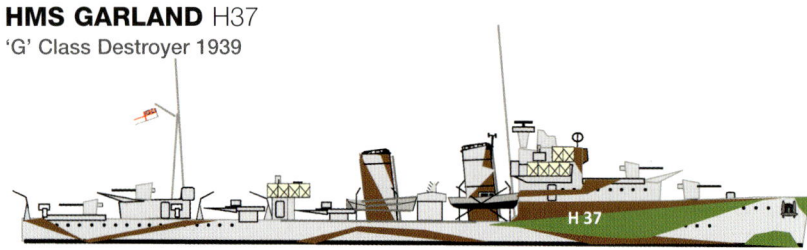

These ships had been built with a completely different war in mind. But fleet actions were few and U-boats the major menace. A very early scheme particularly suited to coastal work. Probably designed by the ship's wardroom and with whatever paint was available or could be scrounged, but it could be an early experimental design for coastal areas. Colours used appear to be 507c, green and brown. Light AA is limited to the usual quad 0.5in MGs upon which so much hope had been placed. The tall mast aft was for radio aerials and was soon removed to save top weight and replaced by spreaders on the funnels or elsewhere. There are very limited ASW facilities aft, but that would soon change.

ORP GARLAND H37
'G' Class Destroyer 1943

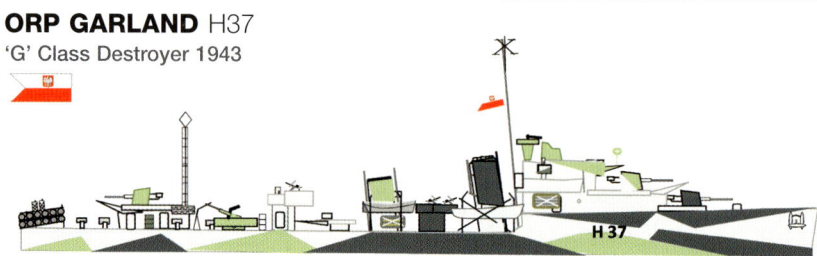

Garland served with the Polish navy in exile for most of WWII then passed to the reformed Netherlands navy in 1947. The scheme shown is an Admiralty light disruptive scheme which breaks up the view of the ship with dark and light shades. It was not a very successful scheme and only used on a few ships. It worked better when the dark panels shown here were themselves changed to light colours. Colours used are 507c, D5 and WA green. As well as the Polish flag she also carries a White Ensign for recognition purposes. She has HF/DF aft and 'Y' gun has been removed to save weight for more ASW equipment. Note the aft funnel has been cut down, also to save weight.

HMS GRENVILLE H03
'G' Class Destroyer Leader 1940

Grenville before radar and using a three-tone grey style of camouflage. She was lost early and is shown with only a few splinter mats added. She still carries the high pre-war mainmast aft. A scheme such as this would have been designed by the wardroom as there were no official directives other than to do something. It would also have been mixed from whatever paint was available.

HMS HOTSPUR H01
'H' Class Destroyer 1940

Hotspur shows a very carefully thought-out design similar to later official styles mixed from available paint. The aft tubes have been replaced by a 3in AA gun but her only other AA consists of quad MGs between the funnels. She still carries the high mainmast aft. It was not uncommon for some ships to use black panels instead of dark grey.

HMS HAVOCK H43
'H' Class Destroyer 1940

A two-tone grey scheme with a sunburst radiating lines from the bow that was intended to cause confusion as to speed. This would also be a very unofficial scheme using 507c and a darker shade achieved by adding black. Interestingly, some German destroyers used something similar later in the war. The red funnel band is a flotilla marking only. There are a few splinter mats added but little else has been changed since the commencement of hostilities.

HMS INGLEFIELD I02
'I' Class Destroyer Leader 1942

Inglefield was a repeat of the 'H' class leader *Hardy* but with quintuple torpedo tubes. She took part in convoy runs to Russia in late 1942 and into 1943. Her camouflage has more blue areas than intended for a WA style. The light blue on the hull also has a black outline to make it stand out, but rather spoils the effect than enhancing it. The aft funnel has been cut down and 'X' gun removed, to be replaced by the 3in AA which had originally been aft behind the second funnel. That would give it a much clearer arc of fire. ASW equipment has been increased but the quarterdeck is very crowded. *Inglefield* kept all her torpedo mounts but the centre tube of each quintuple mount was removed to save weight when she started the Arctic run. There are six 20mm fitted which would have been badly needed.

HMS ICARUS I03
'I' Class Destroyer 1942

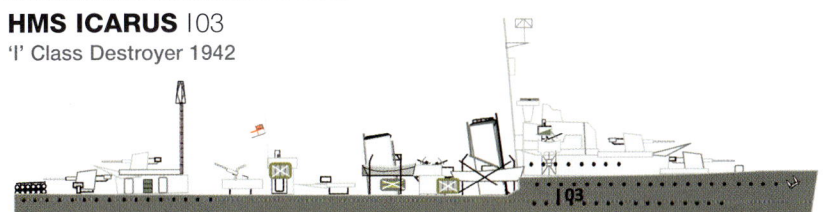

Icarus served with the Home Fleet and wore this scheme whilst stationed at Scapa Flow. It follows the fairly standard idea of a dark 507b hull and 507c pale grey upper works. Note she still carries a full gun armament but has the aft tubes replaced by a 3in AA. There are 20mm singles on the bridge wings and between the funnels. Her DC load is limited and she only has two throwers, yet a HF/DF mast is fitted to the aft deckhouse for triangulating U-boat signals. Type 286P radar on mast. Fleet destroyers had priority for this radar, but escorts had top priority for Type 271 radar.

HMS HURRICANE H06
'H' Class Destroyer 1940

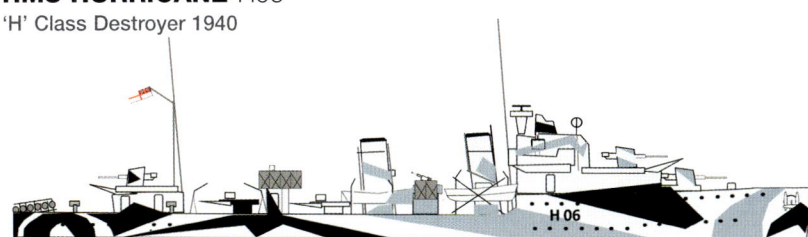

This was a scheme popular for the Home Fleet destroyers, 505c, pale blue and black from available paints. *Hurricane* was originally building for Brazil as the *Japura* but was taken over while still under construction. She completed without 'Y' gun in order to carry more ASW weapons and save weight. Apart from that she is shown here as designed with just a few splinter mats added.

HMS HESPERUS H57
'H' Class Destroyer 1940

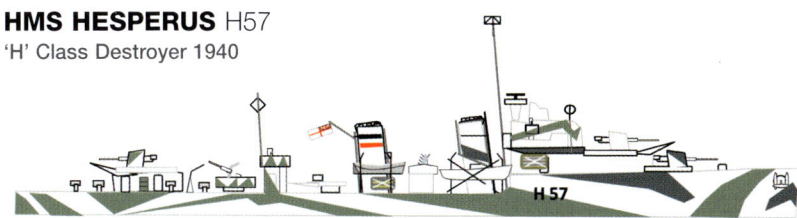

Under construction for an overseas order, *Hesperus* was purchased for the RN during a desperate period. The scheme provides soft tones for a level of concealment rather than the heavy black usually more popular in 1940. It has 507c as the base but with colours similar to MS2 and MS3. Aft funnel markings show her flotilla. There is an early Type 286 radar at the top of the foremast. These ships entered service with some war modifications applied. They were known as the repeat 'H' class officially but often referred to as 'The Brazilians' or even the 'Carmen Miranda class'. Whatever the name, they were desperately needed in a year of heavy losses.

HMS ICARUS I03
'I' Class Destroyer 1944

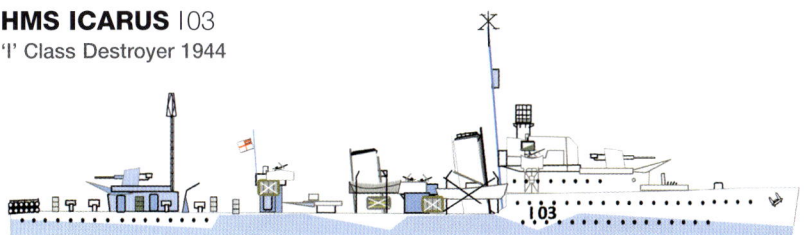

Icarus was given a full ASW conversion in 1944. By that time, many new destroyers had joined the fleet and ships of her type could be converted as leaders for ASW groups. She has a standard WA blue and white WA scheme. Decks would have been 507a. There is Type 291 radar at the foremast. Type 271 radar, which was very effective against U-boats, is carried in a lantern on the bridge. 'A' gun has been replaced by a Hedgehog and 'Y' gun has given way to more DCs. Two more 20mm fitted on the SL platform. Note extra DC throwers and deck stowage. The torpedo tubes often carried one or two Mk X heavy DCs for use on deep-diving U-boats.

'TRIBAL' CLASS DESTROYERS

HMS PUNJABI G21
1941

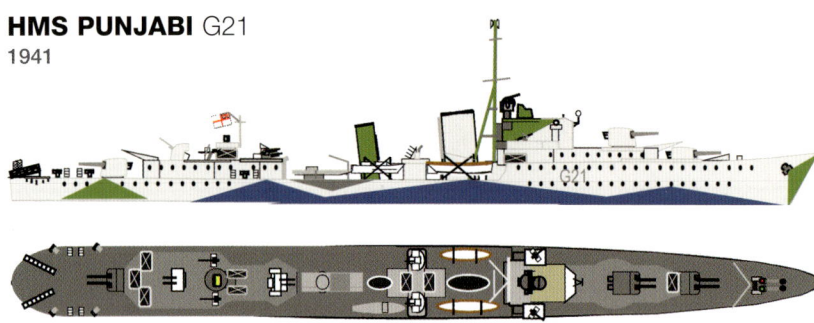

Punjabi was lost in 1942 but is shown here with some changes. 'X' gun has been replaced with a 4in twin AA. She has single 20mm on the aft deck house and in the bridge wings but still has the old quad MGs between the funnels. The scheme is an Admiralty light disruptive type intended to confuse the length and range of the ship. Colours are 1941 blue and 1940 green on MS4a overall. She has fixed Type 286P radar at the masthead and Type 285 gunnery radar on the director. Decks are natural Cemtex. The bridge has wooden slats as these made it easier on the men's feet during long hours on watch.

HMS ESKIMO G75
1942

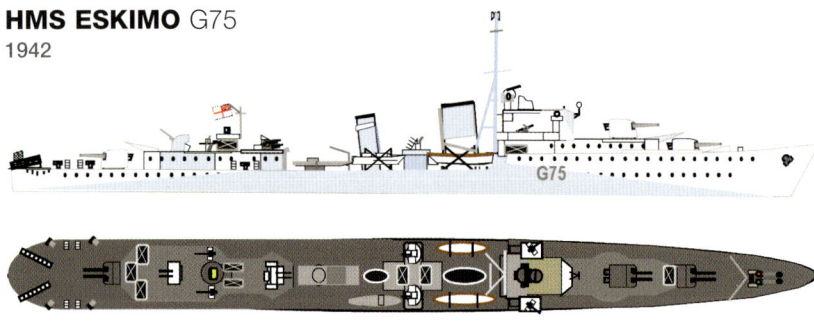

Eskimo is shown in a pale WA scheme of white overall with WA blue. When first seen, this was described in a newspaper article as being 'ghost-like' for Arctic use but, in fact, was for Atlantic work. White and pale blue appeared too easy to see when a ship was in harbour but out in the Atlantic it was the usual day-to-day shade of the horizon when viewed from periscope level, or even a surfaced U-boat. Its real problem was that it was a bit too effective for other ships to keep station on a WA-painted ship. This resulted in the addition of dark panels on the bridge rear. The WA scheme rapidly lost its effectiveness if allowed to become rusty and needed careful upkeep.

HMS ASHANTI G51
1943

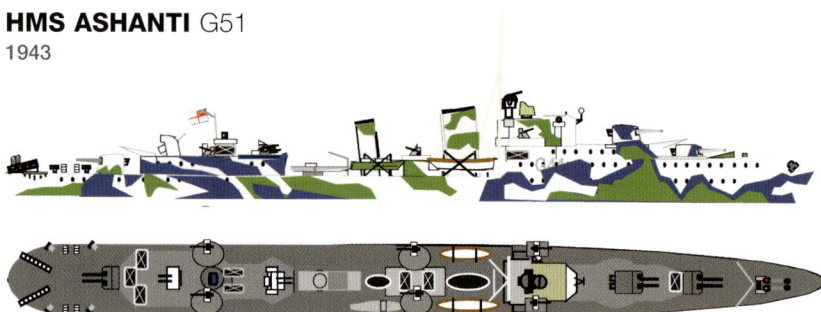

Ashanti wore a confusing disruptive scheme in 1941–2 as shown here. It was a very good example of what the designers would do if allowed to let their imaginations run away with them. The colours are a stark combination of 1941 dark blue and 1940 green on an overall white ship. Her mast was possibly very pale green. This type of scheme was intended to confuse the viewer, rather than hide the ship, but against some backgrounds there would be a level of concealment.

HMS COSSACK G03
1939–40

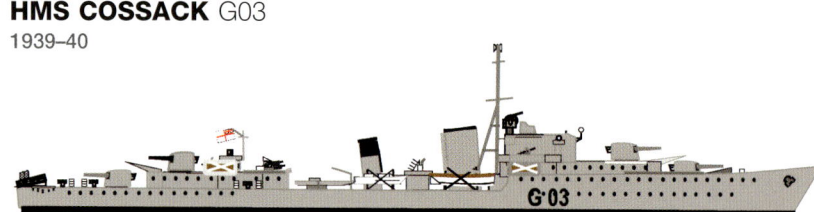

As an early loss, *Cossack* remained in a dull grey scheme achieved by darkening 507c. 'X' gun was not landed and replaced with a twin 4in AA. Her only additions are two 20mm Oerlikon in the bridge wings. She had fixed Type 286 at the masthead at the time of her loss. Note how the black waterline defines the ship, unlike the other illustrations that are in camouflage and do not display a waterline.

HMS GURKHA F20
1939–40

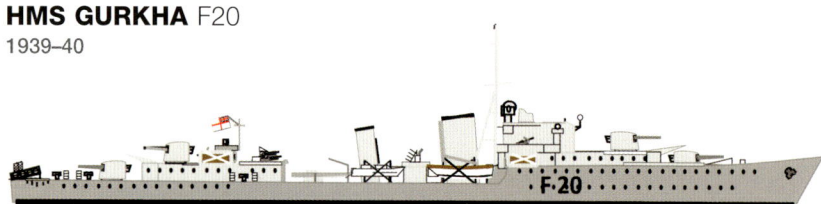

Another early war loss, *Gurkha* has a mid-grey hull and 507c grey upper works. Her mast has also been painted in very pale grey, possibly off-white. She still carries her pre-war pennant number. Once again, the black waterline makes the size of the ship easy to determine but it was hard to persuade their commanders to abandon the pre-war visual smartness and tradition.

DESTROYERS BUILT BETWEEN THE WARS

HMS TARTAR G43
1944

HMS MAORI G24
1941–2

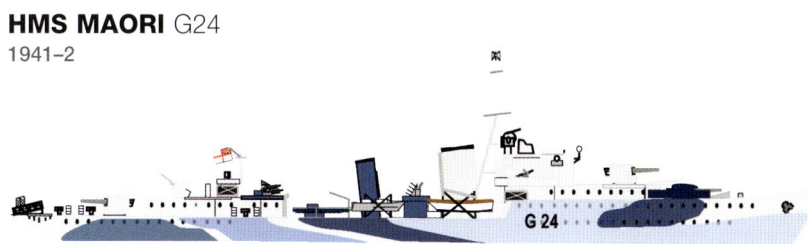

Tartar is shown in a scheme that combines the low visibility of the WA shades with a dark patch to give a shortening effect. It was found that a dark area tended to draw the eye away from other sections in light colours. Colours seem to be overall white, with WA blue, PB10 and a small area of MS4a. She is shown with a lattice mast fitted to carry the increasing amount of radar and other electronic equipment. She has six twin 20mm mounts with those on the bridge wings power-operated.

Maori was lost at the end of 1942 and has some modifications but the scheme is an early Admiralty style that combines light and dark shades to give emphasis on her amidships and lessen the view of other areas. The overall colour is 507c, with areas of WA blue and B5. Radar on the mast is Type 286P, the fully-rotating version. Decks had been dulled with dark grey to make her less visible from the air.

HMS SIKH G82
1941

HMS ASHANTI G51
1944–5

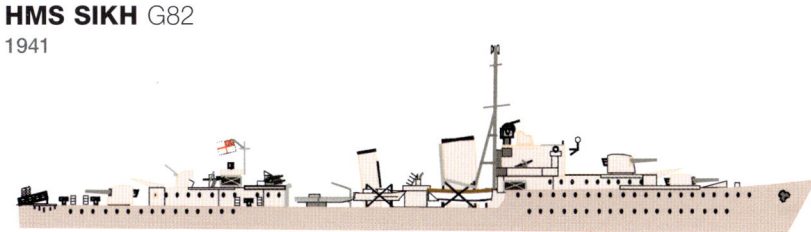

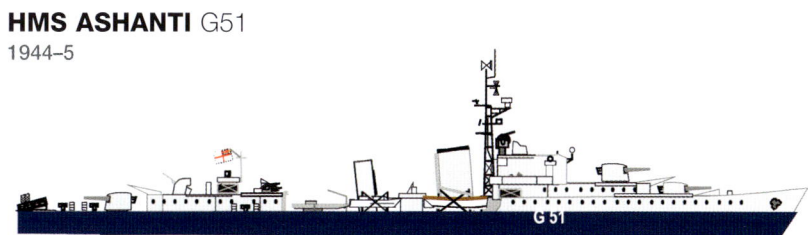

Mountbatten pink was achieved by mixing red lead undercoat with grey. Warships in the Mediterranean often carried it and crews had faith in it more because of their admiration for its designer, Lord Louis Mountbatten. However, in some conditions it was actually more visible than other colours as red tones darken more in dull light such as dawn and dusk. The ship is shown in two shades, light and dark. There is no waterline painted in which helps the effect of the scheme.

Ashanti was one of few 'Tribal' class ships to survive the war. She is shown here in her 1945 appearance with dark blue PB10 lower hull and 507c pale grey upper works. The light AA comprises four twin 20mm and two singles, plus a quad 2pdr. 'X' mount has been replaced by a twin 4in AA. The original tripod mast has been removed and replaced with a lattice type to hold the ever-growing electronics fit: Types 293, 291, 285, 244 and 253 are carried.

HMAS ARUNTA I30
1943-4

HMAS ARUNTA I30
1944–5

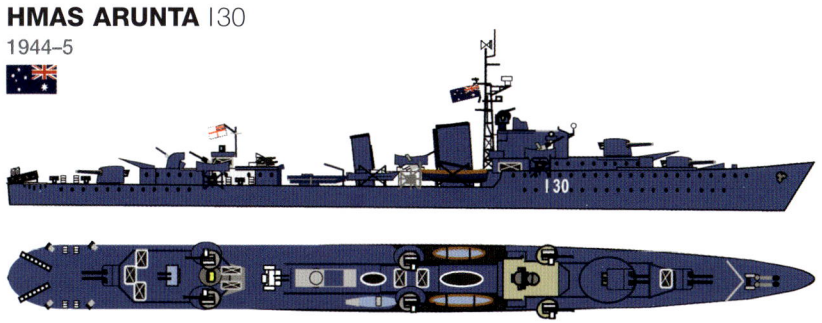

Arunta served in the SW Pacific with the USN but is shown here in an RAN-designed camouflage of MS4a overall and 507a. The scheme was later changed slightly during refits. The ship is shown with six single 20mm AA and the designed quad 2pdr. However, by the time she entered service the need for more AA had been realised and 'X' mounting was replaced by a twin 4in AA. Type 285 radar is carried on the director and the aerial at the foretop is probably for a Type 286. US-type radar was later fitted. Her RDF is shown on the foremast rather than the bridge front.

Arunta at war. She is wearing USN dark blue while serving with the US fleet. Note the lattice mast and the 20mm have been replaced by single 40mm Bofors guns but she retains the quad 2pdr. Her electronics fit is extensive but a mix of British and US types.

HMAS WARRAMUNGA I44
1943

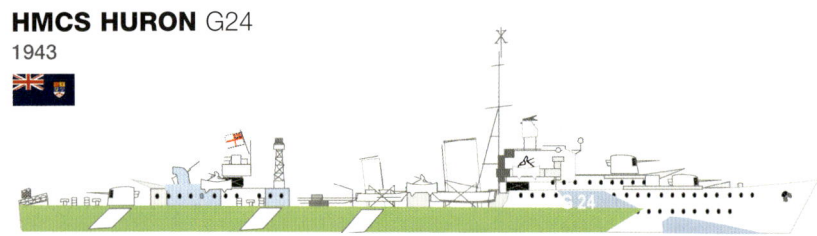

Warramunga saw service with the US Fleet and is painted to match US types. She still has her tripod mast but this was replaced by 1945. US-type blue decks were used. Being so isolated from the UK, the RAN had to rely on American naval paint on some occasions. Due to joint operations, it was also essential to be able to use USN replenishment-at-sea methods.

HMAS BATAAN I91
1945

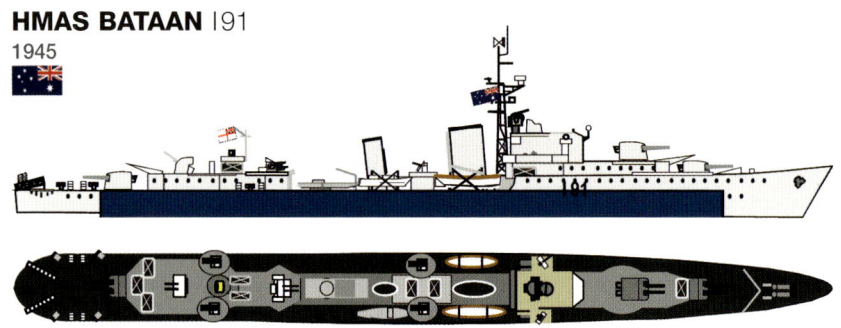

Named in honour of the American defenders of Bataan, the ship was not finished until just before the war ended. She is shown with British-type late war pale 507c grey and PB 10 dark blue waterline. By the time of her completion, the ship was to join the British Eastern Fleet rather than the Americans and is thus painted accordingly.

HMCS ATHABASKAN G07
1942

Athabaskan served mostly in European waters and the Bay of Biscay. The scheme is a typical one for 1942 when many ideas were being tried. The patches of white are to confuse the bow and, at the stern, to confuse speed. Radar Type 272 and the improved Type 271 is carried aft. Type 291 is on the foremast top. There are six single 20mm carried as well as the usual quad 2pdr. 'X' gun has been replaced by a twin 4in AA.

HMCS HAIDA G63
1944

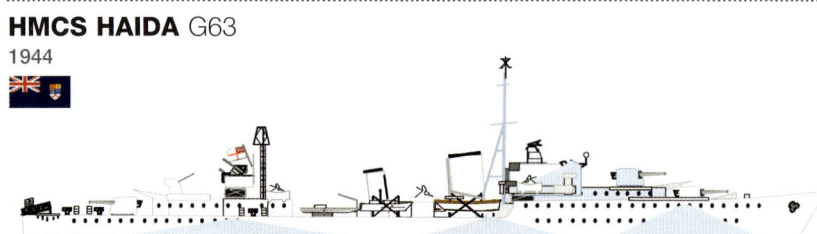

Haida is shown here in late-war fit and WA camouflage of white overall with patches of WA blue. She has 20mm twin power-operated guns and like all Canadian-built 'Tribals' she carries her 2pdr at a higher level in what was the SL position on British ships. She has a gunnery radar combined director, Type 291 at the masthead and HF/DF aft. The very pale shades of this scheme were extremely effective against the average Atlantic skyline when seen from a periscope.

HMCS HURON G24
1943

This is an Admiralty special Home Fleet destroyer scheme worn by *Huron*. It uses a combination of WA blue, with WA green on white, with three white breaks along the green panel. This scheme was lighter than most Home Fleet destroyer patterns. There are six twin 20mm AA as well as the quad 2pdr. There is a HF/DF mast aft. Radar Types 271, 291 and 285 are fitted.

HMCS IROQUOIS G89
1942

Iroquois is painted in an early Admiralty light scheme, a blend of colours that concentrates the eye toward the centre and tries to conceal the rest. MS2 with white and a darkened WA blue. She has eight single 20mm guns and no twins fitted. Like all Canadian 'Tribal' class, her quad 2pdr mount is raised higher on the aft deck house than British sisters. Type 291 radar at the mast head as well as Types 285, 254 and 253.

DESTROYERS BUILT BETWEEN THE WARS

HMS NUBIAN G36
1944–5

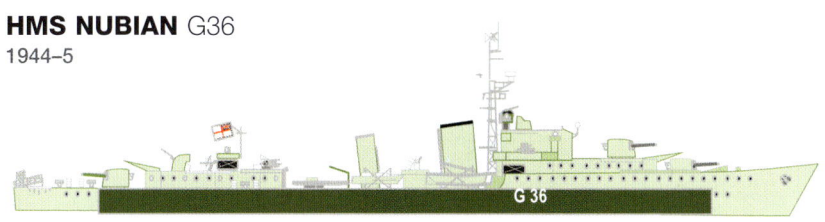

Nubian also survived the war and is almost identical to *Ashanti* in her final layout. However, she is wearing a G45 green panel camouflage on overall WA green in a style that was popular in home waters toward the end of WWII. The light AA comprises a quad 2pdr, four twin 20mm power-operated mountings and also two singles. As they remained fleet destroyers and retained 'Y' gun, these ships were not able to carry as many DCs as some other classes.

'J', 'K' AND 'N' CLASS DESTROYERS

HMS JUPITER F85
1939

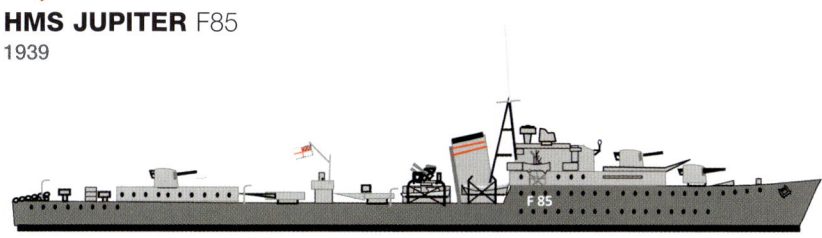
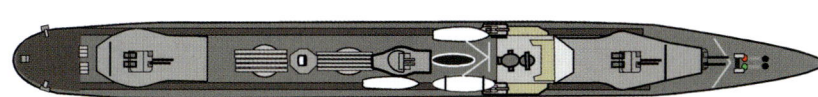

HMS KHARTOUM G45
1940

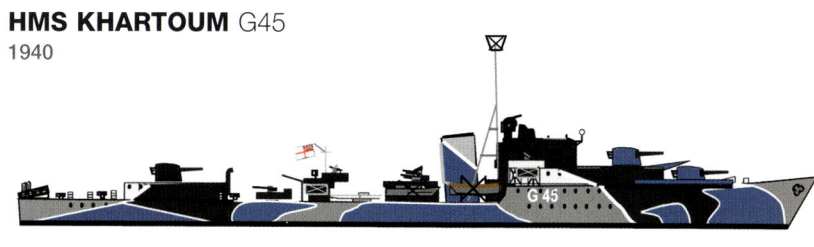
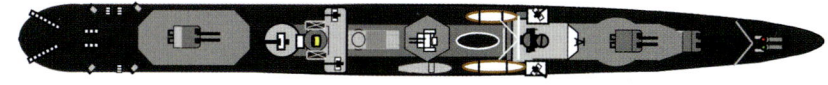

Jupiter on joining the fleet 1938–9. Note mid-grey hull and lighter upper works. She has a black lower mast and pale grey top. Flotilla bands on the funnel. Light AA armament simply comprises a quad 2pdr and quad 0.5in MGs in the bridge wings. As yet *Jupiter* has no radar and carries the pre-war flag superior 'F'. Changed to 'G' in 1940. The paint would be straight from her paint locker, as issued and mixed as required.

There were variations on the idea of shades outlined in white as is shown here. Mid-blue and dark grey are used but the white outline is not as heavy as on some ships. Note that, as with so many fleet destroyers, the black boot topping has been retained for smartness. *Khartoum* has the original quad 0.5in MGs in the bridge wings and has some MG-calibre guns added on the SL platform. There is an early Type 286 fixed radar aerial at the masthead.

HMS JUPITER G85
1940–1

HMS JANUS G53
1940

Jupiter at war. Her scheme comprises a very dark grey overall similar to 507b. As a fleet destroyer, she has retained a black waterline as a hangover of smartness despite the dull grey. The aft tubes have been replaced by a 4in AA. There are single 20mm AA replacing the quad MGs in the bridge wings, but no radar fitted yet. *Jupiter* was typical of 'J' class ships in armament and war paint early in WWII.

Janus is depicted in her own variant of the popular 1941 blue edged white, on MS4a. There is also a small white bow wave. As this style was hard to maintain, the white outline was soon overpainted in the same dark blue. Being so early in the war, she has no radar at all. Apart from having gained a single 20mm in each bridge wing and more DCs, her armament is as built.

HMS JUPITER G85
1942

Jupiter before her loss in early 1942. A dark scheme gives her a very warlike look by applying black and 1941 blue over 507c overall. There is a Type 286 radar at the masthead. Quad 0.5in MGs replaced by 20mm Oerlikons and another pair added on the SL platform. One set of torpedo tubes removed to fit a 4in AA of dubious value. The previous black waterline has been painted out. Destroyers with camouflage schemes were not supposed to have a black waterline as it ruined the camouflage effect by giving a distinctive start and finish to the length of the hull, but this was often ignored to produce a smarter-looking ship. The bridge rear has been extended to form a radar office. There is Type 285 radar on the director and one of the 286 type at the masthead.

HMS JAVELIN G61
1945

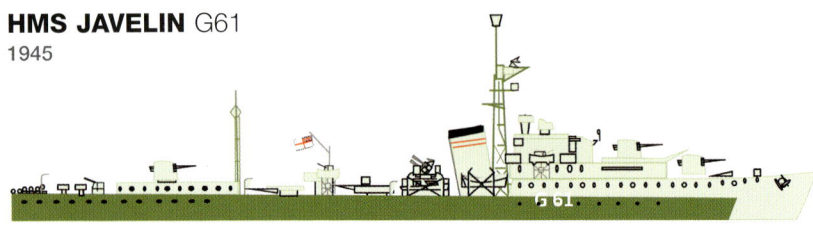

Javelin at the end of the war, one of only two of her class to survive. She has a late-war scheme designed for ships that often operated off Western Europe yet on the oceans as well. Duck egg green over all, with a panel of 1940 green. The tripod mast has been replaced by a lattice which carries an imposing array of radars and aft she has a HF/DF mast. There are twin 20mm in the bridge wings and SL platform and two aft on the quarterdeck. Now a leader, she had a black funnel top. To complement her pale scheme, *Javelin* no longer carries black topping along the waterline.

HMS KELLY G01
1940

Kelly displays an early Mediterranean style. Black on pale grey was very common and often referred to as the Alexandria type. These were paint shades easily obtainable in the region and produced some quite stark results. There was no attempt to hide the ship. It was merely to confuse the viewer. Some were of the opinion that trying to hide a ship at sea was futile and it was best to concentrate on making it hard to identify what sort of ship was being seen.

HMS JAVELIN G61
1942

Javelin has an Admiralty-designed scheme with black concentrated forward, then 1941 blue, and lightened 1941 blue on an overall MS4a. This is the reverse of the system later adopted where dark colours were used aft and then progressed to lighter ones forward. She had landed her aft torpedo tubes and carries a 4in AA in their place. There are single 20mm in the bridge wings and on the SL platform. There is a 20mm aft to counter increasing stern attacks by Axis aircraft. The bridge rear has been extended as a radar office. She has Types 285 and 286 radar. Black waterline boot topping did not fit with the camouflage scheme and has been painted out.

HMS JACKAL G22
1940

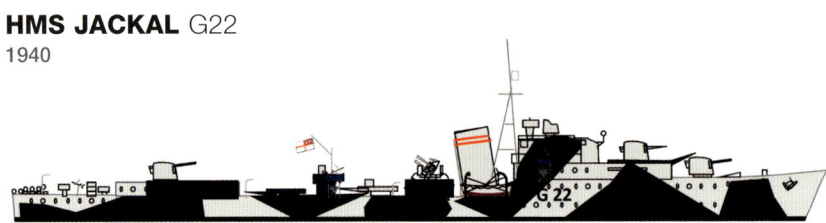

Jackal is shown in a typical Mediterranean Fleet scheme of black on MS4a grey. The use of black is striking and intended to confuse at distance. *Jackal* has single 20mm in the bridge wings and a further single aft on the quarterdeck. The ship retains all torpedo tubes and her scheme is very similar to the 'K' class destroyer *Kandahar* in 1940. The two are often confused. But *Kandahar* changed to the scheme shown late in 1940 or early 1941. *Jackal* has broken the camouflage rule and has a black boot topping along the length of her waterline.

HMS KELLY G01
1941

Lord Louis Mountbatten commanded *Kelly* and became convinced that in some light conditions it was possible to make a ship almost invisible, rather than just confuse the viewer. A shade of pinkish grey was his choice and it was quite popular for a time. It was also easily available as red lead undercoat was mixed in grey paint to get the new shade. There were also dark and medium variants. It was eventually abandoned as Admiralty tests showed it had no particular advantage over other schemes. This ship was the subject on which the WWII movie 'In Which We Serve' was based.

HMS KANDAHAR G28
1940

Kandahar is shown in a black and grey scheme common to the Mediterranean Fleet. It is similar to *Jackal* and probably based on the same idea of creating confusion to make it hard to identify rather than to hide. She has no radar aerials and apart from the addition of 20mm guns is in the same state as when built. These ships had a busy life and it was difficult to find time for upgrades.

HMS KANDAHAR G28
1941

By 1941 *Kandahar* displayed a scheme based on other ideas that were being tried and shows that more variety of paint must have become available. The ship is overall 507c with 1941 blue and B5 areas. She now sports radar at the masthead and on her director. She has had her ASW fit increased and carries a single 20mm on the quarterdeck in a fashion common to the Mediterranean Fleet. Her aft torpedo tubes have been replaced by a 4in AA gun.

HMS KIPLING G91
1940

Kipling displays another line of thought for early war camouflage. 507b grey hull and 507c upper works was reasonably standard, but she also carries a false bow wave of blue on white. This was quite unusual for a British ship and is probably an unofficial scheme. Note the total lack of radar fit. ASW fit is also limited. She has quad 0.5in MGs in the bridge wings, but apart from the quad 2pdr has no other light AA at this stage of the war.

HMS KIPLING G91
1942

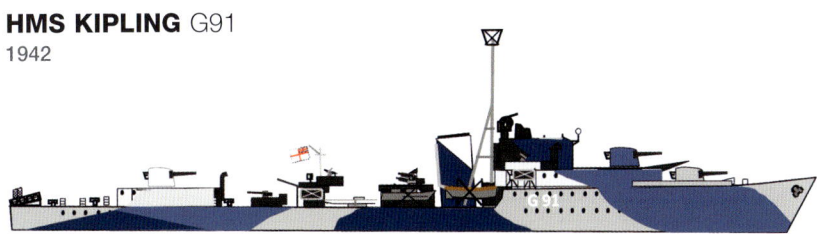

Two years later *Kipling* had an Admiralty scheme with a mix of MS4a grey, white, 1941 blue and a non-standard mid-blue. She has gained radar at the masthead and more ASW fitted aft. The SL platform now has single 20mm port and starboard. The quad MGs have been replaced with single 20mm. The after torpedo tubes have been replaced by a 4in AA.

HMS KASHMIR G12
1940

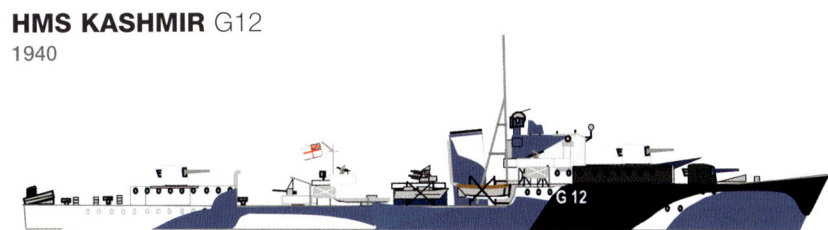

Just prior to her loss, *Kashmir* is shown in a scheme that concentrates dark colour forward and light aft. The white curve forward gives an impression of speed and the amidships one a false impression of where the stern is. The stern itself has been painted out with white. The ship has no radar apart from a Type 285 set on the director. Aft tubes have been replaced by a single 3in AA gun.

HMS KELVIN G37
1945

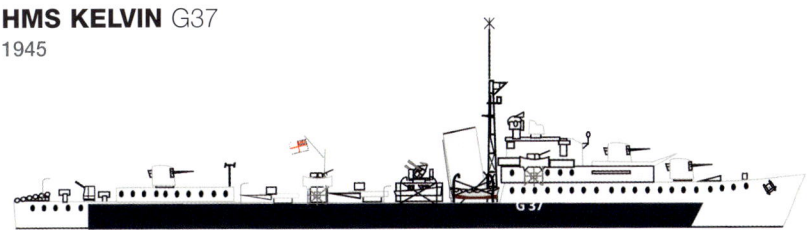

At the end of WWII *Kelvin*, one of the few survivors of her type, has a late-war scheme of 507c grey and B20 dark blue hull panel. She has six twin 20mm AA and, although the aft tubes have been restored, the centre one has been removed to save weight. Note wood on bridge and bridge wings, which was easier on the feet than steel when standing around for long periods. Her tripod mast has been replaced by a lattice and she has an array of radar and electronics.

DESTROYERS BUILT BETWEEN THE WARS

HMS KIMBERLY G50
1940

By 1945 *Kimberley* looked identical to *Kelvin*. But at the time she wore this scheme the war was at its height. On a light 507c overall are patches of a darker grey and blue. During 1940 many non-standard colours were used and it is probable that these were mixed by the crew. Unlike others she has not lost the aft torpedo tubes for a 4in AA. She has single 20mm in the bridge wings. ASW fit is limited. Her camouflage scheme is quite unusual and formed with three colours, but the pattern is almost certainly unofficial.

ORP PIORUN G65
1942

Nerrisa was handed to Poland on completion and became *Piorun* 1940–6. She was returned and given the name *Noble* in 1946. The camouflage scheme is an Admiralty style utilising MS4a dark grey on the hull with an area of 507a. The light grey 507c superstructure contrasts with the others. Note she carried a British pennant number and flew the White Ensign as well as the Polish flag to avoid misidentification.

HMAS NEPAL G25
1941

Non-standard sand and MS1 formed the scheme for *Nepal* during part of her service in the Mediterranean. She later changed to a dark blue panel and light grey as *Nestor* below. The scheme shown would have been very suitable for the very busy duties of the fleet off the coast of North Africa in support of land forces. Note she has single 20mm aft because Axis aircraft often attacked from astern. There are four other 20mm Oerlikons as well as her quad 2pdr mount. A 3in AA gun has replaced the aft torpedo tubes, but was of dubious value. Fixed Type 286 radar is carried at the masthead.

HMAS NAPIER G97
1945

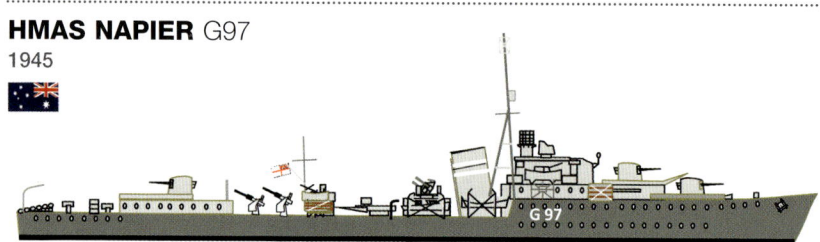

Napier is shown in her later appearance. Dark grey hull and light grey upper works. Aft torpedo tubes not restored after removal for a 4in AA are instead replaced by single 40mm Bofors guns port and starboard. There are twin 20mm mountings in each bridge wing. On the bridge she carries a Type 271 radar lantern. 'X' gun can be traversed across the stern arcs unlike the earlier ships. By the time the 'N' class were built, radar was a standard fit and an office on the rear of the bridge was provided during construction.

HMAS NORMAN G49
1941

Norman entered service with a scheme based around that of *Nepal* but, like her sisters, soon went to a scheme similar to *Nestor*. In this illustration, the ship is in overall non-standard sand, with areas of B6 outlined with 1941 blue. She has Type 285 radar on the director and a Type 286P at the masthead. She has four single 20mm AA. The dark areas of the scheme worn by *Nepal* have been lightened but are edged with the same dark blue grey. The 'N' class were Australian-manned but the ships remained the property of the British Admiralty and the survivors were returned post-war.

HrMs VAN GALEN G84
1941

The 'N' class destroyer *Noble* was handed over to the Netherlands on completion and served as part of the Free Dutch Navy. However, she operated with the RN, wore her original pennant numbers and flew the White Ensign as well as the Netherlands flag. She is shown here in a dull mid-grey all over that was often known as 'Battleship Grey'. She has the usual alterations but aft she carries a twin power-operated 20mm mount. The SL has been retained on a higher level and is flanked by single 20mm. There are single 20mm in the bridge wings.

HMAS NESTOR G02
1941

Nestor saw wide service before her early loss, including hunting the *Bismarck*, operations in Arctic waters, ASW screening of convoys to Gibraltar and a period in the Indian Ocean. Scouting ahead of Convoy HG76, the first victorious convoy commanded by Captain 'Johnny' Walker, she sank a U-boat. But on return to the Mediterranean she was in turn sunk by aircraft. A large number of her crew had come from the Australian destroyer *Waterhen*, also sunk in the Mediterranean. At the time she was painted in the scheme shown. Note she has gunnery radar and improved director. Type 286 at the masthead and 285 on the director. Built in the UK, this destroyer was the only one of the Australian-manned 'N' class never to visit Australian waters. She is illustrated here in overall 507c pale grey with a blue panel, possibly of 1941 blue or B5.

HMAS NIZAM G38
1944–5

On an overall 507c, *Nizam* wears the duck egg blue hull band common to British Indian Ocean Fleet units. Note that she has a full range of radar. But the most interesting feature is amidships where the SL platform has a single 40mm Bofors AA centrally and single 20mm guns lower down each side. In place of the aft torpedo tubes she has single Bofors guns port and starboard. She has twin 20mm in the bridge wings. 'N' class destroyers could traverse 'X' gun fully aft unlike the 'J' and 'K' groups.

3 EARLY WWII DESTROYERS

'L' AND 'M' CLASS DESTROYERS

HMS LIVELY G40
'L' Class 1941

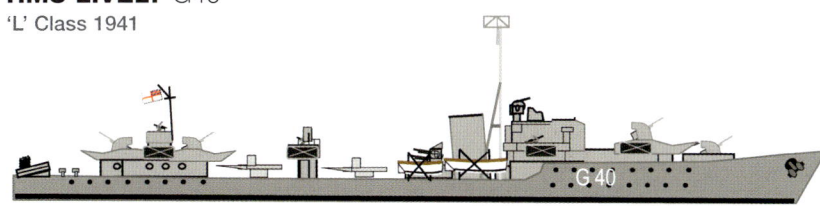

Lively is shown as completed in overall 507b medium grey but with the inevitable fleet unit black waterline that would make the length of the ship very obvious to the observer. There is a quad 2pdr aft of the funnel and six single 20mm: very well-equipped for 1940. The four twin 4in AA mounts were not as efficient as might have been hoped because there was only one director for AA fire. The ship has fixed Type 286 radar at the masthead and Type 285 on the gunnery director.

HMS LOOKOUT G32
'L' Class 1942

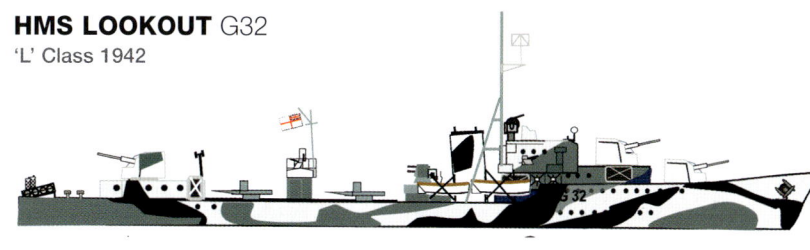
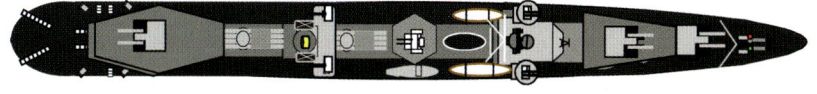

Admiralty designs often used black as a strong colour to catch the eye and distract the viewer from other details. But, unfortunately, black often had the effect of making visible something which might otherwise have gone unnoticed. Nonetheless, on an overall 507c ship, the areas of MS3 and black produces a confusion effect. There were twin manually-operated 20mm in the bridge wings, with singles amidships. A full torpedo tube fit is carried. Type 286P radar is on the mast and the usual Type 285 aerials on the director.

HMS LEGION G74
'L' Class 1942

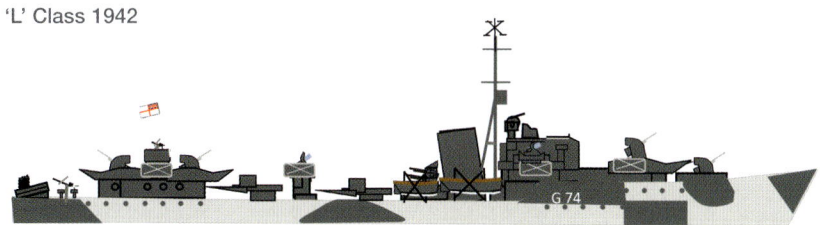

Legion has adopted a rather unusual scheme which is not dissimilar to US camouflage types two years later. A single 507c pale grey with geometric shapes in MS2 is intended to break up the outline and confuse the identification of the ship. Again, it was not an anti-submarine measure like the WA scheme but was to make visual sighting from enemy ships confusing. *Legion* was a constructive total loss in 1942. The AA-armed ships of this type suffered heavy casualties with all becoming war losses or being damaged beyond repair. Note Type 291 radar at the masthead and Type 285 on the director.

HMS LIGHTNING G55
'L' Class 1942

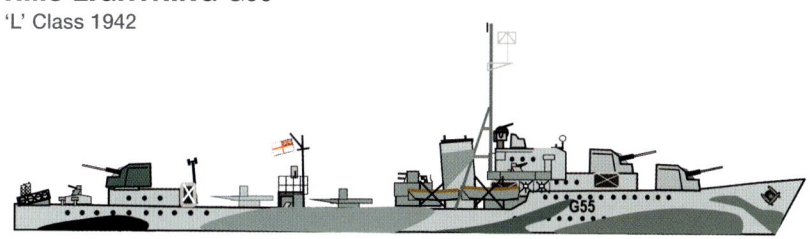

Lightning is shown in an Admiralty light disruptive scheme in early 1942. A range of colours, close in shade, were expected to blend in at a distance and make the ship almost invisible. It only worked in some conditions. On a basically MS4a overall are areas of MS3 and a small patch of MS2. The aft turret is also MS2. I have shown an area of black at the stern but this could also have been MS1. Type 286P radar is fitted as well as Type 285 on the director. Note all torpedo tubes are carried. Light AA are all manual twin 20mm in the bridge wings, on the SL platform and aft on the quarterdeck.

HMS GURKHA (II) G63
'L' Class 1941

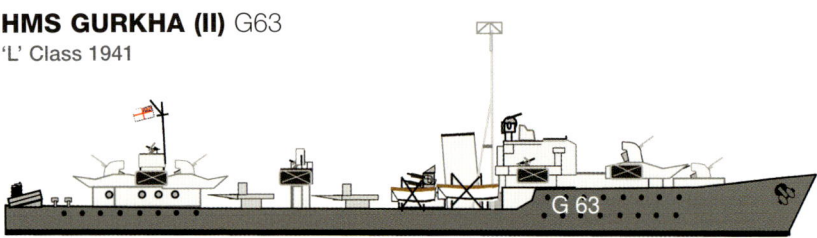

Gurkha (ii) has been completed with a 507a/G10 grey hull and 507c upper works but there is still a black fleet unit waterline to spoil the effect and establish her length. Keeping the ship looking smart was a very hard habit to shake off for many pre-war officers, especially those working with the fleet. At this time, the ship had a very early fixed Type 286 radar at the masthead and Type 285 fitted to the HA director. In addition to the quad 2pdr, the close-range AA comprises four single 20mm Oerlikons. Two more singles were added on the SL platform by the end of 1941.

HMS LANCE G87
'L' Class 1942

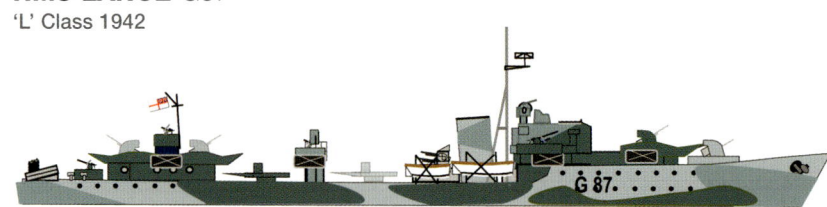

Lance entered service in an Admiralty scheme that was an attempt to use colours of similar shade with the understanding that at a distance they would blend and make the ship difficult to see. This was a measure against being seen by surface ships, not an anti-submarine one. The shades were probably mixed specially for *Lance*. She is shown with Type 286P at the foretop and Type 285 on the director. There are single 20mm in the bridge wings and each side of the SL platform, another on the aft shelter deck and yet another aft on the quarterdeck.

HMS LAFOREY G99
'L' Class 1941

Laforey's first scheme involved a lot of black on MS4a, with some patches of MS2 and seems to draw attention to the ship rather than conceal it. However, from a distance it would have had a confusion effect and make the ship look shorter. The funnel bands are her flotilla markings. Note the aft tubes have been removed for a 4in AA gun to be placed there. There is fixed Type 286 radar at the masthead. Six 20mm Oerlikons are carried.

HMS LAFOREY G99
'L' Class 1943

Laforey not long before her loss following a major refit in the UK. A scheme similar to that being applied to new destroyers of the 'Q' class is worn. Most of the black has gone and what remains highlights areas of MS2 which has become the dominant dark shade. There is a patch of white at the stern for speed deception. Type 291 radar is at the masthead replacing the older type and Type 285 aerials are on the director. There are now eight single 20mm Oerlikons.

HMS MATCHLESS G52
'M' Class 1942

This Admiralty intermediate scheme uses the familiar idea of colours close to each other applied so that they will blend and hide the ship and black to distract the eye. While similar to some Admiralty shades, I believe some of these colours are from a non-standard mix but G45 and MS1 seem to be present. The actual location of colours depended on who marked out the lines and how accurately it was done. Some private shipyards had little experience of this kind of work.

HMS MARTIN G44
'M' Class 1942

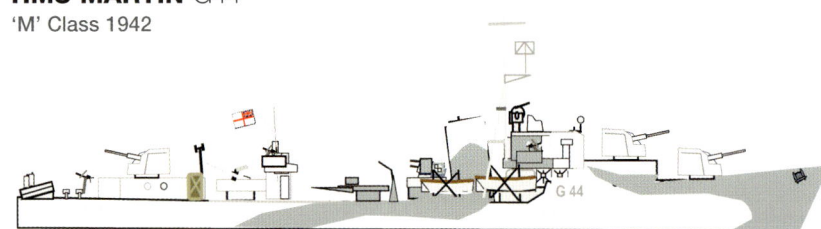

Martin is shown in a WA style probably for a major operation in the Arctic or similar as ships this valuable operated with the fleet and rarely escorted convoys. The pale, ghostly look of a white ship with WA blue would have blended in well with a misty background. She has Type 286P radar but the set was replaced in 1943 as it was too easy for U-boats to detect with Metox.

EARLY WWII DESTROYERS

HMS MUSKETEER G86
'M' Class 1942

Musketeer has no black, although her scheme is an Admiralty intermediate type, and, as a result, the effect is much better. An overall 507c has areas of MS2 and MS3 applied. It is likely very suited for operating with the Home Fleet in the Atlantic, the Arctic or Norwegian Sea. Type 291 radar is at the masthead and the usual Type 285 on the director. Light AA fit comprises 20mm twins in the bridge wings and singles on the SL platform.

HMS MAHRATTA G23
'M' Class 1942

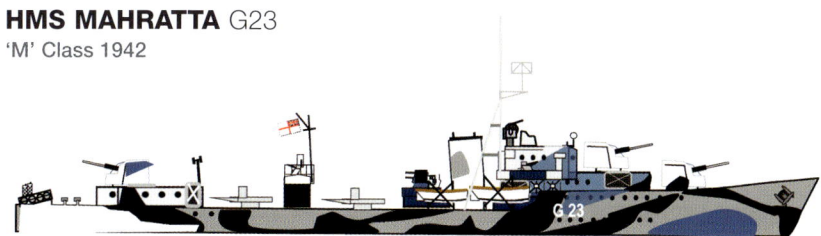

Lots of black in this confusion scheme and this time, with white at the stern, the ship does appear shorter. Light colours above make it look smaller. The concentration of heavy colour can hold the eye and, although there is no doubt it is a ship, may well achieve the aim of confusing a viewer. It is intended for surface camouflage and is not anti-submarine. The colours appear non-standard. Her light AA and radar fit is fairly standard.

ORP ORKAN G90
'M' Class 1942

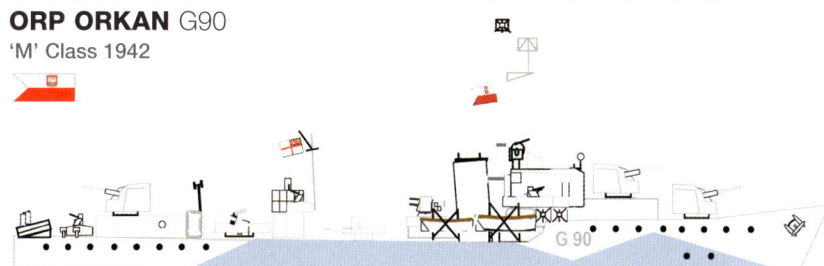

Orkan was Polish-manned and is depicted in a WA scheme of WS white and WA blue but, as she was a fleet unit, this could have been for a specific operation. The WA scheme was one of the most successful ever invented and its effectiveness can be judged by the complaints about near-collisions when trying to keep station on a ship painted in this manner. A twin manually-operated 20mm is at the stern, singles on the SL platform and twins in wings of the bridge. A single 4in AA has been added in place of the aft torpedo tubes.

HMS MUSKETEER G86
'M' Class 1943

This type of scheme was worn by several ships in 1943 when supporting landings in the Mediterranean. It has a good coastal value, but a confusion effect as well. The sand colour could vary from ship to ship depending on the mix and yard applying it. The other shades appear to be WA blue and 507b. Note there is Type 291 radar at the masthead, an excellent set that replaced the Type 286, notorious for the ease with which it could be detected. Manually-operated twin 20mm are in the bridge wings.

HMS MAHRATTA G23
'M' Class 1944

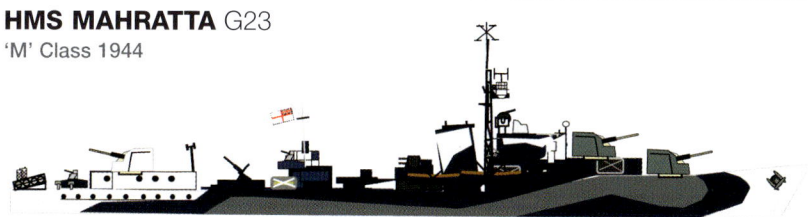

This was a fine scheme worn by *Mahratta* in 1944. Admiralty researchers were now producing better designs. The eye is drawn to the centre; the ends are painted out and the ship appears much smaller than she is. At a distance, it would be very effective as both an anti-submarine scheme or for surface actions. The ship has Type 291 radar at the masthead and Type 292 in a smaller lantern on the lattice with a Type 244 interrogator on top of it. The 4in AA is still carried but the aft tubes were replaced in the same year. The light AA has been augmented by a pair of twin 20mm on the quarterdeck and the same on the SL platform and bridge, to give a total of six manually-operated mounts.

HMS MILNE G14
'M' Class 1942

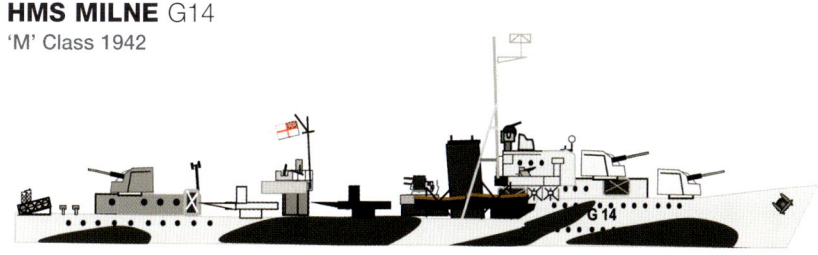

Milne is shown here not long after entering service. The scheme is simple indeed, being MS1 on 507c grey. The grey of the aft deckhouse and 'X' gun could have also been 507c. Type 286P radar is carried at the mast top and Type 285 on the director. There are twin manual 20mm in the bridge wings and singles on the SL platform. Smoke floats are carried on top of the DC racks.

HMS MILNE G14
'M' Class 1943–4

The use of non-standard sand in a high contrast scheme is well illustrated by the second scheme worn by *Milne*. The hull is a non-standard blue green, with dark areas of 507a or MS1 on the hull and lower bridge. The tripod has been replaced by a lattice mast which bears a whole range of electronic equipment from Types 291 and 292 through 244 and 253. There are two single 20mm aft, two more on the SL platform and power-operated twins in the bridge wings. The rather useless single 4in AA has been removed and the tubes reshipped.

HMS MILNE G14
'M' Class 1945

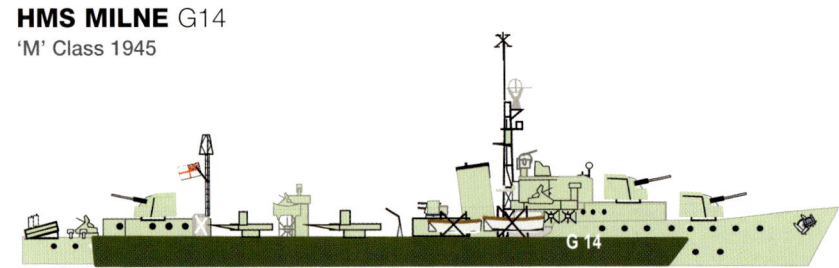

Milne is shown here late in the war and probably in her final warpaint. A G45 green panel on a duck egg green ship was becoming quite common by 1945 with many new frigates completing in that scheme. There is now a HF/DF mast aft, and a Type 277 radar aerial platform on the lattice mast, in addition to the Type 291 set, which is still carried on the mast top. There are six power-operated twin 20mm and a full set of torpedo tubes carried.

'O' AND 'P' CLASS DESTROYERS

HMS ONSLOW G17
'O' Class 1942–3

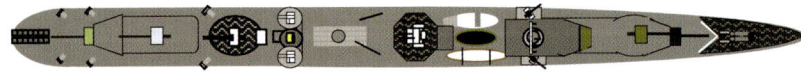

The 'O' class entered service at a time when the RN had suffered terrible destroyer losses. Her main guns are 4.7in singles as designed and probably removed from a war-modified 'A' to 'I' class destroyer. She has a quad 2pdr and twin and single 20mm, with her aft tubes replaced by a 4in AA. *Onslow* later had her single 20mm replaced by twins. Her paint style shows a move toward the later Admiralty standard fleet destroyer scheme evolving and a forerunner of that applied to the 'Q' class. There is a basic WA blue ship forward, with areas of G5, then WA green and non-standard khaki green. Once again, an attempt at the 'two different ships' look.

HMS ONSLAUGHT G04
'O' Class 1942–4

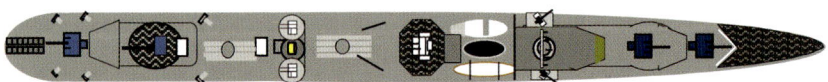

Onslaught shows a move toward a scheme that would be used on the 'Q' class destroyers. The bow is painted out in white as is the lower bridge. The hull is a darkened WA blue with areas of B5. She was a 4.7in gun ship but retains all her torpedo tubes. There are manual 20mm twins on the SL platform. Power-operated twins were provided later and the manual mounts moved to the bridge wings. Radars are Types 285 and 291.

Admiralty standard schemes for various classes often depended on available paint. They might follow the plan but with different shades. This sort of flexibility was necessary as the class entered service at the height of the war and paint pigments were neither constant nor the supply guaranteed.

HMS ORIBI G66
'O' Class 1942–4

Oribi displays a smart camouflage scheme that was designed for War Emergency and fleet destroyers. However, it could vary in colours used depending on what was available. Here she has a three-colour scheme of WA blue overall, with MS4 forward and a non-standard khaki green aft. Twin 20mm manual mounts amidships, singles on bridge wings. Single 4.7in LA main guns. The RN has not yet gained complete confidence in radar and some of the class carry an SL amidships, usually supplemented with 20mm singles on the platform later.

HMS ORWELL G98
'O' Class 1942–4

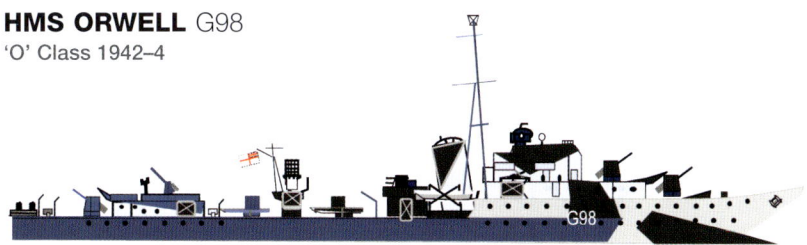

This 4in-armed 'O' class has the designed scheme for her class but in different colours to *Oribi* above. She also carries a radar lantern amidships for Type 271. The Type 286 at the masthead would be quickly replaced by Type 291. This radar fit was more common on 'Hunt' class escort destroyers but unusual for a fleet destroyer. Note that to save weight 'X' gun was unshielded. The shields of the other guns were also of a new pattern. The War Emergency scheme worn has a patch of white at the bow and an overall 507c ship. But there is a PB10 panel on the hull aft as well as patches of MS1 forward and on the bridge. While a War Emergency pattern, there seems to be some intent to retain the 'two ships' look of dark at one end and light at the other.

HMS OPPORTUNE G80
'O' Class 1942–4

Opportune displays yet another variant of the Admiralty War Emergency Destroyer (AWED) design. After a later refit, the blue panel of the aft hull was extended to the bow and MS1 areas forward removed, along with the white bow panel. She carries four HA 4in guns but has a full set of torpedo tubes. 'X' gun has the shield removed to save weight.

HMS OBEDIENT G48
'O' Class 1941–2

Obedient is shown wearing an Admiralty scheme. Pale WA blue aft and on the funnel, while PB 10 separates MS4a forward, which itself has a wave of G10. She was one of her class fitted with single 4in HA guns for AA work. However, she retains all her torpedo tubes, apparently to compensate for the weaker guns in a surface action. She has a Type 271 radar lantern amidships but only single 20mm Oerlikons in the bridge wings. The big deficiency of these ships in the AA role was the single director with Type 285 radar. That meant all guns engaging the same target, or using local control against multiple targets.

HMS OBDURATE G39
'O' Class 1942–4

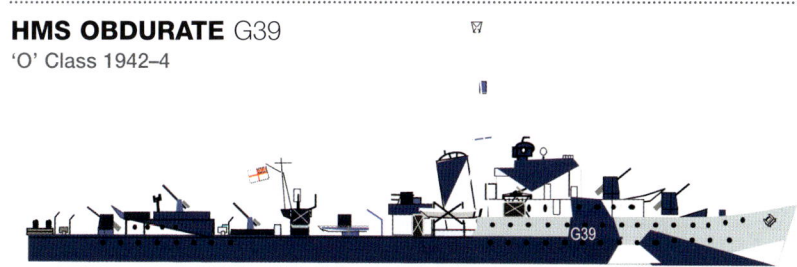

Obdurate was a five-gun 4in AA version of the 'O' class. Her scheme is yet another variant of the official Admiralty design for these War Emergency ships, but much darker. Although official paint shades were specified, wartime demands did not always allow this to be applied. Hence ships might have the same pattern but in different colours. In this instance, there seems to be a lot of B20 in use with white and MS4a. Single 20mm Oerlikons are only carried in the bridge wings, and a quad 2pdr. Radar fit is standard Type 285 on the director and a masthead Type 286P (later Type 291).

HMS OFFA G29
'O' Class 1942–3

The AWED design had many ways it could be used, often depending on available paint, but the forward panels were always black or very dark blue. Here, *Offa* has a WA blue overall colour, G10 areas forward and PB10 aft. There seems to be no white area at the bow as most ships had. She carries 4.7in guns as originally designed. A 4in AA has replaced the aft torpedo tubes. Her quad 2pdr mount is supplemented by single 20mm in the bridge wings.

HMS PETARD G56
'P' Class 1942–4

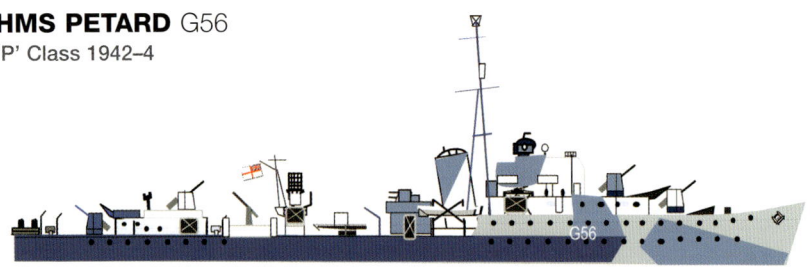

Petard was completed as a 4in gun variant of the intended 4.7in design due to a shortage of guns and a need for AA ships. She has five 4in as the aft tube position has another single 4in. This was soon removed and the torpedoes reinstated. While less powerful than the 4.7in, the 4in guns had a much higher rate of fire. She has yet another variant of the AWED scheme but without the white bow panel.

HMS PETARD G56
'P' Class 1945

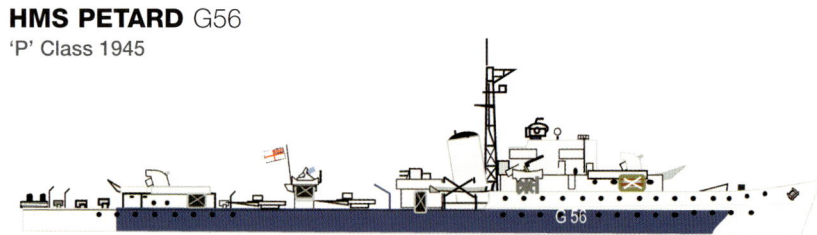

In 1945 Petard underwent a major refit. When building it was thought it might be feasible to give these ships twin 4in AA mounts, rather than singles, which would save weight, but twin mounts were in short supply. However, during refit Petard was given two twin mounts and the singles removed. Note the lattice mast, new radars, single Bofors in bridge wings and twin 20mm port and starboard replacing the SL. Petard displays a typical late-war paint scheme. The dark blue panel was intended to have a forward tilt as shown, but it was not always the case.

HMS PORCUPINE G93
'P' Class 1942

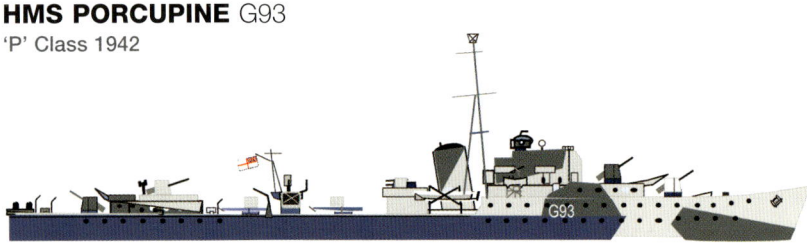

Porcupine is shown in the standard AWED pattern. Colours used are MS4a overall, with PB10 blue panel and B5 sections. This ship was severely damaged and broke in two after only a short active life. On being towed home, the two halves were used for harbour staff accommodation, the forward half named Pork and the stern named Pine. Note she has a full set of torpedo tubes and Type 286 radar at the masthead, Type 285 on the director.

HMS PANTHER G41
'P' Class 1942–3

Panther is shown in an Admiralty light scheme that was suitable for certain regions and misty conditions. Overall MS4a with B6 on the hull and WA blue areas above that. To save weight 'Y' gun is unshielded. Panther was an early loss and probably only ever wore this particular paint scheme.

'Q' CLASS DESTROYERS

HMS QUILLIAM G09
1942–4

Quilliam was originally intended to have a 4in AA gun in place of the aft tubes. However, by the time of her completion these weapons were considered to be of little value. Instead, she completed with two quad torpedo mountings. Radar Type 272 was fitted amidships with 285 on her gun director and 291 on the mast. HF/DF was fitted on the aft deckhouse. The ship had six single 20mm and a quad 2pdr as light AA. The 4.7in guns were low-angle weapons. Her camouflage scheme is typical of those designed by the Admiralty in the mid-war period and features a 507c overall with areas of B5 outlined in black or B15.

HMS QUAIL G45
1942–4

Quail is shown here in an Admiralty intermediate scheme. On 507c overall, she has areas of G45 light olive forward with B30 dark olive amidships. These are divided by a line curving upward, in MS1 olive black. Decks would have been Cemtex or dark grey. The 'Q' class were a war emergency class that used the hull of the 'J', 'K' and 'N' classes, but utilised available single 4.7in low-angle guns. Light AA was limited to a quad 2pdr and six single 20mm. Radar 291 was carried at the masthead, 285 on the director and a HF/DF mast on the aft deckhouse. She was lost in 1944.

HMS QUENTIN G78
1942

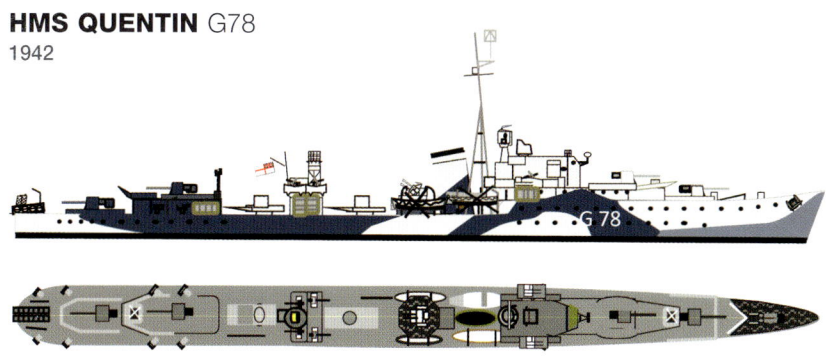

Quentin went straight to the Mediterranean fleet on completion, but her camouflage scheme seemed to be a transitional one between the mid-war swirls of colour and what would eventually become the standard Home Fleet Destroyer scheme. There is a panel of B5 at the bow and B20 over 507c elsewhere. The decks would have been Cemtex faded to grey and other upper surfaces painted in 507b. As the ship was lost within a few months of commissioning it is unlikely that her appearance changed.

HMS/HMAS QUICKMATCH G92
1942

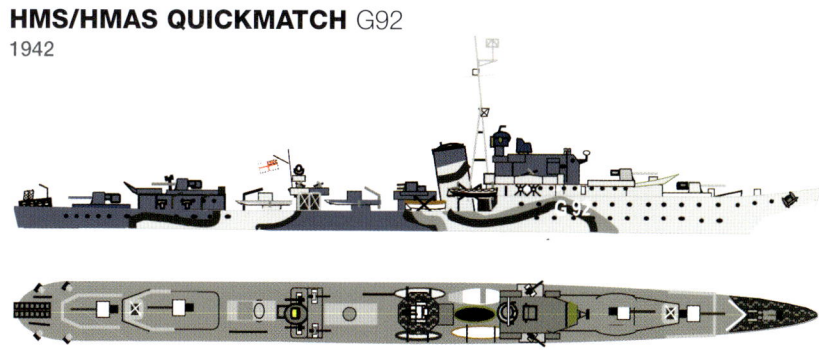

This ship and others of the 'Q' class were Australian-manned but remained owned by the RN. They did not adopt the HMAS to their name until late in the war. The same Admiralty idea of concentration of colour aft to make the ship seem shorter is shown again here but with an overall MS4a, 507a, black and B6 plus a white panel at the bow. Type 286P radar was carried for a short time only, then Type 291, and Type 285 was fitted to the director. Post-war, *Quickmatch* was converted to a fast ASW frigate and served the RAN for many years.

HMS/HMAS QUADRANT G11
1943

Obviously applied in a dockyard, the scheme worn here is almost the same as that of *Quiberon*. Only the colours vary but the intended effect is the similar. This was one of the last official RN camouflage schemes that was outlined in black. Complicated patterns were harder to maintain and the design drift was toward more simple camouflage. The radar and light AA carried was standard for the class. Note the dark grey Cemtex decks with the anchor area painted black. She also had eight DC throwers initially.

HMS QUALITY G62
1942

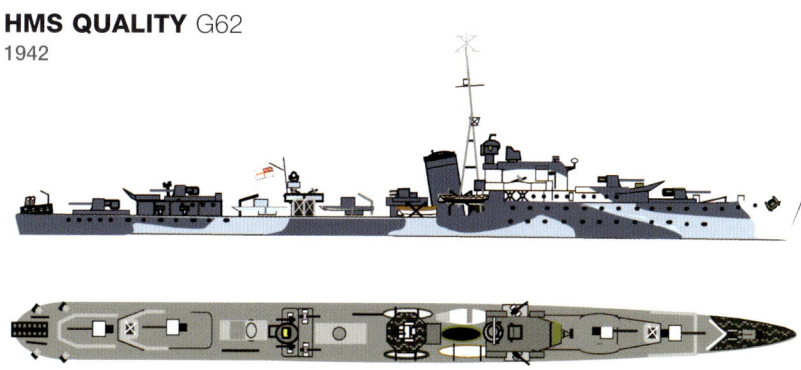

Quality sports a different way of doing almost the same thing as *Quadrant*, but the heavy black outlines are omitted. But for that she is essentially of the same overall style. This could be a dockyard variation or a deliberate attempt to assess different ways of using the same sort of pattern, simplify maintenance etc. All gunnery and radar equipment is standard for the class. The number of DC throwers has been reduced. *Quality* was handed to the RAN in 1945.

HrMs BANKCERT G09
1945

Quilliam became the Royal Netherlands Navy ship *Bankcert* in 1945, named in honour of a Dutch ship sunk earlier in the war. She is shown painted for operations in the Far East with overall WA blue and a very pale blue panel on the hull. HF/DF mast aft. Type 285 radar on the director and Type 291 at the masthead. Note the Dutch flag and RN White Ensign were both flown for recognition purposes.

HMS/HMAS QUIBERON G81
1943

This is an Admiralty dark scheme which takes the colour B5 the length of the ship, but interspersed with white and black. Some WA blue is on the bridge and forward hull. Six single 20mm was the standard fit for this class. There is a Type 291 aerial at the masthead. The usual Type 285 is shown on the director. The 'Q' class were less worn than the 'N' class ships, which were handed back to the RN at the end of the war, and five of this class served in the RAN post-war.

WAR-BUILT DESTROYERS 4

'R' CLASS DESTROYERS

HMS RAPID H32
1944

Rapid is depicted in a scheme that was typical of British ships serving in the Indian Ocean, 507c overall, with a light blue panel. She has only six 20mm AA as, with Japanese forces fully stretched elsewhere, air attack was less common. The blue panel was intended to produce a shortening effect and could vary in colour from a mid-blue as shown here to dark blue. Note that the panel is angled forward which was per regulation and ends at the end of the aft deckhouse. Type 291 or 290 radar is at the masthead, Type 285 on the gun director.

HMS ROTHERHAM H09
1944

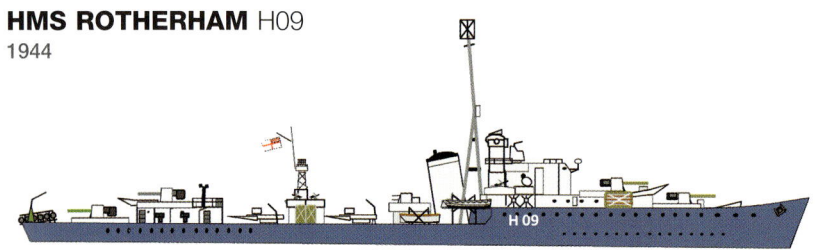

Rotherham is shown here in a scheme adopted by units of the class when they deployed to South African waters, although under the control of the Indian Ocean Fleet. The ship is an overall 507c but the hull is in 1941 blue. Note she has a Type 271 radar lantern raised higher amidships than *Roebuck*. An aerial for Type 290 is at the masthead and the usual Type 285 on her HA director. Some ships of the class received twin 20mm or 40mm Bofors when deployed to the Indian Ocean Fleet, but this ship had six single 20mm.

HMS RAIDER H15
1943

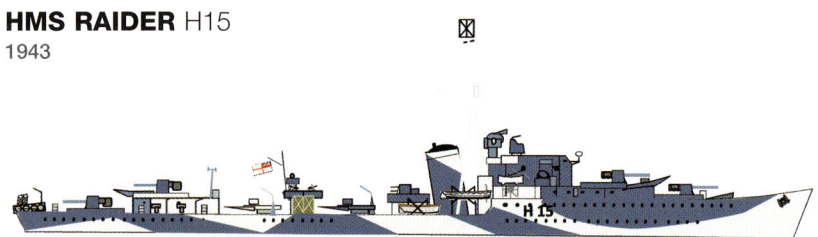

Raider went to the Mediterranean for Operation Husky on completion and is shown here in a disruptive scheme that comprised pale 507c grey with a lightened PB10 blue. Whilst reminiscent of schemes used early in the war, the colours are much lighter. In 1944 she was serving in the Indian Ocean Fleet and changed to the fleet scheme as shown below. She had the standard six 20mm Oerlikons on completion. Type 291 radar is at the masthead along with Type 285 on the director.

HMS ROEBUCK H95
1943

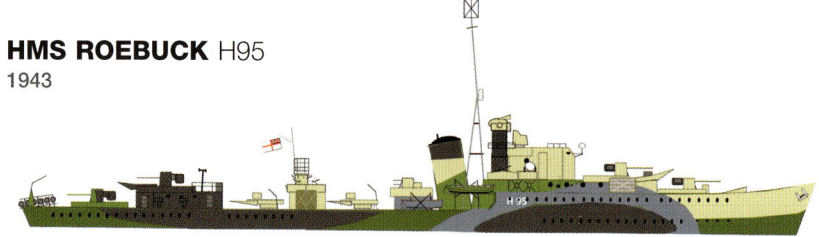

Roebuck completed in a striking Admiralty disruption scheme similar to that introduced on the 'Q' class but in very different shades. It combines a base of dark sand, B5, 507a and 1940 green. Note that this ship had a Type 271 radar lantern set quite low amidships, replacing the SL. Type 290 is carried at the masthead and Type 285 on the director. Despite the radar lantern she still carried four single 20mm on the ex-SL platform as with the rest of her class.

HMS RACEHORSE H11
1943

Racehorse is shown here in an Admiralty light scheme which would have suited her first deployment when she escorted the carrier HMS *Victorious* to the USA for transfer to the Pacific. This type of scheme takes advantage of the generally low visibility in the Atlantic to blend colours together and hide a ship when viewed from a distance. She uses three colours to achieve this scheme, duck egg blue, mid-blue and 507c pale grey. Note that she has a Type 271 or 272 lantern on a foremast platform, which was a very unusual location. Her sisters with this carried it amidships. She has 20mm twin mounts on the bridge wings in addition to the standard six single 20mm AA. The small H-shape mast on the aft deckhouse, shown on most ships, is in fact a galley chimney.

HMS RAIDER H15
1944–5

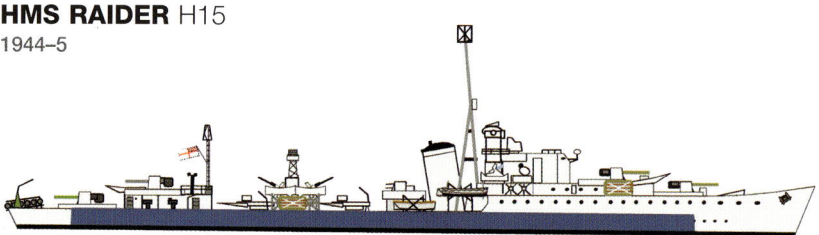

By 1945 *Raider* has had her amidships 20mm replaced by four single 40mm Bofors guns. She has twin 20mm powered mounts in the bridge wings. There is a radar lantern amidships for Type 271 or 272 and on the aft deckhouse a HF/DF mast, one of the few of her class to be fitted with one in that location. The blue panel on her hull extends further aft than the regulations stated and nor it does not tilt forward at the bow end. Tripod masts were standard for this class.

'S' CLASS DESTROYERS

HMS SAVAGE G20
Modified 'S' Class 1943

Savage was the trials ship for the 4.5in twin mount intended for the 'Battle' class destroyers. To make ammunition simpler, the two aft guns were also 4.5in. She was the only one of the class so fitted. The forward turret was a success and adopted for the 'Battle' class. Due to the extra weight forward she did not carry 40mm Bofors guns and instead has six twin 20mm powered mounts. This ship took part in the sinking of the German battlecruiser *Scharnhorst*. The Admiralty disruptive scheme concentrates colour near amidships using a base of white to paint the rest of the ship out. The stronger colours are a curve of G10, a non-standard blue and B20.

HMS SAUMAREZ G12
'S' Class 1943

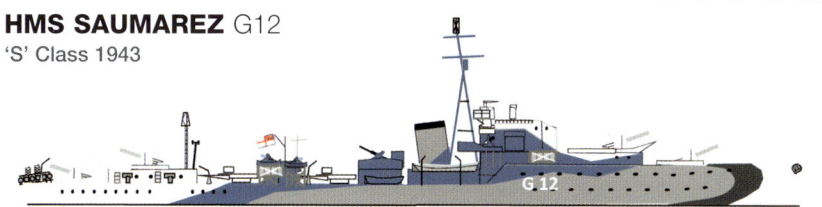

Saumarez was completed in an Admiralty scheme similar to that of *Savage* but utilising MS4 and B5 with a curve of 507a forward. Torpedo tubes and all guns white, as are the bow and stern sections. The effect remains the same. There is a twin 40mm AA aft of the funnel replacing the customary quad 2pdr. There are twin 20mm powered mounts in the bridge wings and on the original SL platform. She carries a HF/DF mast aft and a good fit of radar types. A full fit of torpedo tubes was carried and the old practice of deleting one for a 4in AA discontinued. Most 'S' class mounted 4.7in guns with a new shield with higher elevation. Only *Savage* carried 4.5in guns.

HNoMS STORD G46
'S' Class 1943

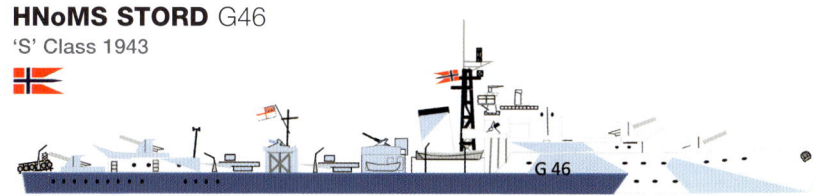

Swift was transferred to Norway on completion and served as the *Stord* until she was lost in 1944. The scheme is a typical one for War Emergency destroyers, combines the blue hull panel and shortening effect with lighter colours, which could be varied from ship to ship and according to available paint. In this case the colours are 507c overall, pale WA blue and PB10. She has a lattice mast which is painted black. Possibly due to shortages, *Stord* mounted only four of the intended six twin 20mm powered mounts. The twin Bofors intended for this class instead of a quad 2pdr is aft of the funnel. The 4.7in gun mounts are of the new pattern introduced with this class.

HMS SAVAGE G20
Modified 'S' Class 1945

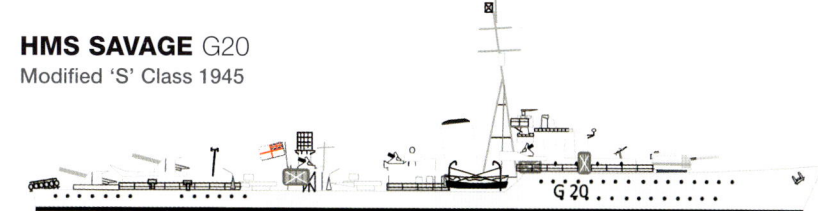

Savage repainted to very pale grey, almost WS white. There were several destroyers in this scheme which dispensed with the pale blue or green of the WA style and relied on white to hide them against a cloudy background or misty conditions. Such schemes were easily ruined by rust streaks. *Savage* served with the Home Fleet during her entire wartime career, screening battleships and cruisers during convoys to Russia, and was the only one of the class to see much post-war service. By 1945 she had gained two single 20mm, side by side in 'B' position.

HMS SAUMAREZ G12
'S' Class 1944–5

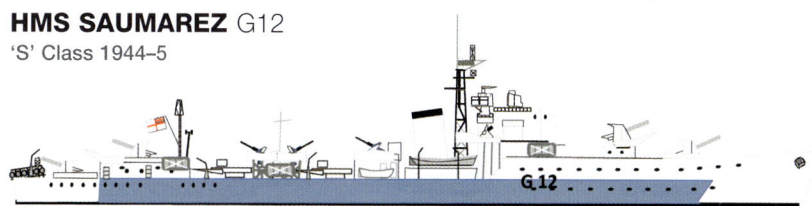

To bear the weight of the growing electronics fit, the foremast has been converted to a lattice type. There were tall and short versions and *Saumarez* had the shorter type. For service with the Indian Ocean Fleet, the typical pale grey 507c with light blue panel was standard. The panel complies with Admiralty instructions; the fore tilted forward and the length being as intended. In recognition of the need to counter Kamikaze aircraft, the ship has four single 40mm Bofors guns on the old SL platform replacing the twin 20mm powered mounts. A twin 40mm is aft of the funnel and twin powered 20mm in the bridge wings. The ensign has been moved further aft, apparently to clear the Bofors guns. Note that it was the practice to paint the lower section of the lattice mast black. The waterline is also black in fleet style, which was against the rules of camouflage for smaller ships but probably a temptation given in to for the ship to look smart.

HNoMS SVENNER G26
'S' Class 1943

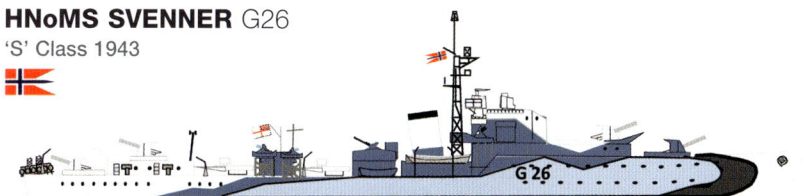

Svenner was to have been HMS *Success* but transferred to Norway on completion. Her scheme is similar to that of *Savage* and *Saumarez* on completion but there is a variation in that the curve of 507a forward is outlined in black. The rest of the colours are WS white, WA blue and B5. She has a standard fit of six powered twin 20mm mountings and a twin 40mm Bofors. The mast is of the taller lattice type rather than the tripod as designed. *Svenner* had a good late-war electronics fit.

'T' AND 'U' CLASS DESTROYERS

HMS TEAZER R23
'T' Class 1943

The 'T' class units went straight to the Mediterranean on completion but were later sent to join the British Pacific Fleet. This shows her on completion for service in an Admiralty intermediate scheme. These always took the same basic form but different dockyards might get the dimensions a bit different and use some of the alternative colours that were prescribed. So, although many of these types may appear the same, one can find differences on closer examination. Here, the overall colour is 507c, with a curve of MS1 forward. The other colours are a non-standard mid-blue with B5. As there was a mid-war shortage of some AA guns, she completed with powered twin 20mm in the bridge wings, a single 40mm Bofors aft of the funnel and four single 20mm amidships. She was one of the class completed with a HF/DF aft. Her lattice mast was lower than some of her sisters.

HMS UNDINE R42
'U' Class 1943

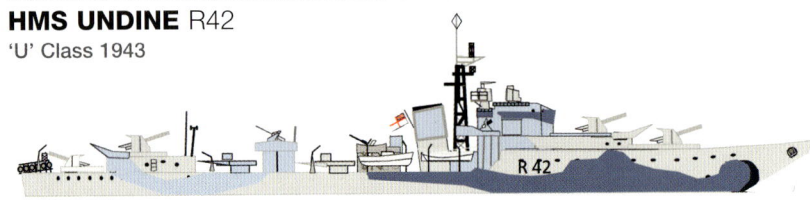

Undine was commissioned in December 1943 in this rather individual scheme. It comprises MS4a overall with a patch of WS white, WA blue and B5. The patch aft of the bow is B15. She soon changed to a single blue panel on MS4a suitable for deployment with the Indian Ocean Fleet and later the British Pacific Fleet. She had a low-type lattice mast painted black, a twin 40mm mounting amidships, a pair of single 40mm aft of the funnel and powered twin 20mm AA in the bridge wings. The 20mm mounts were later replaced with single 40mm AA.

HMS GRENVILLE R97
'U' Class Destroyer Leader Late 1943

Grenville was built as the leader for the 'U' class destroyers. She is shown here in a disruptive camouflage scheme with a combination of B5 on white. The ship completed with the designed tripod mast forward rather than the lattice mast most of the rest of the class had when entering service. She had a particularly tall HF/DF mast aft. The AA armament comprised a twin 40mm Hazemeyer amidships, one single 40mm aft of the funnel and powered twin 20mm in the bridge wings. A SL has been provided aft of the funnel. The first of the class to complete, she saw extensive service.

HMS TUSCAN R56
'T' Class 1945

Tuscan is shown at the end of the war wearing a solid lightened PB10 blue hull and 507c grey upper works; a common style for 1945. Having served in the Pacific, her light AA is strong. There is a twin 40mm amidships, two single 40mm aft of the funnel and she retains a powered twin 20mm in each bridge wing. Some ships of the class carried a single 40mm Bofors in the bridge wings as well. Her lattice mast is of the shorter type. Instead of a HF/DF mast she carries that aerial at the head of the foretop. These ships were intended for warmer climates and not fitted for Arctic service.

HMS TROUBRIDGE R00
'T' Class 1945

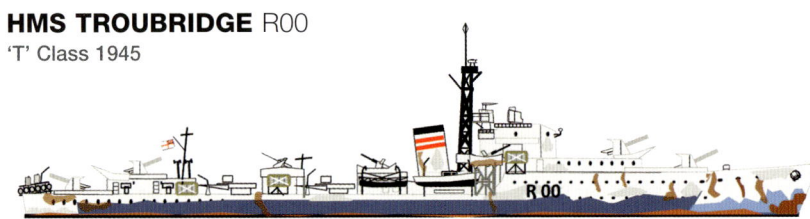

This illustration shows the effects of heavy duty at sea with little time to catch up on paint work. She has obviously had the 507c with dark blue panel style, but this has worn away revealing some pale blue beneath. Rust has added its own shades to the mix. However, it is also notable that the blue panel does not go all the way up to the main deck as was intended. *Troubridge* has a higher-than-usual lattice mast with a HF/DF aerial perched on top. Light AA comprises a radar-directed twin 40mm Hazemeyer amidships, a single 40mm aft of the funnel and single 40mm in each bridge wing, no 20mm being carried in this late-war form.

HMS GRENVILLE R97
'U' Class Destroyer Leader 1944

Before transferring to the Indian Ocean, *Grenville* adopted an Admiralty special scheme which was possibly intended to give the impression of high speed. White contrasts with 1940 green, on an overall MS4a ship, to give an impression of sea and foam. The ship remains almost unchanged except for an extra 40mm Bofors aft of the funnel and the SL has been removed.

WAR-BUILT DESTROYERS

HMS URANIA R05
'U' Class 1944

Urania commissioned in early 1944 and wore a standard Admiralty scheme: in this case, the overall colour is duck egg blue, the central section mid-blue, enclosed with G10. There is a section of MS4a on the lower bridge and funnel. The following year, *Urania* changed to a Pacific style with a blue hull panel. Again, the colours show how different yards could interpret the same scheme or use what paint was available. She has a twin 40mm amidships, powered twin 20mm in each bridge wing and two single 40mm were eventually fitted aft of the funnel. At the top of the lattice mast there is a HF/DF aerial, but also a lantern for Type 272 radar on a platform. This was the lower type of lattice mast. Pennant number is painted in pale blue for low visibility.

HMS URSA R22
'U' Class 1944

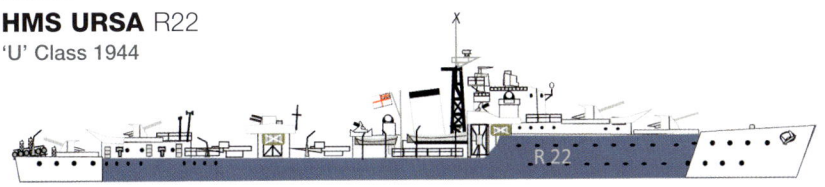

Interpretation of designs was often given an individual touch. Here, *Ursa* shows a rather unusual way of displaying the standard blue panel hull band by extending it to the forecastle deck. It is otherwise positioned correctly and has the forward slope as per instructions. Her AA is as was available, comprising a quad 2pdr amidships, with twin powered 20mm mounts in the bridge wings and two more aft of the funnel. Radar fit is Types 293, 285 and 291. The lattice mast is of the short type. An SL is still carried.

'V' AND 'W' CLASS WAR EMERGENCY DESTROYERS

HMS HARDY (II) R08
'V' Class Destroyer Leader 1943

Hardy completed in a rather unusual Admiralty disruption scheme with dark colours MS4 and B5 concentrated amidships on a 507c hull. All effect is potentially ruined by disregarding instructions not to apply a black boot topping. *Hardy* was intended as the leader of the 'V' class but was lost within five months of commissioning. Her HF/DF mast carried aft was of unusual design. She carried a Type 272 radar lantern on her lattice foremast. Type 244 IFF was carried. Although she had the intended twin 40mm amidships she is shown here with a powered twin 20mm mount in each bridge wing and single 20mm AA on each side of the SL. She and the ships of her group were fitted for work in the Arctic. She was the second ship of the name sunk in WWII, the first being at Narvik in 1940.

HMS ULYSSES R69
'U' Class 1944

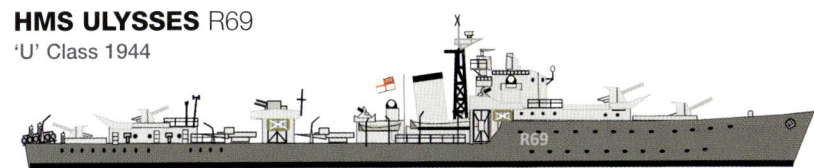

Ulysses commissioned in December 1943 at a time when there were some shortages in weapons due to so many new ships being completed. As a result, she carries a quad 2pdr AA amidships instead of the planned twin 40mm. The low lattice mast was painted black and the small Type 293 radar aerial borne on a platform, with Type 291 at the head. The SL has been placed aft of the funnel. Her other AA is limited to four twin powered 20mm mountings. 'X' mount was given a wide arc forward. She completed in dark grey and mid-grey with black boot topping, but later changed to the typical scheme for service in the Far East. Note that the pennant number is painted in grey and is not as prominently displayed as on *Urchin*.

HMS URCHIN R99
'U' Class 1945

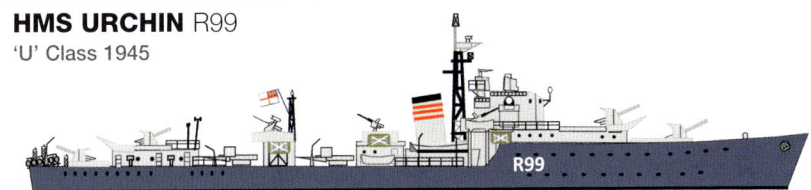

Urchin completed with a twin powered 20mm instead of the twin radar-directed 40mm Hazemeyer amidships. But by 1945 she had received the intended armament. There was also a single 40mm Bofors carried quite high aft of the funnel as well as single 40mm in each bridge wing. The SL was removed. *Urchin* was at the Anzio landings and then went to the Indian Ocean and Pacific Fleet. Her scheme is a PB10 blue hull with MS4a upper works. A tall black lattice mast and the pennant number prominently displayed in large white format. The ship carries HF/DF just forward of the twin Bofors most probably to clear the fire of that mounting on aft bearings. Radar Type 293, and 291 along with 253 IFF are on the lattice mast. Type 285 radar aerials are on the director.

HMS VOLAGE R41
'V' Class 1943

The Admiralty Home Fleet Destroyer Scheme, previously known as the War Emergency Destroyer Scheme, is shown here worn by *Volage* on commissioning. The very dark patch at the bow tended to spoil the effect overall and did not help contribute to the otherwise obvious attempt to place most colours aft and confuse the viewer. It had been thought that a touch of black would concentrate the eye and distract from other details, but on ships where this area was made lighter the effect was better. *Volage* had a quad 2pdr amidships instead of the intended twin 40mm mounting, plus powered twin 20mm in the bridge wings and on the SL platform. She carried Type 291 radar on a pole amidships and Type 296 on the lattice foremast, with the usual Type 285 on the director and HF/DF at the very top of the mast. Type 253 IFF was fitted.

HMS VERULAM R28
'V' Class 1944

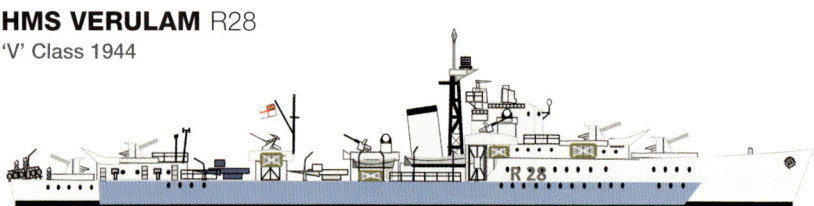

Verulam is shown late in the war with a pale blue panel common to the Indian Ocean during operations off Sumatra. She had a full fit of 40mm AA guns with a radar-controlled twin Hazemeyer mounting amidships, two singles on the SL platform abaft the funnel and two more in the bridge wings. She has a Type 272 radar lantern on the lattice mast as well as Type 285 on the director. The class had been completed fitted for Arctic operations but this was removed to save weight and the ships sent to warmer climes. There is a HF/DF fitting at the head of her foremast. Type 253 IFF would have been fitted. Note the pale pennant number which was common at the time.

HMS VIRAGO R75
'V' Class 1943

Virago completed in an Admiralty intermediate scheme. Unlike her sisters, the lattice mast was painted in pale grey or white which complements the white in her camouflage. PB10 and non-standard mid-blue make up the rest. This was important when operating against U-boats where periscope views were snatched in a few seconds and the calculations of size, distance, speed and angle of aim were all-important. *Virago* carries a twin radar-directed 40mm Hazemeyer aft, and single 40mm Bofors in each bridge wing, but has two powered twin 20mm aft of the funnel. She has HF/DF at the top of the mast and all the latest radar fits.

HMCS ALGONQUIN R17
'V' Class 1944

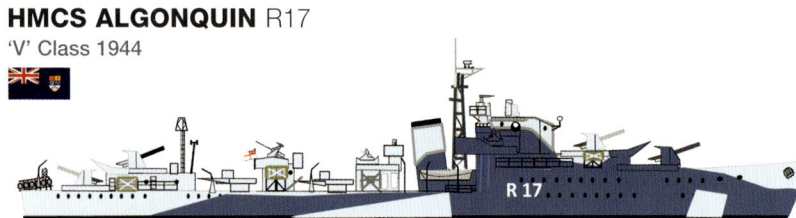

Algonquin entered service with a scheme similar to her sister *Sioux* but changed to this non-standard darker scheme while operating in northern waters. WA blue overall with B5. The pennant number is worn in bold white and very prominent considering the colour of the background. Note she carries HF/DF aft and has a shorter style of lattice mast. Her AA outfit comprises a radar-controlled twin 40mm Hazemeyer and four twin powered 20mm. Type 293 radar is on the short lattice mast and Type 285 on the director.

HMCS SIOUX R64
'V' Class 1944

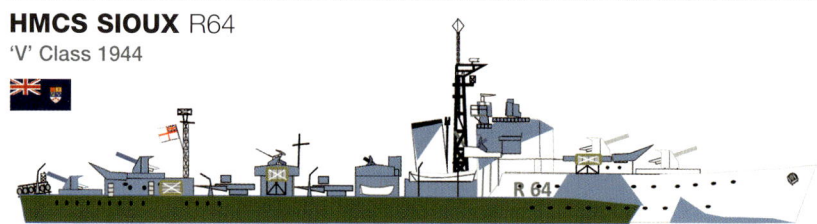

Sioux as commissioned in the Admiralty standard scheme for Home Fleet destroyers. As usual, it varies from other ships but follows the same general pattern. Note she has HF/DF on the top of an extended lattice foremast and Type 293 further down with Type 253 interrogators below. The light lattice mast aft is for Type 291 radar. Unlike *Algonquin*, her pennant number is grey and not as prominent. Four twin powered 20mm mounts are carried as well as a twin radar-directed 40mm. The 4.7in guns of this class had an improved elevation for AA work, but it was still far from ideal.

HMS WRANGLER R48
'W' Class 1944

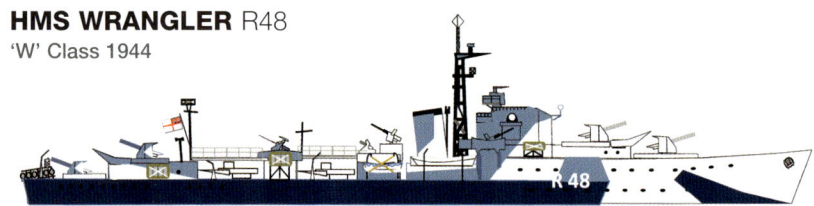

Wrangler completed in July 1944 and wore her scheme with the usual variations as interpreted by the dockyard. In this case, white overall with B20 and mid-blue. Note that there was only one director, which was capable of filling all roles. The HF/DF aerial was at the head of the tall lattice mast which also carried Types 293 and 253 radar. There was a pole mast aft for Type 291. The ship has a full light AA armament comprising a radar-directed twin 40mm Hazemeyer aft, a single manual 40mm Bofors on the SL platform behind the funnel and single Bofors in the bridge wings, as well as two power-operated twin 20mm AA aft of the funnel. The lattice mast is of the taller type and painted in black. By late 1944, the ship had moved to the Indian Ocean and then on to the Pacific, at which time she carried the usual blue panel on the hull typical of that station.

HMS WIZARD R72
'W' Class 1944

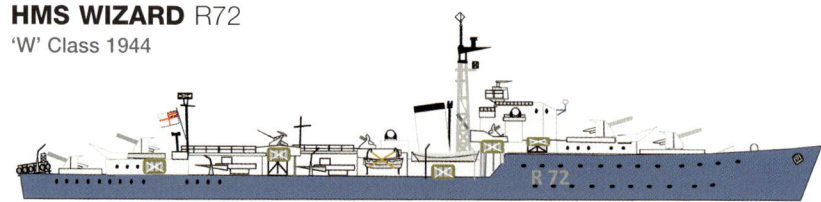

Wizard completed in March 1944 but was badly damaged by the explosion of her own DCs and did not join her sister ships in the Far East. She is shown painted MS4a grey with a PB10 blue hull. Her lattice mast was of the tall version and was grey, except for the top section which was black. It carried HF/DF, Type 293 radar and Type 253 IFF. Type 291 was carried on a pole mast at the fore end of the aft deckhouse. She had her designed armament of a radar-directed twin 40mm Hazemeyer mounting and four twin powered 20mm mountings. Although serving with the fleet and plainly painted, the ship complies with camouflage instruction not to have a black waterline. This class introduced a catwalk to enable crew to pass fore and aft above the torpedo tubes to avoid the danger of moving along the open deck in heavy seas. Note low-visibility pennant number.

HMS WESSEX R78
'W' Class 1944

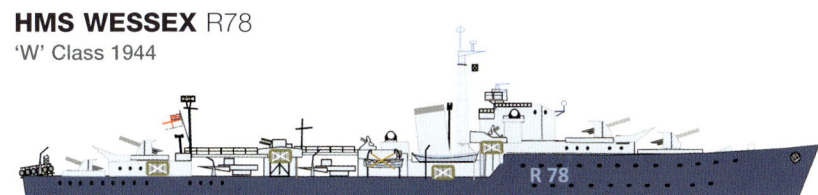

Wessex is shown in a variant of the light and dark scheme with pale WA blue upperworks and dark blue hull. Note the blue low visibility pennant. *Wessex* moved to the Eastern Fleet in 1944 and on to the Pacific Fleet in 1945. She then received all-over pale grey with blue panel on the hull as per *Whirlwind*. Note that, due to a shortage of guns, she carried a quad 2pdr amidships in place of the twin 40mm mount. She still carried twin powered 20mm mounts but these were later replaced by single 40mm Bofors on going to the Pacific. The SL was also removed to make way for a single 40mm AA. Her electronics fit was the same as *Wizard*.

HMS WHIRLWIND R87
'W' Class 1945

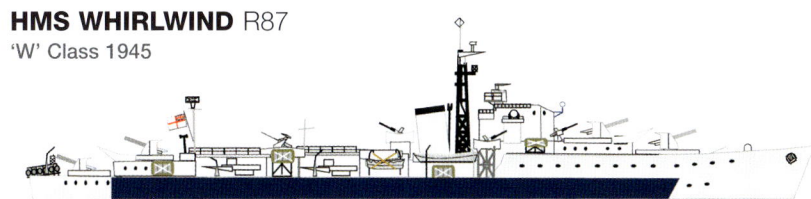

Whirlwind is depicted here in Pacific Fleet colour scheme of pale grey hull and a dark blue centre panel on the hull. This was standard for almost all ships that served with the British Pacific Fleet. Those with the Indian Ocean Fleet had a much lighter blue panel in the same location on the hull. Note she has an all-40mm Bofors armament and seems to have acquired an extra pair of singles which are just aft of 'B' gun, each side of the bridge. This was the last class of British destroyer to carry 4.7in guns. The model fitted had an elevation of 55°, which gave some AA capability, but was still too limited. The increase of 40mm guns was to deal with Japanese Kamikaze aircraft which were hard to shoot down with 20mm guns. Electronics fit as *Wizard*.

HMS ZEBRA R81
'Z' Class 1944

Zebra entered service in the Home Fleet destroyer scheme which again shows there were various interpretations of it with this version concentrating on two shades of green on white. *Zebra* completed with a tall lattice mast bearing HF/DF and numerous radar aerials, but the basic fit was the same as the *Wizard*. She carries a radar-directed twin 40mm Hazemeyer Bofors amidships, but her other light AA comprises four single 2pdr on powered mountings. These ships were intended for the Pacific but, in the event, joined the Home Fleet. The single 2pdr powered guns were considered to have a better knockdown capability than twin 20mm and were used when single 40mm Bofors were not available. Note the new director to control the 4.5in main guns. Delays with these meant that many ships that were otherwise complete had to wait for the directors to arrive and be fitted.

HMS ZEST R02
'Z' Class 1944

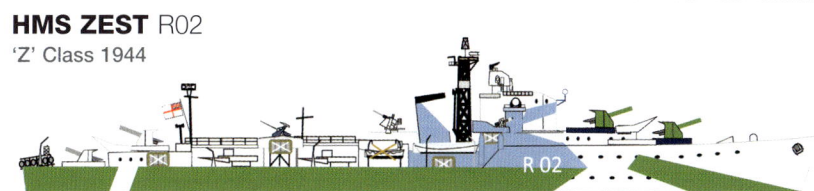

Zest was one of the units with a short lattice mast and on completion was also painted to the Home Fleet pattern, but with some variations specific to her. It has been suggested that variations may have enabled individual ships to distinguished one from another at a distance. Note that, besides the planned twin 40mm amidships, she carried two of the latest model 40mm Bofors singles aft of the funnel and had single 2pdr powered mounts in the bridge wings. The class was the first to carry 4.5in guns as designed main gun armament, replacing the 4.7in which had been in service for many years. However, the mountings were almost identical to the 4.7in mounts of the previous classes and difficult to distinguish from them. Electronics as for *Wizard*.

HMS MYNGS R06
'Z' Class Destroyer Leader 1945

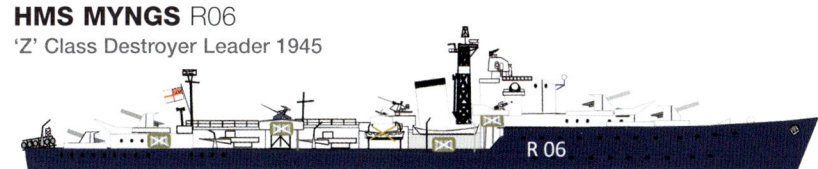

Myngs was another short lattice mast version of the 'Z' class and is shown here in 1945 during the last raids on Norway. The Home Fleet destroyer scheme has given way to a simple dark G5 hull and 507c grey upper works. This was quite standard in home waters by May 1945. Note her very mixed armament. The twin 40mm is amidships but she has single 20mm port and starboard aft of the funnel at a lower level to a single 40mm Bofors. In the bridge wings, she carried the single powered 2pdr mountings that were pressed into service to make up for a shortage of Bofors. These guns had a better knockdown ability against aircraft than the 20mm and were placed on a conversion of the powered twin 20mm mounting. Radar fit as for *Wizard*.

HMS ZODIAC R54
'Z' Class Destroyer 1945

It is unclear if the pale panel on *Zodiac* was light green, blue or grey. However, I have shown her in green as that was becoming a popular colour to use in 1945. The low visibility benefits are quite obvious, only the tall black lattice mast spoils the effect. Like her sister ships, *Zodiac* had a non-standard armament. A twin 40mm Hazemeyer amidships, two staggered single 40mm aft of the funnel and single 40mm Bofors in each bridge wing. That would have made her a particularly well-armed version of the class. Pennant number was in bold black, cut grey or paler shades were permitted with light camouflage schemes. Electronics as for *Wizard*.

HMS ZAMBESI R66
'Z' Class Destroyer 1945

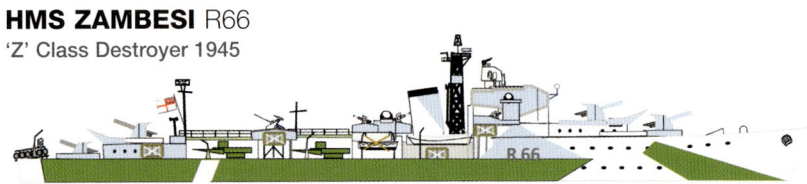

Zambesi has a Home Fleet destroyer scheme but it is interesting in that it does not go all the way to the stern. She was one of the short lattice mast versions and, being painted in black, it does tend to spoil the camouflage effect. The blending of green and blue with white was the optimum combination laid down in earlier colour experiments, but not always available due to wartime shortages. Note that Zambesi has the twin 40mm Hazemeyer amidships, but is otherwise fitted with four single power-operated 2pdr AA guns. Two of these are staggered aft of the funnel, which was a common AA arrangement for the class. Electronics as per Wizard.

HMS ZEALOUS R39
'Z' Class Destroyer 1945

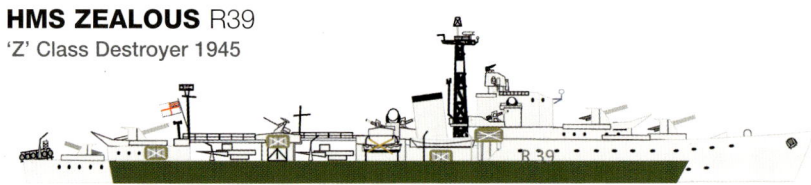

Zealous carried the taller-type lattice mast. Her scheme is typical of late-war ships on completion. Her G45 dark green hull panel has the correct forward tilt specified but not always carried. Besides the twin 40mm Hazemeyer AA amidships she has four single power-operated 2pdrs, one on each bridge wing and another two staggered aft of the funnel either side of the SL. Pennant number is in dark grey. Electronics as per Wizard.

'CA' CLASS DESTROYERS

HMS CAVALIER R73
'Ca' Class 1944

Cavalier was completed to the Admiralty Home Fleet pattern in green and blue on white. This would have suited her duties in the late part of the war in Europe as she was mostly engaged off the coast of Norway and convoys to Russia. The entire 'Ca' group completed with a tall lattice mast and had an impressive array of radar and various aerials. HF/DF is at the top of the lattice, with Type 293 on the platform. Type 253 interrogator IFF system below that. A short mast aft carried Type 291 radar. The ship carries the much improved Mk IV gunnery director which was a little overweight. Production problems meant deliveries were so slow that many of these ships completed and ran trials while still waiting for theirs to be fitted.

HMS CARRON R30
'Ca' Class 1945

Carron at the end of the war. She has the very pale green panel and even lighter green elsewhere. The pale green was known as duck egg and remained popular for a few years even after the war ended. Carron was completed with single powered 2pdr mounts in the bridge wings and the SL platform but these were replaced by 40mm Bofors. Note rockets on 'B' mounting shield. The 4.5in mounts had weather screens attached to the rear to give the crew some protection from sun and rain. Funnel bands spoilt the effect and were only worn if the regional command ordered it. Electronics fit as per Cavalier.

HMS CAPRICE R01
'Ca' Class April 1944

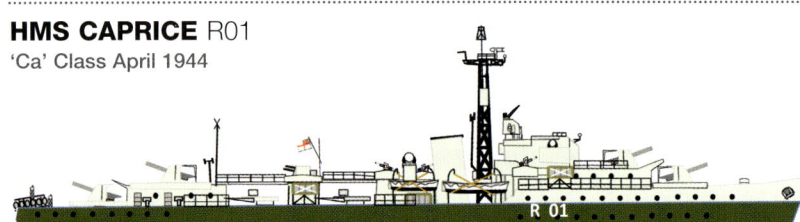

On completion, Caprice was fitted with a quad 2pdr AA amidships as there were no twin 40mm mountings available. Her other light guns comprised four power-operated 2pdr singles. Her mid-green hull was offset with duck egg green to produce a very strong contrast between hull and upper works. The heavy and slowly-delivered Mk IV gun director caused this ship and many others to wait around until it could be fitted. Although overweight, it was to prove not as badly so as the Mk VI that the following groups of 'C' class destroyers would carry. Electronics fit as per Cavalier.

HMS CAPRICE R01
'Ca' Class May 1945

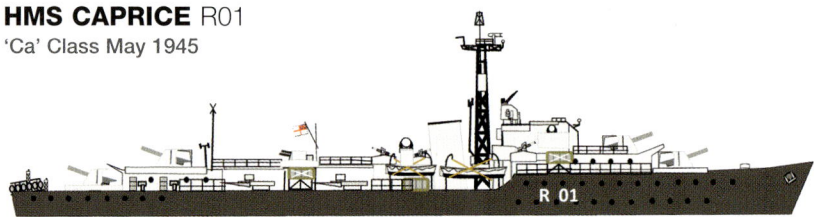

At war's end, Caprice was in a contrasting dark grey and light grey scheme which she would retain post-war and when she went into the reserve fleet. This scheme was easy to apply and maintain and was also adopted by the RCN for many years. Her 2pdr guns had not been replaced with 40mm Bofors by war's end. Electronics fit as per Cavalier. Note that by this time British destroyers were becoming so standard in appearance that the various classes were hard to distinguish from each other.

WAR-BUILT DESTROYERS

HMS CAESAR R07
'Ca' Class 1944

Caesar is shown in the duck egg blue that was becoming a favourite at the end of the war along with its green equivalent. The blue hull panel would have worked well with it in most conditions. Electronics fit as per *Cavalier*. There is a twin 40mm Hazemeyer amidships, but the rest of her light AA are 2pdr guns on powered mountings. She carried a SL aft of the funnel.

HMS CASSANDRA R62
'Ca' Class 1944

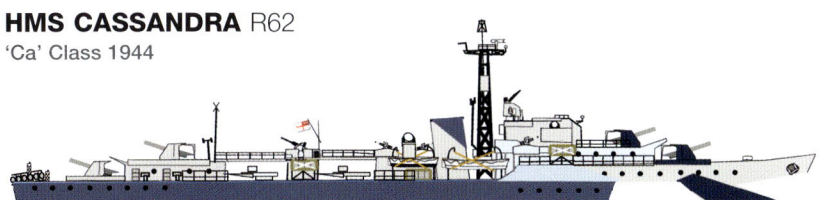

Cassandra is shown in a variant of the Home Fleet destroyer scheme. The presence of single 2pdr powered mounts shows that 40mm guns were in short supply when she entered service. This ship was engaged in convoys to Russia as well as operations off Norway in the last months of the war. She was torpedoed by *U 365*, and lost her bow, but made it to Murmansk where temporary repairs were made. She later sailed to Gibraltar under her own steam for permanent repairs and emerged in a single panel type scheme. Most destroyers were sunk by a single torpedo hit so she must have been sturdily built to survive. Electronics fit as per *Cavalier*.

'BATTLE' CLASS DESTROYERS
HMS BARFLEUR R80
1944

Barfleur is shown in a Home Fleet destroyer scheme. However, note that the blue forward is much paler than the blue used aft of the funnel. This ship and others of her class broke new ground for destroyers with their powerful AA armament. However, there were, as with the previous classes, problems with delivery of the Mk VI director and she initially ran trials without it, then was laid up for a short time until a director became available. This ship did join the Pacific Fleet in time to see action off Japan and was present at the surrender in Tokyo Bay. She has staggered twin radar-directed 40mm Hazemeyer Bofors on the aft deckhouse and two more abreast of each other amidships. There is a single manual type 40mm in each bridge wing and she has a powered single 40mm either side of the bridge front behind 'B' turret. Aft of the funnel, she carried a single 4in gun for firing starshell mostly as any other astern fire was quite limited due to the numerous Bofors mountings. Note there is even a single 40mm on the quarterdeck. Electronics as per *Hogue*.

HMS CAMBRIAN R85
'Ca' Class 1944

Cambrian is shown in the dark blue hull and pale grey scheme the class adopted at the end of the war in Europe and in expectation they would be sent to the Pacific. However, the class did not leave European waters until after the war with Japan had ended. She has an AA armament of a twin 40mm and four single powered 2pdr mounts. Just prior to deploying to the Far East, she had her 2pdr replaced with single 40mm Bofors. Electronics fit as per *Cavalier*.

HMS COMET R26
'Co' Class 1944

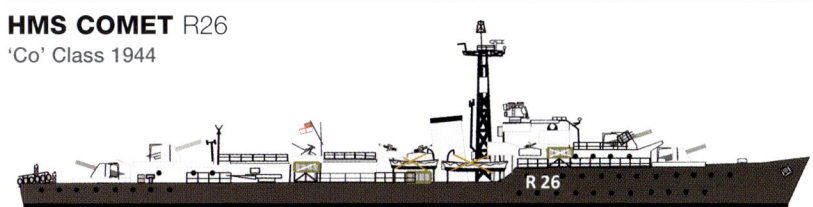

Comet commissioned on 6 June 1945 and was the only 'Co' class destroyer able to see service before the war ended and that only in the closing weeks. This was due to the change to the new Mk VI director which was, again, very slow in being delivered and fitted to ships often otherwise virtually complete. As it was, the Mk VI was so overweight that the ships were forced to land the forward tubes to compensate. The DC throwers were reduced to two and they carried only thirty-five charges, half those previously carried. The weight problem also meant they carried only single manual 20mm Oerlikons in the bridge wings. However, they did have the twin Hazemeyer 40mm AA aft, plus two single power-operated 2pdr guns, later replaced with single 40mm Bofors.

HMS HOGUE R74
1944

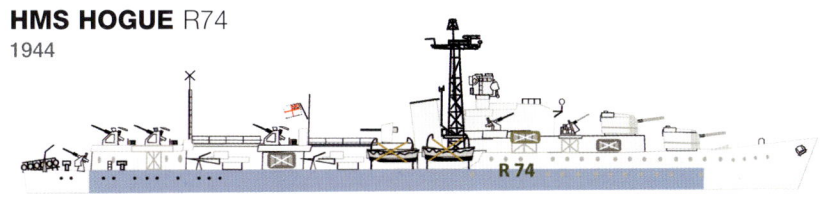

Hogue was completed and ready for service in the Pacific when the war ended. Again, long delays waiting for Mk VI gun directors had been a problem. Her sisters *Armada*, *Camperdown*, *Finisterre* and *Trafalgar* commissioned during the final weeks of the war against Japan but too late to see action. But for production delays with the gun directors and the new twin Bofors mountings, many of these ships would have been in service before the end of the war, as most had been laid down in 1942 and 1943. Only one ship of the first group was laid down in early 1944. The second group completed well after the war or were cancelled and scrapped. The lattice masts were somewhat lower than the 'C' class destroyers for stability. Electronics fit included the new Type 275 gunnery radar on the director, Type 291 on a pole mast, plus Type 293 on the lattice mast which was topped with HF/DF. There was a Type 253 'egg timer' IFF fitted.

5 'HUNT' CLASS ESCORT DESTROYERS

'HUNT I' CLASS ESCORT DESTROYERS

HMS QUORN L66
1940

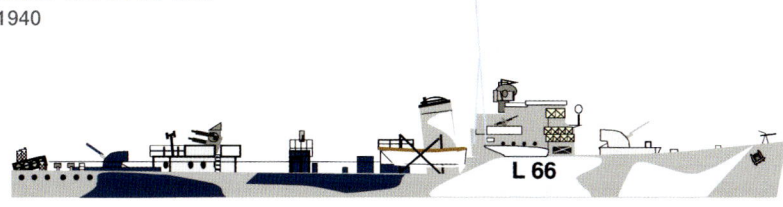

This was probably an unofficial camouflage as it is so early in the war. It appears to be MS4a with areas of 507c and a local dark-blue mix. Nonetheless, dark colours aft made station keeping easier for any ship following behind. The only radar carried is Type 285 on the director. The small H-shaped object on the rear deckhouse is the galley chimney. Stability problems also limited the DC load.

HMS BERKELEY L17
1943–5

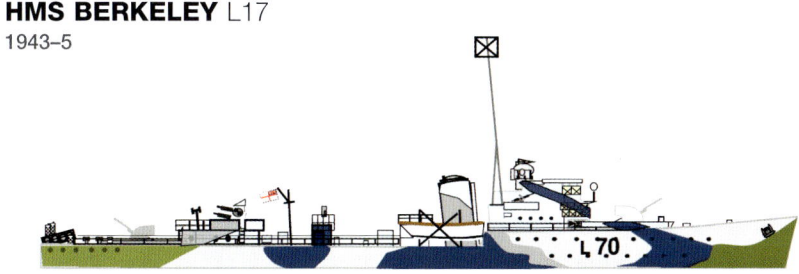

Berkeley displays a form of disruptive camouflage of the Admiralty light type. On a base of 507c, she is shown with 1940 Blue on the hull and a stripe on the bridge, which itself is WA blue. MS4 contrasts with the 507c and there are areas of khaki. She had a Type 291 radar at the masthead and Type 285 on the director. She had a 2pdr on the bow and must have often operated in coastal waters. Attempts to up-gun these ships were frustrated by topweight problems.

HMS QUANTOCK L58
1941

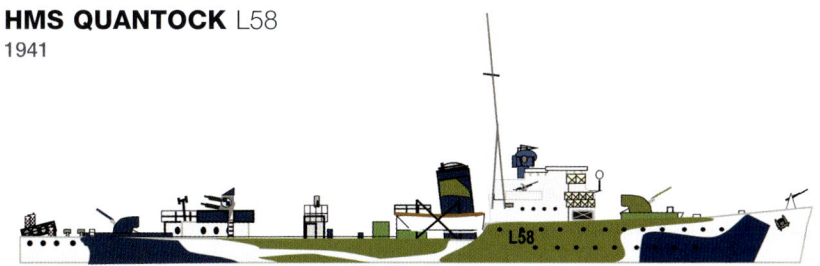

Many 'Hunt' class operated in the confined waters around the UK and this somewhat complicated scheme allows for some effect with a coastal background. The use of 507c pale grey with patches of 1941 blue and khaki provides a certain disruptive effect. Note the 2pdr in the eyes of the bow. Type 285 is on the director but she had no other radar fitted at this time.

HMS WHADDON L45
1942

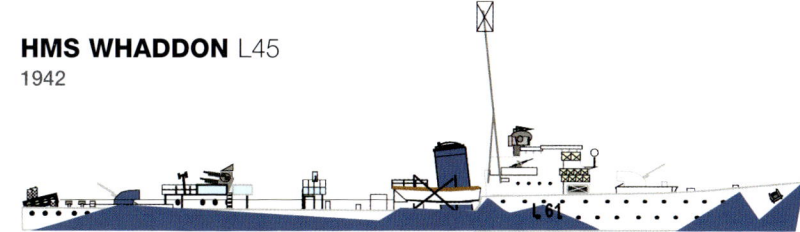

Whaddon has a variation based around the WA scheme but with 1941 blue on white. The intent is probably to make the ship seem lower on the horizon and therefore further away. Radar at the masthead is an early fixed Type 286 and Type 285 on the director. These ships had severe weight problems, hence there are no torpedo tubes and adding additional light AA was not possible. The twin 4in mounts were dual-purpose (DP).

HMS CLEVELAND L46
1941–2

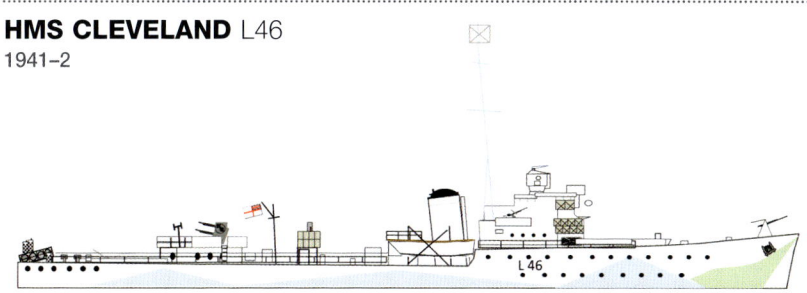

The pale appearance of the WA scheme is clear with the very light WA blue and WA green, on white, worn by *Cleveland*. Splinter mats around the bridge have been painted to fit the scheme. She had fixed Type 286 radar at the masthead and Type 285 on her director. A single director meant the main guns were only able to engage one aircraft at a time or use local control, which was much less efficient.

HMS TYNEDALE L96
1941

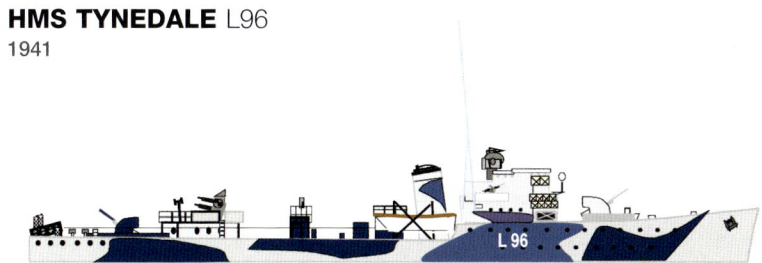

On *Tynedale*, we see colour distributed in a manner such as to give the impression the ship is much shorter or further away by using 507c overall with patches of 1941 blue and a non-standard mid-blue. A torpedo calculation could be thrown out by such a misinterpretation. Although she has Type 285 on her director, this ship was not yet fitted with any other radar. Stability was always a problem for this class.

'HUNT' CLASS ESCORT DESTROYERS

HMS ATHERSTONE L05
1942

This unofficial scheme was obviously intended for UK East Coast or Channel work and a 2pdr in the eyes of the bow suggests operations in areas where E-boats were likely to be encountered. Radar at masthead was probably Type 286, replaced by Type 291 by 1943. The earlier set was discontinued when it was realised German radar detectors could easily pick it up.

'HUNT II' CLASS ESCORT DESTROYERS

HMS BLANKNEY L30
1941

In 1941 *Blankney* wore a scheme of mid-blue on MS4a and 1940 stone, common practice at the time. There is no gun in the eyes of the bow so the scheme was probably not a coastal one. 'Hunt II' class ships carried an extra 4in twin mount but stability problems prevented fitting torpedo tubes. There is no Type 285 radar on the director but there is an early fixed Type 286 set at the masthead. The objects on top of the DC racks are smoke canisters.

HMS AVON VALE L06
1942

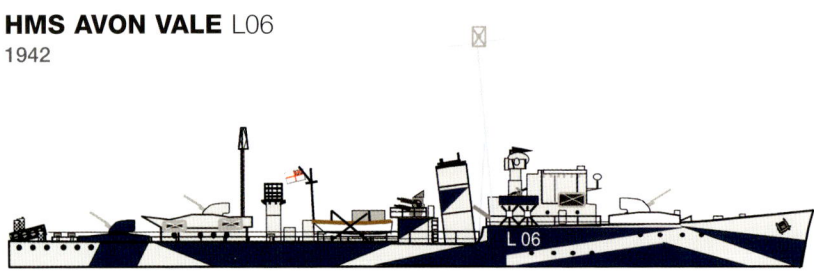

Avon Vale is shown with a quite striking disruptive scheme of 507c overall with 1941 dark blue. Decks would have been 507a or MS1. Note that 'A' gun and its zareba are painted white. There is some similarity to later American schemes. With a HF/DF mast aft, the ship was probably engaged on convoy duty. Type 286 radar at the masthead would soon be replaced by Type 291. By 1943, the use of Type 286 was banned in the vicinity of a convoy.

HMS CATTISTOCK L35
1942–3

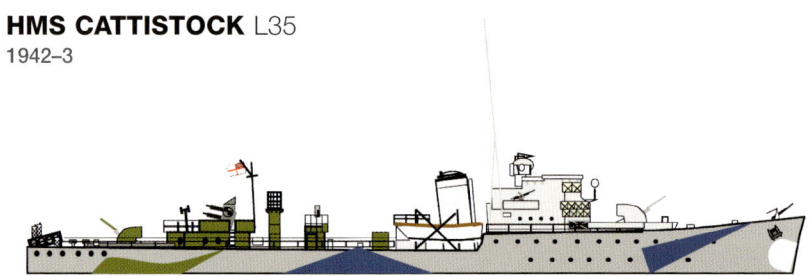

Cattistock is shown with a simple non-standard scheme of around 1942–3. The hull is MS4a with a white patch at the bow, the bridge in 507c. There are two triangular areas of 1941 blue on the hull and an area of khaki which extends to the aft superstructure. The funnel is WS white. This is probably typical of many ideas tried out on various ships in search of the right effect. Note she had a 2pdr in the eyes of the bow for fighting E-boats, so the scheme was expected to be worn in coastal waters. There was the usual Type 285 radar on her director and a lantern for Type 271 carried on a tower just forward of the quad 2pdr mount. Few units of the 'Hunt I' class carried Type 271 due to weight. Apart from the 2pdrs, the only other light AA are single 20mm in each bridge wing.

HMS BLANKNEY L30
1942

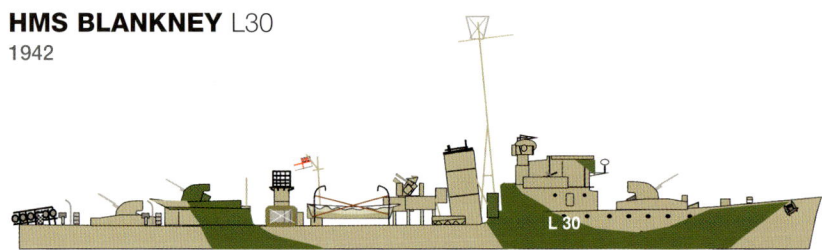

Dark sand and B30 were often used on ships operating in or close to coastal waters. The effect is intended to give some blending-in with the background and provide a confusion effect when seen at a distance. Note there is now a radar lantern amidships for Type 271 and Type 285 has been fitted to the director. There is still a Type 286 set at the masthead.

HMS AVON VALE L06
1944

Avon Vale is shown in an official scheme applied to destroyers in various ways. Here, it uses pale sand, with MS4 on the hull plus B6 mid-grey upper works. She has a Type 271 radar lantern and Type 291 at the masthead as well as Type 285 on the director. While it was possible to upgrade the electronics, stability problems prevented her light AA being increased.

HMS BLANKNEY L30
1943

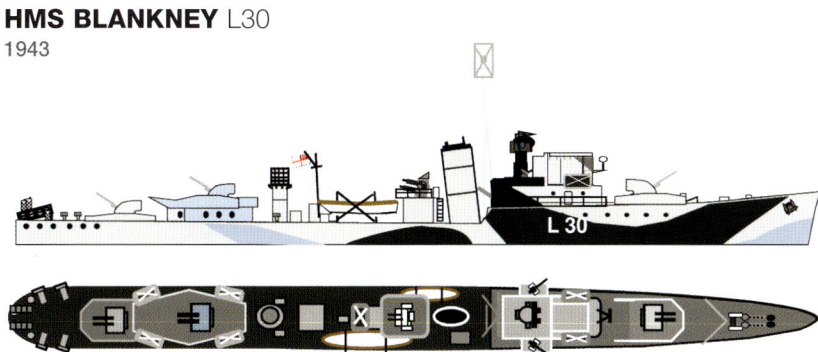

The Admiralty intermediate scheme worn in this illustration was is intended to draw the eye to the dark areas to make the ship look smaller and recognition difficult. The pale 507c grey and WA blue are intended to blend in with the horizon while the areas of dark MS1 confuse the viewer. *Blankney* now has Type 291 radar at the masthead as well as Types 271 and 285. Armament remains three twin 4in DP mounts, a quad 2pdr and two single 20mm as it was not possible to add extra weight to these ships.

HMS EXMOOR (II) L08
1941–2

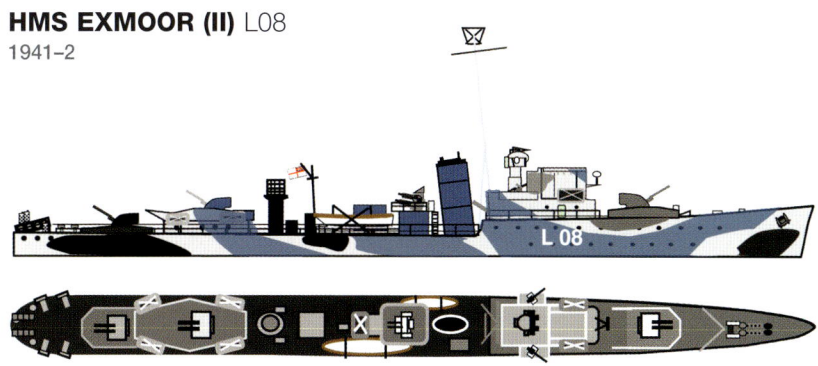

This is an Admiralty dark scheme which was intended to help the ship blend into the background in poor weather, thus more suited for winter. The main colour is 507c, with patches of MS1 and 1941 blue. Electronics fit as for *Hurworth*. The deck can be seen to use MS1 aft with B6 and MS4a on some horizontal surfaces. There are four DC throwers and two racks.

HMS CROOME L62
1942

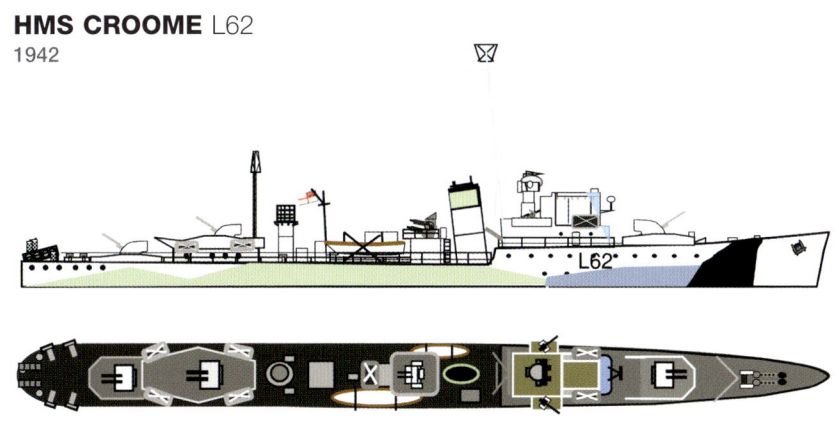

This is very similar to the evolving Home Fleet destroyer design which became standard by 1943. It creates a false impression of where the bow is and makes the ship look shorter. A HF/DF mast shows this ship was almost certainly involved in convoy duty. Other electronics and armament are standard.

HMS BLACKMORE L43
1942

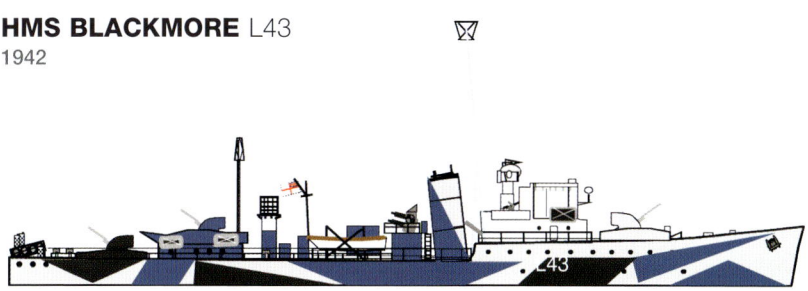

This disruptive scheme carries 1941 blue up from the hull onto the superstructure for maximum effect. The ship is in overall 507c and dark patches of MS1 have been restricted to the hull and aft gun mount. See *Bicester* for a different example. There is no attempt to conceal the ship, just disrupt the general outline and hide its type. The presence of a HF/DF mast means she was on duties involving convoys or the fleet and less on coastal work. Her radar fit is good for the period with Types 285, 286 and 271.

HMS GROVE L77
1942

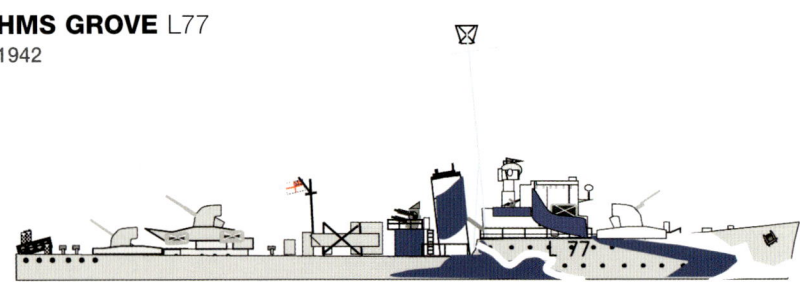

Grove had a very short career before being sunk and is shown here in a scheme similar to the destroyer leader *Wallace*, plus the 'Hunts' *Hursley* and *Chiddingfold*. Local variations to the actual layout and colours occurred often but this one is quite close to *Wallace*. Note how the dark colours draw the eye to the front of the ship, while the white hints at the ship being at high speed. There is Type 285 radar on the director and early Type 286 at the masthead.

HMS CHIDDINGFOLD L31
1942

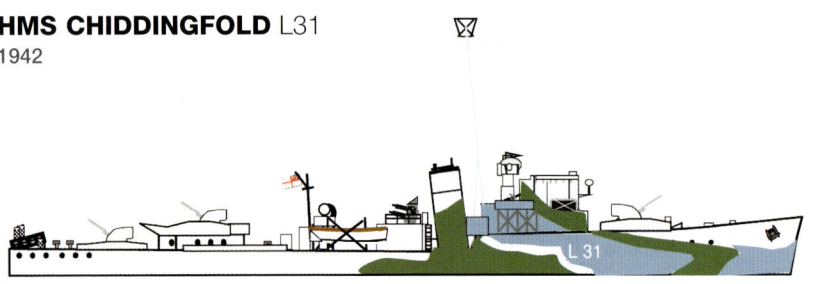

This is a variation on the scheme shown worn by *Hurworth*. The use of white blots out most of the ship while WA blue and WA green at the bow give a 'two ships' effect. As with most ships, schemes could be varied in colour and in minor details to utilise what was available. The ship has Type 285 radar on the director and Type 286 at the masthead.

ORP KUJAWIAK L72
1941–2

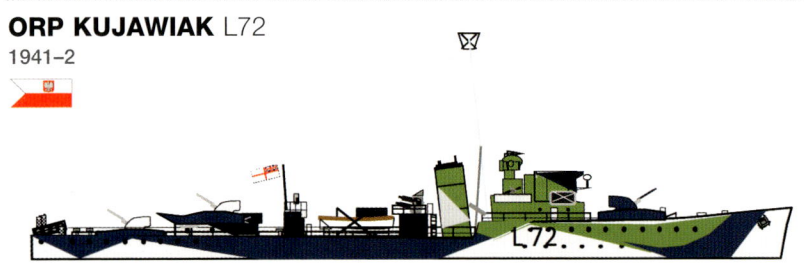

Originally HMS *Oakley*, this ship was transferred to the Free Polish Navy and served under RN operational control during her short life. She is shown here in a dramatic 1941 blue and 1940 green on pale 507c grey camouflage. The effect of the light grey areas on the hull was to create a false impression of high speed. Type 285 and 286 radars are carried.

HMS HURWORTH L28
1942

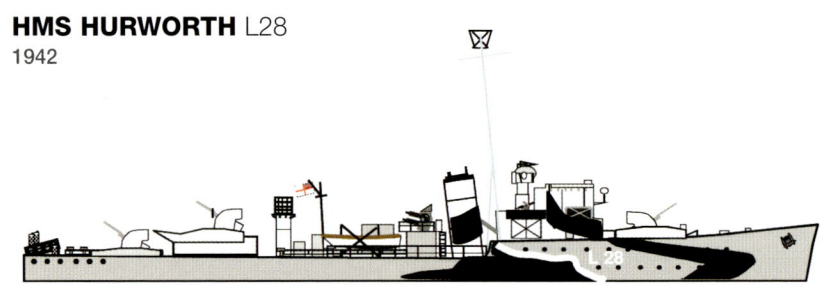

There were several versions of this unofficial scheme, of basically the same idea but the colours used varying from ship to ship. Here, the ship has white upperworks with black outlined white on the amidships section. Her radar fit is good for 1942, comprising a Type 271 lantern, and Types 286 and 285. As usual, only two single 20mm could be fitted due to weight but the ASW capacity was better than the 'Hunt I' class.

HMS BICESTER L34
1941–2

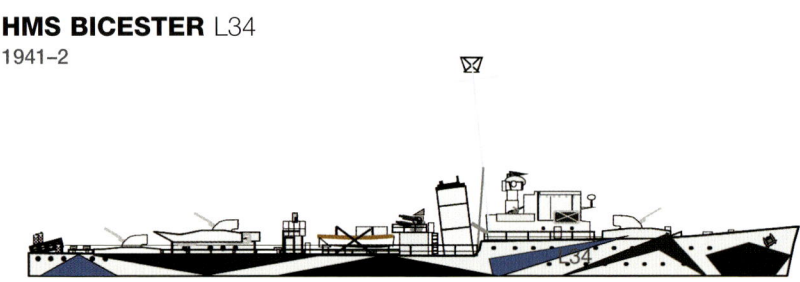

A three-tone pattern comprising black, 1941 blue and 507c pale grey does keep the eye focused on the hull but fails to confuse the ship's true length. However, it could make the superstructure more difficult to identify. All electronics and armament are standard due to the difficulty of upgrading these ships.

RHN THEMISTOCLES L51
1943

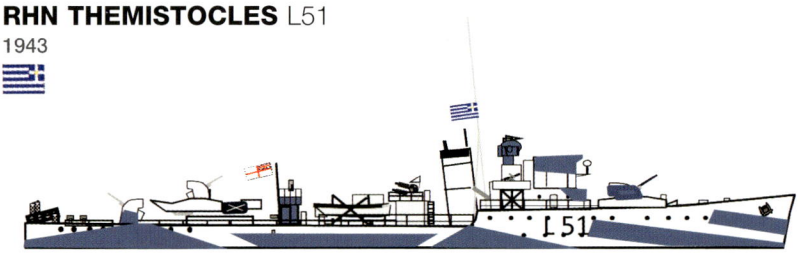

HMS *Bramham* was handed over to the Greek navy in 1943 and is shown here in WS white and mid-blue. This is not a WA scheme, although it borrows much from the general concept. Electronics and armament are standard for her class.

'HUNT' CLASS ESCORT DESTROYERS

HMS BADSWORTH L03
1941

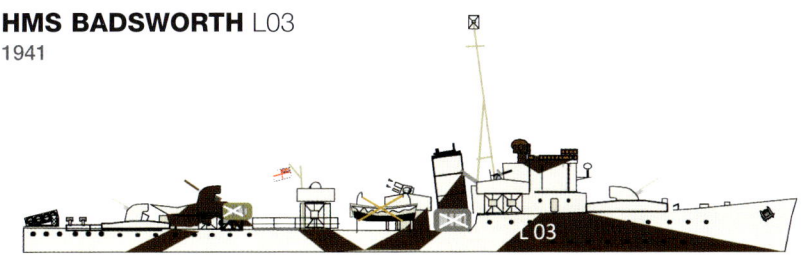

Badsworth is shown here in an unusual pale stone and dark stone camouflage that would be useful while operating in some coastal areas. She is a standard ship of her class, with the usual armament, but has no Type 285 radar on the director, although it would have been fitted later; there is an early Type 286 radar at the masthead.

HMS BADSWORTH L03
1942–3

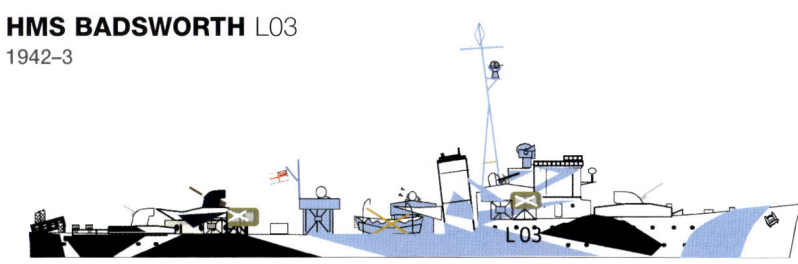

There was a change of scheme in 1942 and *Badsworth* then wore a form of Admiralty disruptive scheme where black was used to concentrate the eye most to the stern to give a false impression of length. She now has Type 285 radar on the director and a Type 291 on the mast. The general appearance can be seen as a line of thought toward the later Home Fleet destroyer pattern.

HMS OAKLEY (II) L98
1943

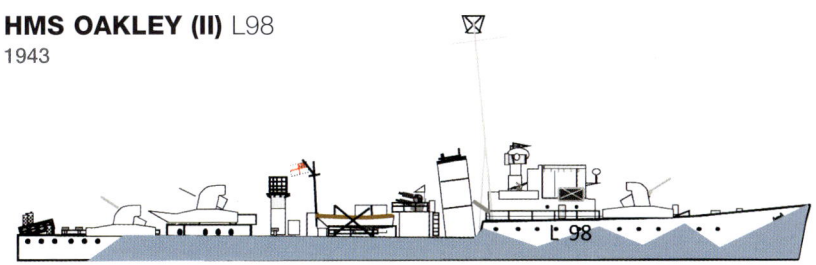

A version of the WA system is shown here as worn by *Oakley*. Green was apparently not available so she is depicted with a white hull and WA blue areas. This ship had been named *Tickham* but was renamed *Oakley* as the first ship of that name had been transferred to Poland on completion. She is show here ready for escort duty and with all radars etc fitted.

HMS PUCKERIDGE L108
1942

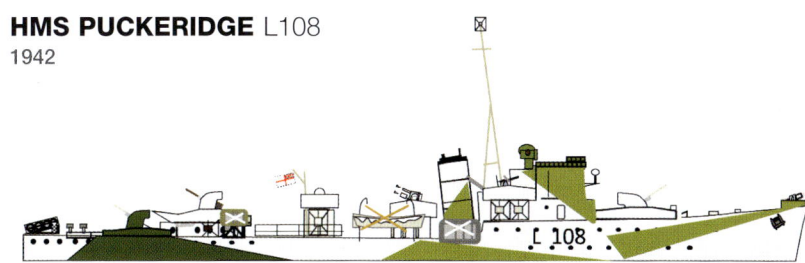

Puckeridge is shown in colours more suited to the East Coast of the UK. The overall colour is 507c with a patch of MS3 aft and khaki forward. She was an early loss and the only radar shown here is a Type 286PU at the masthead. This was a fully-rotating set.

'HUNT III' CLASS ESCORT DESTROYERS

HMS ALBRIGHTON L12
1943

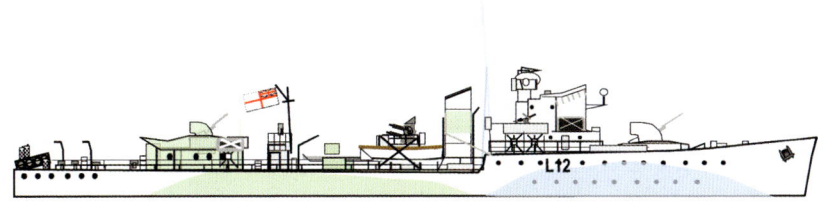

Albrighton is wearing an almost perfect, as-designed, WA scheme of WA blue and WA green on white although with perhaps a little more on the superstructure than the original intent. Dockyards often varied designs and ships' crews carrying out touch-ups might use another colour to repair an area if the original was not available. Rust was the enemy of the WA scheme which relied on its pale colours. This ship was not fitted with a Type 271 radar lantern amidships as were many others.

HMS BLEAN L47
1942

Blean has an Admiralty light scheme which, as usual, concentrates dark colour mostly aft and leaves the forward pale. The colours are white overall, with 507c grey and B6. This was the first 'Hunt' group to carry torpedo tubes for fleet work but to do so they had to revert to a two twin 4in mount configuration. Type 286 radar is on the mast and Type 285 on the director. A twin torpedo mount is carried amidships. By the time this group were in production, many of the stability problems of the early ships had been addressed, but the design was small overall and difficult to expand on. Hence, like those before, the light AA was restricted to a quad 2pdr and two single 20mm.

'HUNT' CLASS ESCORT DESTROYERS

HMS EGGESFORD L15
1943

Eggesford is shown here in a dull dark grey overall, probably 507b. Although AA ships, these vessels carried only two 20mm Oerlikons along with the quad 2pdr. At the time of design, heavy AA such as the twin 4in were considered the main priority. It was only with war experience that the need for a stronger close-range AA armament was realised. A Type 271 radar lantern is carried amidships on a quite extensive office, with Type 286 at the masthead and Type 285 on the director.

HMS MELBREAK L73
1942

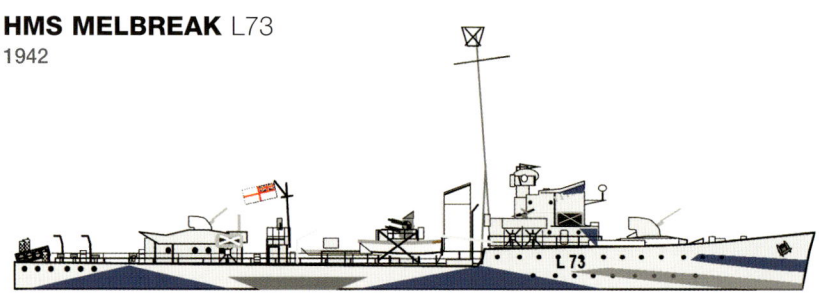

Melbreak is shown with one of the schemes often used with WA colours, but here in 1941 blue and B6 over 507c. Note the funnel is white as is the aft gun shield. This class were fitted with torpedo tubes to enable them to operate as fleet destroyers if required, a duty that was sometimes called for in the Mediterranean in particular. *Melbreak* is shown with Types 286 and 285 radars. Note the distinctive bridge of the 'Hunt III' group.

HMS HAYDON L75
1943

Haydon is camouflaged with 507c, MS4a, 507a and 1941 blue. Having been completed mid-war she carried radar as part of the design. The provision of only a single director still limited heavy AA fire to a single target unless inefficient local control was used. This ship did not carry Type 271 radar but had Type 286, later replaced by Type 291, and the usual Type 285 for the director.

HMS EASTON L09
1943

This is a somewhat blotchy disruptive scheme using MS4a and 1941 blue over 507c. The radar lantern is the smaller one for Type 272 (an improved 271) with a Type 244 IFF interrogator aerial on top of it. Type 291 radar is carried at the top of the mast and Type 285 on the director. A single 20mm AA has been added on the quarterdeck to deal with low-level aircraft attacks from astern.

LA COMBATTANTE L19
1944

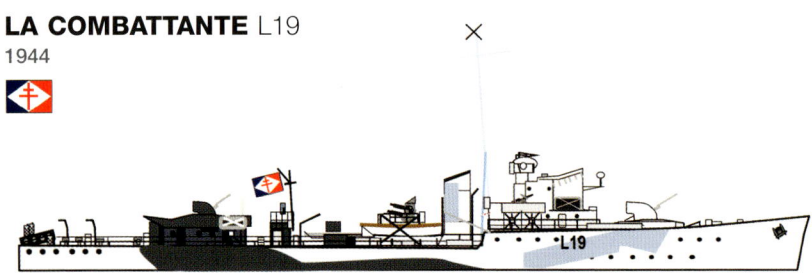

HMS *Haldon* was transferred to the Free French Navy (FFN) but was lost in 1945. Her scheme is based around WA blue and 507b grey on white overall. Like all ships operating under RN control, she wears the White Ensign as well as the FFN flag. Radar fit is Types 291 and 285. Armament is standard as built.

RHN ADRIAS L67
1943

Surprisingly, dark colours can work well in hot areas and HMS *Border*, transferred to the Greek navy as *Adrias*, is shown in 507b with patches of white amidships. The wearing of her national flag as well as the White Ensign was common under RN operational control. Radar fit would be Types 291 and 285. She did not carry a lantern-type radar.

'HUNT IV' CLASS ESCORT DESTROYERS

HMS BRISSENDEN L79
1943

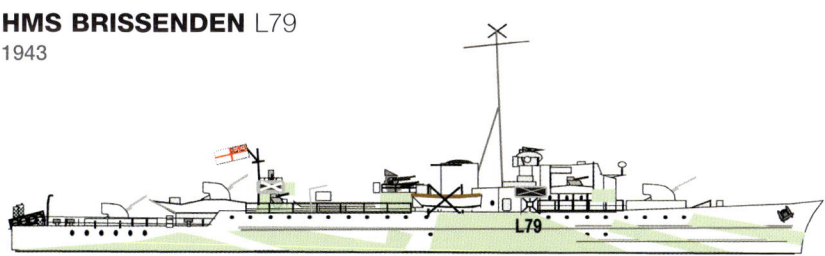

HMS BRECON L76
1943

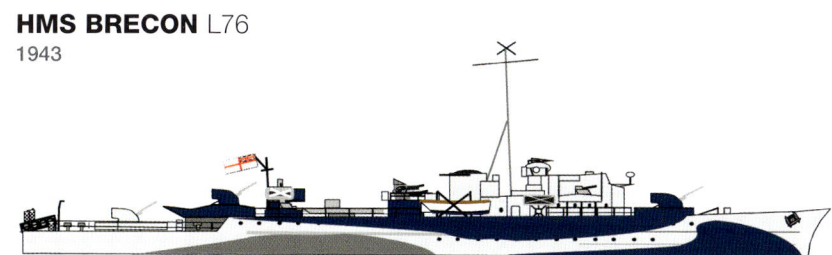

The 'Hunt IV' class ships originated from complaints of poor stability with the earlier groups. An independent design was allowed to proceed, in order to see if it could address the problems. Stabilisers were fitted but not popular. The forward deck was continued well aft to provide more accommodation and undercover movement fore and aft. They not only carried torpedoes but had four twin 20mm and a full fit of three twin 4in AA, the only 'Hunt' group to be stable enough for such a full armament. *Brissenden* is shown in a late-war use of overall white with WA green irregular areas. These ships were arguably the best of the 'Hunt' class, carrying a full armament but with good seakeeping qualities. However, they were more expensive and, with large numbers of other ships entering service, only two were built.

Brecon was the only other unit of the 'Hunt IV' class and is shown here in an Admiralty disruptive scheme of three colours. 507c forms the base with areas of 507b and 1941 blue. These ships were experimental and late entering the war but the principles behind their long, protected upper decks were carried over into post-WWII frigate designs. They were designed for radar and carried Types 291 and 285. Their powerful light AA armament was a distinct improvement over earlier 'Hunts'.

EX-FRENCH VESSELS IN RN SERVICE

HMS MISTRAL H03
Bourrasque Class Destroyer 1942

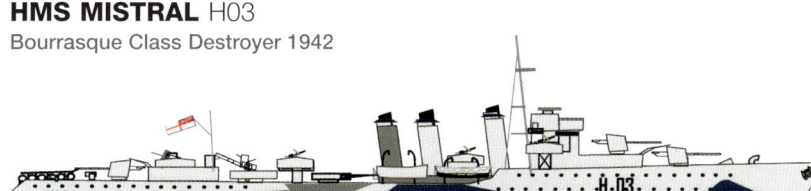

HMS LA MELPOMÈNE H56
Pomone Class Torpedo Boat 1940

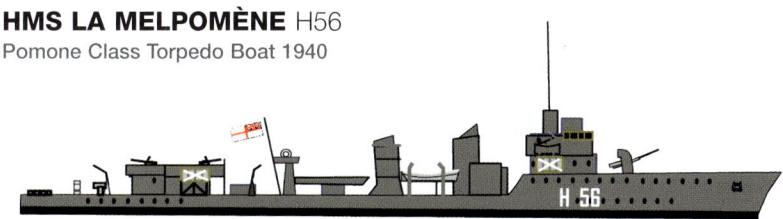

The French destroyer *Mistral* was seized in 1940 and put into service with the RN. Her guns were replaced by British 4.7in due to a lack of ammunition and a need for common supply. She has a fairly standard RN destroyer fit with the aft tubes replaced by a 3in AA gun. There is a single 2pdr on the aft deckhouse but she has a single 20mm Oerlikon on the former SL platform, two between the funnels and one in each bridge wing. The paint scheme was MS4a as a base with 507b and 1941 dark blue. No radar is shown on this drawing but Type 286P then Type 291 were carried.

How do you make a captured French ship look less French? Well, the answer with *La Melpomène* seems to have been to paint her in overall 507b dark grey, the very reverse of what she wore when the ship was in French service. These ships had very poor stability and after the capsize of *Branlebas* in the English Channel with heavy loss of life they were relegated to secondary duties. There were attempts to transfer them to the Dutch and the Poles but it seems nobody really wanted them, not even the Free French who rejected transfer to them. *La Melpomène* has 2pdrs aft, 20mm in the bridge wings and a British 4in forward. No radar is carried.

6 SLOOPS

SLOOPS

HMS ROSEMARY U14
Old 'Flower' Class Sloop 1940

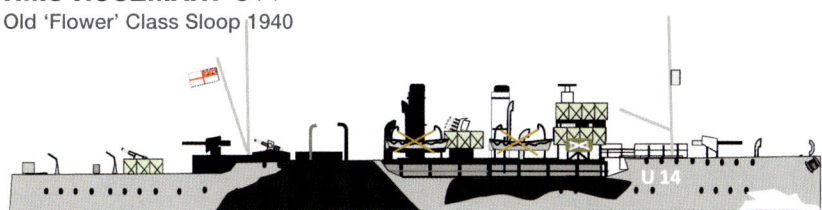

A hastily-applied unofficial scheme probably using what was available. False bow waves were popular and easy to apply. Quad 0.5in MGs added between the funnels and a 2pdr on the quarterdeck. Lewis guns from her armoury are on the bridge and other MG-calibre weapons probably added if available. The U-boat crisis had not yet started so her main fear was from air attack. There are splinter mats on the bridge and protecting the AA guns. She had two DC throwers but no stern rack. Flag superior of the pennant changed from 'P', then to 'L' and finally to 'U14' in 1940.

HMS FOXGLOVE T43
Old 'Flower' Class Sloop 1918

This illustration shows how these ships used 'dazzle' camouflage in WWI rather than the more subtle colours of WWII. Note, however, that most of the dark colours are concentrated toward the stern of the ship and the lighter ones forward, hopefully giving the impression of being two ships not one. This type of scheme was entirely devoted to confusing the aim of a submarine commander during his brief glimpses through a periscope. The schemes were not intended to hide the ship, just confuse as to size, course and type. They were time-consuming to maintain but research showed that crews felt something was being done to protect them and they therefore raised morale.

INDIAN SLOOPS
HMIS PATHAN K26
'PC' Class Sloop 1939

Previously HMS *PC 69* built in 1918, this ship transferred to the Indian marine service in 1921. She is shown as she appeared for most of her service life, as a training ship. She was overpainted with 507c grey in 1940 and was senior ship of the escorts based on Bombay. However, *Pathan* operated in the colours shown during the first months of WWII. The ship is shown with her two 4.7in guns relocated to the centreline and the 12pdr AA moved to the bow. Apart from that, she had only a few MGs as AA defence. She was sunk on 23 July 1940 after an internal explosion, but the Italian Navy claimed it was due to a torpedo from one of their submarines based in the Red Sea.

HMS LUPIN L19
Old 'Flower' Class Sloop 1939

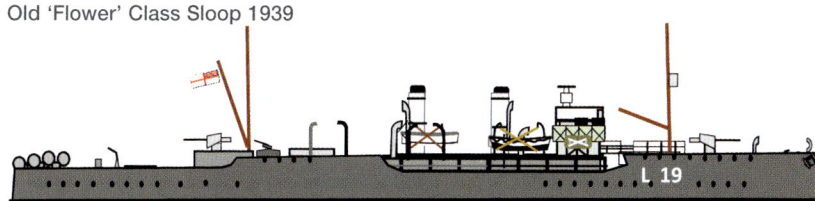

This ship is shown with a 507b dark grey hull and 507c grey funnels. The original armament of two LA 4in with two single 2pdr AA port and starboard is still carried. Lewis guns on the bridge were probably from her own equipment. Splinter mats added to the bridge. Note the DC rack aft with only four charges and only two DC throwers, typical for the start of the war before the U-boat menace really developed. Masts are varnished wood. Pennant changed to 'U19' in 1940.

HMS FOXGLOVE L26
Old 'Flower' Class Sloop 1940

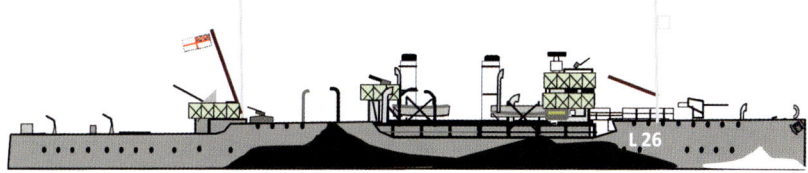

Black areas added onto a dark grey hull with pale 507c funnels and superstructure made for a simple camouflage that could be applied from the ship's own paint locker. There were no regulations so each ship could do its own thing. The false bow wave was common in WWI and junior officers of that period were now commanding ships, so it was no doubt an idea easily recalled from personal observation. Note the aft gun replaced by a 12pdr AA and four twin Lewis gun mountings. *Foxglove* was a constructive total loss in July 1940. Pennant never changed to intended 'U26'.

HMIS CORNWALLIS L09
Azalea Class Sloop 1939

Originally completed as HMS *Lynchis* in 1917 to a decoy merchant design (Q ship), intended to fool submarines into attacking on the surface. Before WWII, the armament was placed on the centreline and she served as a sloop. As shown here, she has been painted in MS4 with black areas on the hull and a false white bow wave. AA guns were limited to a single 12pdr aft and four sets of twin Lewis guns. Depth-charge traps can be seen under the aft gun and she has throwers as well. Even the older ships of the Indian navy played a vital role in 1939–42 until newer vessels became available. A sister ship built as *Pansy* in WWI was requisitioned by the RIN and served under the same name. Two RN vessels of this type were both lost 1941–2: *Cornflower* at Hong Kong, and *Laburnum* at Singapore.

HMIS CLIVE L79
1944

Clive is shown in a scheme based on a pale blue hull panel but, for some reason, it only ran from bow to below the aft superstructure. She was otherwise mostly white. Two old LA 4in guns were the main armament. AA armament comprises one 2pdr on the aft superstructure and one each side of the bridge front. There were also MGs. She had a good supply of DCs aft and was a very active unit in the early part of the war.

'24' CLASS SLOOPS
HMS SILVIO T05
1919

This illustration shows HMS *Silvio* as handed over to Australia from the Reserve Fleet, still in her WWI dazzle scheme, and is included to illustrate how drastically different the ideas of late WWI were in comparison to those of WWII. The '24' class sloops were built to look like they could be steaming in either direction. To confuse which was the bow and which was the stern when seen from a periscope, the anchor at the stern was fake and painted on, the aft bridge was a dummy and some units were completed with the mast before the funnel and others with it aft as shown. They could carry thirty-nine DCs, which was very impressive for WWI, and made 17 knots. *Silvio* became HMAS *Moresby* and, like others of her class, was converted to a survey vessel.

HMS HERALD T73
1941

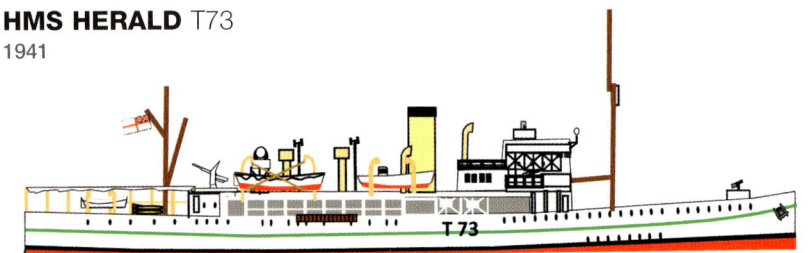

Originally HMS *Merry Hampton*, this ship was renamed HMS *Herald* and then converted to a survey ship. She was at Singapore when the Japanese entered WWII. In poor mechanical condition, she was rearmed with a 12pdr on the aft deckhouse and MGs forward and on the bridge wings, but otherwise little altered. When it was obvious she could not escape, she was taken out to a mud bank and scuttled. The engines were wrecked and as many fittings as possible removed, and then the ship opened to the sea to fill with water. Her condition was such that the RN did not consider she was worth the Japanese repairing. Even the scuttles had been removed. She is shown here in her survey ship paintwork, which was apparently not overpainted prior to her scuttling.

HMIS LAWRENCE L83
1944

Built to act as a sloop, gunboat or, more often, a yacht for senior British officials, *Lawrence* was immediately called up as an escort once WWII broke out, particularly against Italian units stationed in the Red Sea. Her scheme is unusual and almost certainly locally designed. The overall colour appears to be 507c and there are patches of B5 at the waterline. The other colours were probably unofficial. This ship was very active and spent a lot of time patrolling various British Indian Ocean possessions. Without any AA at the start of the war, she is shown here with a quad 0.5in MG aft, 20mm Oerlikons each side of the bridge front and an Army-pattern single Bofors on the quarterdeck.

HMAS MORESBY J54
1943

Moresby was called up as an escort in 1942 when Japanese submarines appeared off the Australian east coast. Her scheme here is a mix of blue and greys, probably 1941 blue and B5, while the overall colour is either an individual mix or 507c. She has had a lot of extra superstructure added and the dummy bridge removed. A single LA 4in gun is carried forward and she has a 12pdr AA on the aft deckhouse. Just aft of this are twin Lewis guns, there are more on the top of the bridge, which has a lot of splinter-mat protection, and two single 20mm Oerlikons aft of it. *Moresby* resumed her survey duties later, sometimes in areas of the South Pacific still in enemy hands.

HEIYO
1944

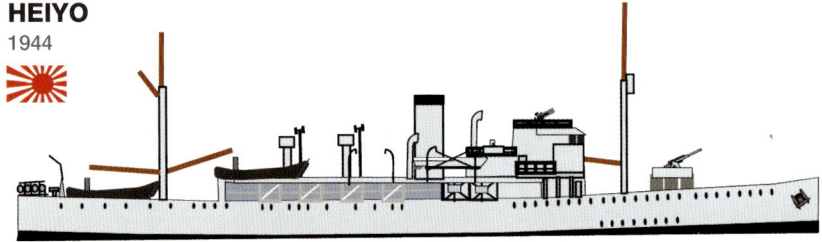

Desperate for escort vessels, the Japanese raised the scuttled HMS *Herald* for reuse. She is shown in a bluish-grey Japanese scheme with black waterline. A Japanese 3in AA is forward and 7.7mm MGs on the bridge. Other MGs were probably carried. She not only escorted merchant vessels but could carry stores aft to resupply various garrisons, hence the Daihatsu landing craft carried. Mechanical condition was poor, and speed only about 12 knots, but she carried DCs aft and was quite active until sunk by a mine in November 1944. The aft mast was of the merchant-ship goalpost type.

SLOOPS

POST-WWI SLOOPS

HMS BRIDGEWATER U01
Bridgewater Class, 1941–2

These two illustrations of the same ship show how research can be confusing at times. *Bridgewater* has a similar camouflage scheme in 1943 but does not carry her pennant number. The overall scheme is MS4a with areas of 1941 blue. She had a Type 271 radar lantern fitted to the bridge. There are single 20mm Oerlikons either side of the bridge front but she still carried a quad 0.5in MG aft of the funnel. Both main guns are 4in AA, the aft LA gun having being replaced just before the war. The square openings along the side of the hull were for ventilation as most sloops were intended to serve in hot climates but were not air-conditioned. These were, of course, kept closed at sea, while many of the portholes were overpainted to match the camouflage scheme. There are eight DC throwers.

HMS BRIDGEWATER U01
Bridgewater Class, 1943

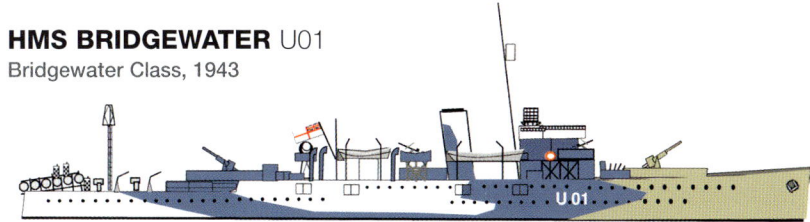

A year later, and after a refit, the ship carries almost the same camouflage scheme except the bow has been repainted in non-regulation dark sand. The MS4a grey areas are now white. Quad 0.5in MG mounts have been replaced by 20mm AA. There are changes to the bridge and funnel but the main section on the hull has been repainted during refit and the pennant painted in. To save weight, the Type 271 lantern has been lowered. However, a Hedgehog has been fitted to starboard and aft of the forward gun, plus *Bridgewater* now carries a HF/DF mast aft. The number of DC throwers has been reduced to four to save weight and to fit in with new doctrine that had done away with the fourteen-charge pattern.

HMS SANDWICH L12
Bridgewater Class, 1939

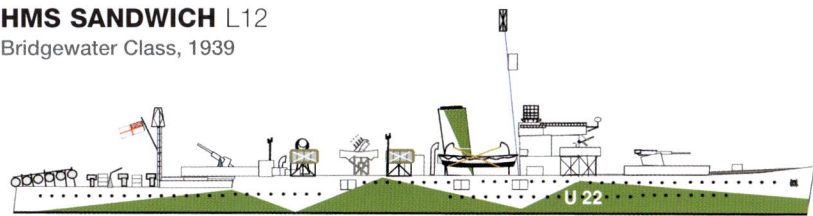

This sloop was at Hong Kong when war broke out and continued to operate in peacetime colours until she was given a quick ASW fit, repainted grey and sent home to the UK for escort duty in the south western approaches. The fittings show how the Admiralty had presumed most sloops would be required for minesweeping duty. Some ships carried ASW equipment stowed, but able to be fitted if needed; *Sandwich* having some small DC droppers and four charges. However, she did have ASDIC. Both guns were altered to HA 4in in 1938 and the 3pdr saluting guns replaced by two quad 0.5in MGs amidships. There were no other AA weapons apart from any MGs in the ship's armoury.

HMS SANDWICH U12
Bridgewater Class, 1943

Sandwich saw considerable service on North Atlantic convoys as well as to Gibraltar and Freetown. She is shown here in a WA scheme which she seems to have worn for much of her wartime career. Type 291 radar at the masthead as well as the typical Type 271 lantern on her bridge. She has four single 20mm Oerlikon AA guns and Hedgehog. The quad 0.5in MGs amidships were only removed and replaced by 20mm guns during her May 1943 refit. The ship is carrying double the usual number of Carley rafts, with four per side. Pennant changed from 'L' to 'U' in 1940.

HMS HASTINGS U27
Hastings Class, 1941–2

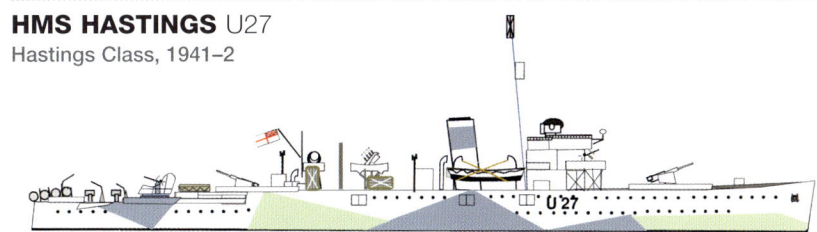

There were few changes between the *Bridgewater* and *Hastings* groups. *Hastings* is shown here on Atlantic convoy duty in 1942. She is in the typical WA green and WA blue on white. The pennant number was in black.. The 20mm gun right aft has a frame restricting its train to avoid shooting-up other parts of the ship. She does not mount a Hedgehog in this illustration but one was fitted in July 1942. A Type 286 radar aerial is shown at the masthead.

HMS HASTINGS U27
Hastings Class, 1943

Hastings is shown wearing an Admiralty dark scheme which includes a low-visibility grey pennant number. The shades provide a nice blend of G45, MS3 and mid-blue. Unusually, the quad 0.5in MGs have been retained amidships. The director has been replaced by a tower for Type 271 radar and there is Type 291 at the masthead. A Hedgehog is placed right forward ahead of 'A' gun; one of the few ships to have such an arrangement. A HF/DF mast sits on the quarterdeck.

HMS FOLKESTONE U22
Hastings Class, 1941

Folkestone is shown here when on Atlantic convoy duty in 1942. She is in a darker shade of 1940 green on white, with a prominent pennant number. Her forward gun has a half-shield to save weight but provide at least some protection at sea. There is a quad 0.5in MG mount amidships and a pair of 20mm each side of the bridge. She only fitted the aft 4in AA in 1941. The forward gun is a LA weapon only. There is a cluster of ASW equipment aft and the original bulwarks reduced. There is also a HF/DF mast. She does not mount a Hedgehog in this illustration but one was fitted in July 1942. There is Type 286M radar at the masthead and a Type 271 lantern on the bridge top.

HMS FOLKESTONE U22
Hastings Class, 1942

After refit, *Folkestone* emerged with an Admiralty disruptive scheme then becoming common. The overall colour was 507c with a blue tint, B5 and black. The use of black was to contrast with the lighter areas. Her deep black funnel top shows her to be an escort group leader. Both 4in guns are HA but the forward mount has a full shield fitted. There is a Hedgehog to starboard and aft of the forward gun. The quad 0.5in MGs have been replaced by two single 20mm mounted port and starboard. There is a Type 291 radar at the masthead and Type 271 on the bridge. The DC throwers have been reduced to four. In 1944, rockets were added to the side of the forward gun shield.

HMS SCARBOROUGH U25
Hastings Class, 1943

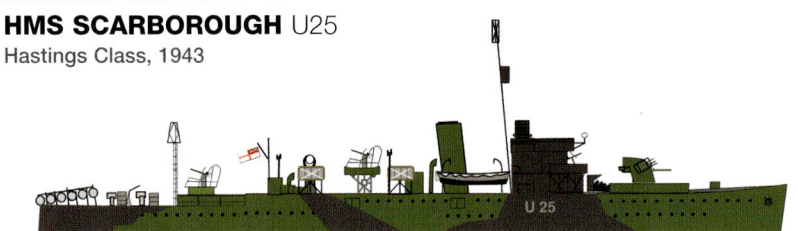

Scarborough wears a simple design of 507a grey on B30. She has lost the aft gun, replaced by a pair of 20mm AA, likewise the 0.5in MGs amidships, which, with those in the bridge wings, gives her a total of six Oerlikons. The weight saved has been used to give 'A' gun a full shield providing better protection for the crew. There are rockets on the side of this and a Hedgehog aft of the mount. Type 271 radar is carried on the bridge, Type 291 at the masthead and a HF/DF mast on the quarterdeck. Two or more of these with a convoy allowed a cross-reference fix on a transmitting U-boat.

HMS SHOREHAM U32
Shoreham Class Sloop, 1943

Shoreham is shown here in a simple scheme of black, white and MS3. There is Type 291 radar at the maintop and a Type 271 lantern on the bridge. Both guns are HA 4in. The 20mm at the front of the bridge have no side cover and she has the usual quad 0.5in MGs port and starboard amidships. There is a Hedgehog fitted aft of the forward gun mount and the DC throwers aft to enable a fourteen-charge pattern. Some of these were later removed. The provision of HF/DF was considered more valuable than the aft gun.

HMS FOWEY U15
Shoreham Class Sloop, 1941

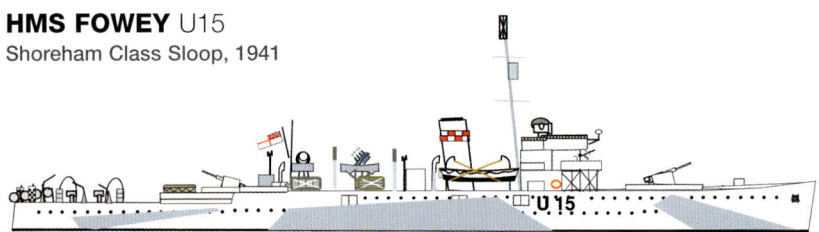

Fowey is shown as she appeared on Atlantic convoy duty in 1941 in a fairly standard WA scheme. Note the tug hoops over her DC area, probably to make it easier to tow home damaged ships. An early Type 286 radar was at the foretop. Both guns had half-shields to save weight and the original bulwarks aft were removed for the same reason. Light AA armament is standard for her type, with 20mm forward of the bridge and quad MGs side by side amidships. A director was carried on top of the bridge. This ship received a HF/DF mast aft in 1942 and the towing hoops were removed.

HMS FOWEY U15
Shoreham Class Sloop, 1945

At the end of the war, *Fowey* is shown with a green panel against a light green hull and upperworks. The forward gun has a shield and rockets attached to each side. The quad MGs have gone and been replaced by single 20mm port and starboard. There is Type 291 radar at the masthead and a US type on the bridge. This ship spent the majority of its career serving in the North Atlantic on convoy duty but did spend a short time in the Mediterranean.

SLOOPS

HMIS HINDUSTAN L80
Lengthened Hastings Class Sloop, 1940

Hindustan entered the war in the white and buff of most British ships in the Far East and quickly changed to pale 507c grey. She was a lengthened *Hastings* type sloop but was equipped with old 4in guns from scrapped destroyers and had no other guns. This left the ship with no AA at all, so therefore a quad 0.5in MG was added amidships and various other MGs. It is said she received a pair of 20mm in 1942 but records are scarce. The ship was not equipped with ASW equipment or ASDIC when war broke out and these were fitted at Bombay in September 1940. Her pennant was changed from 'L' to 'U' late in 1940 as with RN ships.

HMS FALMOUTH U34
Dundee Class Sloop, 1943

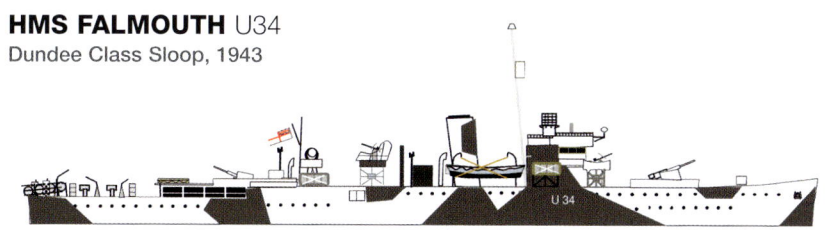

Falmouth is shown as she appeared when serving out of Bombay. The bright light of the Indian Ocean was particularly suited to very high-contrast camouflage schemes. This utilised 507a dark grey on white or 507c to provide a confusion effect when seen at long ranges in high heat haze conditions. This ship never received a HF/DF mast and spent most of her career on Far Eastern and African stations where U-boat intercepts were less likely. Her bridge has been modified and upgraded. The 20mm guns are now much further forward and bridge windows increased. Apart from a Type 271 lantern on the bridge she seems to have no other radar.

HMS WESTON U72
Dundee Class Sloop, 1944

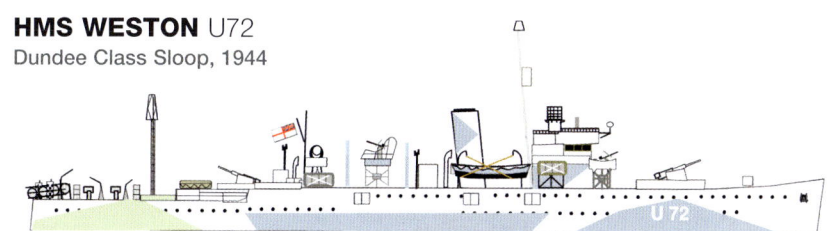

Weston is shown here late in the war in a full WA camouflage scheme. The bridge has undergone some modifications and the 20mm moved forward to give a better ahead-fire arc. The HA 4in guns have half-shields to provide some weather cover. Way aft is a HF/DF mast. This was the only ship of the four in her group to carry one. Her amidships MGs have been replaced by single 20mm. There is Type 271 radar on the bridge and Type 291 at the masthead.

HMS BIDEFORD U43
Shoreham Class Sloop, 1941

Bideford was on the China Station when war broke out and returned home urgently. She is shown here with a dark grey hull and very pale upperworks, possibly white or 507c. The foremast is topped by an early fixed Type 286 radar. Both main guns are HA 4in. There are MGs in the front of the bridge wings and a quad 0.5in MG amidships. She has a really formidable range of DCs aft.

HMS DUNDEE U84
Dundee Class Sloop, 1941

On occasion, camouflage areas were highlighted. *Dundee* is shown with such a scheme. The superstructure is MS4a with B30 hull and 1940 G45 green at the waterline with a black edging. Highlighting was used for a time but then dropped in favour of allowing colours to blend together. The scheme was worn while the ship served on UK East Coast convoys and with the northern escort force. Note that the 20mm on the bridge were not as far forward as most other sloops. *Dundee* is shown with Type 286 radar on the foremast. There are quad 0.5in MGs amidships. The ASW fit was not all that extensive and minesweeping davits and a winch were still fitted at this time.

PRE-WAR SLOOP CLASSES
HMS GRIMSBY L16
Grimsby Class, 1940

The *Grimsby* class were intended to be better armed than previous sloops with an increase to 4.7in guns and a 3in AA forward along with the then standard quad 0.5in MG amidships. While on the China Station she was refitted for service in very cold waters, with the intention of wintering in northern China. On the outbreak of war, she was recalled and allocated to the Rosyth escort force. Soon sent to the Mediterranean and Red Sea, she was sunk during the evacuation of Crete and thus was little altered before her loss, other than possibly receiving some MGs in the bridge wings. There was no radar shipped. Her scheme is a simple dark grey with mid-grey but it is possible a camouflage scheme designed by the wardroom had been applied by the time of her loss. She is shown here with a false white bow wave which is from an anecdote told by a former crew member and may not be exactly correct. Note the 3in AA has no shield fitted.

HMS ABERDEEN U97
Grimsby Class, 1943

Aberdeen was engaged on North Atlantic and African convoy duty for much of the war and is shown here in an Admiralty light scheme which was intended to allow the colours to blend in at a distance and provide a certain amount of invisibility from surface view. It combines MS4a grey with washed-out 1941 blue and a pale blue that could be a washed-out B6. The forward gun has been removed and replaced by a Hedgehog. The 4.7in aft has been retained as well as the 3in AA. The ship mounts four 20mm and has a HF/DF mast aft. Radars Types 291 and 271 are fitted.

HMS FLEETWOOD U47
Grimsby Class, 1942

Fleetwood is shown here in an Admiralty light scheme worn when engaged on convoy duty out of the UK, mostly on the Gibraltar and Freetown routes. Three colours are almost certainly the same as *Aberdeen*. Note that this ship introduced the twin 4in AA to sloops and was considered a valuable AA unit on UK east coast convoys initially. The lack of a gun in 'B' position has enabled two single 20mm Oerlikons to be shipped there instead. She has the usual singles in the bridge wings as well as a further single per side at the break in the foredeck. There is a HF/DF mast carried well aft. Hedgehog was also fitted late in 1943.

HMS LOWESTOFT U59
Grimsby Class, 1942

This ship is shown in a WA scheme which, like on *Wellington*, has been highlighted with a thin black line. This was quite contrary to the intent behind the scheme where the idea was for the blue and white to blend together against the horizon when seen from a periscope, an important part of the design. It is probable that some dockyard thought it looked more effective highlighted. That is probably so in harbour but, at sea, the WA scheme was intended to fade into the background rather than any one part of it stand out. *Lowestoft* had completed as a standard *Grimsby* but later rearmed with twin 4in AA guns which were more useful than the original LA 4.7in guns.

HMS LEITH U36
Grimsby Class, 1944

Leith is shown here in 1944 with a textbook WA scheme without highlighting. The only unusual thing is that the pennant number has been painted well forward of where it is supposed to be and rather similar to the way Canadian ships showed theirs. This could be due to a dockyard refit in a yard not familiar with the regulations. There is now a HF/DF aft and single 20mm guns have finally replaced the quad 0.5in MGs which had been retained up to 1943. There is a Hedgehog forward. The ship has four DC throwers and is fitted for a standard eight-charge pattern.

HMS MILFORD U51
Grimsby Class, 1944

Milford spent much of her career operating out of Freetown before and during the war. However, she returned to the UK late in WWII as the ship had been hard used and was becoming worn out. She is shown here in a camouflage of grey and blue-grey while serving in the north of Scotland attached to the Submarine School. Her aft gun has been replaced by a single 20mm AA giving her a total of five. There are Types 271 and 291 radar fitted.

HMS WELLINGTON U65
Grimsby Class, 1942

Named after a New Zealand port rather than a UK one, as was the previous custom, it was intended that the ship would spend much of her time on that station. She did so pre-war and sailed for her war station at Singapore in 1939. However, she was soon ordered to the UK where she was engaged in convoy duty in the Atlantic for most of the war. Her early-type WA scheme is unusual in that the edges are highlighted but only slightly. This was seen from time to time but was not common. This ship was still extant in 2013 on the Thames at King's Reach in London. Note that, as shown, the ship has bulwark protection around the guns and eight DC throwers aft to enable the fourteen-charge pattern to be fired. This was later found ineffective as some DCs countermined others before they reached the two-layer depth intended and some throwers were then removed.

HMAS WARREGO U73
Grimsby Class, 1941

Warrego is shown in a dark confusion scheme comprising locally-procured dark blue over MS4a grey on the hull and 507c grey above that. Although the waterline is painted in, it has a false bow wave to give the impression of speed. The quad 0.5in MGs are mounted in 'B' position and there are 20mm in the bridge wings but, apart from MGs, she has no other light AA. Both main mounts are twin 4in AA and, although there is a director, it has no radar fitted. There is a radar of British type fitted on the mast, probably Type 286 or a similar model.

HMAS SWAN U74
Grimsby Class, 1943

By mid-war, *Swan* has adopted an Admiralty-type confusion scheme but probably of local design. The overall shade is MS4a with some patches of black on the hull in addition to areas of B5 or washed-out blue. Having to face heavy Japanese air attacks, she has a single 40mm Bofors before the bridge and temporarily carried one on the quarterdeck as shown here. There are also six single 20mm carried. She is shown with Type 285 radar on the director and Type 286PU on the mast.

HMAS PARRAMATTA U44
Grimsby Class, 1941

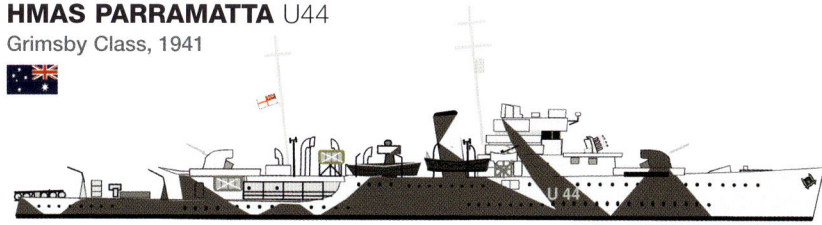

Parramatta is shown here in a scheme typical of ships in the Red Sea and Mediterranean: simple 507a grey on 507c grey, but great care was taken to ensure that the geometric lines ran true from hull up into superstructure and on the funnel etc. However, she still has her black waterline painted in. This indicates a Mediterranean Fleet scheme, most of which were from locally-derived ideas. Admiralty schemes usually instructed the waterline not to be painted in. The quad 0.5in MG mount is in front of the bridge, while two 20mm Oerlikon AA are in the bridge wings. It was common for Australian ships in the region to add MGs that had been abandoned, or unwisely left unattended, to their AA armament for as long as ammunition could be found.

HMAS WARREGO U73
Grimsby Class, 1945

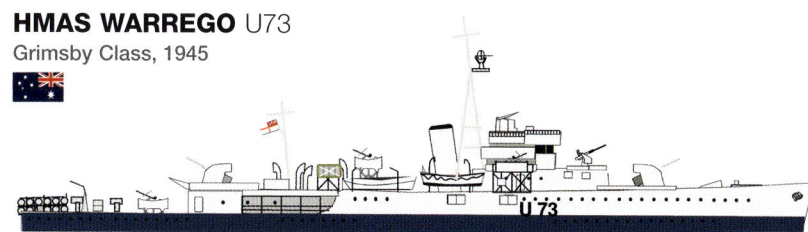

Warrego at the end of the war is in a typical blue-panel hull design typical of the Pacific Fleet. She now has a tripod mast to support heavier radar, which was probably a late version of Type 291, and she has Type 285 on the director. There is a single 40mm before the bridge and no less than six 20mm Oerlikons. The purpose of the dark hull camouflage was to confuse a viewer as to how far away the ship was. It could give the impression the ship was hull down when in fact it was closer. Scheme is probably B20 with 507c grey.

HMAS YARRA U77
Grimsby Class, 1942

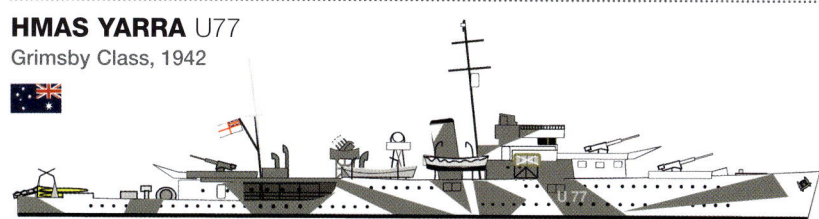

Yarra is shown here in an unofficial early-war scheme typical of the Indian Ocean and Red Sea where she mostly operated. The 507c with 507b medium grey areas is intended not to actually hide the ship but to make identification difficult. She has three single HA 4in guns and the quad 0.5in MGs are mounted aft like British *Grimsby* class ships. There is no radar fitted. *Yarra* was involved in an action in the Red Sea when Italian destroyers tried to intercept a convoy she was escorting but were driven off. She was sunk by the Japanese heavy cruisers *Atago* and *Takao* and two destroyers in a gallant but hopeless defence of a convoy of refugee ships escaping from Singapore. Only thirteen men were later rescued.

HMIS INDUS U67
Grimsby Class, 1942

This is taken from a drawing lent to the author some years ago. There are very few wartime photographs of the ship but the general style fits with the thinking of officers who applied unofficial camouflage in the Far East. The colours are 507c and black. The forward 4.7in gun is mounted on 'B' deck to provide extra staff accommodation forward. She is reported to have shipped a 3in AA in 'A' position to save time instead of adopting the same layout as the rest of the class. With only single 20mm in the bridge wings and a quad 0.5in MG aft, she was overwhelmed by a Japanese air attack.

HMS GORELESTON Y92
Banff Class Cutter, 1941

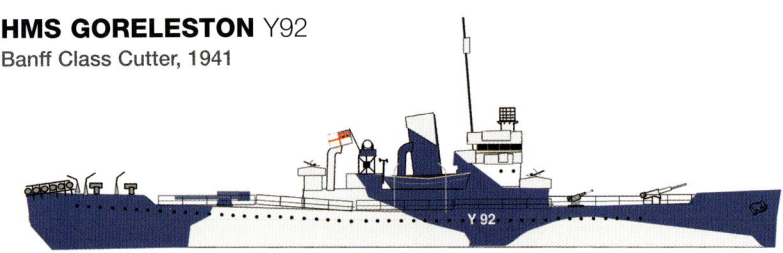

Goreleston was a large US Coast Guard cutter handed over to the RN under the Lend-Lease programme. She wears a very simple scheme of 1941 blue and pale 507c grey intended to break up her outline. Very roomy ships that could handle heavy seas well, they were popular with British crews and spent most of their service on the Freetown and other African routes because of their excellent radius of action. *Goreleston* has a single LA 5in gun forward plus single 3in AA in front of the bridge, all of US pattern. She also has 20mm singles in front of the bridge and on the aft deckhouse.

HMS ENCHANTRESS U56
Bittern Class, 1938

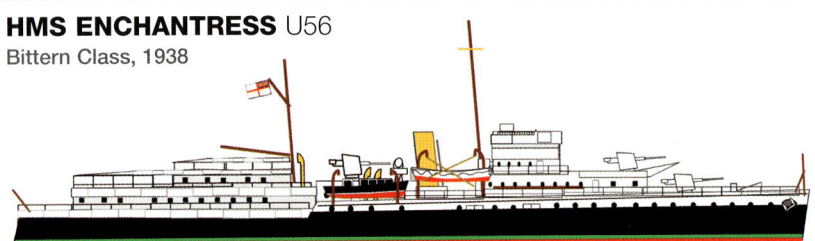

Enchantress is shown here as completed as an Admiralty Yacht, in Victorian livery. She has three 4.7in guns, of which the one mounted in 'Q' position was removed for the 1937 Coronation Review. Note the black hull with green over red boot topping, white upper works and buff funnel. Masts are varnished wood. The motor boat carried has a black hull with white boot topping over red. Areas aft have canvas overhead cover. Her accommodation aft was expansive and lavishly furnished for use by the Admiralty Board. She also served as the official yacht for the Silver Jubilee of King George V.

HMS ENCHANTRESS U56
Bittern Class, 1943

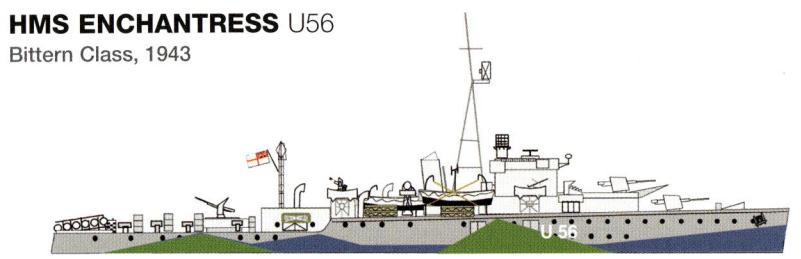

By mid-war, *Enchantress* looked very businesslike with a heavy DC load aft and a Hedgehog aft of 'B' gun. There are 20mm single Oerlikons in the bridge wings and single 2pdr guns amidships replacing the quad MGs. A HF/DF mast has been added on the aft deckhouse. Type 271 radar is on the bridge and Type 286PU on the mast, soon replaced by 291. The camouflage scheme is unusual and is an apparent mix of ideas providing a unique style. The hull is B6 and there are areas of 1940 green and 1941 blue. Her upper works are very pale, probably 507c but possibly WS white.

HMS WALNEY Y04
Banff Class Cutter, 1941

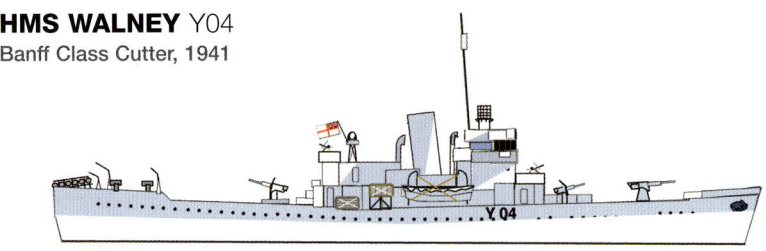

Walney displays a very interesting combination of WA blue and WS white arranged in an unusual reverse manner. She was a little different to some of the others and had a single LA 5in up forward, two 3in AA in front of the bridge and another one aft. She has three 20mm AA, arranged two forward of the bridge and one on the aft superstructure. British Type 271 radar is fitted to the bridge. As there was no rating for a cutter in the RN, these ships were referred to as large sloops.

HMS ENCHANTRESS U56
Bittern Class, 1941

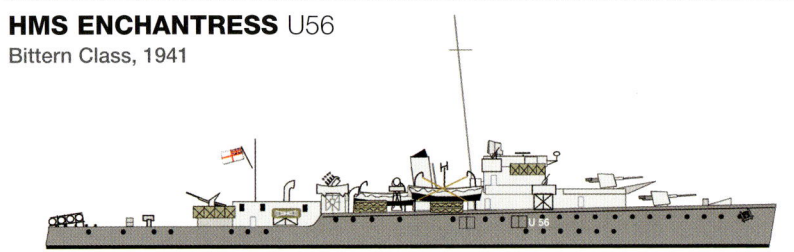

With no need for an Admiralty Yacht in wartime, *Enchantress* was quickly prepared for combat. Her armament forward stayed the same but, instead of a third 4.7in aft, a 3in AA was added. Amidships, she had a pair of quad 0.5in MGs but otherwise her close AA was limited to a few MGs. There are depth charges on the quarterdeck but not the number that would be expected of a sloop by 1941. Camouflage is a simple B6 grey hull and pale 507c upper works. There are splinter screens around the bridge and 3in AA gun, plus piled Carley floats on the boat deck. The funnel has been capped.

HMS ENCHANTRESS U56
Bittern Class, 1945

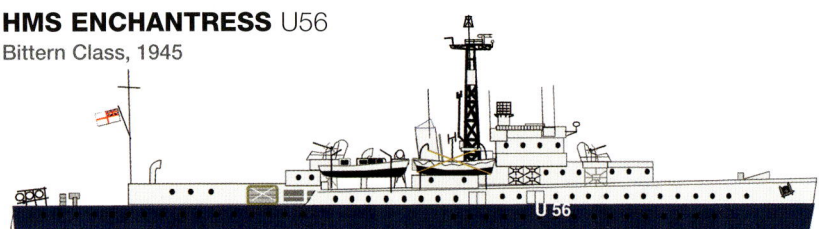

Because *Enchantress* retained some of the extra accommodation from her Admiralty Yacht days, she was chosen to become a Landing Ship HQ (Small) for use in the Far East. For this, she landed her main guns and was equipped with only four single 20mm Oerlikons. There is an aerial for advanced Type 291 radar on the mast and Type 271 on the bridge. US-type radar is at the mast-head. There are numerous aerials for the communications boost required in her new role. Having only reached Colombo when the Japanese surrendered, *Enchantress* was ordered to continue and to use her communications in the reoccupation of Japanese-held areas. Note there are a small number of DCs carried just in case they were needed. Her hull is in PB10 and the rest 507c.

SLOOPS

HMS BITTERN L07
Bittern Class, 1940

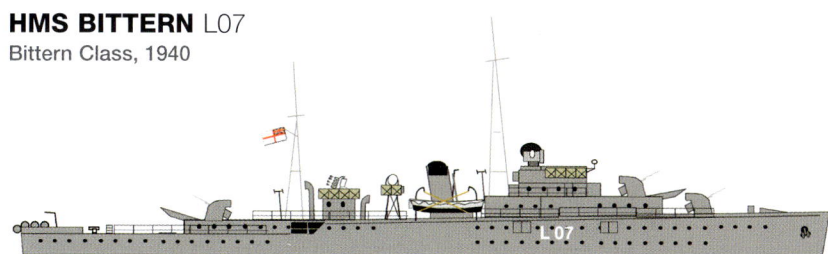

Bittern is shown in overall 507b grey adopted by many ships on the outbreak of war; the scheme worn when she became an early loss to air attack off Norway in 1940. It had been thought that the six 4in AA would prove formidable against air attack and she was allocated to protect troopships. However, it was quickly found that the mounts could not track fast enough against low-flying aircraft, despite their effectiveness against those flying high. Close-range rapid-firing weapons were needed and *Bittern* had only one quad 0.5in MG amidship. With only one main director, they could also only engage one aircraft at a time. Note the sparse early war appearance, considering that later her sisters carried large numbers of DCs and were fitted with as much light AA as possible.

HMS STORK U81
Bittern Class, 1943

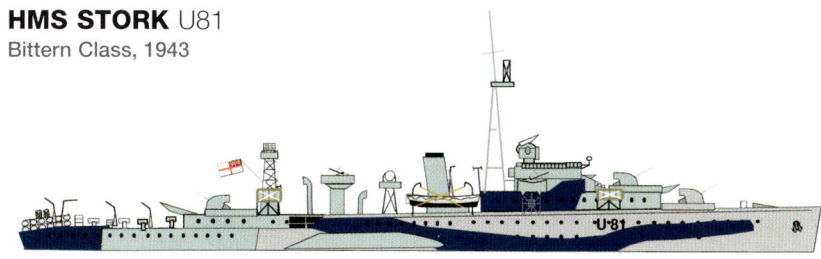

Stork is shown here in mid-war state in an Admiralty intermediate scheme. Colours are MS3, PB10 and B55. Note the Type 271 radar aerial on a lattice mast aft, and Type 291 on the mast. The ASW load aft is considerable. *Stork* was a famous U-boat killer and had a Hedgehog on the port side of 'B' mount. There were single 20mm in each bridge wing and another pair amidships. There are eight DC throwers shown plus a double rack and spare reloads near each thrower.

HMS AUCKLAND U61
Egret Class, 1941

Auckland was to have been completed as a survey ship for New Zealand waters, hence her name was changed from *Heron*. She was heavily armed with four twin 4in mountings but her close-range AA was limited to two quad 0.5in mounts and MGs. She was lost on the Tobruk run in 1941 and had no major alterations from completion. *Egret* and *Pelican* were completed to the same form. Her scheme shown here comprised MS4 on the hull with a slightly lightened version above that.

HMS STORK U81
Bittern Class, 1940

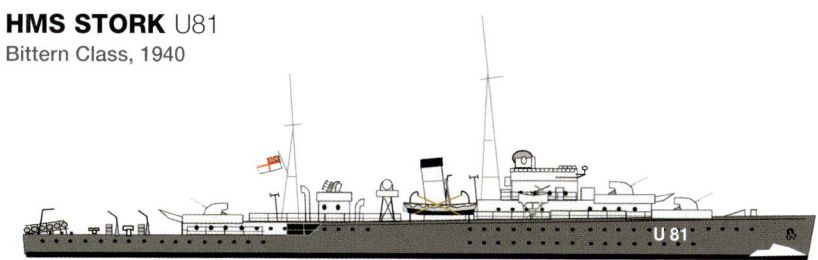

Converted to her designed form from service as a survey ship when the war started, the *Stork* appeared in the Norway campaign in simple dark grey hull and pale grey upperworks. There was little time to apply anything more elaborate. As a regular navy ship she retains her black waterline, not even a false bow wave being allowed to interfere with it. Most sloops kept regular navy crews for most of the war, unlike other ships that were filled with ratings listed for hostilities only. For this reason, they were always counted on for that extra bit of efficiency and old habits such as a smart turn out stayed too. The ASW armament is quite light compared to the view of her in 1943 (below).

HMS STORK U81
Bittern Class, 1945

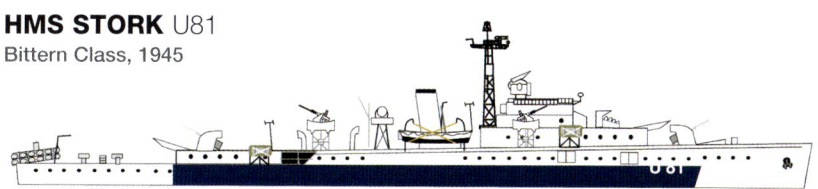

Stork underwent repairs and extensive refits several times during the war and, as a result, was in quite good condition by 1945. This shows her 1945 state when the ship was preparing to sail to the Pacific. 'B' mount has been removed and the Hedgehog has replaced it. The tripod mast has been replaced with a lattice type with radar and HF/DF fitted. The 20mm have all been removed and instead the ship has single 40mm Bofors in the bridge wings plus another amidships. The scheme is white or washed-out 507c with a PB10 panel.

HMS EGRET U75
Egret Class, 1942

Egret is shown here while on convoy duty the year before her loss to a German guided missile in the Bay of Biscay. She was the first warship to be sunk by this weapon. The tall aft mast has gone and she now has quad 0.5in MG mounts port and starboard. There are single 20mm in the bridge wings and there is a single 2pdr which was carried on the quarterdeck for a short time. Not long after, the quad MGs were replaced by single 20mm and the 2pdr was removed. There is a Type 286 radar at the masthead and the director has Type 285. A Hedgehog has been added to the port side just aft of 'B' mount. She has HF/DF aft. The paint scheme is typical of the WA colours.

HMS PELICAN U86
Egret Class, 1942

Pelican is shown in a rather nicely-done WA scheme. Note that it is not only low visibility but that the angles of the blue and green tend to draw the eye to the centre of the ship and thus have the shortening effect that other camouflage schemes also tried to bring about. Against a typical North Atlantic skyline, this was very hard to see when viewed through a periscope. The ship has a tower for the Type 271 radar lantern aft, Type 286 at the masthead and Type 285 on the director. She has single 20mm AA in each bridge wing and amidships there are two quad 0.5in MGs. All four twin 4in AA mounts have been retained. The pennant number is carried unusually far forward.

HMS PELICAN U86
Egret Class, 1945

Pelican is shown in the usual Eastern Fleet style with washed mid-blue panel and a washed-out 507c overall. Her pennant is now much more correctly positioned. 'X' mount has been replaced by a quad 2pdr AA and she has four single 20mm as well. She retained her tripod mast to the end, though it does appear to have been strengthened, and atop it is fitted the HF/DF aerial. The Type 271 radar has gone but she has Type 291 or later on the foremast and Type 285 on the director.

HMIS SUTLEJ U95
Modified Bittern Class, 1941

Sutlej was the first of the four Indian ships to complete and is shown here with a PB10 blue hull and 507c pale grey upper works. The pennant is large but in low visibility grey. She completed with three twin 4in AA, a single quad 0.5in MG amidships and single 20mm in each bridge wing. She has Type 285 radar on the director and Type 286 at the masthead. As well as a good ASW load aft, she has been fitted with Hedgehog to port and aft of 'B' mounting.

HMS PELICAN U86
Egret Class, 1943

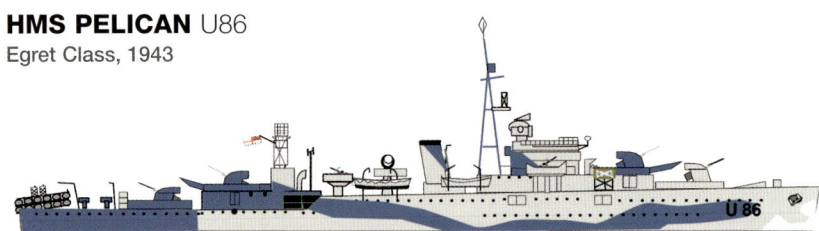

Pelican is shown here in an Admiralty intermediate scheme of B6 and PB10, including a false bow wave of unusual height. She still has her pennant number well forward on the hull. The quad MGs have been replaced by single 20mm AA giving a total of four. A Hedgehog has been mounted to port and aft of 'B' gun mounting. There is an aerial for HF/DF at the masthead. She has Type 285 radar on the director and Type 291 on the mast as well as retaining the Type 271 tower and lantern aft. All four main gun mountings are still carried.

WAR-BUILT SLOOPS
HMIS GODAVARI U52
Modified Bittern Class, 1943

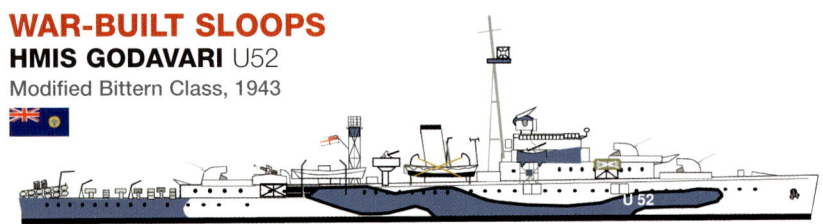

Godavari and her sisters came between the improvements in the *Bittern* class and the later *Black Swan* class, and has gained from the design of the latter although intended to be ships of the former group. Here, *Godavari* wears a class design of Admiralty intermediate type that was intended for sloops in the mid-war period. The central section of 1941 blue is highlighted with a black line. Despite being in camouflage, the ship has a prominent waterline. The light AA comprises two twin 20mm power mountings amidships, single 20mm in the bridge wings and two single 2pdr on the aft deckhouse. Note the amidships tower for Type 271 radar and Type 291 on the mast. The director has Type 285 radar fitted. Depth charge armament is substantial but there is no Hedgehog.

HMIS NARBADA U40
Modified Bittern Class, 1943

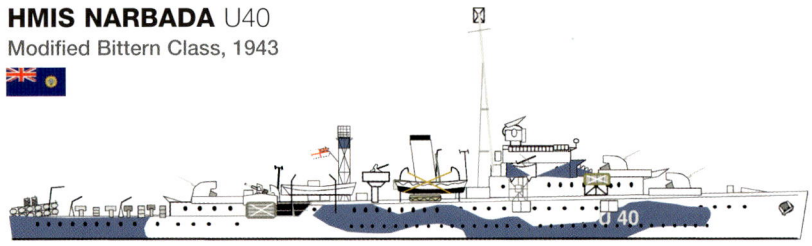

Narbada has the same Admiralty-designed scheme for the class as *Godavari*. But note how the instructions could be seen and interpreted in different ways. *Narbada* does not have her central area highlighted in black and, like that on the bridge, it is not exactly the same shape, though similar. This depended on the men allocated to measure and mark the ship ready for painting. *Narbada* has Type 291 radar at the masthead, Type 285 on the director and Type 271 on a tower amidships. Armament is the same as *Godavari* except the Hedgehog is carried aft of and to port of 'B' mounting.

BLACK SWAN AND IMPROVED BLACK SWAN CLASS SLOOPS

HMS IBIS U99
1941

This camouflage was an inspired scheme that was certainly very unusual. There are some aspects that follow the Admiralty design for sloops, mainly the outlined forward section. But the areas amidships and aft are quite unofficial and probably a local idea. The hull is MS4a but she also has areas of MS1, MS2 and MS3 as well as white. *Ibis* had completed with four twin 4in AA guns but, before entering service, the aft mounting was removed and replaced by a quad 2pdr to give the ship a better volume of close-range AA. There was a quad 0.5in MG amidships and single 20mm in each bridge wing. She was lost during the Operation Torch landings. Type 285 radar is fitted to the director and early Type 286 fixed radar at the masthead.

HMS WOODCOCK U90
1943

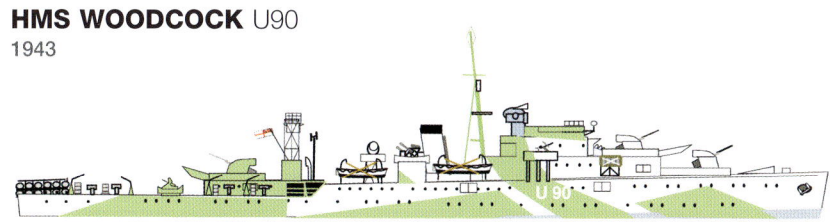

Woodcock is shown here in a WA green version of the WA scheme with, unusually, a pale WA blue waterline area and director. While guidelines were given on how to apply these schemes, the exact composition could depend upon which shipyard marked out the hull for painting and their interpretation of what was required. She has a quad 2pdr AA port and starboard amidships, two twin 20mm on the quarterdeck and two single 20mm in the bridge wings. There is HF/DF at the foretop, a Type 271 radar lantern on the lattice mast aft and Type 285 on the director.

HMS CRANE U23
1943

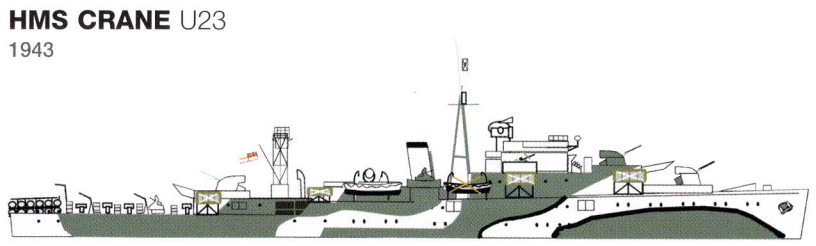

Crane wears an Admiralty intermediate scheme somewhat similar to that popular with some new destroyers of the same period. Forward sections of the MS3 are highlighted with black, but the black is not carried up from the hull onto the superstructure. She has a light AA of four twin 20mm AA and two singles. Types 271, 291 and 285 radar are fitted. As well as a very heavy DC fit she also has a split Hedgehog aft of 'B' mounting.

HMS WHIMBREL U29
1943

Whimbrel is shown in a pale WA blue and white WA scheme typical of ships on Atlantic convoy duty. She has a Type 271 radar lantern on a short lattice mast aft and Type 291 on the mast, as well as Type 285 on the director. AA armament is excellent. Besides her three twin 4in AA there are twin 40mm port and starboard amidships, two twin 20mm mounts on the quarterdeck and single 20mm in each bridge wing. The ship has an extensive ASW fit including Hedgehog. The lower half of the tripod mast was black.

HMS AMETHYST U16
1943

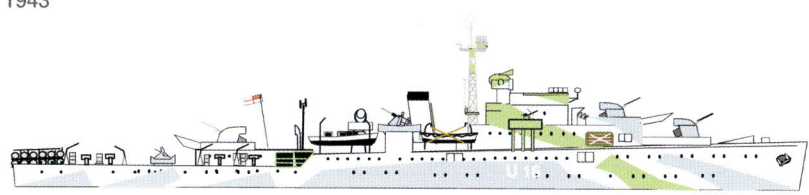

Amethyst is shown in a very unusual variation of the WA scheme. Instead of the lines being straight, they have kinks and variations. The colours are still WA green and WA blue on white. This ship has twin 40mm AA port and starboard amidships, two twin 20mm AA on the quarterdeck and single 20mm in the bridge wings. She has a lattice mast which enables the Type 271 radar lantern to be carried high. The only other radar is Type 285 on the director. There is a HF/DF aerial on top of the mast. This ship gained post-war fame in the 'Yangtze Incident'.

HMS WOODPECKER U08
1943

Woodpecker is shown in an Admiralty intermediate scheme with a combination of shades. The hull is mostly MS4a with areas of MS2 and MS3. There is, however, a white panel aft to disguise her length. The forward guns have been painted out in white, as has the aft mount and the stern. There is a Type 271 radar on a stump lattice aft, Type 291 on the mast and Type 285 on the director. She has Hedgehog fitted. In addition to the three twin 4in AA mounts, she has twin 20mm port and starboard amidships, the same on the quarterdeck and single 20mm in the bridge wings.

HMS BLACK SWAN U57
1942

This illustrates just how simple a WA scheme could be. The bulk of *Black Swan* is white and the areas of pale WA blue quite limited. The Type 271 radar lantern is carried aft, Type 285 on the director and there is a HF/DF aerial at the masthead. Note that this ship carried a quadruple 2pdr AA on the quarterdeck as well as four single 20mm. There is no Hedgehog fitted as yet.

HMS HIND U39
1944

Hind in an Admiralty intermediate scheme that concentrates colour aft and with the bow painted out in white. The curves in this type of scheme were thought to give an impression of speed. The colours used are probably MS2 on washed-out MS3. Being completed late, this ship has a very heavy armament compared to earlier sloops. There are four twin 20mm and two singles, plus there are two single 40mm Bofors AA on the aft deckhouse. Type 291 radar is on the mast which is topped by a HF/DF aerial and Type 285 on the director. The camouflage scheme seems to have been at least partly carried across the deck as well.

HMS CYGNET U38
1943

Cygnet is shown in an Admiralty dark scheme similar to the *Erne* as shown above, but there is the addition of pale WA green which is also carried onto the aft superstructure and gun mount. Interestingly, the pennant number is large and bold in white rather than trying to blend in. Note there are quad 2pdr mountings port and starboard, just aft of the funnel. There are single 20mm in the bridge wings and another on the quarterdeck.

HMS BLACK SWAN U57
1945

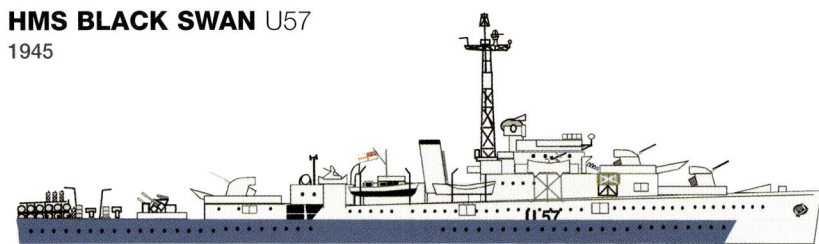

Black Swan in Pacific scheme at the end of the war. The ship is in overall 507c light grey with a PB10 blue panel. The panel is sloped at the front as per instructions, but extends all the way to the stern. Some ships ended the panel at the aft gun mount, others had the panel run for the whole length of the hull in the American style. Note that she now has a lattice foremast to carry all the latest radar and electronics which has enabled the stump lattice and Type 271 lantern aft to be removed. The light AA has been altered with a twin power-operated 20mm mounting at the break of the foredeck. The quad 2pdr on the quarterdeck has been retained.

HMS ERNE U03
1942

Erne is shown with an Admiralty dark scheme that concentrates all dark areas forward to confuse the size of the ship and with the addition of two additional light areas near the bow to suggest a bow wave. This sort of scheme was very effective in that it made it hard for the human eye to pick out the lighter areas when seen from a distance. The pennant is also low visibility to blend in with the scheme. Overall colour is a washed-out MS3 with MS2.

HMS WILD GOOSE U45
1943

Wild Goose was a famous U-boat killer and is shown here in a textbook WA scheme but the areas of WA green and WA blue are quite extensive. See *Black Swan* in WA scheme for an example of how simple it could be. Radar fitted is Type 271 in a lantern on a stump lattice aft with Type 285 on the director. There is a HF/DF aerial at the masthead. Her light armament comprises four twin 20mm and two singles. There is a Hedgehog forward.

HMS STARLING U66
1944

One of the most famous U-boat killers, *Starling* was the leader of the ASW hunter group led by Captain Walker RN. Here, she shows the deep black funnel top band of an escort group leader on a scheme of similar colours to the *Cygnet* and *Erne*. The pennant is very prominent in bold white. Her light AA comprises four twin 20mm and two singles. Types 271, 291 and 285 radar are carried with an aerial at the masthead for HF/DF. This ship sank or shared in the sinking of no less than sixteen U-boats while part of the 2nd Escort Group.

HMIS CAUVERY U10
1943

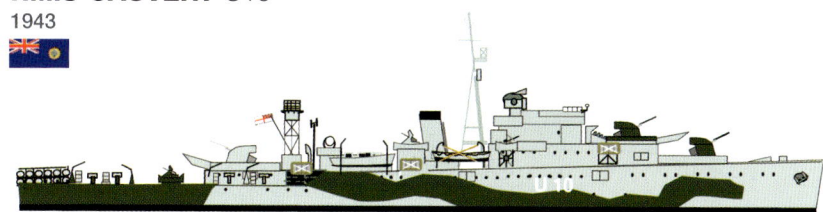

Cauvery entered service in 1943 and was completed to one of the schemes currently in use for RN ships in home waters. Her overall colour is a washed-out green and areas of B30. This was later changed to a blue panel on a light grey hull when the ship was refitted at Bombay in 1944. Ships of the Royal Indian Navy were equipped and operated the same as RN vessels and under the control of the Admiralty. The crew were mostly Indian with a mix of mostly British officers and some senior ranks. This was a cause of resentment among many of the Indian crew who felt that the British received preferential treatment and promotion opportunities. They were quite efficient if not always happy ships. *Cauvery* displays Types 291, 271 and 285 radar. The twin 20mm AA were later replaced by single 40mm Bofors.

HMS MERMAID U30
1944

Mermaid entered the war in 1944 and appeared in a very low visibility scheme of lightened G45 green on WA green. This was, of course, not possible early in the war due to a shortage of green pigment and the requirements of other armed services but, by 1944, it was again available in quantity and some of the original ideas behind the WA scheme were able to be implemented. However, instead of green on white, the choice was as shown. Not long after completion, the twin 20mm amidships were replaced by twin 40mm. She has Type 277 radar on the lattice mast, the usual Type 285 on the director and a HF/DF at topmast position.

HMS LAPWING U62
1944

You can't even trust the dockyard mateys. HMS *Lapwing* left the basin after fitting out on the Clyde with a nice late-war scheme that would suit her for convoys to Russia. But the pennant is wrong. It reads 'U pt 62'. Obviously, an inexperienced painting crew received a note that meant the ship used the letter 'U' with pennant '62'. This was possibly abbreviated on the note as 'U pt 62'. So that is what they painted on the side of the ship! Being in a basin, the crew would have had no opportunity to see the handiwork of the painters. But no doubt she was not far out into the Clyde before someone signalled to point out the error, or to enquire if this was a new style! No doubt her First Lieutenant who was responsible for checking what the painters did was very embarrassed. Nonetheless, the overall paint job looks good and probably suited Russian convoy duty well. The ship has a standard armament for the class and full late-war radar installations. The lower hull is in B20 but the upper colour may be either B5 or a specially-prepared mid-blue. On the lattice she carries the latest Type 277 radar, Type 285 for her guns and HF/DF. A Type 253 IFF is also carried.

7 FRIGATES

FRIGATES

HMS MONNOW K441
1943

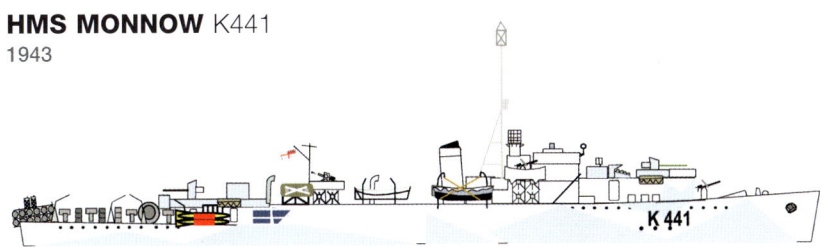

Monnow is shown in a full WA scheme of WA blue and WS white. The Hedgehog has been moved to 'B' position and is of the split type either side of the gun. There is a HF/DF aerial at the masthead and the Type 271 radar updated to Type 272 on the bridge. There are two single 2pdr amidships. Main armament comprises two LA 4in guns. The quarterdeck is crowded with ASW weapons as well as minesweeping gear.

HMS WYE K371
1944

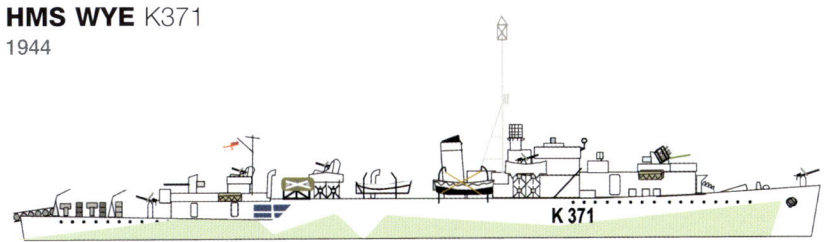

Wye is in a WA green on WS white scheme which was the first-choice colour of the designer. Wartime shortages, however, usually meant that pale blue was used instead. This ship carries single-level DC racks aft. There are five single 20mm in the standard positions and another in the eyes of the bow plus one on the quarterdeck. The DC throwers have been reduced to four due to the fourteen-charge pattern no longer being used. There is also no minesweeping equipment so the quarterdeck is far less crowded. Note rockets on the forward gun mount. The bridge-top radar lantern is for Type 272. It probably had a Type 244 IFF interrogator on top by the end of 1944.

HMS DART K21
1943

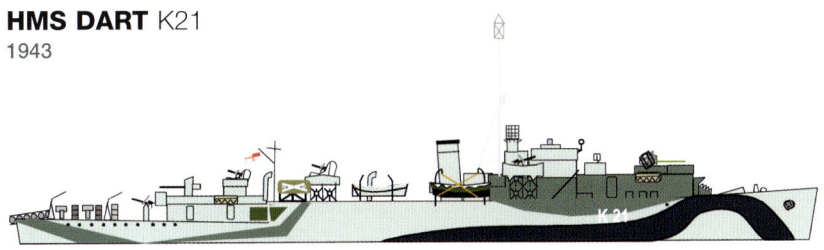

Dart is shown here in a scheme similar to that of newly-built destroyers completed in the same period. The overall colour is a washed-out MS3 with areas of MS2 and G10. She has a pretty standard fit for 'River' class vessels except her DC throwers have been reduced to four in line with the new smaller patterns in use after discarding the fourteen-charge one. There are single 20mm in the bridge wings, sided amidships and on the aft superstructure. There is a single 20mm on the quarterdeck. Note rockets on the shield of 'B' gun. Radars fitted are Types 271 and 291.

HMS ROTHER K224
1942

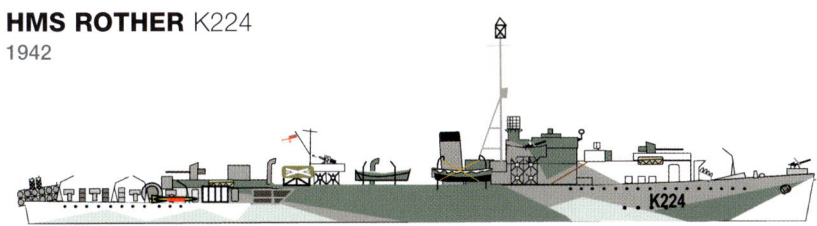

Rother is shown in a dark scheme used during 1942. Colours include white, B6/B30, and MS3. Note that she is fitted for minesweeping which the Admiralty had insisted on in the design in case that was required. However, most had that removed fairly quickly. Note the Hedgehog in 'A' position, which proved very wet. There are single 2pdrs port and starboard plus 20mm in the bridge wings. The two single 4in were LA only, with no AA ability. The 20mm Oerlikon in the eyes of the bow was to engage German E-boats. The deep black funnel band shows that the ship was the leader of a group. Radar fit is standard for the era with a late version of Type 286PU at the masthead and Type 271 on the bridge.

HMS AVON K97
1943

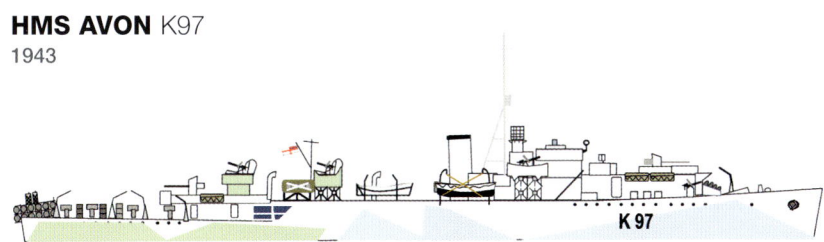

Avon has had the minesweeping winch and associated gear removed and is shown in a standard WA camouflage scheme. The ship still has Hedgehog right forward but there are single 20mm just aft of it either side of the forward deckhouse. There are 20mm in each bridge wing, two more port and starboard amidships and a single superfiring over 'X' gun. There are eight DC throwers and there is a double-layer DC rack with smoke floats on top. The only radar is the Type 271 in a bridge-top lantern.

HMS EXE K92
1943

Exe is shown wearing a WA scheme where WA blue is limited to the hull only with everything else in white. Her close-range armament includes seven 20mm AA. The cluttered quarterdeck has a double DC rack and eight throwers for the fourteen-charge pattern. This ship was not fitted with HF/DF at the top of the mainmast on completion. There is a Type 271 radar lantern on the bridge, as was standard for the 'River' class, but no other radar carried at this time.

HMS JED K235
1944

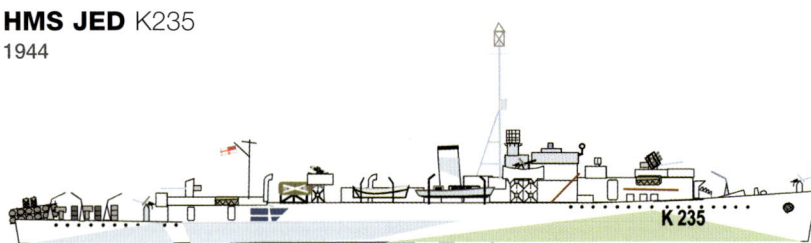

Jed is shown in a two-colour WA scheme more or less to the preferred style of the designer. This ship was at the D-Day landings. It is evident the ship was involved in work close inshore as there is a single 20mm mounted in the eyes of the bow for use against E-boats and other coastal craft. There are 20mm Oerlikons in the bridge wings and one on the quarterdeck, but amidships she mounts two single 2pdr AA on powered mountings. Type 272 radar is carried with HF/DF at the masthead.

HMS ETTRICK K254
1944

Ettrick is shown in a WA scheme that adds some variety by having a central panel of blue which extends to the funnel and some upper areas. There is a single 2pdr in the eye of the bow, single 20mm in the bridge wings and on the aft superstructure, but she has twin 20mm powered mountings amidships. These were not fitted to all 'River' class ships although it was intended it be done if possible. There is HF/DF at the masthead and a full ASW fit aft, giving the usual cluttered look. Her only radar is a lantern for Type 271 or 272.

HMS AIRE K262
1943

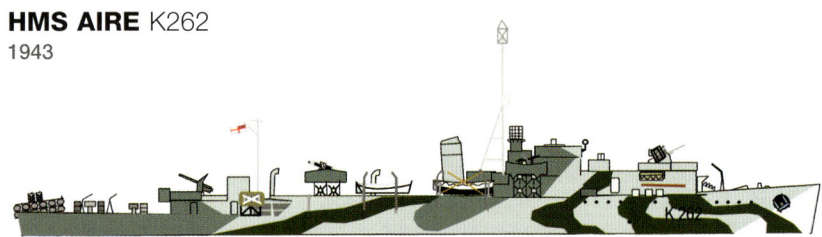

Aire is shown wearing an Admiralty scheme in washed-out MS3 overall with areas of MS3 and MS1, but with white at the bow. The ship has a Canadian-style armament of a twin 4in AA in 'B' position and a 12pdr AA aft. Single 20mm in the bridge wings, but single power-operated 2pdr mounts are in the gun tubs amidships. The usual HF/DF at the masthead and a Type 272 lantern on the bridge make up her main electronics. There would have been a tiny Type 244 aerial on top of the lantern.

HMS BALLINDERRY K255
1944

Ballinderry is shown in a WA green on white scheme in 1944, including the bow-chaser 20mm, but not only has retained a cluttered quarterdeck, it actually includes no less than ten DC throwers. That would enable up to an eighteen-charge pattern, but such an extensive fit was being reduced by 1944 when it was realised that, if too many charges were dropped at once, some countermined others which in consequence reduced the effectiveness as well as wasting depth charges. Her radar lantern for Type 272 probably carried Type 244 IFF on the roof. HF/DF is at the masthead.

HMS NITH K215
1944

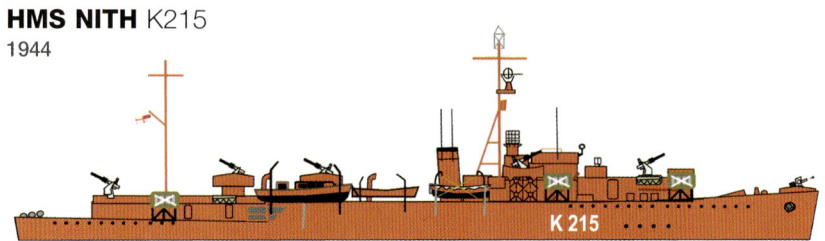

Nith is shown painted in overall 'red lead' as she was on D-Day, 6 June 1944, after having been converted to a Brigade HQ ship. This was to actually make her more visible, not less, during the landing operations. That enabled the Army Brigade being directed to more easily see her. It is not Mountbatten pink, it's straight undercoat! The main guns have gone and the ship carries only light AA. There are seven 40mm Bofors guns, and an anti-E-boat 2pdr at the bow. Note that extra accommodation and boats have been added and there are more communications carried, hence the whip aerials. Radars Types 277 and 272 and HF/DF are fitted.

HMCS ROYAL MOUNT K677
1944

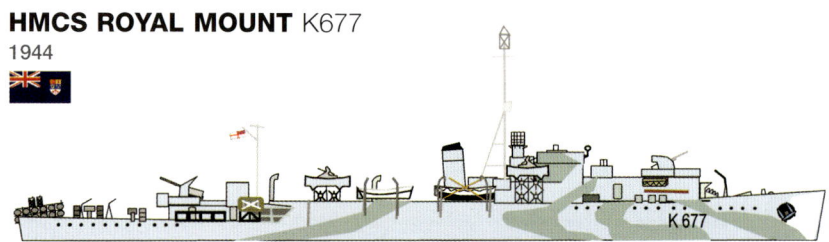

Royal Mount is shown in a scheme similar to that of *Aire*, but in lighter tones and somewhat rearranged pattern. It appears to be WA blue overall, with a very washed-out MS3 over it. The ship mounts four twin powered 20mm AA with no singles at all. There is a twin 4in AA forward and single 4in AA aft. Canada operated more 'River' class than the RN. A lantern for Type 271 is on the bridge but possibly to be replaced by Type 272. HF/DF is at the masthead.

HMCS WENTWORTH K331
1944

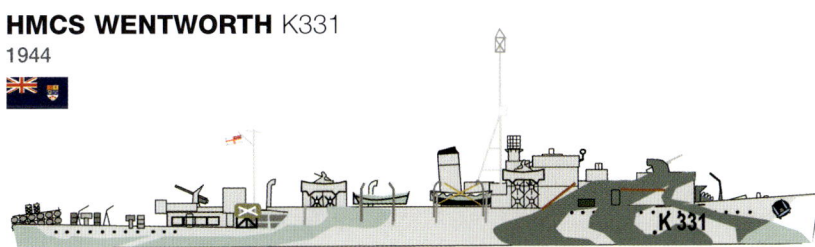

Wentworth carries another variant of the scheme popular with Canadian ships at the time this ship entered service. More and more were serving in the European theatre rather than exclusively the Western and Central Atlantic. The concentration of MS2 forward over a MS4a base is deliberate. Placing only washed-out MS3 aft gives the 'two ships' look seen in other schemes. A touch of white forward is to confuse her speed. Correct size and course were vital for U-boat commanders to make an accurate firing calculation. The more the scheme confused them the better. Light AA and electronics as per *Royal Mount*.

HMCS TORONTO K538
1944

Toronto has a pale scheme that is intended to blend in and can be considered a later type of Atlantic convoy camouflage scheme. It was probably intended to fit two needs. Note that like nearly all Canadian 'River' class she has four twin power-operated 20mm AA mountings. The gun in 'B' position is a twin 4in AA and the aft gun a single 4in AA. Occasionally a 12pdr had to be substituted.

HMCS SWANSEA K328
1945

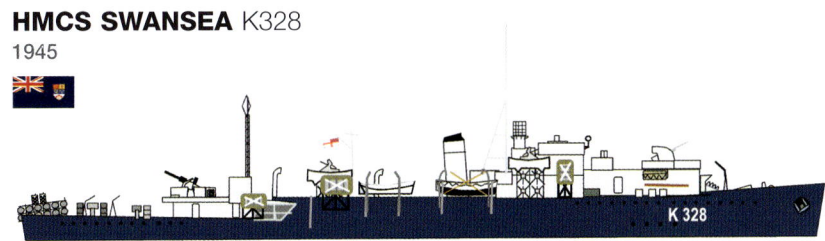

Swansea was a Canadian unit modified for service in the Pacific. For this, the ship has been painted in a scheme of B20 hull and 507c grey upperworks. There is a twin 4in AA forward and a twin 40mm Bofors aft. The guns in the bridge wings and amidships are power-operated twin 20mm AA. Note that the HF/DF aerial has been moved from the foremast to a special lattice aft. She retained the Hedgehog and a full complement of DCs. The only radar is the Type 271 set as the American SU set planned had not been delivered by the time of her Pacific refit.

HMCS ANTIGONISH K661
1944

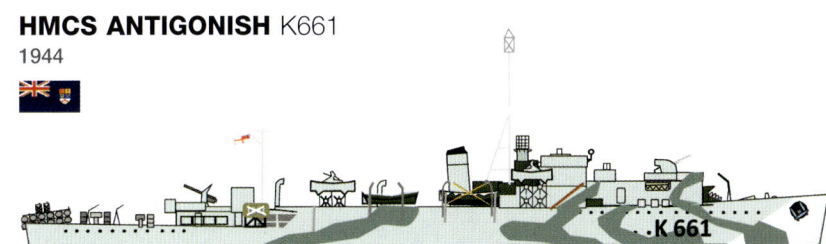

Another interpretation of the Canadian 'River' scheme similar to *Wentworth* and *New Waterford*, but in variations of colour and the actual shapes depending on where the dockyard marked out the lines for the painters to fill in. Usually, the crew merely touched up these schemes and any major change took place in a dockyard. Between refits, it was up to the crew to keep paintwork fresh and thus, the simpler it was, the easier for them to do that during short breaks from convoy duty. Electronics and light AA as per *Wentworth*.

HMCS NEW WATERFORD K321
1944

Many of the Canadian 'River' class completing in 1944 were finished in variations of the scheme shown rather than the WA scheme. This dark-on-light type effect does throw emphasis on the forward part of the ship with intent to mislead the viewer. With fewer submarines active and ships operating in more coastal areas such as the Normandy beaches and the English Channel the main danger was from E-boats and air attack, plus a need to take shore batteries into account. The colour overall is MS4a with dark patches of MS1. Electronics and light AA as previous ships.

HMCS LEVIS K400
1944

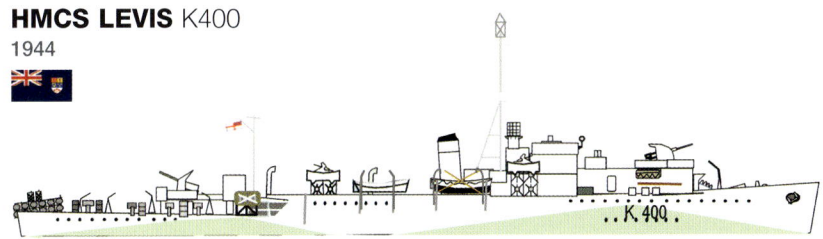

Despite a tendency to design later schemes, the WA type remained very common on convoy duty because it was so effective. The intent was to make the ship blend in with the average Atlantic horizon and thus be hard to see from a periscope. Indeed, it was often hard to see from other ships and, if operating in close formation, could be quite, hazardous to station-keeping. Her guns, ASW fit and electronics are standard.

LA DÉCOUVERTE K370
1944

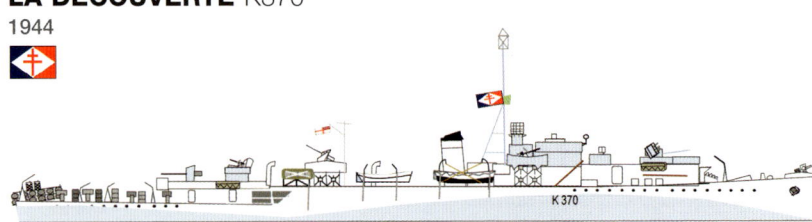

The French operated six 'River' class frigates under RN control and all were very busy in the Channel, especially during the Normandy landings, which they supported. Her intended name had been *Windrush* and she was the third of her class to commission as a French vessel. The scheme is based on the WA style but with a long double-curving WA blue panel and some sections of the upperworks in the same. Note there are port and starboard single 40mm Bofors amidships where 20mm were usually positioned. Interestingly, she has a 2pdr bow chaser. Electronics as per the previous units.

HMAS GASCOYNE K354
1943

Gascoyne displays some RN influence but in blues more suited for the Pacific areas where the ship was likely to operate. There is British Type 271 radar on the bridge but an Australian-pattern GW warning at the masthead. No HF/DF is shown. The ship has single 4in AA guns in similar shields to that of the standard British twin mount. There are eight single 20mm Oerlikons in total.

HMAS DIAMANTINA K377
1943

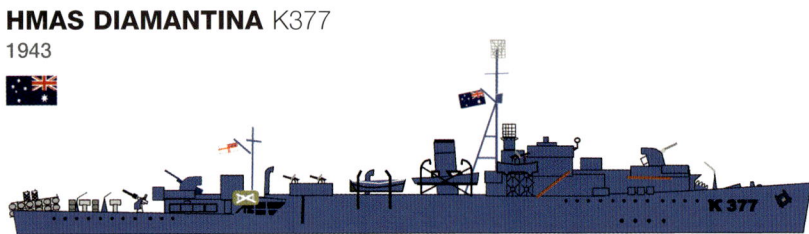

Diamantina is in overall blue for operations with the US Navy. The pennant number is in bold black but still not prominent. There is a single 40mm on the quarterdeck, four single 20mm amidships and single 20mm in the bridge wings. Australian and RN radar carried. US radar was to have been provided for compatibility purposes and easy replacement or repair of parts but it was not available on completion. The main guns are single 4in AA. Like all Australian ships, the White Ensign was flown aft and the national flag at the mast.

HrMs JOHAN MAURITS VAN NASSAU (II) K251
1944

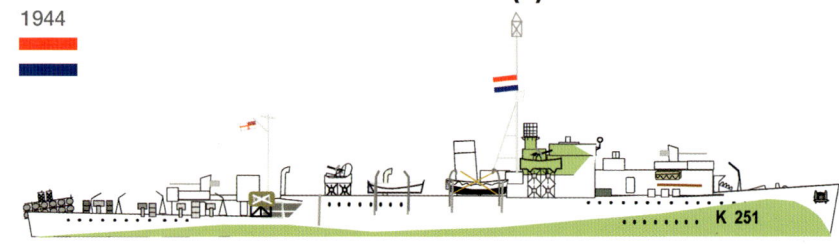

Named in honour of an early sloop of the Royal Netherlands Navy sunk during the war, this ship is shown in a WA scheme of somewhat darker green which has been carried up onto the bridge area as well. She is otherwise plain WS white all over. The decks were dark grey. British-built, she carries single 20mm AA and single LA 4in guns fore and aft. The ASW fit enables large patterns to be laid such as used by hunter-killer and support groups when pursuing a known U-boat contact to destruction. Electronics as previous units.

HMAS GASCOYNE K354
1945

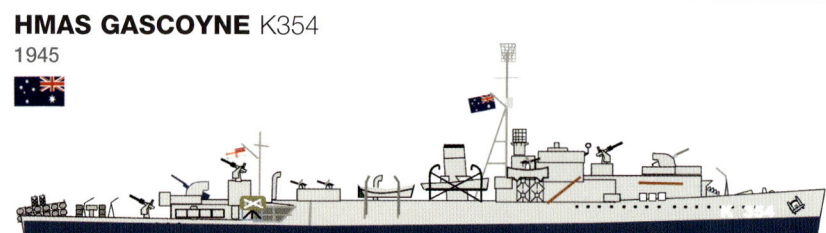

By 1945, *Gascoyne* was dressed to work with the British Pacific Fleet, and has adopted the regulation scheme, but, interestingly, right aft it does not go all the way up to the quarterdeck. The ship's decks were very dark grey. Since 1943 the AA has been upgraded. There is a single 40mm in front of the bridge, a second behind 'X' gun and another on the quarterdeck. There are still six single 20mm but they were soon to be replaced by four twins. Radar fit remains the same.

HMAS BARCOO K375
1945

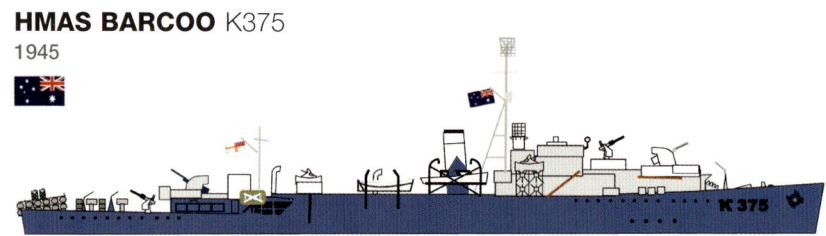

Barcoo has an interesting combination of styles with a dark blue hull and pale grey upper works yet some areas, such as the forward gun and the funnel, in white. There are single 40mm AA on the quarterdeck and before the bridge. The other light AA comprised four twin 20mm power-operated mounts. Vessels of this type spent most of their time in New Guinean and other South Pacific waters, mopping up Japanese garrisons and preventing supplies getting through to them.

'CROWN COLONY' CLASS FRIGATES

HMS ANGUILLA K500
1944

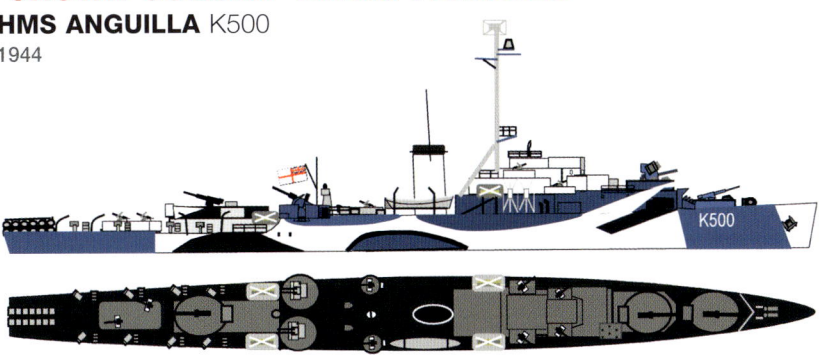

HMS ASCENSION K502
1944

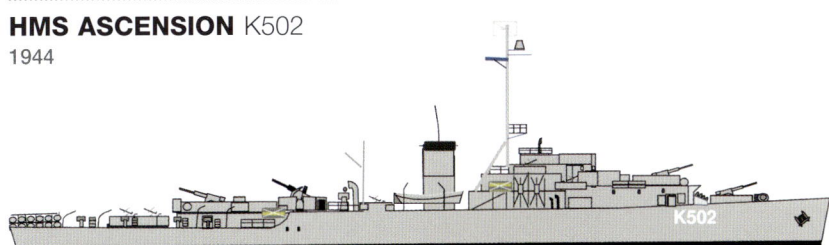

Ascension is shown in MS4a grey which particularly highlights the very few portholes these frigates had in comparison to the 'River' class from which they evolved. The USN preferred air-conditioning and an unbreached hull to assist with damage control. This ship has two additional 20mm just aft of the funnel, giving a total of eight such weapons as well as the two twin 40mm. The 3in guns were of US standard type, which were of moderate value in the AA role but were totally useless against a surfaced U-boat as they could not penetrate the thick pressure hull.

HMS SOMALILAND K594
1944

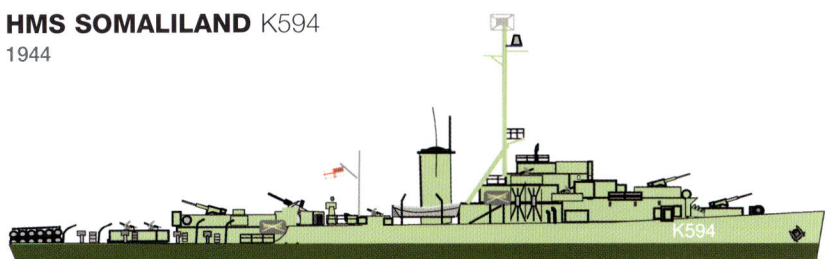

Somaliland wears a version of the late-war British scheme worn by many escorts during the last months of WWII. This would probably have been applied in a British dockyard during refit as US-built ships were delivered in schemes more familiar to the USN. The lower hull is in dark green and the upper areas in G45. Early machinery defects were overcome and these ships were both fast to produce and expendable as their cost was quite low compared to other escorts built in the UK. These ships have whip aerials which were uncommon with British ships.

Anguilla is shown as delivered in a US-style camouflage of black and dark blue on white. These ships were essentially 'River' class frigates built in American yards but with equipment and weaponry altered to USN standards. They were known as the *Ashville* class in US service. They were armed with the same 3in gun as American destroyer escorts, a pair of twin 40mm, and four to six 20mm. Radar was American type SL and with SA at the masthead. A RN modification is the fitting of a shield to 'B' gun as this also allowed rails to be placed on the sides for rocket flares.

HMS CAICOS K505
1945

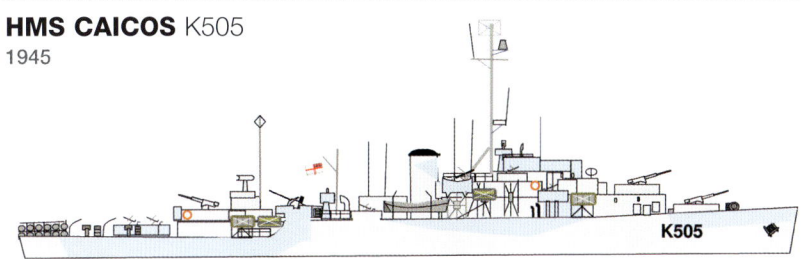

Caicos was converted to a fighter direction ship in 1945 but retained her ASW capability. She was employed in detecting V1 flying bombs launched against the UK from the Netherlands and directing fighters to intercept them. The ship was intended to be deployed to the British Pacific Fleet but was still in European waters when Japan surrendered. Her very pale scheme of WA blue and 507c was to help against the only two major threats remaining, German coastal U-boats and E-boats, any Luftwaffe air threat being by then almost negligible. Additional superstructure was fitted aft of the bridge and, as can be seen, there were many radars, electronic intercept equipment and communications aerials added.

HMS SARAWAK K591
1944

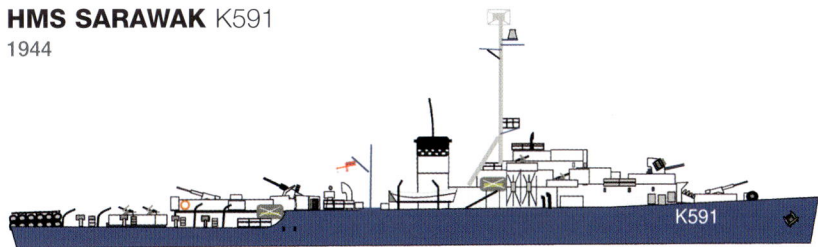

Sarawak is shown after her first refit. A shield has been added to 'B' gun along with the associated rocket flare projectors. The check band on the funnel indicates her escort group. The paint scheme has been simplified to a PB10 hull with 507c upperworks. Some changes to schemes came about due to pressure on dockyards and shortage of men which meant the easier to maintain, the better. The ships of this class were built in incredibly short times but they suffered machinery defects at first. There are four 20mm clustered around the bridge and two on the quarterdeck. The twin 40mm at the break of the foredeck was a far superior fit to British-built ships.

'KIL' CLASS PATROL ESCORTS

HMS KILBRIDE 5 02
1944

The USN developed a corvette-type escort of their own, known as PCEs. Some of these were made available to the RN and at first were referred to as BEC. *Kilbride* was therefore known as BEC-2 when first commissioned, but the Admiralty was not keen on ships being un-named so they chose to allocate names based on the 'Kil' class built at the end of WWI. This ship wears a camouflage of MS2 on WS white and spent most of her time based on Gibraltar. There is no funnel, the ships were diesel-powered and the fumes were exhausted via the black vent that can be seen on the hull between the two single 40mm aft. The ships were well armed with a 3in AA forward, two single 40mm aft and single 20mm in each bridge wing. ASW fit was strong, including a Hedgehog forward.

HMS KILMARNOCK 5 11
1943

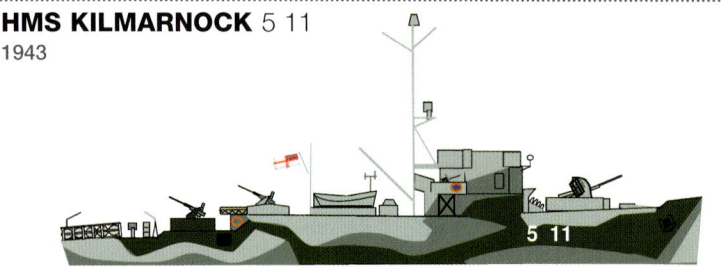

HMS KILCHRENAN 5 04
1944

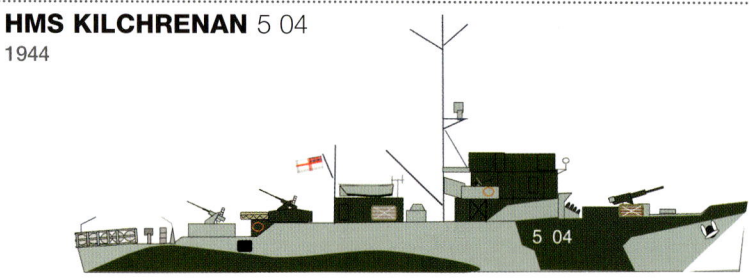

Kilmarnock served mostly on the Gibraltar to West Africa run and wears a camouflage that could have been American or British. The colours seem to be MS1, MS2 and MS3, which would have been quite good against an African background as most duty was to escort coastal convoys. Radar carried was US type SL and they had IFF fitted as well. This ship took part in the sinking of *U 731* in May 1944, the only success for this class. The Admiralty chose not to give these ships flag 'K' as part of their pennant because the numbers with that letter were getting into the many hundreds. But it did apparently cause some confusion at first.

Kilchrenan is seen here wearing a RN camouflage scheme that would have been applied after she reached a British yard for refit. The colours are MS3, dark green and white. The class were built 1,000 miles inland at Chicago and had to sail down inland rivers to finally reach the sea. Most of the class spent their time operating along the coast of West Africa back and forth to Gibraltar. They were smaller than the RN's 'Flower' class corvettes but much better armed for AA defence. They also had a respectable ASW armament. Their service life was short, all being returned to the US in 1946.

'LOCH' AND 'BAY' CLASS ASW FRIGATES

HMS LOCH ECK K422
'Loch' Class 1944

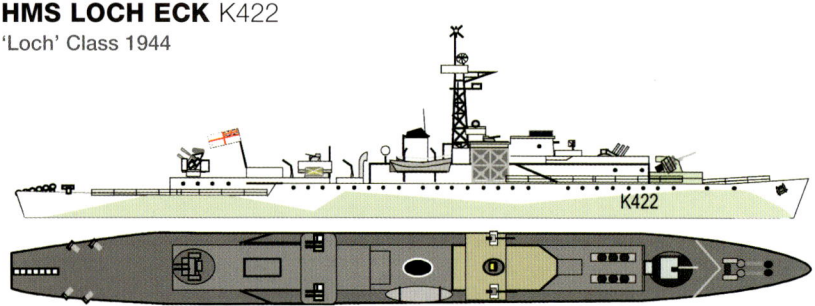

HMS CARDIGAN BAY K630
'Bay' Class 1945

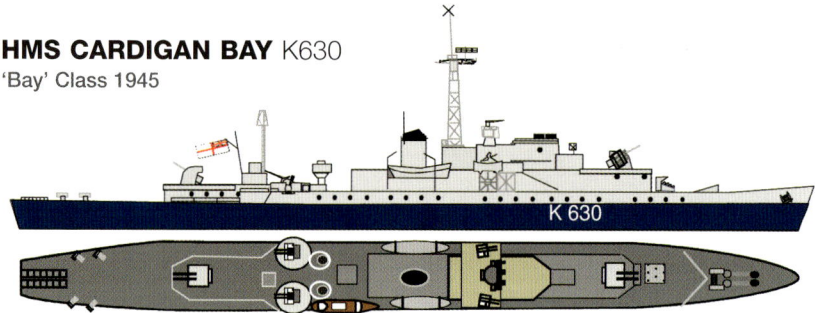

Loch Eck took part in the sinking of three U-boats. It was rare for one to escape once a 'Loch' class had made contact. The scheme is a fairly standard WA scheme with rather more green on the hull than was usual on escorts a year or two earlier. Note the simple uncluttered deck layout. Dark grey Cemtex decks. The wood on bridge areas was for watch crew comfort. Type 277 radar is carried on the lattice mast with HF/DF at the top.

The 'Bay' class were essentially 'Loch' class ships converted for service in the Pacific where more AA firepower was needed. The change of design caused a delay in completion and only six were in service before Japan surrendered. None saw any action. *Cardigan Bay* is shown in a typical Pacific scheme as worn on completion. Hedgehog and a larger DC armament was provided in lieu of Squid. There is a HF/DF mast aft. On the lattice foremast she carried Type 293 radar on a projection and Type 271 at the mast top, with Type 285 on the gun director. There are director tubs for the twin 40mm, each of which has Type 282 radar.

FRIGATES

HMS LOCH GLENDHU K619
'Loch' Class 1944

Loch Glendhu is shown with the standard late-war scheme for escorts in the European theatre and Atlantic escort. This ship sank *U 1024* in April 1945 just before the end of the war. The 'Loch' class were deadly against conventional submarines and would have been fairly effective even against the Type XXIs then entering service with the Kriegsmarine. Type 277 radar on the lattice mast and HF/DF is at the masthead. These ships carried ASDIC that gave an accurate reading of the depth of a submarine target and the percentage hit rate was very high. Only two DC throwers and fifteen charges were carried. Light AA comprises a quad 2pdr aft and four twin manual 20mm mounts.

HMS LOCH DUNVEGAN K425
'Loch' Class 1945

Loch Dunvegan took part in the sinking of two U-boats. She is shown here in a scheme intended for the Pacific Fleet, with a blue panel on light grey hull and upperworks. Many ships were to proceed to the Pacific and Indian Ocean in 1945 when the Battle of the Atlantic was over. It was common to carry rockets on the forward gun mount in this period. Light AA and electronics are standard fit.

HMCS LOCH MORLICH K517
'Loch' Class 1944

This ship was built in the UK but handed to Canada on completion and was among the first 'Loch' class to join the Battle of the Atlantic. The ship is shown here in a WA blue and WS white WA scheme. Armament and electronic fit was the same as British ships. She served out of Londonderry with the 9th Escort Group with Canadian 'River' class frigates on Atlantic and Eastern Atlantic duty.

HMS LOCH KILLEN K391
'Loch' Class 1945

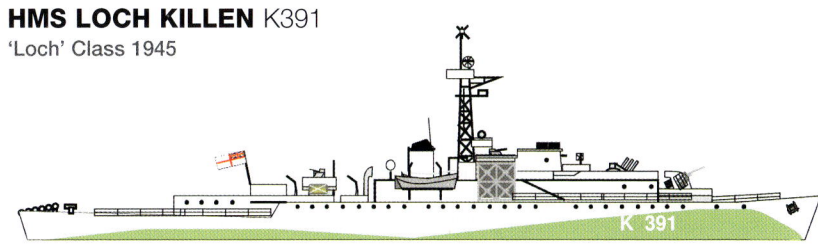

Loch Killen took part in the sinking of three U-boats in the last year of WWII. The success rate of this class was very high due to the double Squid mounted in 'B' position. She has a WA green on white scheme with curved areas rather than angled panels. There is a single 4in forward with rockets attached to the shield. She has a quad 2pdr aft and four twin 20mm AA.

HMS LOCH FYNE K429
'Loch' Class 1945

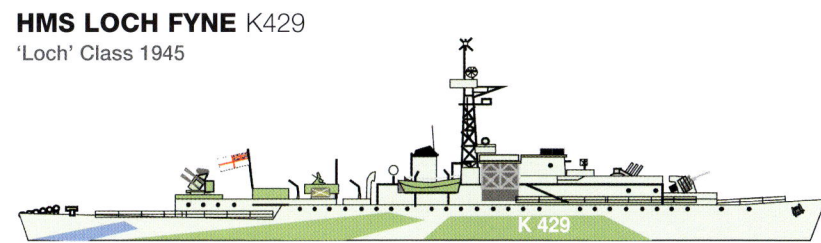

Loch Fyne completed too late to score any sinkings in the European theatre but took the surrender of ten U-boats when the war ended. She then adopted a paint scheme similar to *Loch Dunvegan* and proceeded to the Pacific but had only reached Colombo when Japan surrendered. I have shown her in a late-war version of the WA scheme with patches similar to those worn by earlier ships, except she has it applied to a pale green overall instead of the more common white. Light AA and electronics are as standard.

HMCS LOCH ALVIE K428
'Loch' Class 1944

Loch Alvie was commissioned into the RCN in August 1944 and took part in two convoys to Russia as well as operations in the Atlantic and European theatre. She is shown here in a very simple WA scheme of overall white with just two WA blue panels on the hull. *Loch Achanalt* also served in the RCN. The names of these ships were not changed as Canada had a large Scottish immigrant population that could relate to the names. Guns and electronics the same as RN ships.

'CAPTAIN' CLASS FRIGATES

HMS BICKERTON K466
'Captain' Class (Long Hull Group) 1944

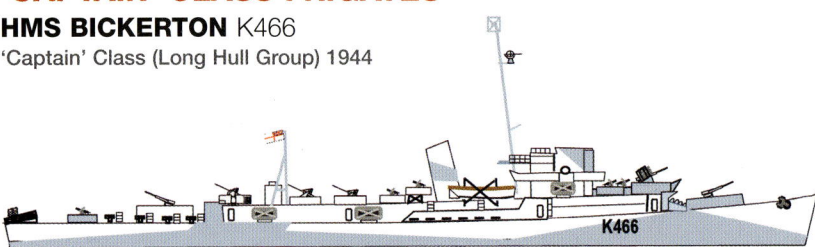

Bickerton is shown repainted to RN standards for Atlantic escort duty. It is a variant of the WA scheme in WA blue. 'B' mount has been given a shield to provide cover so that rocket flare rails can be fitted. There are 20mm AA each side of the bridge front, four more aft of the funnel. There are staggered single 40mm Bofors amidships and a twin Bofors on the aft deckhouse.. For some reason, this ship is carrying a British Type 277 radar on the mast and Type 291 at the masthead. US radar was a more normal fit.

HMS BAZLEY K311
'Captain' Class (Short Hull Group) 1944

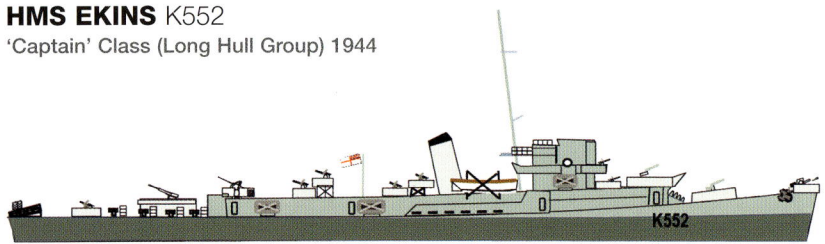

Bazley is also shown in as delivered condition with a US-applied paint scheme. Note that this class had a lower funnel which did give them a slightly smaller look but the difference in size between the long hull group and short hull was not much at all. It was merely to accommodate different machinery. SC-2 and SL radars would be normal fit.

HMS EKINS K552
'Captain' Class (Long Hull Group) 1944

Ekins is shown when operating as a support ship for coastal forces in the North Sea and approaches to the English Channel. She has an incredible thirteen 20mm guns, and the usual twin 40mm, but also has a single 2pdr mounted in the eyes of the bow for use when chasing E-boats. The 3in guns of these ships were useless against submarines and not all that much better against aircraft. Her scheme appears to be MS2 and MS3 with some washed-out MS3.

HMS GOODALL K480
'Captain' Class (Short Hull Group) 1943

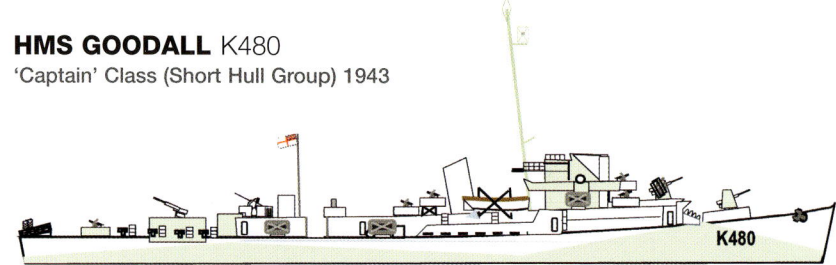

Known in the USN as the *Evarts* class and to the RN as short hull 'Captains', this shows *Goodall* on Atlantic duty in a very pale green and white scheme. The light AA comprises a twin 40mm Bofors and no less than nine 20mm at a time when many British fleet destroyers were lucky to have six. The only thing that ruins this very pale scheme is that the pennant number is painted in black. SC-2 and SL radars would be normal fit.

HMS BENTICK K314
'Captain' Class (Long Hull Group) 1944

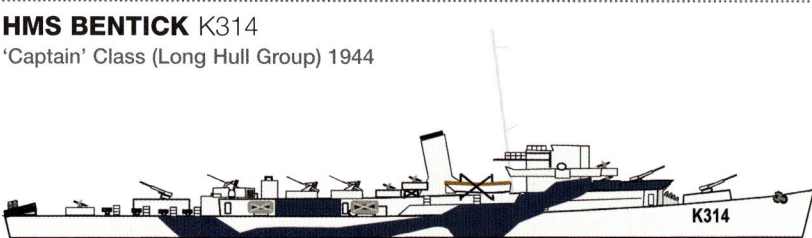

Bentick is shown as delivered in a camouflage design provided by the dockyard in the US that built her. Not long after arriving in the UK this was painted out and a WA-type scheme applied. The colours were probably USN haze grey and dark blue. SC-2 and SL radars would be the normal fit.

HMS LAWFORD K514
'Captain' Class (Short Hull Group) 1944

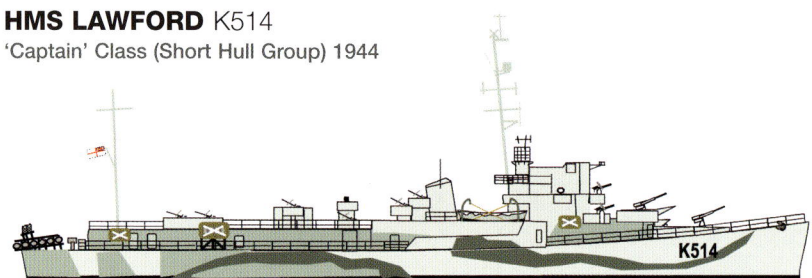

Lawford was a short hull version that was given a special conversion to act as a HQ ship for the Normandy landings in June 1944, during which she was sunk by air attack on the 8th. The scheme was unique to this ship. Accommodation and HQ facilities take up most of the aft superstructure which has also been extended. The aft gun has been removed, along with the twin 40mm, but she had fifteen 20mm. American SU radar is carried as well as a lantern for Type 272 with a prominent Type 244 IFF on top of it. The provision of a mainmast aft was to allow for a wide spread of aerials as well as whip antenna.

CORVETTES 8

KINGFISHER CLASS COASTAL ESCORT SLOOPS, LATER RE-RATED AS CORVETTES

HMS KITTIWAKE L30
1940

HMS SHELDRAKE L06
1939

Sheldrake is shown in the 507a dark grey many ships adopted on the outbreak of war. The class were considered the latest thing for coastal ASW work but were very poorly armed for what they would face. Note the only AA armament is a single Vickers MG aft. The forward gun is an old LA 4in gun with no AA ability. They were too complicated for mass production; by the end of WWII they were totally obsolete. No radar.

HMS PUFFIN K52
1940

Kittiwake is shown in 507b grey during the summer of 1940. Due to increased air threat, a quad 0.5in MG has been added aft and there are a pair of twin Lewis guns on the aft deckhouse. She carried other Lewis guns in the bridge wings. The only concession to camouflage is that the black waterline has been painted out. No radar carried.

Puffin is shown wearing one of the numerous unofficial schemes that were left to the ships' officers to design. Waterline black on MS4a, with some patches of white would have been easy to achieve from her own paint locker or existing local dockyard stock. The scheme had black centrally in a patchwork form intended to confuse, while the white areas created an impression of speed. The main gun was an old low-angle 4in. The light AA was restricted to a quad 0.5in MG aft and two twin Lewis guns. ASW gear is limited.

HMS MALLARD K42
1943

HMS KINGFISHER K70
1942

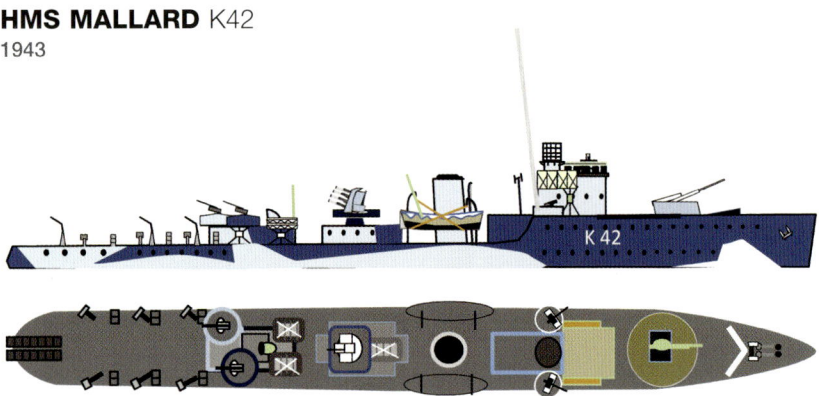

Mallard shows a 1941 blue on WA blue experimental scheme with false bow wave. Her quad 0.5in MG has been moved amidships. There are two single 2pdr on the aft deckhouse and single 20mm AA in the bridge wings. The aft deck was made clear for a good load of DCs and throwers. The shield of 'A' gun has been removed and replaced by a zareba. Type 271 radar is carried.

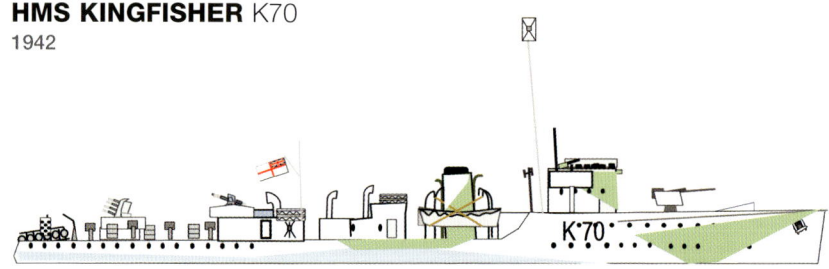

Kingfisher is illustrated in a WA-type scheme although the ship mostly worked elsewhere. Note the AA increase. There is a quad 0.5in MG well aft and single 2pdr on the aft deckhouse. Twin Lewis guns in the bridge wings. The old 4in has been given a half-shield to save weight. A Type 286 fixed radar aerial is carried at the masthead.

HMS KITTIWAKE K30
1943

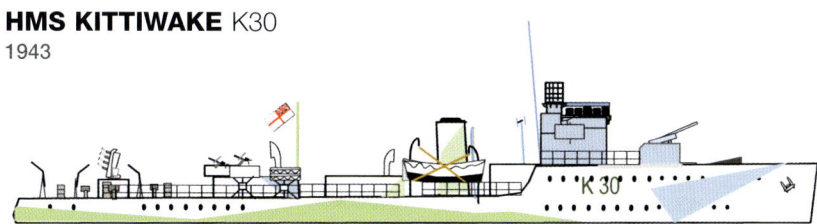

Kittiwake in 1943 shows further improvements. Some of the deckhouse area has been removed to save weight. There is a Type 271 radar lantern on the bridge but set on a low pedestal due to stability problems. There are offset single 20mm on the aft deckhouse, twin Lewis guns on the bridge wings and the 4in has been given a half-shield. The paint scheme is a WA type of MS white with WA blue and WA green.

HMS KITTIWAKE K30
1945

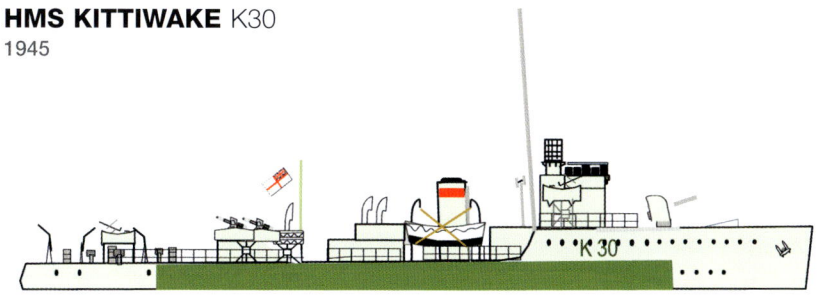

As the war neared its end, *Kittiwake* adopted a simple dark green panel on the hull in a scheme then fairly common. Her AA has changed again. There is a single 20mm aft, single 2pdr AA on the aft deckhouse and she has 20mm in each bridge wing. There is a Type 271 radar lantern but, because of topweight problems, most of these ships had to carry it as low as possible. The old 4in gun has been replaced by a newer type in a full shield.

HMS SHEARWATER K39
1943

Shearwater has a scheme typical of some of her sisters. Green was in short supply but, as these ships spent a lot of time in coastal waters, they may have been given priority. Somewhat unusually, she has a patch of dark MS2 at the waterline amidships on what is otherwise a standard WA scheme. There is a Type 291 radar at the masthead. This could be carried high as it was lighter than the Type 271 set and its associated equipment. These ships had very little reserve stability, which limited how much extra AA they could be given.

EARLY 'FLOWER' CLASS CORVETTES

HMS GARDENIA M99
1940

Gardenia was one of the first 'Flower' class completed. The flag superior on her pennant number is 'M' but was changed to 'K' the same year. She has two masts and the original bridge, and was painted in plain 507b grey with a peacetime-type black waterline. The life rafts are in civilian colours. The bridge is protected by splinter mats and there is a prominent external degaussing cable. The AA armament comprises two single Lewis guns on the bridge, and a twin Lewis gun mount where the 2pdr was intended aft. There are only two DC throwers. There is a single LA 4in gun forward.

HMS AUBRIETIA K96
1940

Aubrietia was one of the early 'Flower' class fitted for minesweeping as well as ASW, making her quarterdeck very crowded. The 4in gun forward had no AA ability. Her AA comprises a single 2pdr amidships, single Lewis guns in shields aft of the 2pdr, and two more on the bridge. Flag superior is now 'K' instead of 'M'. The camouflage scheme is almost certainly unofficial, using dark 507a grey on light 507c, yet it is close to the sort of pattern that would be worn later in the WA colours.

HMS HIBISCUS K24
1940

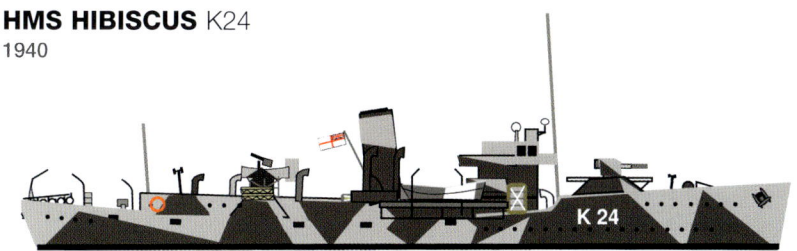

Hibiscus is shown in her early form with an unofficial camouflage scheme intended to confuse. With special colours hard to obtain, the ship has been painted in simple dark 507b grey and B6 grey, but it is quite effective as a confusion scheme. The only light AA are Vickers MGs in the 2pdr tub. Probably Lewis guns on the bridge. She had modernisation refits in 1941 and 1942 including Type 271 radar. There is no crow's nest. Depth charges are limited and only two throwers carried.

HMS HIBISCUS K24
1941

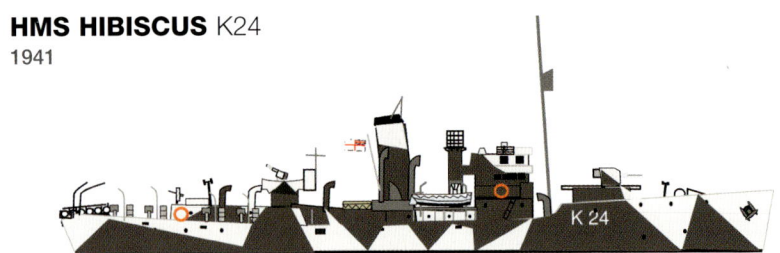

Hibiscus is shown a year later than overleaf. The overall pattern remains the same but a change to pale 507c grey makes the contrast much more dramatic against the dark 507b. The ship has a Type 271 radar lantern behind the bridge, not on it as was more usual. The 2pdr gun has been fitted and Lewis guns at the rear of the aft superstructure. Note the dramatic increase in DC throwers, reload racks and rails with more capacity. There are changes to the rigging with the adoption of 'spreaders' for aerials and removal of the stump after-mast. These changes helped with clearing AA arcs of fire.

USS SPRY EX HMS HIBISCUS PG64
1942

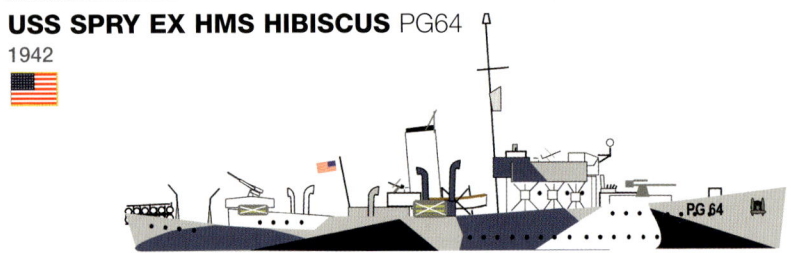

Hibiscus was transferred to the USN during the 1942 emergency known to the German U-boat crews as 'The Second Happy Time'. The US was caught without sufficient escorts and was forced to ask the RN for help. Some corvettes and ASW trawlers were transferred as urgently as possible. The USN did not like the WA scheme and preferred their own. *Spry* is shown with this. The USN has replaced the Type 271 radar lantern with their own type SG. There is a US 4in gun forward and a 3in AA aft, 20mm AA in each bridge wing and two more aft of the funnel.

HMS PRIMULA K14
1942

Primula, serving in the Mediterranean, is shown with a very dark 507a hull and 507b grey upper-works. Note that the pennant number is very small and in dull grey. Two sections of the superstructure have been extended out to the sides for more accommodation. The 3in AA forward has no shield and, although the other AA is similar to *Peony*, *Gloxinia* and *Azalea*, it is not arranged exactly the same. This seems to be standard for ships that refitted at Gibraltar. *Primula* has Type 271 radar on the bridge top and was fitted for acoustic minesweeping. The radar lantern was placed rather low.

HMS HIBISCUS K24
1942

In early 1941 *Hibiscus* was given the major upgrade planned for all 'Flower' class. To improve seaworthiness and provide more accommodation amidships, the forward well deck was filled in and the foredeck carried aft to the 2pdr. The mast was behind the now lowered bridge on which there was a single 20mm, the Type 271 radar lantern was now part of the bridge structure and a Hedgehog added aft of the 4in gun. *Hibiscus* was given a WA camouflage scheme on completion of the refit. She was in this state when handed to the USN.

HMS AZALEA K25
1941

This is an unofficial camouflage using light stone and light blue on a dark grey hull, with a false bow wave and a false wash at the stern. The ship is fitted for acoustic minesweeping with a boom at the bow with noise hammer. *Azalea* is fitted for operating in areas where air activity was intense, such as the Mediterranean, with an unusual range of weaponry. Forward is a 3in AA, there are twin Lewis guns on the bridge, aft of the funnel there are single 20mm port and starboard, the 2pdr position has been given to a quad 0.5in MG, the single 2pdr is at the rear of the after deckhouse and there is a French 25mm above the DCs. There is just the base for a Type 271 radar lantern and no crow's nest.

HMS ABELIA K184
1942

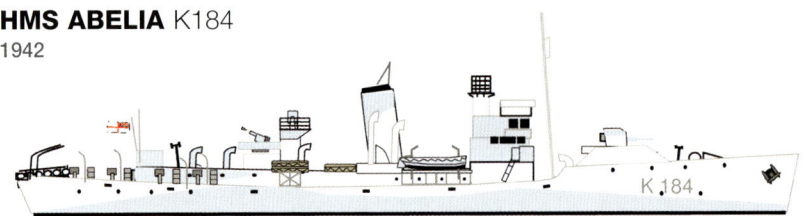

Abelia was one of the first corvettes to adopt the WA scheme of very pale WA blue on a WS white ship. The application is not all that standard, but effective. It is somewhat spoilt by the provision of a black waterline as shown here, which was completely against instructions. Her armament is single LA 4in gun forward and a single 2pdr amidships. There were probably Lewis guns brought out of the armoury if required. The lantern for Type 271 radar sits rather high and, while giving good coverage, did little to help stability on a class known for their heavy rolling even in moderate seas.

HMS GLOXINIA K22
1942

Gloxinia sported a fantastic false bow wave well above any speed a corvette could possibly reach. One presumes that, as this was an unofficial scheme, someone aboard or at the dockyard had an artistic talent! Her LA 4in gun was retained forward, but the intended pom-pom position was taken up by a 3in AA. The 2pdr pom-pom itself was placed at the after end of the deckhouse, with a clear arc of fire astern. There are also single 20mm in the bridge wings. She was not fitted for minesweeping and in 1942 has not yet received the major upgrade many of her sisters had been given, or completed with. A Type 271 radar lantern is on the bridge, but somewhat lower than usual.

ALYSSE K100
1941

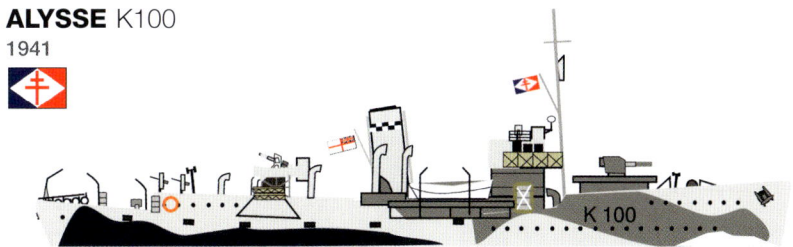

Alyssum was handed over to the Free French on completion as *Alysse* but was sunk the following year. Here she wears an early unofficial scheme of two greys and black with a white bow wave. She has no painted-in waterline. Although shown flying the flag of the Free French, it was usual to fly the White Ensign as well to avoid identification problems. An early war loss, she was never modified.

HMCS HEPATICA K159
1942

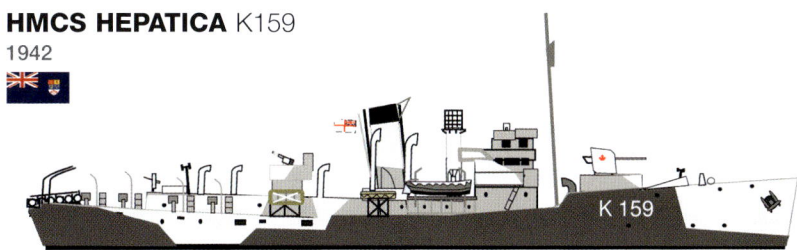

Hepatica has an unofficial scheme intended to alter the apparent profile, with the dark hull concentrating the eye. In some photographs she looks a bit strange as the bridge appears too skinny, due to the censor eliminating the radar but, for some reason, deleting sections of the bridge as well. Note the Canadian maple leaf symbol on the forward gun: this started to appear quite early but there seems to have been indecision on where it should be placed as some ships carried flotilla markings. The black funnel top indicates a flotilla leader. The tall Type 271 radar lantern platform was necessary due to the high early bridge. Most corvettes had bridge and lantern lowered later for better stability.

HMS PEONY K40
1941

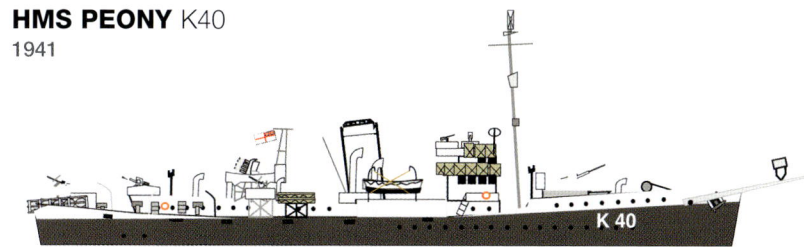

Peony is shown with a dark grey hull and pale upperworks while based at Gibraltar. Dark blue was not used at this time as many Vichy ships had a dark blue hull. As with *Gloxinia*, the AA armament was increased considerably. However, instead of the French 25mm over the DCs, she had a 20mm Oerlikon. The concentration of guns aft is because of the Italian tactic of aircraft attacking from the stern. There is a fixed Type 286 radar at the masthead, not a common fit for corvettes and later replaced by the usual Type 271 lantern on the bridge. Although the well deck has not been filled in, there was some extra accommodation amidships with the superstructure extended out to the sides. She changed to the dark blue central panel in 1943, rather than a full dark grey hull.

HMCS AGASSIZ K129
1941

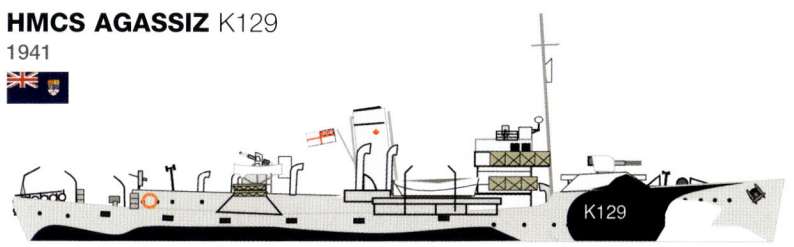

Agassiz was one of the first of the Canadian 'Flower' class to enter service and is shown here in an unofficial scheme using greys and black with a white patch at the bow. This was a common theme even though not official. There may have been some guidelines but generally it was left to the officers of the ship or the dockyard to design a scheme and they seem to have followed similar ideas, possibly through seeing or copying others. *Agassiz* has a 2pdr aft in the British-design position. Later units had the 2pdr aft end of the deckhouse. There is a maple leaf symbol on the funnel.

HMCS ARROWHEAD K145
1941

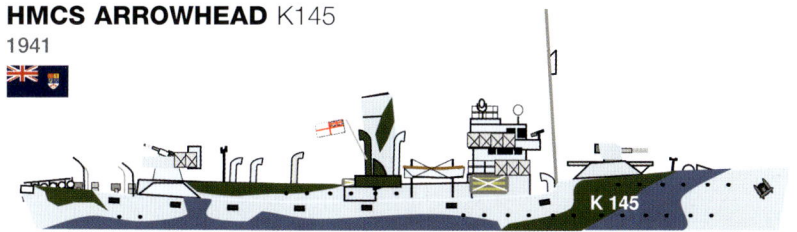

Arrowhead is shown here as completed and wearing colours later part of the Admiralty light scheme. White with a dash of blue achieved the pale shade, darker grey with a dash of blue achieved the dull blue-grey. The green was probably achieved from an army paint or adding grey to Brunswick green. It is unclear if this was an early use of the Admiralty light scheme, or just a coincidence. The only light AA carried comprises 2pdr aft and single MGs at the front of the bridge wings.

HMCS SHAWINIGAN K136
1941

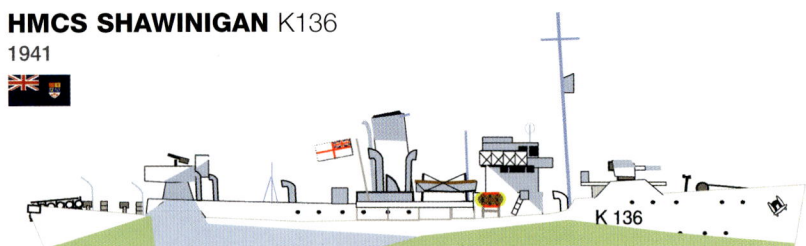

Shawinigan was one of the first Canadian corvettes to be completed wearing the RN-type WA scheme. Some viewed this with caution at first as it seemed to make the ships far too visible in harbour. It was at sea where the value could be seen. Hence there was a tendency for some yards to make the blue and green a few shades darker than the designer intended. Note that this ship completed with only a Vickers MG in the pom-pom position aft and no other light AA at all. Civilian-colour life rafts were also part of original equipment. There is no radar fitted.

HNoMS NORDKYN K193
1941

Buttercup was transferred to Norway as *Nordkyn* in 1942 and is shown in original configuration but with the new WA scheme in WA green on a white hull. Someone has had the sense to read the instructions and has not painted in a black waterline. *Nordkyn* has had a 20mm added to each bridge wing and Type 271 radar fitted to the top of the bridge. The rest of her armament is standard.

HMS GENTIAN K90
1942

The omission of a black waterline makes the dull grey of *Gentian* more effective. The crew obviously painted it out when she left dock after the major bridge alterations she had one. Note the escort group red and white band and the pennant number in white rather than black as on *Convolvulus*. Although the forecastle deck has not yet been extended aft, the ship has received a new, lower bridge and a Type 271 radar lantern on top. Lowering the height of these ships was a priority as they rolled so badly in their original form. There is a 20mm on the bridge wings at the front and below it an SL platform which was not standard to the modifications on others of this class. There is a twin Lewis gun mount on the aft deckhouse to supplement the 2pdr pom-pom.

HMS ALISMA K185
1942

Alisma received a partial modernisation in 1942 and is shown here in a version of the WA scheme using blue on a white hull. The darker blue is probably a local mix as someone thought the original was too light and could not be correct. The new bridge is lower and has been widened to give more room, with a single 20mm in each wing. Type 271 radar is fitted on a small lattice. The foredeck has not yet been carried aft, but the new bridge is closer, and passing between the forward mess decks therefore easier. However, going aft still involved passage along an open deck.

HMS CONVOLVULUS K45
1941

Convolvulus is shown in overall dark grey with a black waterline. No attempt at camouflage at this point. However, she has undergone a partial rebuild with the forecastle extended aft to provide cover for crew moving from the seamen's accommodation forward to other positions on the ship, as well as allowing some additional accommodation to be added. There are single 20mm Oerlikons in the bridge wings and the usual 2pdr AA aft. Depth charge fitting was standard for 1941. Note that, for some reason, the pennant number is painted aft as well as in the usual position forward.

HMCS ORILLIA K119
1941

Orillia is shown here as completed and opposite as rebuilt according to war experience. Here, there is a dark blue panel of unusual shape. The top of the funnel is painted out in light blue as is the forward gun and the mast. The only AA carried is a single 2pdr aft. There would probably be MGs on the bridge if needed. The effect of this scheme is to create a dark area which will confuse as to the size and distance of the ship. Painting the funnel top out in pale blue is probably to add to the effect. Note the galley funnel aft, a most inconvenient place as the crew's quarters are in the forecastle.

HMCS ORILLIA K119
1941

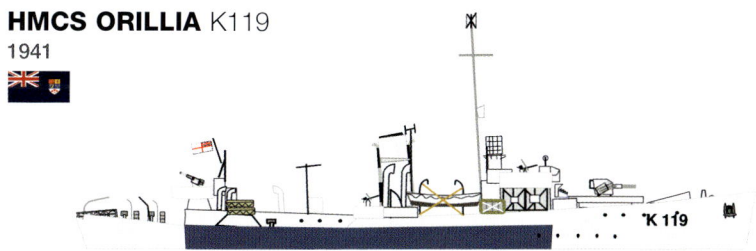

Orillia has had a total refit with a lowering of the bridge and forward gun and the foredeck carried aft to allow easier movement and provide extra accommodation. The ship carries a Type 271 radar lantern but at a lower level than some earlier ships. There is a Hedgehog just aft of the main gun. The 2pdr aft is no longer the only AA as there are 20mm guns in the bridge wings and at the break of the foredeck. There are spreaders amidships to help with aerials and the galley funnel is attached to the front of the funnel. SW2C Canadian radar is at the masthead. Type 271 British radar is on the bridge. The ship is painted 507c overall with a 1941 blue panel on the hull.

NADA K81
1944

Nada was originally HMS *Mallow* and was transferred to Yugoslavia in 1944. This ship had been given most of the modifications but, as she was to serve in air-dangerous waters, was given extra 20mm Oerlikon AA. There are six altogether plus a single 2pdr. The 4in gun has rocket rails on the shield. Type 271 radar is on the rear of the bridge. There is a Hedgehog fitted aft of the gun. She became *Partizanka* after the war. The hull is 1941 blue and the rest of the ship 507c grey.

HMS CAMPANULA K18
1943

By 1943 many early 'Flower' class were coming out of refit almost completely rebuilt. The scheme here is a standard WA type but has the unusual addition of a dark MS 2 triangular patch at the bow. As per instructions, the black waterline has been omitted and everything is as pale as possible. To aid station-keeping in close formation, some ships had a dark colour applied to the stern, the rear of the bridge or the funnel. *Campanula* has also been given the newer lantern for a Type 273 radar which was lower and smaller. There are single 20mm Oerlikons in the bridge wings and the usual 2pdr aft.

HrMs FRISIO K00
1944

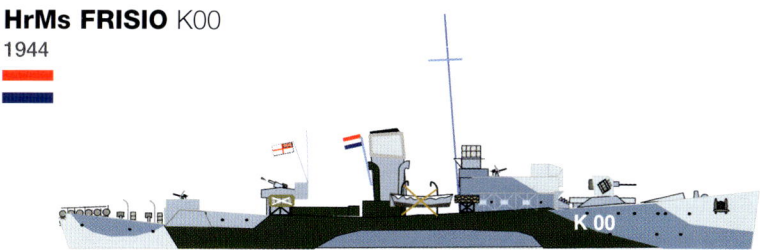

Netherlands corvette *Frisio* was originally HMS *Carnation* before being transferred in 1943. She is shown with full 'Flower' class modifications and is wearing an Admiralty intermediate scheme. Type 273 radar with its smaller, lower lantern is on the bridge and it can be seen that every effort has been made to lower the height of the vessel for better sea-keeping. A Type 244 IFF was added to the radar lantern roof. There is an ASDIC cabinet on the front of the bridge as well as more shelter for those on watch. Hedgehog is fitted aft of the 4in gun which itself has rocket rails fitted.

HMCS ALGOMA K127
1943

Algoma has an Admiralty intermediate light scheme based on blue-greys in order to blend with a range of different backgrounds to help conceal the ship. The problem with the design of camouflage is always that one can never be sure what the weather conditions and general background will be. Thus Admiralty schemes, while attractive to look at, often failed to have the intended result. They were further hampered because many of those involved in the design did not go to sea and therefore had to rely on the reports of others as to how various schemes worked. *Algoma* has Canadian radar at the foretop, which was regarded as ineffective in use and easy for a U-boat to detect.

RHN APOSTOLIS K84
1943

Hyacinth was transferred to Greece in 1943 after modernisation. The foredeck has been carried to amidships, the bridge lowered and improved, as well as a Type 271 radar lantern added. The ship has Hedgehog fitted and a total of six 20mm AA as well as the single 2pdr due to service in the Eastern Mediterranean, which was regarded as an air-danger area. The scheme is a variation on the PB10 blue hull and 507c light upperworks style.

HNoMS SOROY K197
1941

Intended to be HMS *Eglantine*, this ship was handed to Norway on completion and is shown here in late 1942 with all the modifications of the class. The bridge is larger but much lower, has a Type 271 radar lantern but the mast remains in front of the bridge. There is a Hedgehog aft of the main gun. The foredeck is extended aft and the ship wears a WA scheme. The darker area under the bridge is the same blue but in shadow. To try to overcome this, that area was sometimes painted an even lighter shade and very high-gloss paint used. *Soroy* would have flown the White Ensign as well as the Norwegian flag while with the RN.

USS TEMPTRESS, EX HMS VERONICA PG69
1942

HMS *Veronica* was transferred to the USN after receiving her major refit and upgrade and is shown here with a few modifications. The 4in gun is now a US type, there is a 3in gun aft and the 2pdr has been replaced by a single 20mm. The RN Type 271 radar was retained for a time, probably due to USN shortages. The scheme is vastly different from the WA scheme the ship wore on her handover, with black and dull blue now predominant. White has been retained. The US classed her as a Patrol Gunboat and thus her pennant is 'PG 69', which is shortened to a small '69' near the bow. This drawing illustrates the quite different line of thought from the RN as shown in the Norwegian-manned *Soroy*.

HMS LOTUS K93
1942

Lotus is shown here in a WA scheme. The darker green on her stern is because as she is fitted for minesweeping, other ships will need to keep station on her and the darker green will make her easier to follow. Collisions and near-collisions were a hazard of the WA scheme if ships had to sail in close formation. Note that she had early Type 271 radar on a very high platform and the bridge, while to the new shape, is also very high. Hedgehog is fitted high as well. There is an SL platform each side of the bridge, possibly something to do with minesweeping, and her only light AA is a 2pdr pom-pom aft. The booms at the bow are for influence minesweeping.

HMS VIOLET K35
1942

An Admiralty light scheme is shown worn by *Violet* late in 1942 after her major refit and rebuild. It again attempts to draw the eye to a dark colour and so miss vital details of what the ship really is. There were situations in which this scheme worked but, in general, it overlooked the persistence of the observer in making a point of seeking out other salient features. The ship has had a very strong AA upgrade with no less than six 20mm Oerlikons added, somewhat incredible when often fleet destroyers had less. She was probably bound for the Mediterranean where air attacks were frequent.

PA 2
1944

This is included for the interest of the reader. I cannot guarantee the accuracy of the actual colours of this drawing nor the full pattern. It is based on a sketch I made in 1970 during a conversation with an German ex-naval officer whose E-boat shared a berth with a ship that he had understood to be a captured British corvette. The sketch was prepared by showing him various German ships in camouflage until he found one that he thought looked like it. But the photographs were black and white. His recollections could have been of any one of the four. I have no doubt it was a 'Flower' class ship he had seen and he was certain it was one of the French construction units as no other ship of the class was ever captured. The scheme is similar to German ships based on the French coast. *PA 2* was the ex 'Flower' class corvette *Hallebard*, building at St Nazaire along with three others. All were launched by November 1940 and all lost to allied forces. The scheme was intended to hide against a coastal background. It was said that the 'Flower' class would roll on morning dew, but these ships with this armament would not have been comfortable even in coastal waters. German 4.1in forward, two single 20mm behind it. A quad 20mm is on top of the bridge, a twin 37mm amidships with another quad 20mm aft of that and a single 37mm further aft. The ship has four DC droppers each side.

MODIFIED 'FLOWER' CLASS CORVETTES

HMS BETONY K274
1943

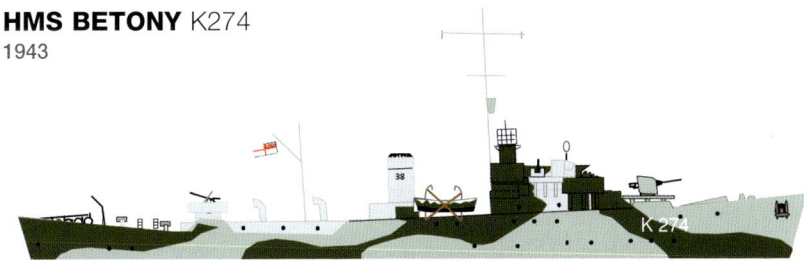

Subtle differences in shade mark the Admiralty light scheme of *Betony* on completion. The WA blue funnel and upperworks blend with the washed-out MS3 of the hull, both of which are offset by MS1 areas designed to focus the eye. These schemes had limited success because the natural tendency of the human mind is to try to make sense of what the eye appears to be seeing. There are only three 20mm fitted and no 2pdr. She was transferred to India as *Sind*. Unlike most of the group, she has no funnel cap. The hull has more sheer and the foredeck is carried well aft.

HMCS FOREST HILL K486
1944

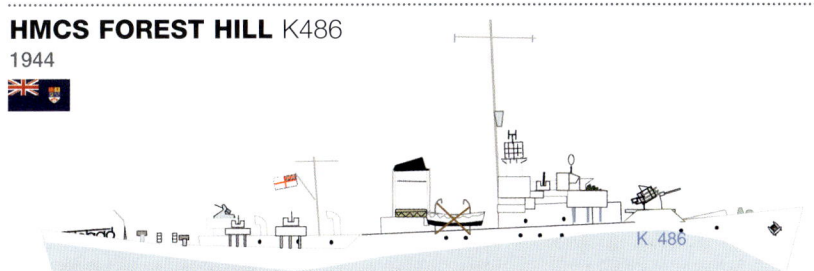

Forest Hill is in a standard WA scheme. The pennant number is in blue and sits under the forward gun. Many Canadian ships carried this well forward in the American style. It is in a reduced-size format rather than the larger, bolder type. The increase of AA could be because these ships were intended to serve on the Pacific coast of Canada. Electronics are as for *Charlock*.

HMNZS ARBUTUS K403
1945

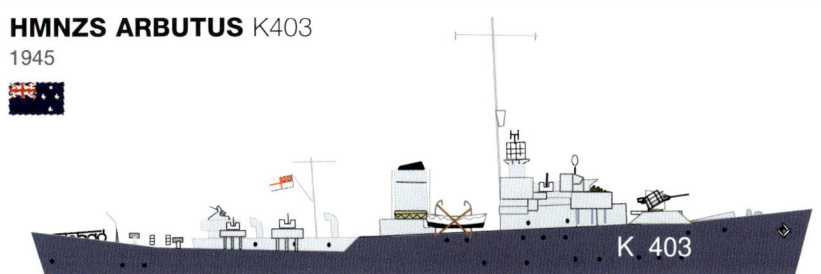

Arbutus served in the RN for a time before being transferred to the New Zealand navy in 1945. The ship is shown as she appeared by the end of the war with B6 upper works and PB10 blue hull. Surprisingly, the pennant number is large, bold and in white. Electronic equipment is the standard fit and AA armament is quite strong compared to the early 'Flower' class.

HMS CHARLOCK K395
1944

Charlock displays an interesting variation on the WA scheme. The blue is darker and covers a much larger area of the ship, suggesting that it was possibly intended with convoys to Russia in mind. She has a powered twin 20mm AA aft and four single 20mm as well. The forward gun now carries rocket launchers on the shield as standard. These ships were considered dry and comfortable compared with the earlier 'Flower' class. Radar on the bridge is Type 271Q with a Type 244 interrogator on top for IFF. The class were designed to have a funnel cap as shown here, but not all did.

HMCS LONGBRANCH K487
1944

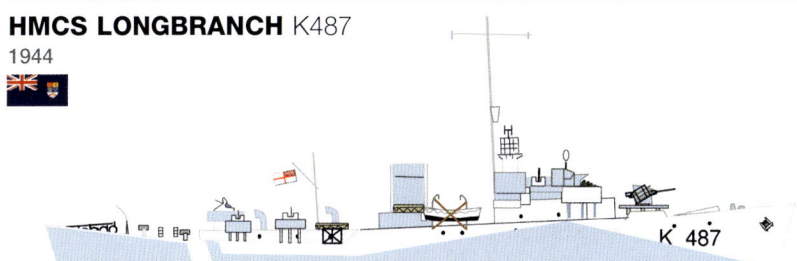

Longbranch is shown in a Western Approaches scheme with an unusual break in the hull layout aft. Note the dramatic increase in AA over the original 'Flower' class. There is a powered twin 20mm where the 2pdr had previously been, plus six single 20mm. The ASW capacity of these ships was similar to the original 'Flower' class but the Hedgehog has been lifted up higher to keep it drier and for greater safety firing forward. Note this ship has no funnel cap. Electronics fit as above.

HMCS BELLEVIEW K332
1944

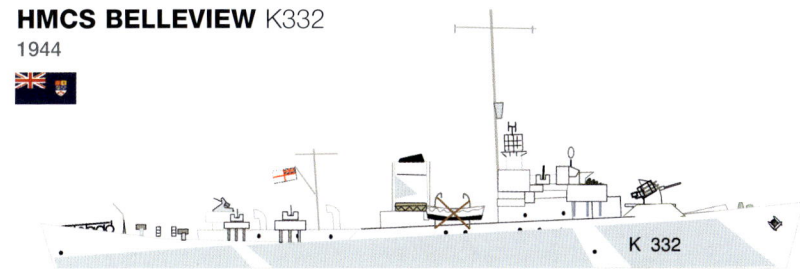

Belleview displays one of the alternative ways of applying the WA scheme via panels that had a white gap between them. This ship had a funnel cap which was black and spoilt the overall camouflage. Type 271Q radar was carried on the bridge along with Type 244 IFF on top. By this period of WWII, lots of larger and more capable ships were coming into service but some yards could not build bigger ships, thus some corvettes were continued with in case they were needed.

USS ACTION PG86
1943

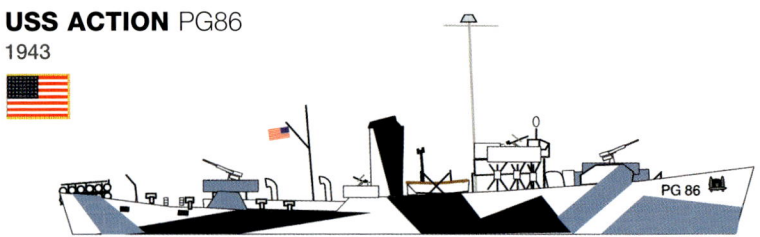

HMS *Comfrey* was transferred to the USN in 1943 as part of a reverse Lease-Lend deal to help the Americans deal with the appearance of long-range U-boats off their east coast. Considering the USN's mass production of escorts, this is rather surprising. Instead of a Type 271 radar lantern a US-type SL radar is carried at the masthead. Armament is two 3in AA and four single 20mm in the bridge wings or abaft the funnel. Note the interesting difference between US camouflage ideas and those of the RN. No attempt is made to hide the ship, instead the aim is to confuse the viewer.

USS INTENSITY PG93
1943

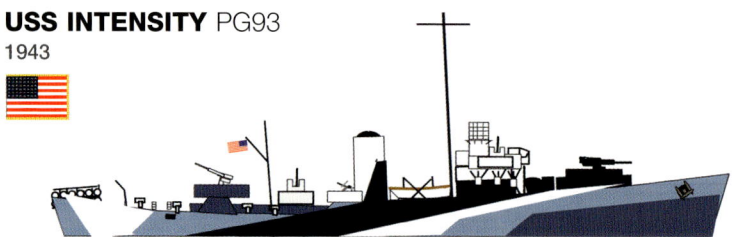

Intensity was to have been HMS *Milfoil* but was handed to the USN on completion. The British main guns have been replaced by a US 4in and a 3in AA. Surprisingly, this ship continued to carry her British Type 271Q radar for some time as shown here. Light AA of six single 20mm is shown. Once again, the quite different approach to camouflage is shown and makes an interesting comparison to the RN schemes most 'Flower' class wore. The scheme makes no attempt to hide the ship but instead to provide some confusion as to size, type and distance. It is therefore an ASW scheme.

'CASTLE' CLASS CORVETTES
HMS KENILWORTH CASTLE K420
1943

Kenilworth Castle entered service in the WA scheme in common with most of her class. Intended to replace the 'Flower' class they were larger but could be built in yards too small to build frigates. She took part in the sinking of two U-boats. Although they only had a single Squid forward, they were almost as effective as the 'Loch' class frigates and certainly more so than the 'Flower' class. They had HF/DF, which was unusual for corvettes. The ship had four manual twin 20mm AA and a single 4in gun which had rails for flare rockets on the shield. The older Type 271 radar lantern is on her lattice mast with Type 244 IFF below it.

HMS HADLEIGH CASTLE K355
October 1943

Hadleigh Castle was the first of the class to enter service and the much more spacious design greatly impressed 'Flower' class crews. There is only one DC rail aft and they only carried fifteen charges – Squid was such a successful weapon they were rarely used. The ships also carried the Shark missile, a round fired from the 4in gun and which could penetrate the pressure hull of a U-boat. Guns less than 4.5in or 4.7in had been found incapable of achieving this even at the closest ranges. The older Type 271 radar lantern is at the head of the lattice mast. The 20mm twins are manual mounts.

HMCS PETROLIA K498
1944

Petrolia is in darker shades and even a reversion to the earlier style of a panel near the bow. Darker blue was often used by ships on the western side of the Atlantic and in colder waters. Type 272 radar is fitted with 244 below it and HF/DF on the pole mast rising from the lattice. The 20mm mountings are all power-operated.

HMS BAMBOROUGH CASTLE K412
1945

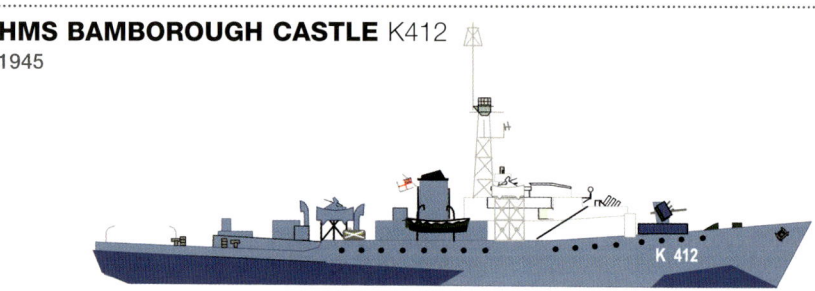

Resplendent in PB10 blue and mid-blue on white, *Bamborough Castle* was set for duties with convoys to the Arctic. This is unusual as most of her class were in standard WA schemes. The newer Type 272 radar is carried on the lattice mast with Type 244 just below it. HF/DF is at the head of a pole mast on the lattice. The 20mm are power-operated twin mounts which were effective enough but weighed almost as much as a single 40mm which had better range and hitting power.

HMS CARISBROOKE CASTLE K379
1943

This is typical of the flexibility and variations of the WA scheme where green was preferred but could be combined with pale blue or, in case of a shortage, either could be used. Squid is carried in 'B' position. This was a weapon that was deadly to WWII-type submarines and so successful that only a few DCs were carried aft. The lattice mast had a smaller Type 272 radar lantern on top with a HF/DF aerial above that. There are rails on the gun shield for illumination rockets. The pennant number is blue. The twin 20mm are power-operated mounts.

HMS CAISTOR CASTLE K690
1944

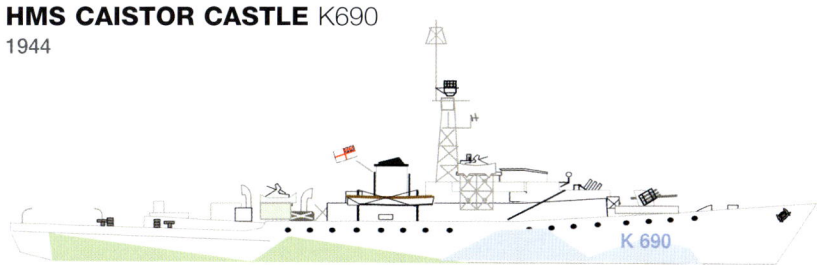

Caistor Castle is shown wearing a pale WA scheme with the regulation triangular areas along the waterline, except for an unusual rectangular section amidships. There is the new smaller Type 272 radar lantern at the top of the lattice mast instead of the Type 271 of earlier classes. Type 244 radar is on the front of the mast. Like most 'Castles', this ship has four power-operated twin 20mm AA, considered sufficient for Atlantic convoy duties by 1944 but they were given space for extra guns if needed. A Bofors could be placed on the quarterdeck if required. The class used the same machinery as the 'Flower' class but with improved boilers and were a knot faster as well as more likely to be able to maintain full speed due to the improved hull form. They were the only RN corvettes retained in service after the end of WWII.

HNoMS TUNSBERG CASTLE K374
1944

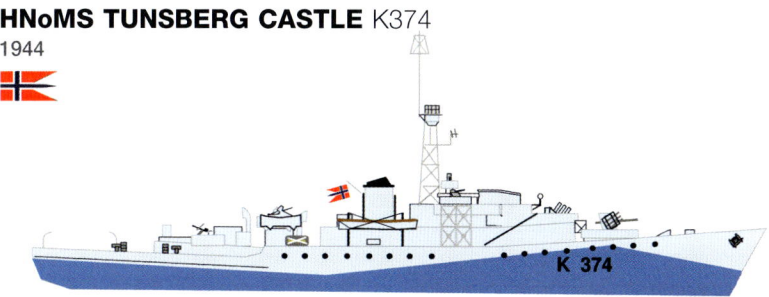

One 'Castle' class corvette was transferred to the Norwegian navy but lost within eight months. Other than to Canada, this was the only ship of the class ever transferred to any other navy. Squid technology was shared with the US which chose not to use it. Squid was a weapon that was considered top-secret when first introduced and, once detected, a U-boat rarely escaped. Note that this ship has twin manual 20mm in the bridge wings, single 20mm right aft on the deckhouse, and power-operated twin 20mm amidships. Unusual but probably a case of what was available.

HMCS BOWMANVILLE K493
1944

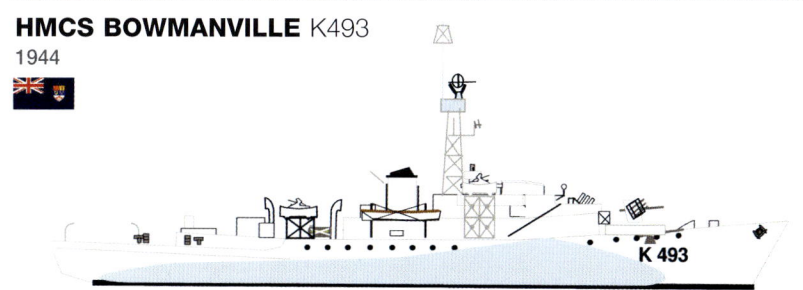

Canada was to have mass-produced 'Castle' class corvettes but, with the war obviously drawing to a close, this was cancelled and instead some of the RN production were transferred to the RCN. Note *Bowmanville* has Type 277 radar on top of the lattice mast and Type 244 on an extension below it. A tall pole carries HF/DF to the highest point on the ship. The paint scheme is typical as delivered from a British yard, being a standard WA scheme. Painting instructions have been ignored and a black waterline provided. 20mm are powered mountings.

9 MINESWEEPERS

MINESWEEPERS

OLD 'HUNT' CLASS MINESWEEPERS
HMS PANGBOURNE J37
1941

Despite their age, the 'Hunts' were valuable until new-built sweepers could be brought into service. *Pangbourne* was given 12pdr AA fore and aft, plus 20mm before the bridge as well as on the aft deckhouse. There were also MGs on the bridge. This indicates that the ship served in rather air-dangerous waters. Her scheme is an unofficial disruptive type utilising dark blue, black and mid-blue on white, with most procured locally. Note she has acoustic sweeping gear in the bow. More up-to-date minesweeping gear has been fitted aft. There are a limited number of depth charges, with a single dropper each side of the quarter.

HMS ABERDARE N49
1939

Aberdare shows how the 'Hunt' class minesweepers looked at the start of WWII. There is an LA 4in gun forward, a single 12pdr AA positioned aft and a single 2pdr AA on the aft deckhouse. There are twin Lewis guns forward of the bridge. She wears a peacetime grey. Note the waist is uninterrupted amidships. Extra accommodation would soon be added below the lifeboat area. Her minesweeping gear is of the WWI gallows type and she has no ASW capability at all. These ships were coal-burners.

HMS ALBURY J41
1942

By 1942 *Albury* was wearing a scheme based around the general ideas of the Admiralty disruptive type. She is fitted for acoustic minesweeping but has more conventional gear aft. Her AA comprises two 12pdr, a single 20mm forward of the bridge and a quad 0.5in MG aft. There are also MGs on the bridge. Depth charges are limited to two per side in traps, indicating that the coastal U-boat threat no longer exists. However, they were occasionally used to detonate some mines that were difficult to sweep.

HMS KELLETT J05
1941

Kellet displays an interesting scheme which is possibly the appearance of a smaller ship on the side via the dark areas. It is almost certainly an unofficial scheme but quite effective. Aft, the old sweep gear has been replaced and she carries a reasonable number of DCs in traps as well as a single thrower each side. The ship has two 12pdr AA and single 20mm fore and aft as well as MGs on the bridge. No radar fitted. Part of the waist has been filled in to provide more accommodation.

HMS SALTASH J62
1940

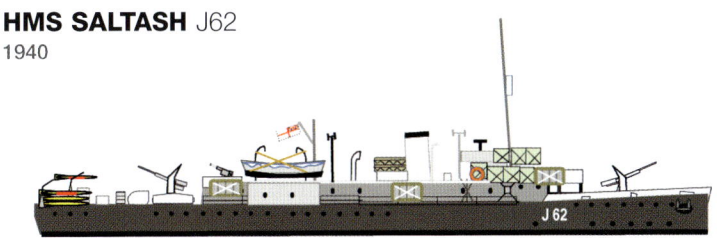

Saltash is shown here very early in the war, with a dark hull and pale upper works, yet her AA has been heavily increased, indicating she was probably operating on the East Coast of the UK where air attacks were heavy and frequent. She has 12pdr AA fore and aft, a single 2pdr on the aft deckhouse and a 20mm Oerlikon forward of the bridge. There are MGs on the bridge as well. She has already had part of the waist filled in for more accommodation.

HMS SUTTON J78
1942

Sutton is wearing an Admiralty intermediate scheme with black area forward that was typical of that type of camouflage. She is fitted for acoustic minesweeping as well as conventional type. Guns are both 12pdr AA, plus a single 20mm forward, a 2pdr aft and MGs on the bridge. These ships retained splinter protection for some time as they operated in dangerous areas.

HMAS DOOMBA N01
1939–41

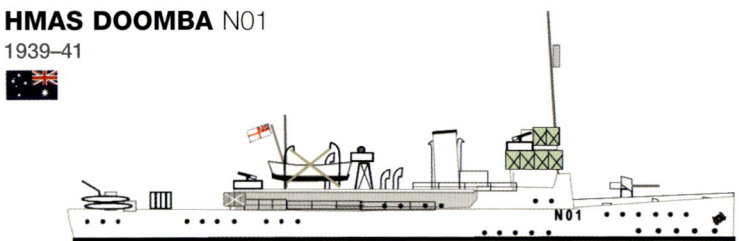

HMS *Wexford* was sold out after WWI and purchased for use as a ferry operating around Brisbane, Australia. When WWII broke out, she was requisitioned by the RAN and commissioned as a minesweeper. She retained her civilian name of *Doomba*. Her original pennant number was 'N 01' but was changed to J01 in 1940. She is shown here with a single old LA 4in gun forward, Vickers MGs aft and Lewis guns on the bridge. Her colour scheme is not white, but a very pale grey which was adopted for most minor Australian warships in the first years of the war. Her old minesweeping gear had been removed during civilian service and she therefore re-equipped with standard WWII-type gear. The mast is before the bridge which had a very high open conning position on top.

HALCYON CLASS MINESWEEPERS
HMS BRAMBLE J11
1942

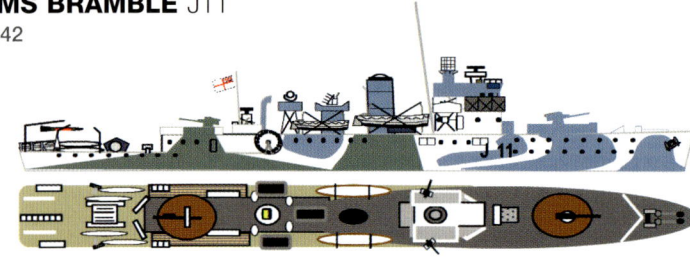

Built immediately pre-war, the *Halcyon* class were always highly thought of. The crew were initially all regular navy and they were kept so busy in so many theatres of war that the thinning of crew with war-hostilities ratings was deliberately kept slow. The class also spent a lot of their time engaged with convoys to Russia and *Bramble* was sunk in an action with German destroyers.

HMS SALAMANDER J86
1943

Salamander was the last ship of the first *Halcyon* group, all of which had an LA 4in forward and a 4in AA aft. Light AA has been increased to four single 20mm Oerlikons as well as the quad 0.5in MG amidships. The scheme is a mid-war Admiralty light type which concentrated dark colour toward the stern to ease station-keeping and light colours from amidships forward. Type 271 radar is on the bridge.

HMAS DOOMBA J01
1943–4

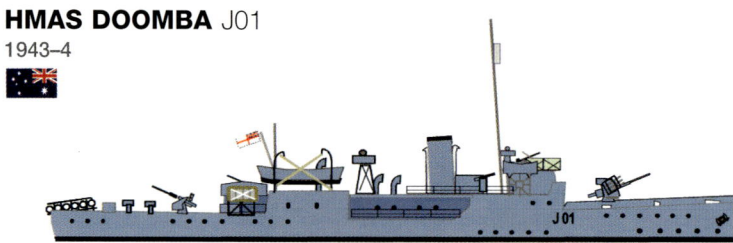

When Japanese submarines became active off the east coast of Australia, the RAN converted the *Doomba* to an ASW escort. She was in Sydney at the time of the Japanese midget submarine attack on that harbour and sighted one. She is show here later when serving as an escort on the east coast and to New Guinea. The old 4in has been replaced by a more modern gun which even has rocket rails on the shield. There is a single 40mm Bofors AA on the quarterdeck and a Vickers MG mounting on the aft deckhouse. On the bridge wings, there are single 20mm AA with twin Lewis guns on deck just aft of the bridge. There were forty-six DCs carried in racks and four throwers. Her nick name was 'Smokey Joe' because, being a coal-burner, she was noted for the great masses of smoke she gave off when on convoy duty.

HMS HARRIER J71
1941

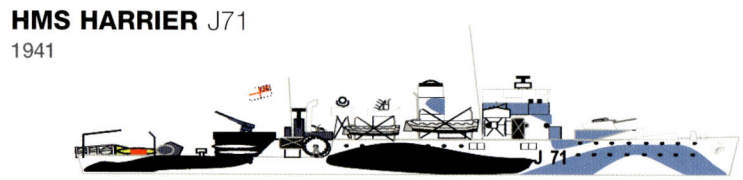

Harrier is shown wearing an early disruptive scheme that was common for such ships as they could be called on to work in many areas at short notice. They worked with convoys or clearing known fields or with the fleet. She was an early ship of the class and has an LA 4in forward and an HA 4in aft. The light AA comprises a quad 0.5in MG amidships and two single 20mm at the break of the foredeck. There are also single 20mm in the bridge wings. Note the ship has been given a half-shield to the forward gun to give at least some sort of protection in heavy seas. Although there is full minesweeping gear aft, these ships had sufficient DCs to act as escorts, which they frequently did. There are only two DC throwers and a single rack.

HMS GLEANER J83
1943

Similar in layout to the WA scheme, this is nonetheless an Admiralty light type in a range of greens. Generally, some dark colour was best placed at the stern as these ships had to work in close formation where it was easy to collide and careful station-keeping was necessary. *Gleaner* is shown with single 20mm in the bridge wings and a quad 0.5in MG amidships. These ships were kept very busy and tended to retain their older weapons longer. Both main guns were DP 4in from completion.

MINESWEEPERS

HMS HALCYON J42
1941

Halcyon is shown in a very pale WA scheme. There is no radar on the bridge yet but Type 271 was fitted later. Note the rear gun has been replaced by two single 20mm on the aft deckhouse. There are single 20mm in each bridge wing and the usual quad 0.5in MG amidships. This weapon was restricted when firing astern due to the position of the SL platform. 'A' gun has a half-shield.

HMS SHARPSHOOTER J68
1942

This early Admiralty light scheme concentrates dark colour around a pale central triangle in a reverse shortening effect that seems to be an attempt to produce two ships instead of one. Note these ships have retained the rangefinder on the bridge as it was very useful in taking range bearings to mark out the parameters of a swept area or the edges of a minefield. The aft gun has been replaced by a pair of 20mm side-by-side and the quad 0.5in MGs have been moved further aft to give a clearer field of fire.

BANGOR CLASS MINESWEEPERS

HMS EASTBOURNE J127
1941

Eastbourne wore 507b overall during 1942 with no other camouflage. Note the ship had a quad 0.5in MG mount aft and a 3in AA forward. The bridge and the aft AA position were protected with splinter mats. This ship was of the longer hull, reciprocating-engine type. There was no radar fitted.

HMS BRITTOMART J22
1944

Brittomart is shown painted to an Admiralty light scheme with sweeping curves of MS3 slate green and 1941 blue, on an overall duck egg blue. She was fitted with two 4in HA guns as built. In this illustration, quite late in the war, the ship had landed her quad 0.5in MGs and gained single 20mm in each bridge wing.

HMS JASON J99
1941

Jason is shown in an Admiralty dark scheme. Sea experience showed that it was best if a scheme concentrated dark colours aft and lighter colours forward. The boom at the bow is for sweeping acoustic mines that were detonated by noise. The boom has a noise-maker that causes sound ahead that imitates a ship passing over the mine. This should detonate the mine safely before the sweeper reached it. This was not always so as the Germans would set some to have a delayed detonation and thus catch the sweeper.

HMS BRIDPORT J50
1941

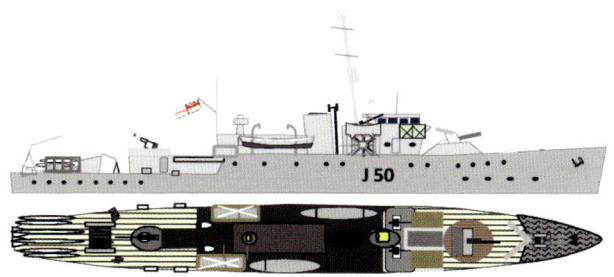

Bridport was a diesel-engine version of the *Bangor* class. These ships were a few feet shorter than the reciprocating or turbine-engine versions. She has a single 2pdr aft and 20mm Oerlikons in the bridge wings. Many *Bangors* only had MGs in 1941. Although fitted with ASDIC the ship had only four DCs in droppers. There were no other ASW weapons.

HMS SEAHAM J123
1942

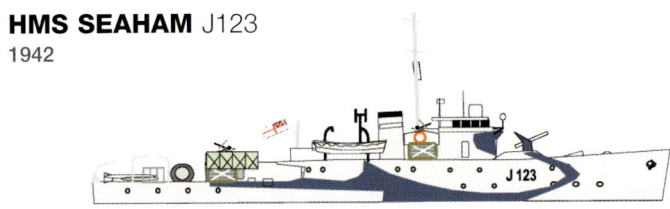

Seaham displays an early and simple form of Admiralty light scheme while operating as a minesweeper in the English Channel. She has three 20mm Oerlikons and the usual single 3in forward. She has no radar and the only DCs are two per side on dropping traps. The platform on top of the bridge was an open conning position

HMS SEAHAM J123
June 1944

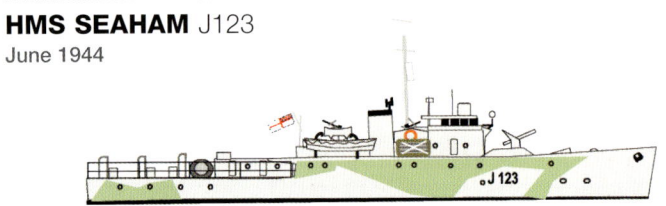

The impending operations off Normandy resulted in a need for more fleet tugs but, as those existing were already short in number, this ship was converted as a rescue tug. She has no minesweeping or ASW weapons. Her aft 20mm has been moved amidships.

HMS ARDROSSAN J131
1943

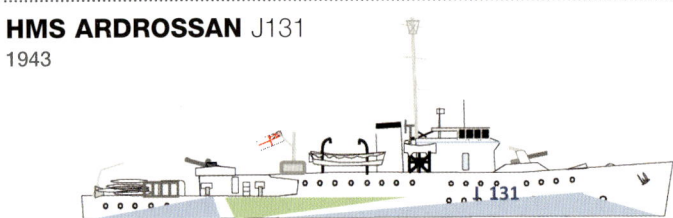

This ship is in an almost perfect WA scheme as the designer intended – blue and green panels on a basically overall white ship. The role in helping convoys in and out is shown by her two DC throwers and a supporting reloads rack. Minesweepers often met convoys at sea as they approached the UK and swept ahead of them.

HMS BANGOR J00
1945

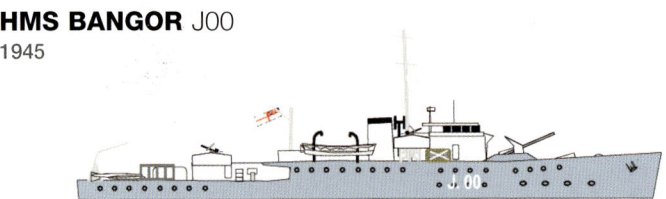

Bangor, the lead ship of her class, is shown here at the end of WWII. The entire hull was painted duck egg blue and the rest of the ship white. *Bangor* was armed with a 3in forward as well as single 20mm guns in the bridge wings and another aft. She carried only two DC throwers and had not been fitted with radar of any kind. She was transferred to Norway in 1946.

HMS WORTHING J72
1942

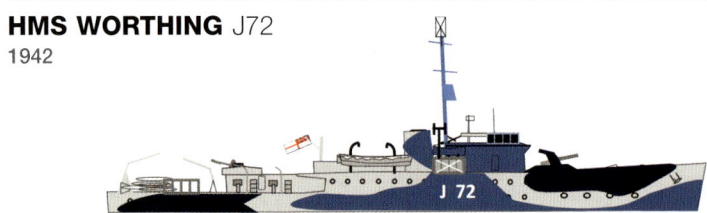

This ship is illustrated in an Admiralty dark disruption scheme. The contrast in colour utilises 1941 blue and black on MS4a hull for a confusion effect. She had two DC throwers per side. The spare racks of depth charges, plus loading davits, indicates that she took part in escort duty from time to time in addition to minesweeping. This may be why, at this early period, the ship is carrying a Type 286PU radar aerial at the masthead. Many ships of the *Bangor* class went through the war without any radar being fitted.

HMS BEAUMARIS J07
1942

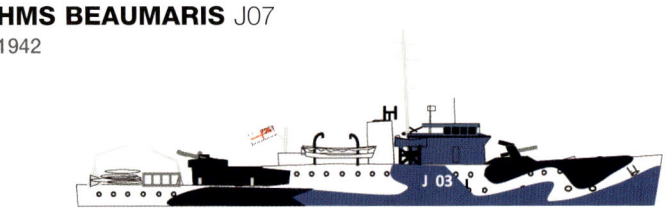

This ship wears an Admiralty disruptive scheme along the lines of the *Worthing*, but uses white instead of pale grey. There were many experimental schemes sent to sea and tried out for effect. A problem for designers was that they were shorebound and often had little chance to see the effect of the schemes they designed on ships at sea.

MINESWEEPERS

HMS WHITEHAVEN J121
1944

Very unusual and probably unofficial, but this scheme does make the ship look more like a tug than a minesweeper. Perhaps that was the intention or, once again, it was a local interpretation of more regular schemes. Her light AA is comprised of three single 20mm Oerlikons.

HMS MIDDLESBOROUGH J164
1942

Middlesborough is shown in a mid-war light scheme combining B5 on a white background to produce a breaking-up of the outline. She has a 12pdr AA forward. Light AA comprised a single 2pdr aft and a single 20mm in each bridge wing. No radar was fitted.

HMIS ORISSA J200
1944

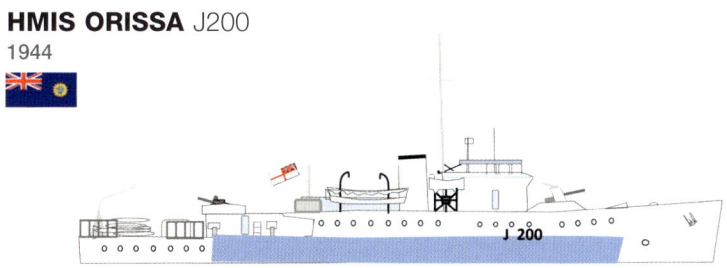

Originally HMS *Clydebank*, this ship transferred to the Indian Navy on her completion and is shown in the typical scheme for ships stationed in the Eastern Fleet. An unusual feature is the manual twin 20mm aft and single 20mm in the bridge wings.

HMIS RAJPUTANA J197
1942

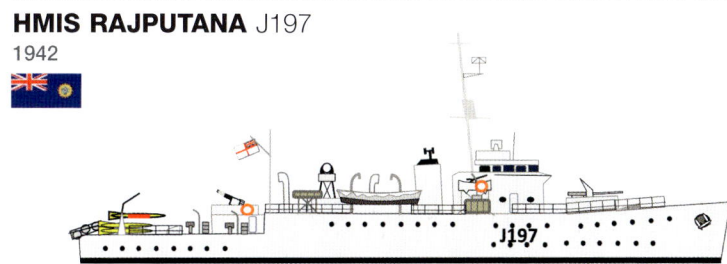

Lyme Regis, transferred to India in 1942, wearing a simple 507c grey scheme with black waterline. Later, while serving in the Indian Ocean, she had a mid-blue panel added to the hull in the manner common for British and Commonwealth ships in that region. At transfer she had a 3in DP forward, a single 2pdr aft and single 20mm Oerlikon guns in each bridge wing. Her pennant is unusual in that there is no gap between the letter 'J' and the number. The radar on her mast was a 286PU, which may have been replaced from 1943.

HMCS INGONISH J69
1944

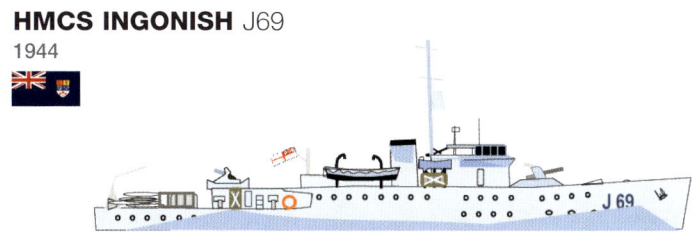

Ingonish utilises two shades of blue to create her low-visibility effect. It has its origins in the WA scheme but taken to a complete blue style. The ship has gained a twin 20mm AA aft and has single 20mm in the bridge wings. There are two DC throwers per side and she carried more charges than the RN ships did. Pennant number at the bow in US style.

HMCS GUYSBOROUGH J52
1943

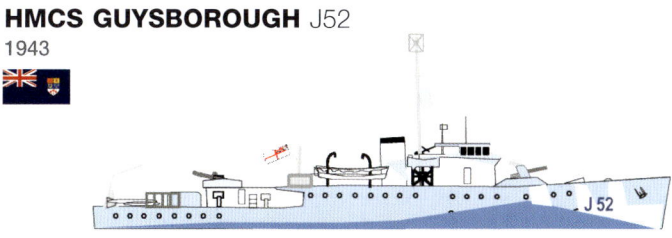

Another Canadian blue on blue with white for this ship is quite different than that seen in most other navies. Note that the pennant number has been placed near the bow in an almost USN fashion. It is also in blue to maintain the camouflage effect. This ship has radar at the foretop, probably of Canadian origin.

HMCS RED DEER J255
1943

Red Deer also has a very Canadian version of the British WA-type scheme using two shades of blue and patches of white. This ship is also equipped as an escort rather than a minesweeper. As usual, the pennant number is placed well forward in the US manner.

HMCS CLAYOQUOT J174
1943

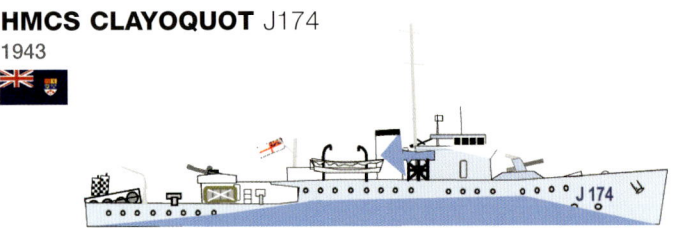

Clayoquot is finished mostly in two shades of blue but with just enough white patches to create confusion. She was obviously engaged on escort duty as many Canadian *Bangor* class were, as can be seen by the ASW outfit. Minesweeping gear is not even shipped. Some of these ships did have such equipment stowed below in case of a need to convert back to their original role, but many went through their entire service without streaming a sweep.

W 101
Captured Bangor Class Minesweeper 1945

HMS *Taitum* was under construction at Hong Kong when the Japanese captured the city. Although *Taitum* and her sisters *Waglan*, *Lantan* and *Lyemun* were barely started, the IJN found the plans and the material for their construction. They therefore built all four, one as an escort, one as a merchant vessel and the other two as minesweepers. However, by 1944 ASW escort was just as important as minesweeping. During construction, the Japanese altered the profile of these ships to avoid them being fired on by their own forces. *W101* certainly carried far more AA guns than her UK sisters. She has a LA 4.7in gun forward, a twin 25mm before the bridge, single 25mm each side of the bridge and there are two twin 25mm on the aft deckhouse. She carries eight DC throwers. There is a Japanese radar on the foremast. Only the original *Bangor* dimensions remain! *W 101* was lost in March 1945.

HMCS THUNDER J156
1944

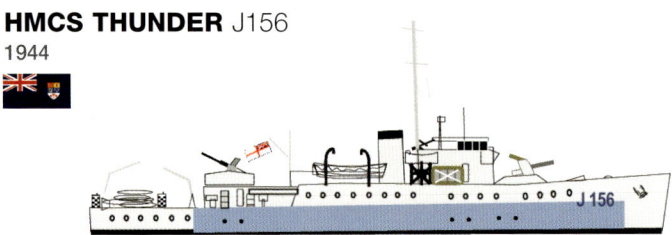

Thunder is fitted for minesweeping but still carries a reasonable DC ability. At some point, the 2pdr AA has been replaced by a single 40mm AA aft but her other guns are standard issue. Her scheme comprises a simple blue panel on the hull.

HMCS MEDICINE HAT J256
1943

Medicine Hat has combined later RN ideas of mixing green with blue to produce a very unusual pattern that builds to a point and give a shortening effect. Her armament is quite standard for the type with a 12pdr forward, two single 20mm in the bridge wings and a single 2pdr AA aft. She is fitted as an escort, not a minesweeper.

ALGERINE CLASS MINESWEEPERS
HMS ACUTE J106
1944

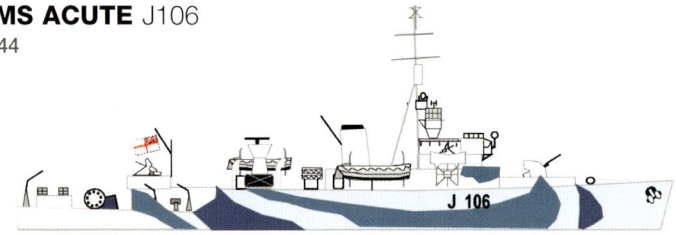

Acute is shown in an Admiralty light scheme that was borne by many of the *Algerine* class minesweepers. The scheme relies on a series of colours of slightly darker shades, placed on an otherwise completely white ship. Many of the principles are the same as the WA scheme but it is a much more elaborate system that came in various shades according to the ship and the yard that applied it. The ship has Type 272 radar on the bridge and Type 291 at the masthead as well as Type 244. The large rangefinder is to help in plotting the position of minefields and swept channels. *Acute* had powered twin 20mm in the bridge wings and aft. Her original name had been *Alert*. This class of minesweeper was based on the design of the very successful *Halcyon* class but using war experience to introduce improvements. They were far better at their role than the *Bangor* class being much larger and with a roomy sweep deck aft.

MINESWEEPERS

HMS BRAMBLE J273
1944

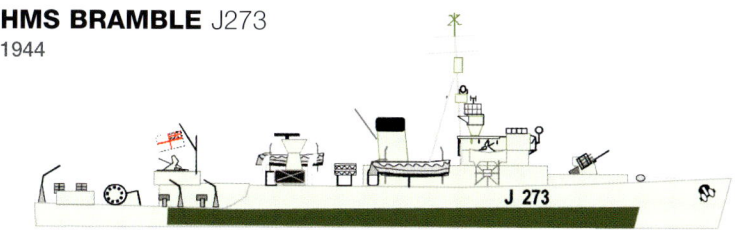

Bramble has standard armament and equipment for the *Algerine* class but is shown here in duck egg green overall with a 1940 green panel on the hull. Green had been in very short supply earlier in the war but by 1944 various schemes based on it were being seen. Type 291 radar is at the masthead and Type 272 on the bridge with Type 244 IFF atop the lantern.

HMS ALGERINE J213
1942

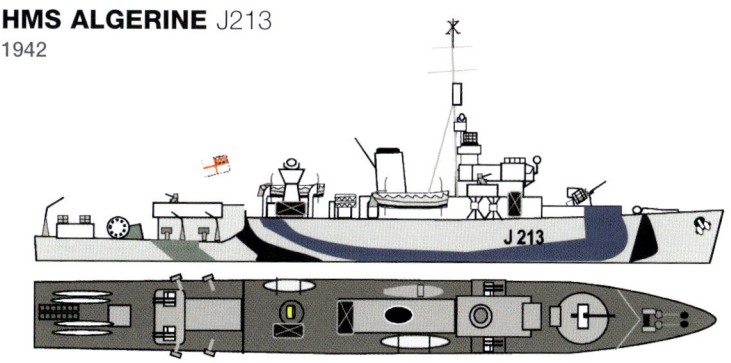

Algerine is shown in the class camouflage design but again the shades used are varied. Black makes up the darkest colour and is offset by blue and green on a grey hull, yet white upper works. Types 271 and 291 radar are carried.

HMS CHAMELEON J387
1944

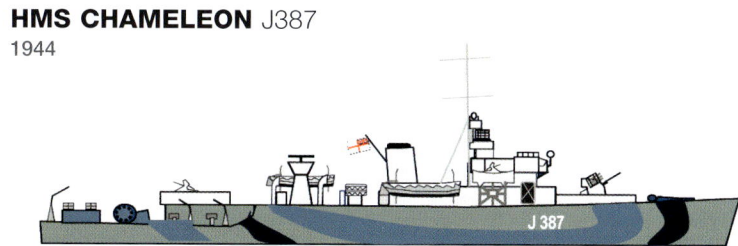

Chameleon had an Admiralty dark scheme intended to confuse and yet have a high level of blending-in with a dull background. Due to the very nature of their duties, most minesweepers spent a lot of time in coastal waters and dull schemes were suitable for such a background. *Chameleon* has two powered twin 20mm AA aft and another in each bridge wing. The older Type 271 radar lantern is on the bridge.

HMS ROWENA J384
1943

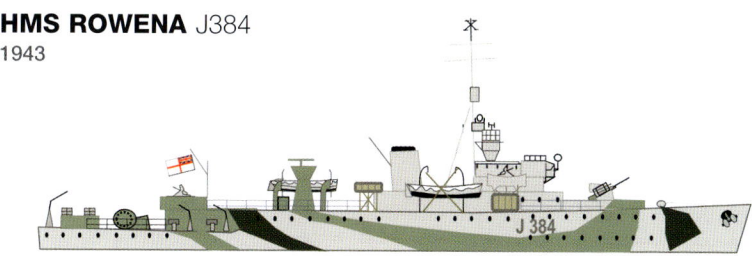

Rowena shows another version of the scheme designed for this class that is also shown on *Acute*. The ship was MS4a overall, with areas of MS3 slate green and MS1 olive black. The light AA comprised three powered twin 20mm AA. The 4in main gun forward had rocket flare racks attached to the shield. There were three rails each side of the mount so a total of six flares could be fired to fall in a pattern ahead of the ship, lighting up a wide area. This was helpful when dealing with E-boats and other small craft. Radar Types 272 and 291 with Type 244 IFF on top are carried.

HMS ALARM J140
1943

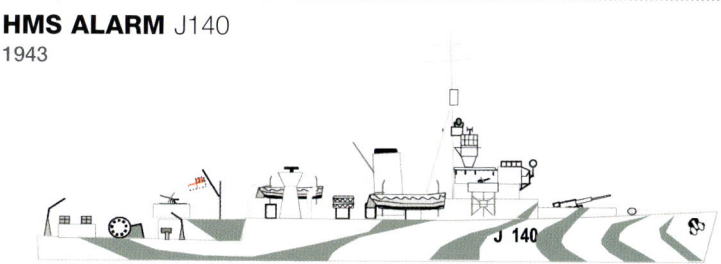

Alarm is shown in a scheme based on the ideas of the pale WA scheme but trying a pattern of pale colour instead of the more familiar pale blue or green panels. Alarm had two single 20mm aft side by side on the deckhouse. There were also single 20mm in the bridge wings. Unlike her sister ships, the *Alarm* has no shield on the 4in gun. A Type 272 radar lantern is carried with Type 244 IFF on top.

HMS RECRUIT J298
1943

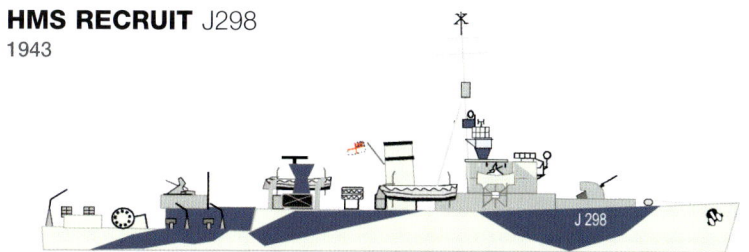

Recruit is shown in a high-contrast scheme that uses two shades that are very similar but a third that is far darker. These schemes were intended to blend in with low-visibility conditions such as mist and rain. She is depicted with two powered twin 20mm on the aft deckhouse and one in each bridge wing. Type 291 radar at the masthead and Type 272 on the bridge with Type 244 IFF on top of the lantern.

HMS HOUND J307
1944

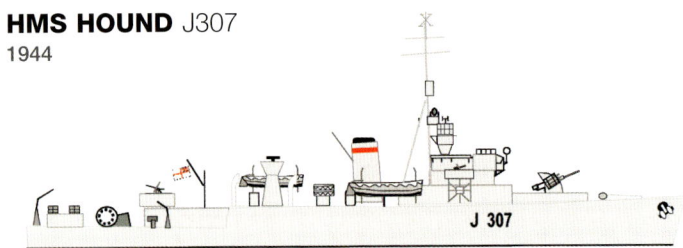

Hound was completed in a very pale grey only a few shades darker than white. Type 272 radar is on the bridge and Type 291 at the masthead. Type 244 IFF is on the Type 272 lantern. Some of this class completed with rocket rails on the forward gun shield to enable them to fire a six-flare pattern to illuminate enemy coastal forces and other targets.

HMS BRAVE J305
1944

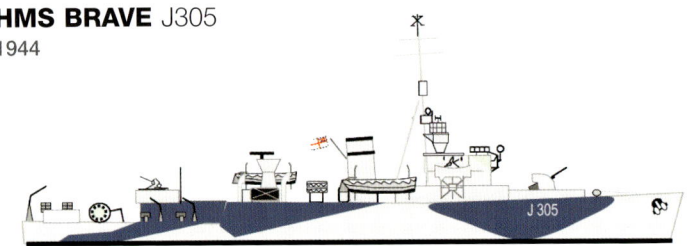

Brave is shown in a simple scheme of pale grey with areas of mid-blue. Toward the end of WWII it was more and more common for ships to adopt schemes that required less maintenance. Complicated camouflage was time-consuming to keep freshened up and needed a wider range of paint. Simple schemes were therefore efficient for ships that spent a lot of time at sea and had less time for in port maintenance. *Vestal* had power-operated twin 20mm side by side on the aft deckhouse and a mount in each of the bridge wings.

HMS FRIENDSHIP J398
1944

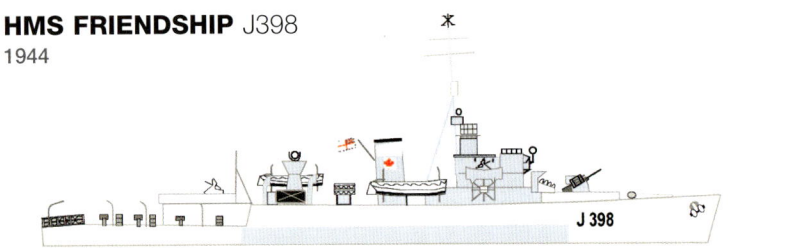

The *Algerine* class escort vessel *Friendship* wears an unusual combination of styles in this illustration. On a white ship, there is a pale blue panel amidships but sections of the upper works are also painted in the same shade. There is a white area at the top of the funnel. All the pale blue was apparently concentrated amidships as the aft deckhouse and twin 20mm guns are in white. Radar carried is Type 271 in a lantern on the bridge plus Type 291 at the top of the foremast. AA armament appears in photographs as the designed four twin power-operated 20mm. However, on some ships the after guns were replaced by two single 40mm Bofors.

HMS CADMUS J230
1944

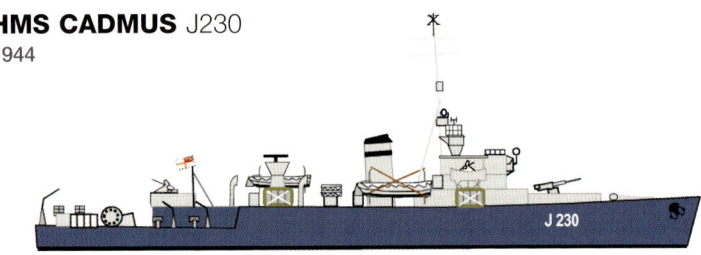

Cadmus is shown in a typical late-war style of a dark blue hull and mid-grey upperworks. This was a simple scheme to apply and maintain on a busy ship. Note that the deckhouse aft has also been painted blue as an extension from the hull but items on the sweep deck are in grey. *Cadmus* was one of the few that were completed with a funnel cap. The black band marks her as a flotilla leader.

HMS REGULUS J327
1943

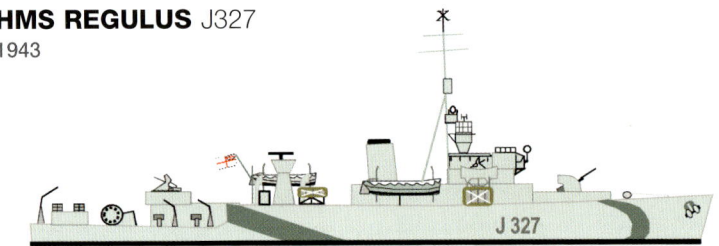

Regulus is shown with another very simple camouflage scheme that is based on the apparent class standard, but omits the centre section (see *Rowena*, *Algerine* and *Chameleon*). *Regulus* was Canadian-built for the RN and was lost in 1945. The ship is fitted with the planned armament of four twin power-operated 20mm AA.

HMCS KAPUSKASING J326
1944

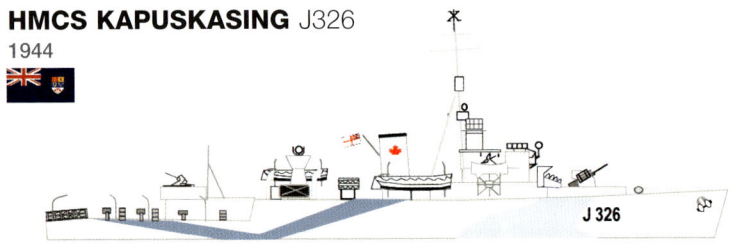

Canada built many *Algerine* class ships for the RN but only operated a few with the RCN. All those it manned were used in the escort role rather than as minesweepers. Canada had built many *Bangor* class and felt they thus had a quite sufficient number of the minesweeping type. Note there is no minesweeping gear aft and instead the ship carries lots of DCs. Up forward, there is a Hedgehog fitted aft of the main gun mount. With many of the *Bangor* class also operating as escorts, these larger vessels made useful leaders for such groups. The camouflage scheme is of Canadian origin but based on common ideas of a white ship with blue areas to provide a difficult target for a U-boat to sight from a periscope.

BATHURST CLASS CORVETTES/MINESWEEPERS

HMAS TOWNSVILLE J205
1941

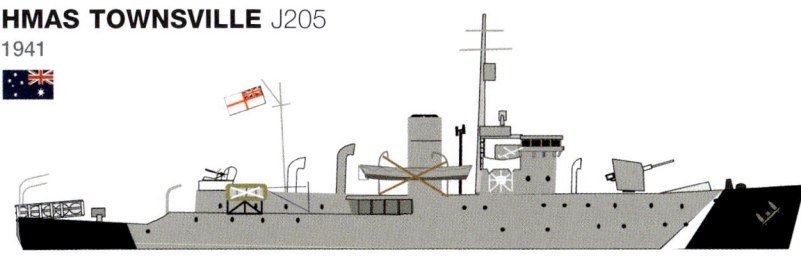

Townsville was equipped and operated as an anti-submarine corvette during most of her service. The class were Australian-designed and built but were somewhat of a cross between a 'Flower' class corvette and a *Bangor* class minesweeper. Sixty were built, of which the twenty units intended for the RN were manned by the RAN and commissioned as Australian ships. The camouflage scheme seems to be rather unique to this particular ship – B6/B30 grey with black and white. There is a LA 4in forward and the light AA comprises three single 20mm. Forty-two DCS were carried.

HMAS PIRIE J189
1943

Pirie is depicted in the dark blue colour often adopted when working in the South Pacific war zone in cooperation with the US Navy. *Pirie* is fitted as an ASW escort. She is armed as standard with a 4in gun forward and three single 20mm, but has MGs in front of and on top of the bridge. These small ships sailed into some heavily-contested areas. There was no radar fitted in 1943.

HMAS BURNIE J198
1942

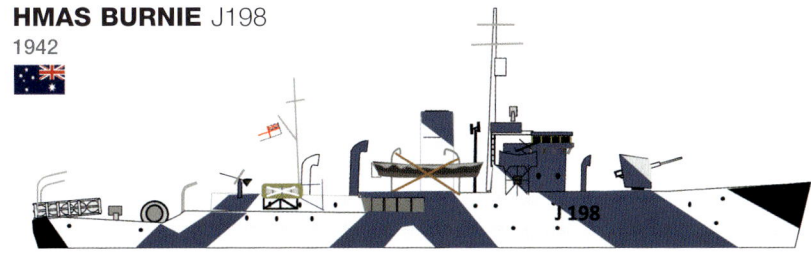

Burnie as she appeared at Singapore 1942. The overall colour is 507c with areas of B20 and black. Most of the schemes used by these ships were unofficial until around 1943-4. *Burnie* has some minesweeping gear fitted but is also equipped for ASW escort. Her light AA comprises three single 20mm Oerlikon, but MGs were also used. In the desperate days of the fall of Singapore, these ships were very busy, but the bulk of the class were still under construction.

HMAS MILDURA J207
1942

Mildura was another ASW version of the *Bathurst* class but with a different mark of 4in gun and smaller shield. Note there is no radar carried and the light AA armament is restricted to three single 20mm Oerlikons. Much later, *Mildura* shipped minesweeping equipment and took part in sweeping operations right through to the Korean War. It was not always the case, but at the time of construction these ships were fitted with a 4in gun if intended as an escort or a 12pdr if the role was to be a minesweeper. The scheme is 507c overall with patches of B6/B30 grey.

HMAS PIRIE B249
1944

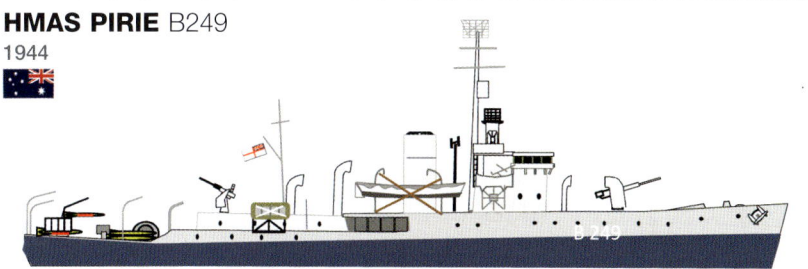

Later in the war, *Pirie* has adopted the dark blue lower hull very common to American warships. The 20mm aft has been replaced by a single 40mm Bofors. There is now British Type 271 and US SC radar. While the *Pirie* served with the British Pacific Fleet she was given the pennant 'B 249'. Most of the ASW gear was replaced by minesweeping equipment.

HMAS LISMORE J145
1941

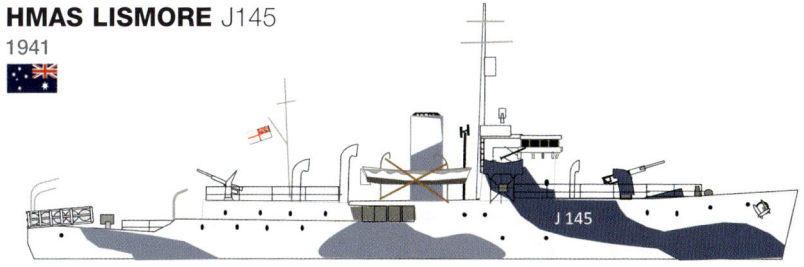

Lismore is depicted in the scheme worn by the ship when serving in the Mediterranean with the RN. MS507c is the overall shade with patches of 1941 blue and B5. *Bathurst* class ships were a very important reinforcement for the hard-pressed British who had such heavy demand on escorts for the Atlantic that few could be spared for elsewhere. These little ships, with their weak armament, escorted, swept for mines and did work in the Red Sea as well. Note this ship had a 12pdr AA aft until all her 20mm were available. There are 20mm singles in the bridge wings.

HMAS TOWNSVILLE J205
1942

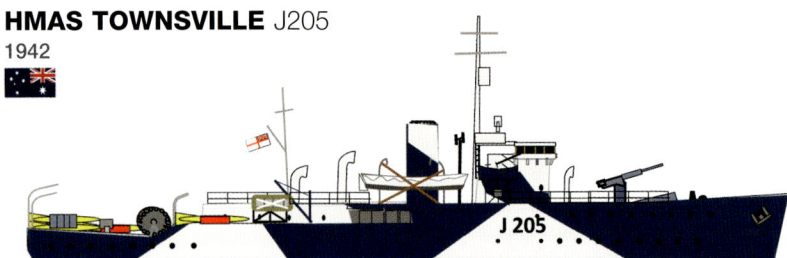

Townsville has a camouflage scheme well suited to the Pacific, using PB10 on 507c grey. There was no shield to the gun when completed and, as drawn here, 20mm singles have been fitted in the bridge wings. It is probable that rifle-calibre MGs were also used if needed. This unit was fitted and used for minesweeping, but in the RAN the class were always called corvettes.

CATHERINE CLASS MINESWEEPERS
HMS STEADFAST J375
1944

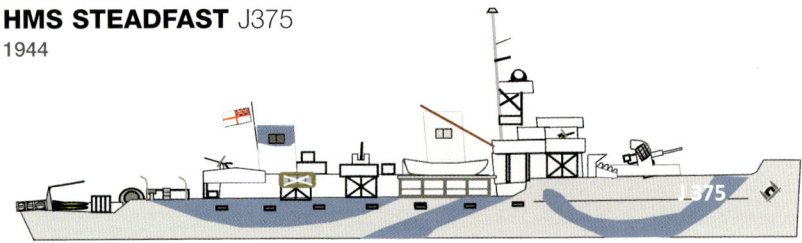

Steadfast was a US Raven/Auk class minesweeper provided under the Lend-Lease agreement. She is shown here with a very light scheme that was a mix of white, MS4a and mid-blue, and was probably as delivered. The RN has placed a small shield on the 3in gun so it could be provided with rocket flare launchers. There are six single 20mm AA carried and some ASW capability including a Hedgehog, as well as minesweeping gear. American SL or SU radar was carried.

HMS CATHERINE J12
1944

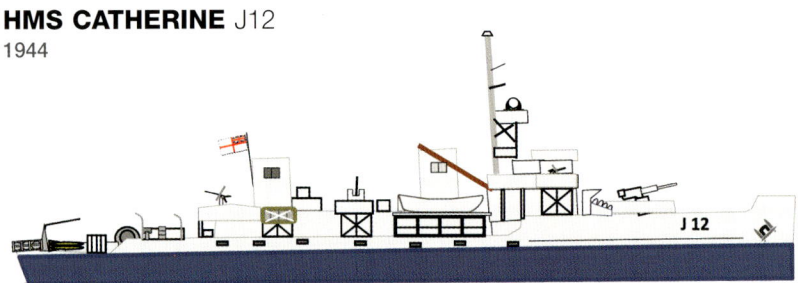

Catherine is definitely in as-delivered condition including US-style paintwork. The boom behind the bridge was for handling the boats and later replaced. These ships had a heavier ASW capability than most British minesweepers, including a Hedgehog forward, but the DCs aft tended to crowd the sweep deck. There are six single 20mm and a 3in AA.

HMIS BENGAL J243
1942

Bengal is shown in a striking black and white camouflage which would have been well-suited to the Indian Ocean. She was built in Australia for the RIN and was mostly intended for use as an escort vessel. Note, unlike the Australian-manned ships, there is a single 2pdr AA aft as well as the single 20mm AA in the bridge wings. Her main gun was a single 4in. This ship fought a heroic battle to defend a convoy against two large Japanese merchant raiders, sinking *Hōkoku Maru* (eight 6in and two 3in) and driving the *Aikoku Maru* (eight 5.5in) off. The Japanese ships also had four torpedo tubes each. Seldom has a ship won against such overwhelming odds.

HMS GRECIAN J352
1945

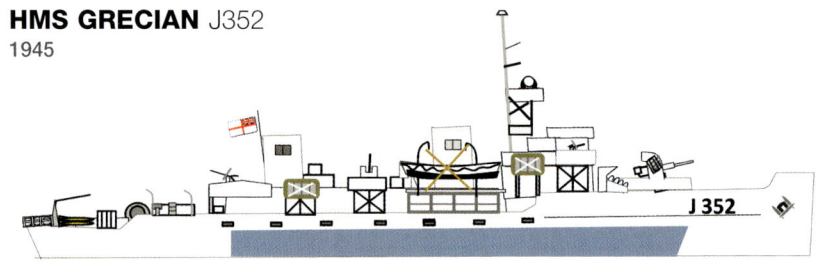

Grecian shows her end-of-war appearance with a pale blue panel on an otherwise entirely white ship. The boat boom has been replaced and RN-type boats added. This ship also has a 12pdr shield fitted to the US 3in AA gun to allow rockets to be fitted. Light AA is the standard six single 20mm.

MOTOR MINESWEEPERS
MMS 12
1941

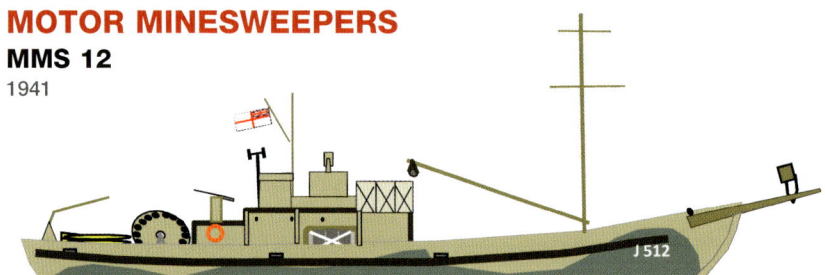

Motor minesweepers (MMS) operated in coastal waters other than when on passage from one area to another. Camouflage therefore concentrated on a coastal background, MS3 slate green and locally-procured khaki. These small, manoeuvrable craft were slow but could get into areas the large minesweepers could not. *MMS 12* as shown is armed only with a twin 0.5in MG mounting and has equipment to sweep moored or acoustic mines. The box-like structure by the galley funnel was an armoured cabin where crew members could shelter during air attacks.

MINESWEEPERS

MMS 16
1942

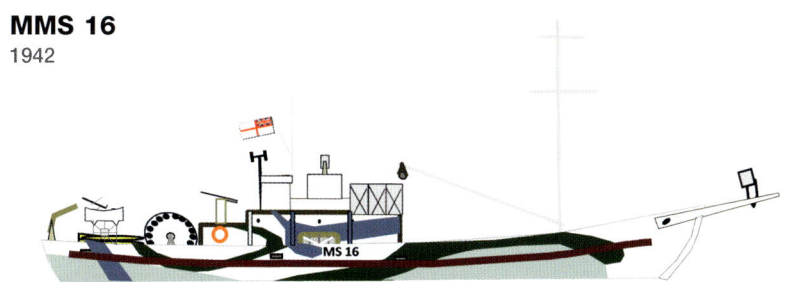

MMS worked in many dangerous areas but only those that did tended to wear camouflage as maintenance of it was a problem with just a twenty-man crew. Those in areas less prone to enemy aircraft and fast attack craft were usually just grey. This vessel is overall white, MS1 and MS3. There is also some mid-blue. *MMS 16* is shown with a 20mm aft as well as the twin 0.5in MGs. Some of these ships displayed a pennant number and some used the name of the ship very small, as shown here.

MMS 248
1942

This scheme was obviously an attempt to make the hull look lower and the vessel further away. Probably a defence against enemy coastal batteries or fast attack craft. As this sweeper is armed with two 20mm, it can be presumed it operated in an area of high enemy activity as most of this type of MMS landed their 20mm guns and were only MG-armed. As a later vessel, it has some changes to layout and the rubbing strake goes all the way to the bow. On a white ship, there is MS3 and a small amount of 1941 blue.

MMS 1022
1944

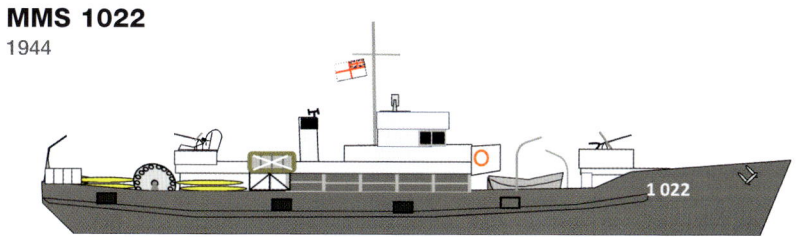

An easy solution was chosen for *MMS 1022* by simply providing a grey 507b hull and MS4a grey upper works. By the time these vessels were coming into service, air attack was unlikely as the Luftwaffe was far too busy on other fronts. But E-boats were still active and some measure was felt necessary so single 20mm Oerlikons were carried fore and aft. Many of these longer MMS were transferred to allied navies; nine to the Netherlands, two to Norway and six to the USSR.

MMS 1044
1944

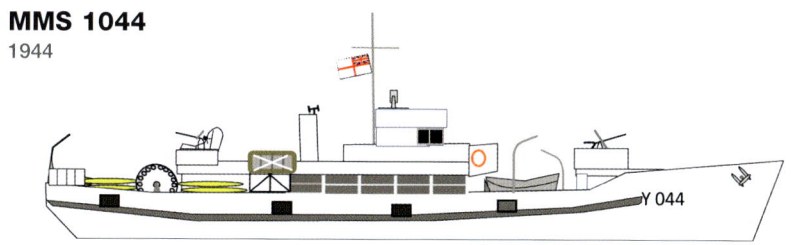

Most long-hull MMS seem to have completed in very pale grey, almost white, but with the rubbing strake painted dark grey. In misty conditions while sweeping coastal waters, this would have been quite effective as camouflage. Note the pennant is displayed as 'Y 044'. Many MMS seem to have had a pennant that was the last three numbers of their title but with 'Y' as flag superior.

BRITISH YARD MINESWEEPERS

BYMS 2022
1944

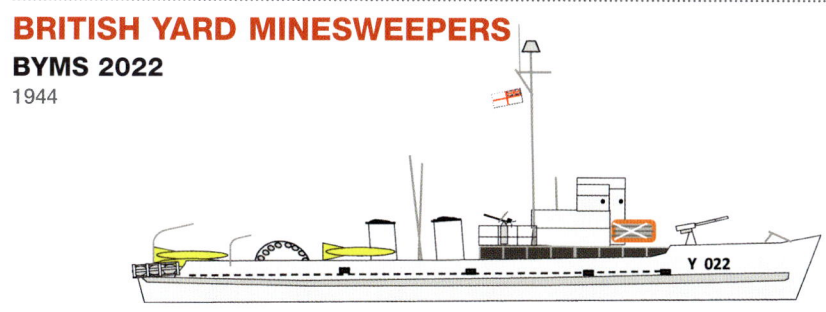

BYMS 2022 is shown in very pale grey, which seems to have been the favoured scheme for those in RN service. This unit has the short foredeck as built. Note that these ships had limited ASW capability but nonetheless more that usually carried by RN ships of similar type. SL radar is carried at the masthead.

BYMS 2070
1944

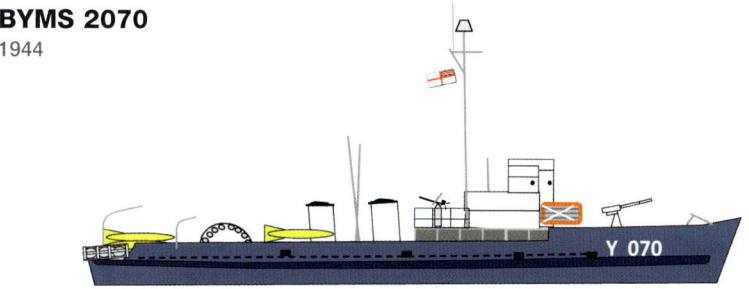

BYMS 2070 was a US-built coastal minesweeper supplied under the Lend-Lease programme. They were more manoeuvrable than the British-built MMS types. Some of those serving in the Mediterranean were given a PB10 blue hull and MS4a upperworks. Most others were left plain grey. They were armed with a 3in DP forward and two single 20mm on the bridge. Note this unit has the foredeck extended further aft to provide more accommodation.

BYMS 3244
1945

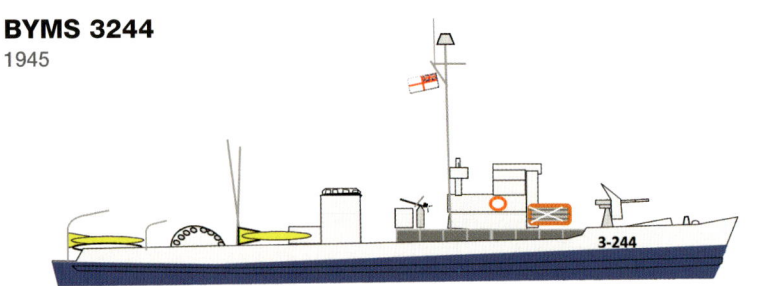

BYMS 3244 is depicted in typical dark lower hull and pale upper works and may have even been delivered in that from the US builders, using USN paint. The ship was of the later single-funnel type BYMS and remains unmodified except for the gun which has had a British-type 12pdr shield added for crew protection. This suggests she may have been expecting to operate in an area where enemy coastal forces were still active.

KIWI CLASS MINESWEEPERS
HMNZS TUI T234
1944

Tui in Pacific War camouflage in 1944 with very dark blue hull and 507c upper works. The black band on the funnel shows the ship as a flotilla leader. There are single 20mm in the bridge wings and another aft. Rather a light armament considering that the air war off the Solomons was so intense. The radar on the short lattice aft is British Type 293. Note the flag superior and pennant is of trawler-type

HMNZS MOA T233
1943

Moa is shown in a drab overall blue US-type camouflage whilst working with the USN in the Solomons campaign where she sank the Japanese submarine *I-1* with her sister ship *Kiwi*, only to be herself sunk two days later by air attack. There is a Type 271 radar on the lattice amidships and she is shown carrying three single 20mm guns as well as the LA 4in forward. There were four MGs available for AA etc, as well.

HMS QUEEN OF THANET J30
'Racecourse' Class Paddle Minesweeper 1943

This ship and her sister *Queen of Kent* were built in WWI as paddle minesweepers but sold out. Requisitioned for WWII, both ships spent the war as minesweepers despite many other paddlers being altered to AA ships. Paddle minesweepers, with their shallow draft, were so valuable they took part in minesweeping in European ports during 1945, particularly Antwerp. The ship is shown here in a scheme that would be quite suitable for coastal operations. The overall colour is 507c with MS3 and 1940 Stone.

HMNZS KIWI T102
1942

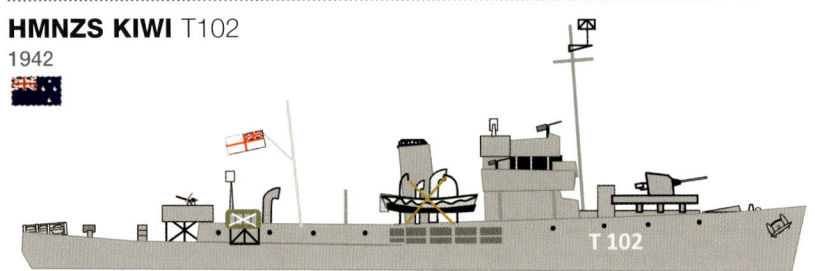

With the possibility of war in the Pacific, New Zealand decided to order a class of small corvette-type vessels built by a UK trawler yard. Although they were given trawler-type pennants they were intended to perform a similar role to the *Bathurst* class in the RAN. *Kiwi* is shown here during operations off Guadalcanal where she and a sister ship sank the Japanese submarine *I-1* on 29 January 1943 in a depth charge and gun duel, finished off with a ramming attack. Radar is Type 286PU. *Kiwi* is painted in overall B55.

HMNZS KIWI T102
1944

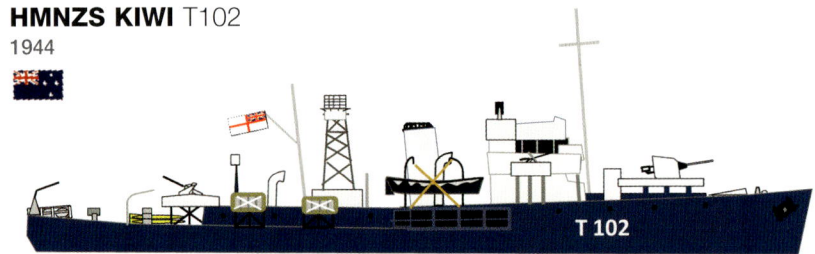

Kiwi is shown in 1944 with PB10 hull and 507c upper works. The radar on the lattice is Type 271Q. With a 4in gun, 20mm in the bridge wings and a 40mm aft, this ship is as well-armed as most corvettes in the RN. Although able to act as minesweepers, these ships spent most of their war in and around the Solomon Islands and other areas of the South Pacific.

TRAWLERS 10

HMS NORTHERN GEM FY194
ASW Trawler 1941

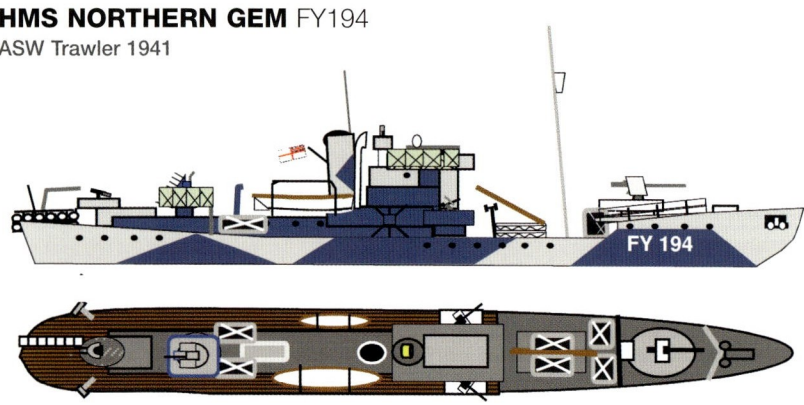

There were several vessels in this group requisitioned for the RN as ASW trawlers. Built for deep-sea fishing in rough seas, they made useful escorts in northern waters. The ship is shown in MS4a and 1941 blue. Her bow was useful when operating in pack ice. She carries a 4in forward, single 20mm in the bridge wings and a quad MG on a bandstand aft. She also has twin Lewis guns at the rear of the aft deckhouse. The ASW fit is quite standard for a trawler. Splinter screens are in use. The limited power-generation capacity of trawlers meant they needed a special ASDIC set and radar that could run on such low power.

HMS NORTHERN FOAM 4.76
ASW Trawler 1942

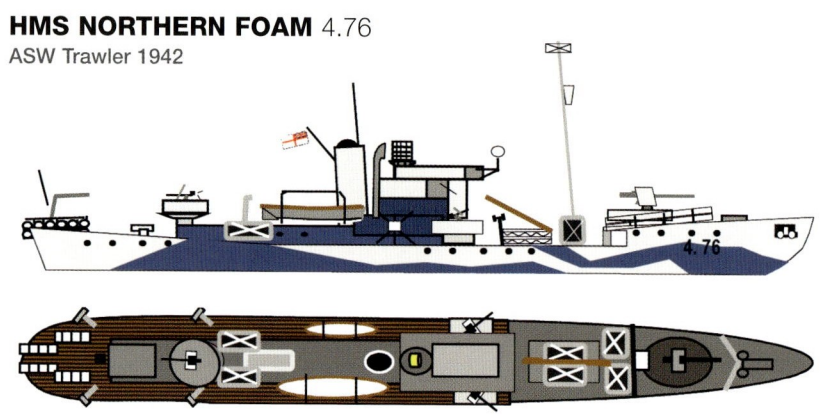

This 'Northern' class trawler wears a scheme similar to *Northern Gem* but with 507c grey as the main overall. She still carries her early armed boarding vessel pennant number but has a Type 271 radar lantern on the bridge. The MGs aft have been replaced by a single 20mm Oerlikon. Her ASW fit includes two DC racks, four throwers and spare charges, so can deliver quite a good pattern. She has trawler-type Type 286PU radar fitted on the mast top.

HMS NORTHERN PRIDE FY105
ASW Trawler 1940

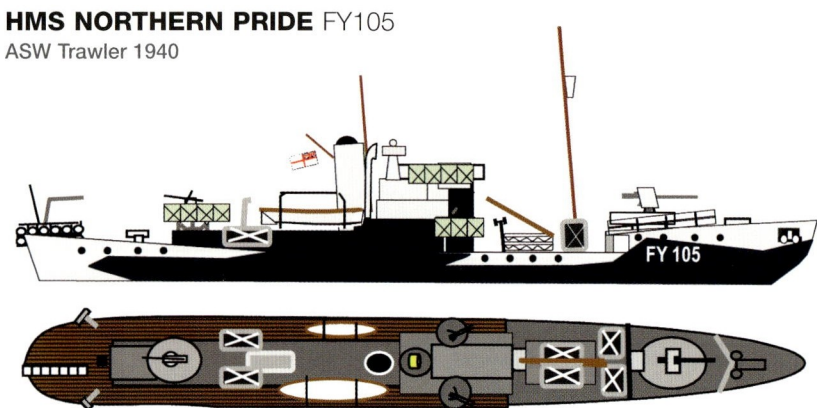

This 'Northern' class trawler wears a scheme which is probably unofficial. The overall colour is 507c but the dark area is either black or very dark blue. Considering the shortages of paint, black is the most likely. In this early-war form she has no radar. Her AA is limited to a single 2pdr aft and twin Lewis guns in the bridge wings. Her ASW is typical of trawlers with a single DC rack and two throwers. The bridge and AA positions are protected by splinter screens. The 4in guns for these ships came from WWI weapons that had been kept in storage.

HMS BUTSER T219
'Hills' Class ASW Trawler 1942

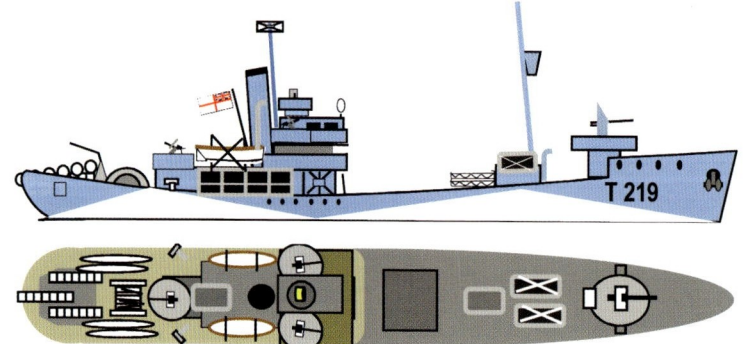

This 'Hills' class trawler was built for the RN during the war and entered service just before the war in the Atlantic turned in the Allies' favour; she wears almost a reverse of the WA-type scheme with mid-blue uppermost and white on the hull. Type 286PU radar is fitted, which was quite a rarity for trawlers in 1942. The three single 20mm AA were only fitted late in 1942, prior to which she had carried MGs only. The forward gun was a 12pdr. For a trawler to be so well fitted late in 1942, we can presume that she must have undergone a major refit just when all the right things were available. The large fish well was in presumption that the class would be sold for commercial trawler use after the war.

HMS YESTOR T222
'Hills' Class MS Trawler 1942

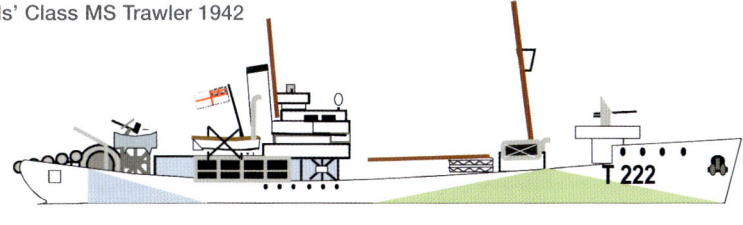
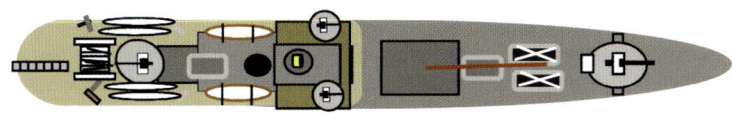

The 'Hills' class were built in 1941 for the RN and intended for sale for civilian use post-war. *Yestor* is shown here wearing a typical WA scheme of WA blue and WA green on WS white. She entered service with a 12pdr forward and three 20mm AA as designed. The ship is fitted for minesweeping as her main role. However, these ships, particularly those on minesweeping duty, were low-priority for radar and none is fitted in the illustration.

HMS SIR TRISTAM T229
'Round Table' Class MS Trawler 1943

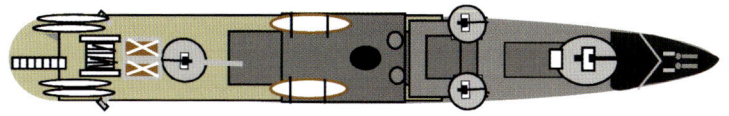

Sir Tristam saw service with Western Approaches and is shown here in a typical WA scheme. Its simplicity against the average Atlantic Ocean background was very effective and hard to see from a periscope. Note the 20mm at the bridge have been moved forward to allow a better arc of fire. The fish hold has accommodation built over it. Type 286PU radar is fitted. The ship is fitted for minesweeping duty. Note the large wooden-deck working areas, which were more comfortable for the crew than steel or Cemtex.

HMS SIR GERAINT T240
'Round Table' Class MS Trawler 1942

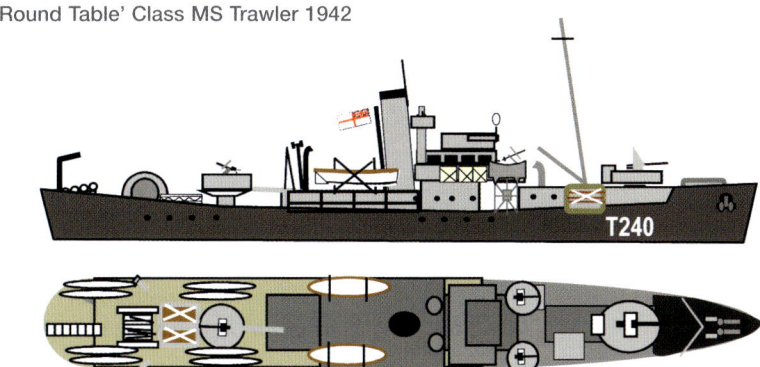

The 'Round Table' class mostly entered service in 1942. *Sir Geraint* is shown with a very simple B20 hull and 507b grey upperworks. She was fitted for minesweeping as well as ASW duty. Despite being designated for ASW duty, the vessel has no radar fitted. Note that the aft 20mm is in a raised tub and had a small walkway between it and the aft deckhouse. The SL platform near the front of the funnel was a feature of this class.

HMS BURRA T158
'Isles' Class MS Trawler 1943

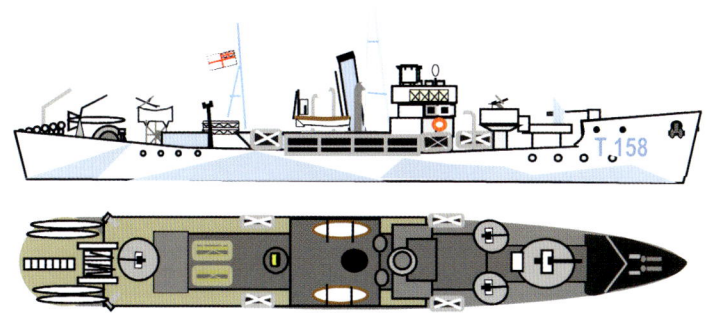

Burra is depicted in a WA scheme. Even the pennant number was painted in blue for low visibility. Note there are minor differences in layout because this large class were built in a variety of yards. Most of the 'Isles' class were fitted for minesweeping and were heavily engaged in that work. In this illustration the vessel has a base platform for Type 271 radar on the bridge but it is not yet actually fitted. Installations such as this were often completed across one or two refits to prevent the vessel being out of service too long.

HMS ISLAY T172
'Isles' Class MS Trawler 1943

Islay is shown with a WA scheme. The 'Isles' class were the largest single class of trawlers built for the RN during WWII. They were used for many duties including ASW escort, minesweeping, dan laying and as rescue ships for convoys. In this illustration *Islay* is shown with the Type 271 radar lantern fitted but no other radars or special electronics. The armament fit is standard as designed.

HMS CALVAY T383
'Isles' Class Dan Layer 1944

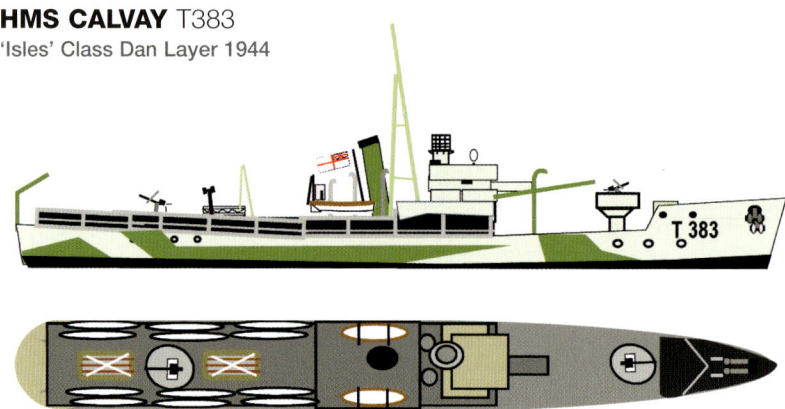

Calvay was one of the 'Isles' class trawlers converted to a dan layer in support of mine-clearing operations. The armament was reduced to only two 20mm AA as by 1944 the threat of air attack had been greatly reduced in the areas she would operate in. There was a Type 271 radar lantern on the bridge. Her paint scheme reflected her mostly inshore work and concentrates on two shades of green that were popular toward the end of the war. The numerous 'Isles' class were versatile ships, which made them good value for money.

HMS ARRAN T06
'Isles' Class ASW Trawler 1943

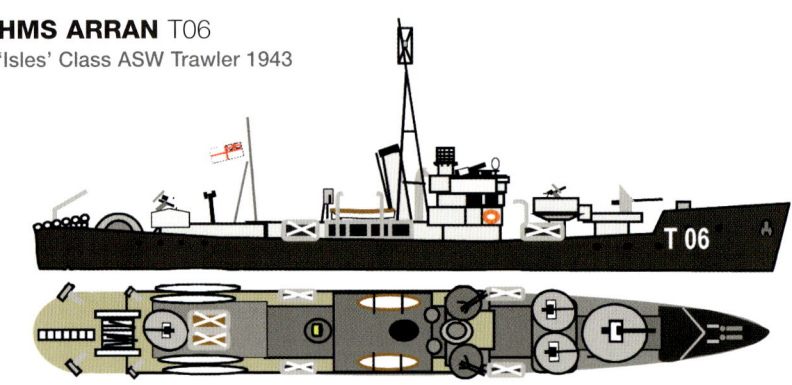

Arran spent much of her time on ASW escort duty to West African ports. She wears a dark MS1 hull and pale 507c upper works. There was a Type 271 radar lantern on the bridge, with Type 290 at the masthead. A 12pdr forward and three single 20mm AA was the designed armament. Twin MGs are depicted on the bridge wings which were not standard, but the author knew one of her commanding officers and he had them installed. While in harbour, he personally used the port mount to shoot down a low-flying German Ju 88 during a surprise attack before the rest of the ship's crew could get to action stations. Her crew were of mixed nationalities which complicated giving orders as some had to be issued in English, and then translated into two other languages before they could be carried out. The boatswain was considered a valuable multi-lingual asset. This problem was apparently not unusual with some RN naval trawlers due to manpower shortages.

HMS FOXTROT T109
'Dance' Class ASW Trawler September 1940

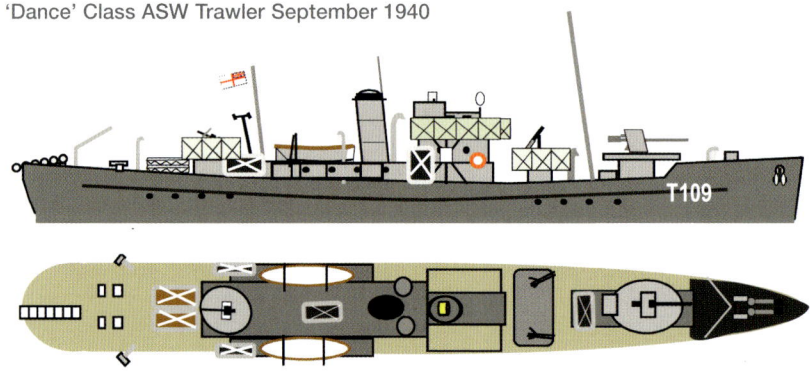

Rushed to completion to counter the U-boat menace, *Foxtrot* entered war service with twin Lewis guns forward instead of the planned 20mm. She had an old 4in forward, which was standard for ships intended for ASW duty, and a single 20mm was mounted aft. *Foxtrot* is shown in a very dull standard dark grey and mid-grey, which were probably dockyard-mixed. No minesweeping gear was fitted as she was intended for escort duty. Despite limited capabilities, these little ships performed dangerous and valuable duties with Atlantic convoys, often in weather when they would not even have been at sea in peacetime.

HMCS MISCOU T277
'Isles' Class ASW Trawler 1942

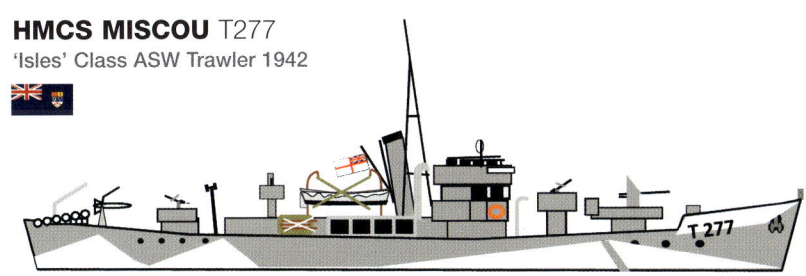

The Canadian Navy preferred more regular warships, with the *Bangor* class preferred as small escorts. However, some of the 'Isles' class they built for the RN were retained as escorts. *Miscou* is shown fitted for ASW and minesweeping. Her camouflage is somewhat unusual, utilising WS white on 507b grey to perhaps give the impression of speed when being observed by a U-boat. The armament is standard but no radar had been fitted up to the end of 1942.

HMS KERRERA T200
Early 'Isles' Class ASW Trawler 1942

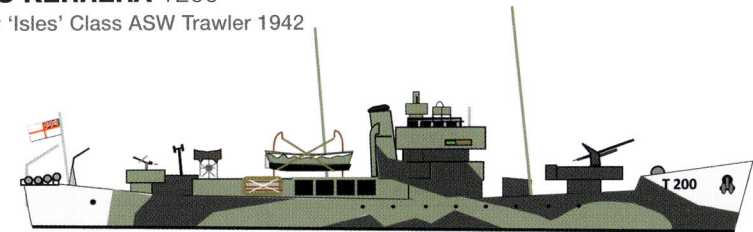

Being built in multiple yards, the 'Isles' class were not always identical. Here *Kerrera* lacks the light tripod masts of later vessels. She has the foremast in front of the bridge as per the original design and a short mast amidships. The ensign is flown from a staff over the depth charges. She is painted in an Admiralty light design with the bow and stern painted out with WS white and the central area in MS3 and MS2. The 4in forward was of non-standard type, two single 20mm were carried on the centreline aft and MGs were mounted in the bridge wings.

HMS GRENADIER T334
'Military' Class ASW Trawler June 1944

Grenadier is shown in MS507b all over with PB10 blue-grey, which was a scheme suitable for many areas. Showing the capacity for these vessels to be up-gunned, she has an extra pair of 20mm Oerlikon guns in front of the bridge. She has Type 290 radar on her tripod mast.

HMS COLDSTREAMER T337
'Military' Class ASW trawler 1945

This class were the ultimate war-built Admiralty trawler design. Her scheme is a typical late-war variation using dark green on light green and indicates the vessel was probably engaged in coastal escort duty in the later part of WWII. The designed armament of a 4in gun forward and four single 20mm Oerlikon AA was carried but there was room to increase that if necessary. The bridge design and layout was considered as good as any corvette and she had a strong ASW armament.

HMAS MARY CAM FY48
Minesweeping Trawler 1943

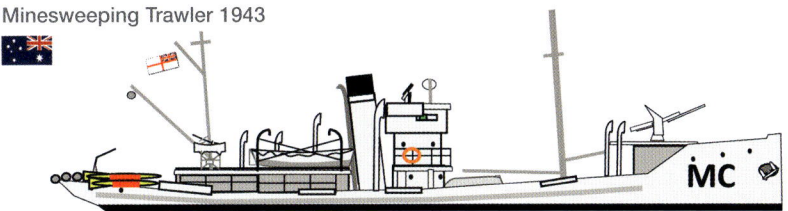

Mary Cam was one of many small trawlers taken up for minesweeping around Australian ports. Serving in regions where the weather was often very hot, the RAN painted most of its auxiliaries in very pale grey. Those in more northern areas usually adopted very dark blue, like US ships, or very dark grey. The ship had a single 12pdr forward, two 20mm aft and single MGs on the bridge wings.

HM DRIFTER ARCADY FY1598
Minesweeper 1940

Very small trawler-type vessels, drifters were handy for minesweeping in harbours and close inshore; areas larger units could not reach. Conversion to naval use often involved simply swearing the existing crew into the RN and giving them a course in how to sweep for mines. Often later replaced by YMS vessels, they then returned to fishing. *Arcady* retained her civilian black hull. She may have been brown before her upper works were painted a grey similar to B55. Masts remain in varnished wood. There is a single 20mm AA forward, but many of her type only carried MGs.

HMS MORRIS DANCE T117
'Dance' Class ASW Trawler 1941

Morris Dance at least had her three 20mm Oerlikon AA fitted in 1941. Some trawlers waited much longer to get those high-priority weapons. The unofficial paint scheme is based around black, grey and white, all of which would have been readily available. Radar is still something for the future. Splinter mats cover the bridge and some guns in case of strafing by aircraft. They gave only limited protection and were later removed to save weight. There was a full ASW fit with no minesweeping gear.

HMS COTILLION T104
'Dance' Class ASW Trawler June 1943

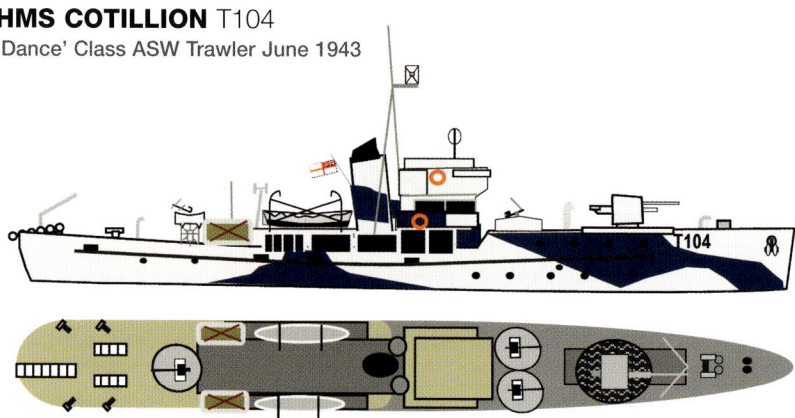

During a major refit *Cotillion* had her funnel capped and the forward well deck filled in for more accommodation. The bridge was enlarged and a 4in of a later pattern fitted. All three 20mm AA guns were fitted although there had previously only been one. The ASW fit is strong. The mast was moved aft of the bridge to improve visibility forward and Type 290 radar placed on it. The mast was also converted to a tripod. She is now more like a corvette than a trawler. Her paint scheme has probably been applied in the dockyard and comprises a dark B20 blue with 507c grey on all other surfaces, compatible with wartime escort vessels.

HMS ELLESMERE T204
'Lake' Class ASW Trawler 1942

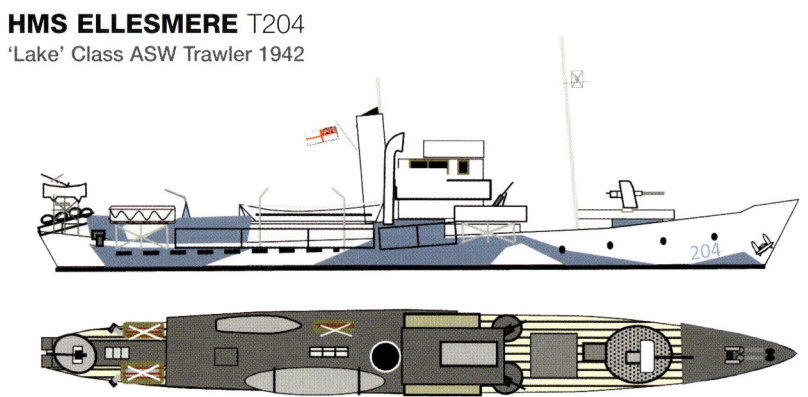

Only six 'Lake' class were built. They followed whale chaser lines more than trawler type, proving to be cramped and too small for the job even though quite fast. The crowded area at the stern made handling DCs difficult and the single 20mm AA carried was perched above it. The low freeboard aft made them very wet, but they were designed to operate in difficult waters and this unit is shown in a variant of the WA style. Type 290 radar was carried on the mast.

HMS NOTTS COUNTY FY250
Minesweeping Trawler 1940

Notts County was taken into service in the early days of WWII and was typical of hastily fitted-out ships. The merchant service varnished wood bridge remained. She had an old WWI 4in gun fitted forward and single Vickers guns on the bridge, twin Lewis guns amidships and a quad MG aft. This would have been considered an extensive AA fit for this type of vessel in 1940. Aft she has some minesweeping capability but the rapid escalation of the U-boat war required the fit of DCs to be increased. Her paint scheme was totally unofficial and has some areas of white on the hull.

HMNZS TAWHAI T348
Minesweeping Trawler 1944

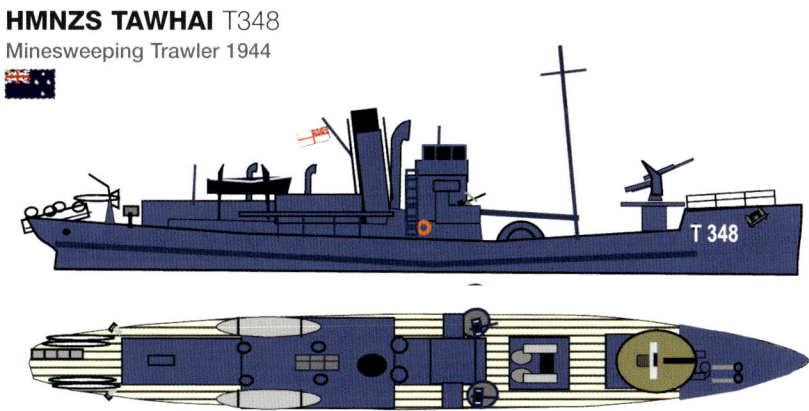

New Zealand built four 'Castle' class trawlers for magnetic minesweeping. They were of mostly wood construction over steel frames. The colour scheme is typical of US standard and this ship was probably painted using USN supplies. The four ships looked antiquated but were actually built from 1942–4. They were armed with a 12pdr gun forward and two single 20mm Oerlikon AA on the bridge wings. The minesweeping equipment was up-to-date and effective. No radar was fitted.

HMNZS KILLEGRAY T174
Minesweeping Trawler 1942

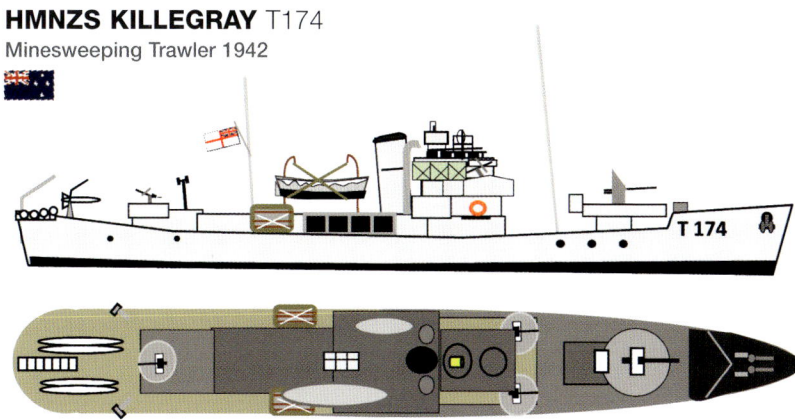

New Zealand received four minesweeping trawlers of the RN 'Isles' class, but there were differences in general appearance. The forward 20mm were placed on the front of the bridge and the funnels were thicker. The RNZN chose to use a scheme of very light 507c grey with a prominent black waterline as shown here.

HMNZS SOUTH SEA T08
Minesweeping Trawler 1941

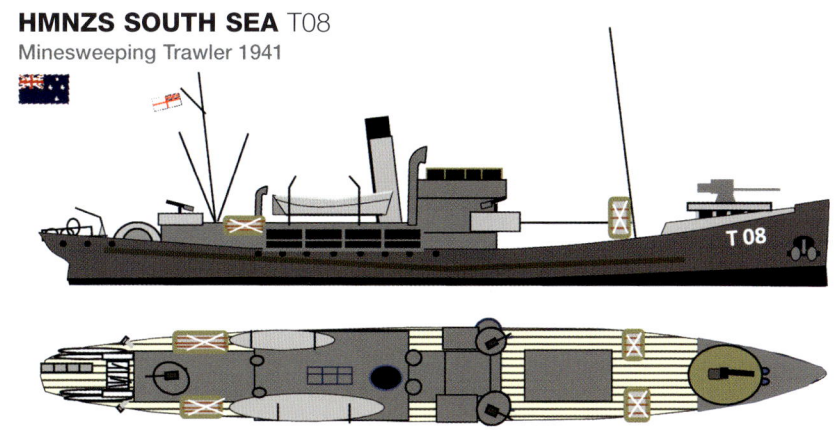

This old trawler was built in 1912 but was taken up for service as a minesweeper when WWII broke out. She is shown in a drab grey scheme that became more battered and rusty as time went by. Her only armament comprised a very old 4in gun and three Vickers machineguns. There were a few depth charges carried.

HMS KINGSTON OLIVINE FY193
ASW Trawler 1941

Although an ASW unit, this requisitioned trawler still carried a minesweeping winch aft. Her scheme was a simple and workmanlike dark and mid-grey which was probably easily available and not necessarily RN standard. There is an old single 4in at the bow, but her forward 20mm are mounted over the former fish hold. She has two twin Lewis guns on the bridge wings and another single 20mm aft. There is no radar carried but her ASW outfit is quite good with four DC throwers, one rack and some deck reloads.

HMS DELPHINUS FY846
Minesweeper 1940

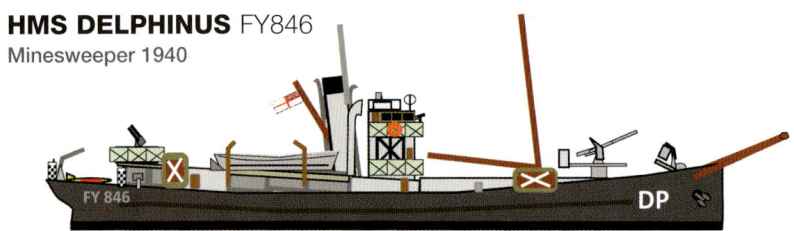

Delphinus is shown configured for influence minesweeping. Her dark grey hull is probably a local mix and she has retained brown masts. The influence hammer is prominent near the bow. There is limited sweep gear aft and she has port and starboard DC throwers. The main gun is an old 12pdr; there are a pair of 0.5in MGs aft and single Vickers MGs in each bridge wing. A very unusual feature is the pennant number carried aft. 'DP' forward is an abbreviation of her name. Possibly this was some sort of local arrangement in the area she was serving if there were lots of similar trawlers.

HMS LIBERIA FY1826
Minesweeper 1942

As illustrated, *Liberia* appears to have received some dockyard attention, providing her with an Admiralty style camouflage. It could, however, have been unofficial and the style merely copied. Rather surprisingly, she was given a black boot topping along the waterline with the camouflage carried down over it. Colours used are MS3 slate green, B30 dark olive, with MS4a overall. Many trawlers never received a standard camouflage scheme, which suggests her duties may have taken her well away from mundane tasks around the UK coast. She has the usual 12pdr forward; however, her AA was limited to a twin 0.5in MG mount aft, and single Lewis guns in the bridge wings.

HMS STOKE CITY FY232
ASW Trawler 1943

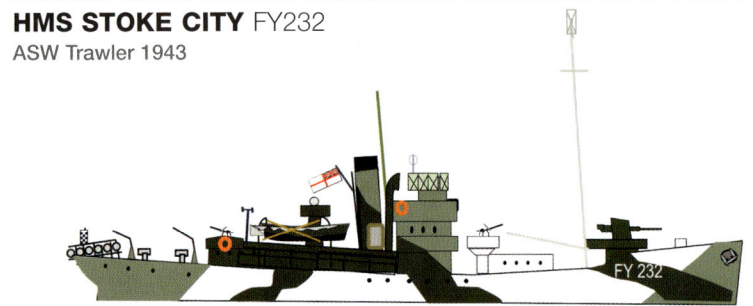

Stoke City was taken up for ASW duty in 1939. She is illustrated in this 1943 view, painted to an unofficial scheme based on white, B30 dark olive and MS3 slate green. The armament was fairly standard for escorts, with a single 4in and three 20mm AA. Type 290 radar is shown at the masthead. Trawlers were usually at the bottom of the list to be fitted with radar but the Type 290 set was designed for them because their electrical output was less than other ships.

HM DRIFTER GILT EDGE FY963
Minesweeper 1940

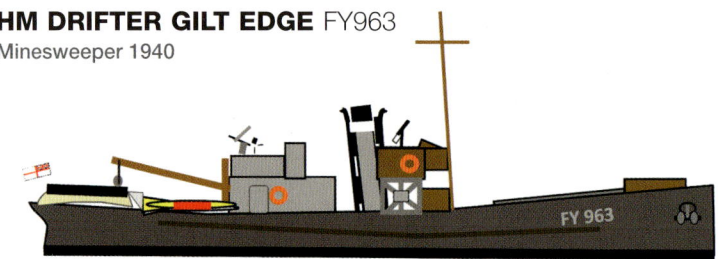

Painted in two tones of grey that were probably locally mixed, *Gilt Edge* still retains some brown areas on the bridge. There is a black naval-style waterline. She carried a 20mm Oerlikon aft and single Vickers MGs on the bridge wings. There was no ASW equipment. The funnel marking indicated which flotilla she belonged to. The pennant FY963 was applied in pale grey not white.

HMS BLAAUWBERG FY32
ASW Whale Chaser 1940

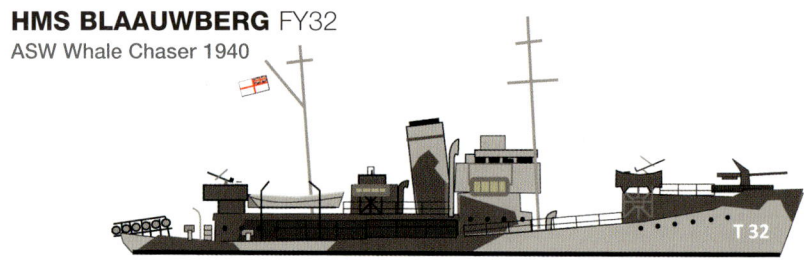

Blaauwberg was a South African whale chaser converted to an ASW escort. She is shown with a simple application of MS4a and 507a/G10 or a local-procurement dark grey. The low freeboard aft would have made her very wet but the hull form was intended to give more speed than the usual trawler type. She had two single 20mm mounted side by side just aft of the 12pdr gun mounted at the bow, and another single 20mm aft. When first taken into service, there were MGs instead of the 20mm. As these ships did not operate in areas where German aircraft were expected, they did not carry splinter mats as protection against strafing. The pennant number placed so far forward is non-standard and was a T flag superior, rather than FY, as she was an ASW vessel.

HMAS BINGERA FY88
Patrol Vessel 1944

With a vast coastline to protect and few ships to call on, Australia was forced to call up almost everything available. Hence *Bingera*, not a trawler but a recently-built coastal trading vessel, was requisitioned as an ASW patrol ship. Previously, she had been painted pale grey with a heavy black waterline. She later served as a stores vessel and she is shown here in the typical dull blue adopted when going in New Guinean waters. Her actual pennant number was 'FY 88' but, like many Australian ships, she carried a combination of letters for visual identification.

HMS OTHELLO T76
'Shakespearian' Class ASW Trawler 1942

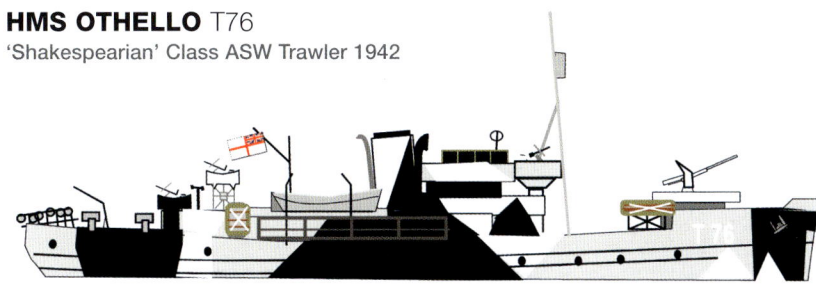

This scheme uses black to concentrate the eye and even features two false white bows, possibly in the hope of tricking the viewer into thinking there are two ships very close to each other. Remember a U-boat captain only had seconds in which to view a target and lower his periscope to avoid being seen. This style of camouflage, while never official, was fairly common in the Mediterranean Fleet. Bright sunlight does affect vision in a very different manner than the duller conditions of the Atlantic. Hence the black areas would be confusing in bright light, but would be far too prominent in dull light. *Othello* has the usual 12pdr forward and two 20mm either side of the bridge, but aft the single 20mm are placed on the centreline rather than side by side.

HMAS GOONAMBEE FY94
Minesweeping Trawler 1942

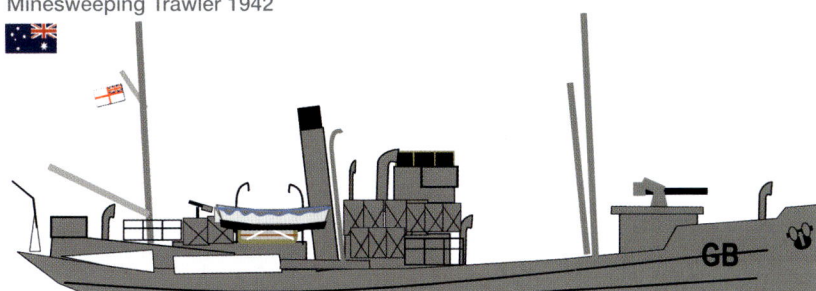

Despite her very weak armament, the *Goonambee* sailed into some dangerous waters during WWII. While employed in areas subject to the advancing Japanese forces, she was painted dark grey all over in a colour similar to B55. There was little opportunity to provide any other sort of camouflage. Her decks remained mostly unpainted wood, but the hold areas and forward section were dark grey. Her armament was limited to an old 12pdr forward and a single Vickers MG aft. *Goonambee* also carried four DCs. She was engaged in the hunt for Japanese midget submarines that attacked Sydney Harbour, helping to destroy one. She was later painted in the very pale grey of most Australian minesweepers.

HMS VIZALMA FY286
ASW Trawler 1940

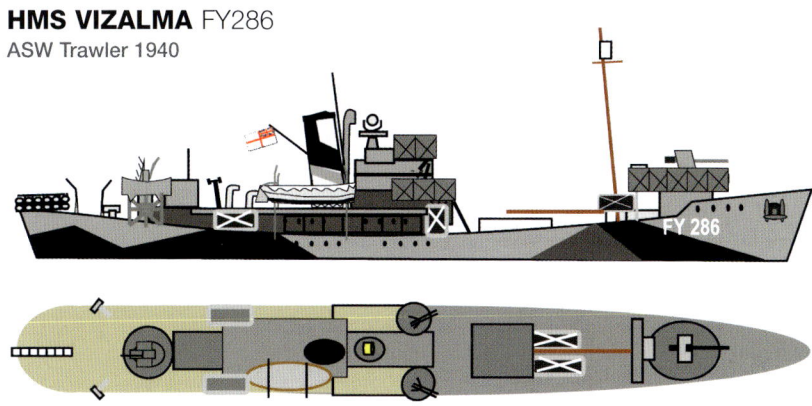

Vizalma was quite a large trawler taken up for escort duty. She is shown wearing a very early camouflage scheme which was probably based around whatever paint was available to the crew or the dockyard that converted her for naval use. AA guns were limited to a quad MG aft and Lewis guns in the bridge wings. She had no minesweeping capability. The bridge was raised for better visibility. No radar was carried.

HMS NORTHERN DUKE 4.11
ASW Trawler 1941

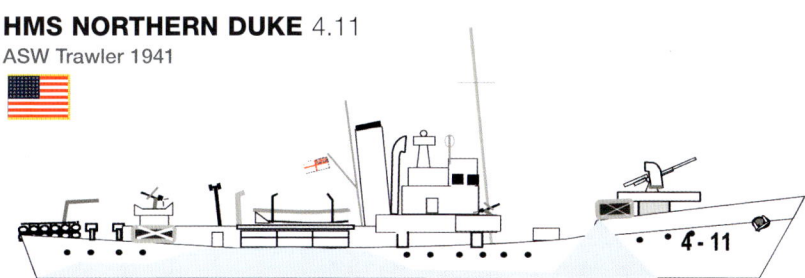

Northern Duke differed in design from others of the requisitioned 'Northern' class trawlers. The ship had a high Atlantic bow, making her drier and well suited for convoy operations. The scheme shown here is a typical WA one of white overall with WA blue. When the US entered WWII, its east coast was ravaged by German U-boats in what was know to them as 'The Second Happy Time'. To help the USN overcome the onslaught, this ship was one of several vessels lent to the US Navy via reverse Lend-Lease. But they proved so useful that the USN retained them in service even after their massive building programme was churning out hundreds of new ships. The *Northern Duke* was not returned until 1946. The illustration shows her with a 4in gun forward, a single 20mm well aft and singles in each bridge wing. In USN service, the ship was painted with a dark blue hull and light grey upperworks.

11 AUXILIARY AA SHIPS

AUXILIARY AA SHIPS

HMS SPRINGBANK F89
1941

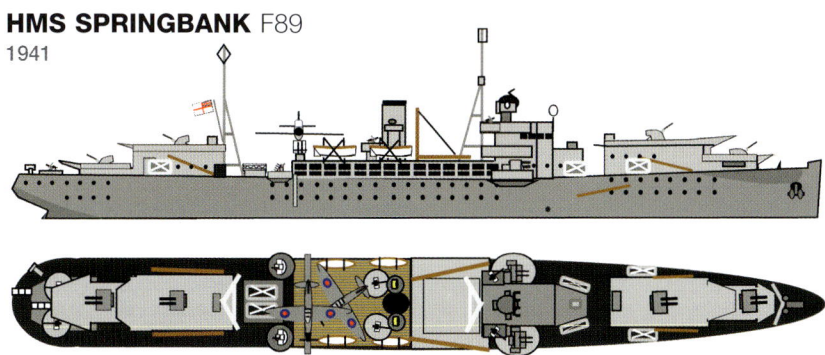

This Bank Line steamer was fitted with a powerful AA armament and a catapult-launched naval Fulmar fighter which could not be recovered. A spare could also be carried. In this form, she was referred to as a Fighter Catapult Ship (FCS) as well as an AA vessel. Merchant ships with a catapult only carried aircraft of RAF origin and were referred as CAM or catapult merchant ships. *Springbank* was lost late in 1941 as shown here in a standard merchant-type scheme of dark grey hull approximating B55 and MS4a grey upperworks. The director was fitted with Type 285 radar and there was a Type 286 at the head of the foremast.

HMS ALYNBANK F84
1943

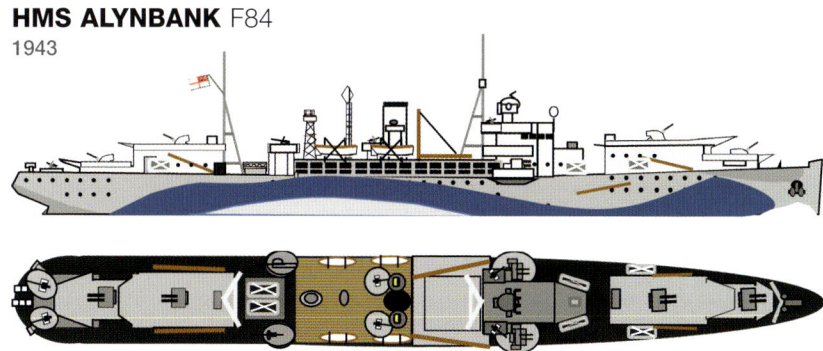

Alynbank lasted longer than her sister ship but was never fitted to carry aircraft. Here, in 1943, she has Type 285 radar on the director and a tower amidships for a Type 271 lantern, as well as another for HF/DF. The quad 0.5in MGs were replaced by single 2pdr AA but the six single 20mm and two quad 2pdr remained the same. Her scheme comprises three shades; MS4a on the hull and 507c superstructure, with 1941 blue wavy line. Thoroughly worn out by extensive convoy duty, the *Alynbank* was stripped of her guns in 1944 and was one of the ships scuttled on D-Day to help form an artificial harbour.

HMS POZARICA 4.261
1942

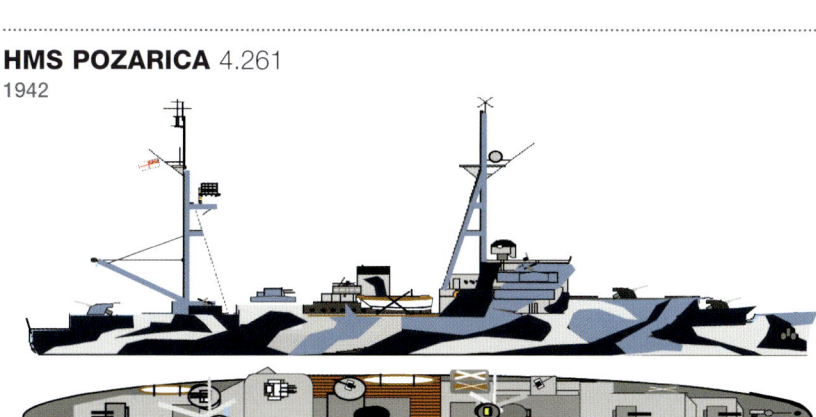

This ship has had a similar conversion to her sister *Palomares*. This ship spent a lot time at Murmansk and on Russian convoys. The scheme is an Admiralty disruptive type suitable for Russian waters. There was an overall colour of MS4a with areas of B15 and a washed-out dark 1941 blue. Ships such as these were so fully converted as to be as well-fitted as many regular warships, and gave valuable service. There is no Type 285 radar on the director in this illustration but it was fitted at some stage. Type 291 radar is at the foretop with a Type 271 lantern on the aft tripod mast. The ship has three twin 4in AA mounts, two quad 2pdr, a manually-operated twin 20mm and four singles. This was a formidable AA armament that made these ships as valuable in a convoy as a cruiser or battleship.

HMS PALOMARES F98
1941

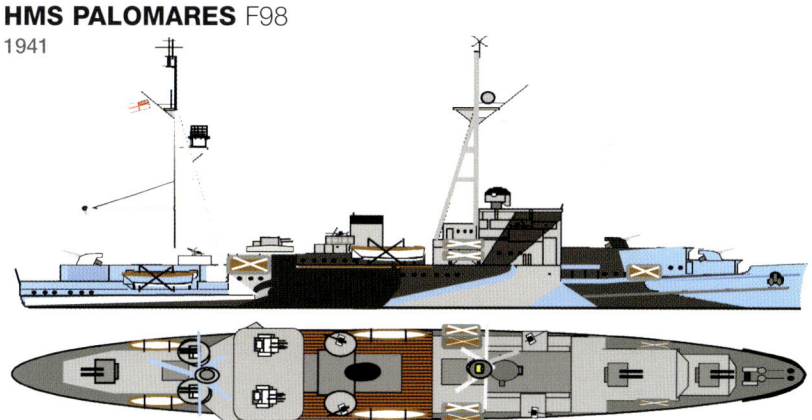

A former fruit ship. the *Palomares* gave good service and is shown in a disruptive scheme very suited for northern service. These ships were chosen because fruit ships were generally faster than most merchant vessels. The armament of this ship was the same as her sister *Pozarica* but her camouflage scheme was quite different, as can be seen. Note that an area of the boat deck was wood planked but other horizontal areas were one of two shades of grey.

HMS JEANIE DEANS J108 (4.29)
Auxiliary Paddle AA Ship 1940

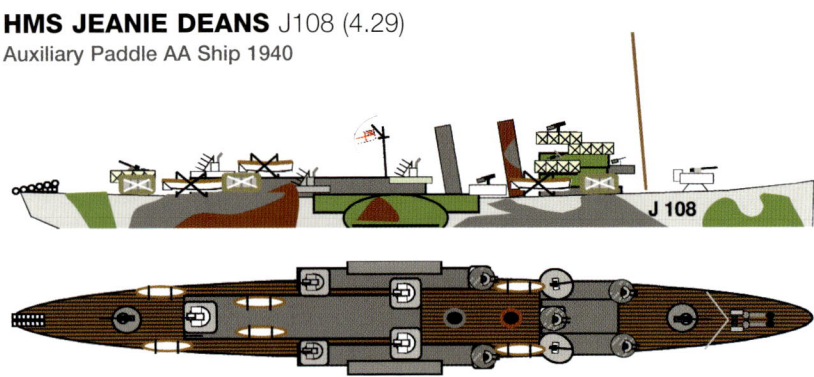

The pre-war day tourists had gone and lots of light AA guns covered the decks of this old paddler in 1940 for the escort of coastal convoys. A shallow draft meant she could work in confined waters to protect small colliers and freighters. She started the war as a minesweeper as her pennant number indicates. There were single 2pdrs fore and aft plus two single 20mm in the bridge wings. There were four quad MGs and no less than seven twin Lewis guns in various positions. Her scheme is unofficial being intended to blend in to a coastal background and was almost certainly made up from paints available at the port she operated from. Her actual pennant number as an AA ship was 4.29; but she carried her old one for a time after reassignment from minesweeping.

HMS EMPEROR OF INDIA 4.237
Auxiliary Paddle AA Ship 1940

Overall 507b grey was worn by this old paddler. Her AA armament was mostly of light weapons, but numerous. The role of this ship was to defend against air attack in shallow waters and harbour entrances where enemy aircraft often laid mines. The ship had started the war as a minesweeper before conversion to AA duty. She was built in 1906 and worn out by 1943 when relegated to harbour duty only. Her pre-war role had been as a ferry and in the tourist trade. She had served in WWI as a RN minesweeper under the name HMS *Mahratta*.

HMS ROYAL EAGLE 4.239
Auxiliary Paddle AA Ship 1940

Camouflage with what you have available would have almost certainly been the case with the *Royal Eagle*. A pre-war pleasure steamer, she was one of many ships very hastily converted to AA ships in 1940. The overall colour is 507c and the patches are local procurement khaki. German bombers used the Thames as a route for low-level attacks on shipping in and out of the Port of London. She has a quite formidable armament for her size: six single 2pdr AA, six single 20mm AA, three Boulton Paul aircraft-type MG turrets, two other MGs and aft there are two Unrotated Projectile (UP) launchers for wire-trailing AA rockets. Grey under stern and paddle boxes is area in shadow, not part of the scheme.

HMS MAPLIN F107
Fighter Catapult Ship 1941

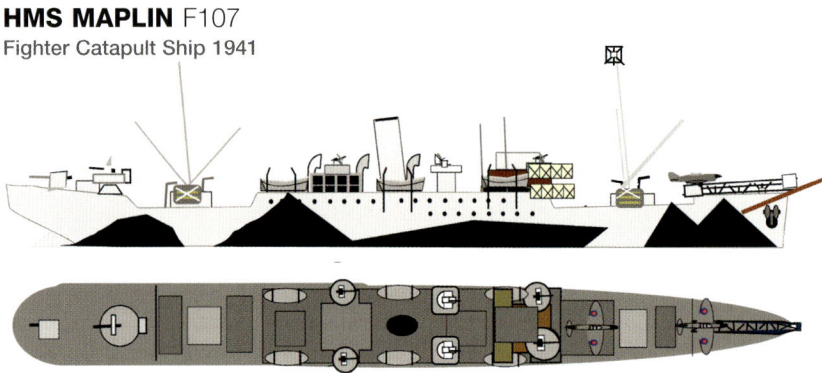

After the fall of France in 1940 convoys crossing the Atlantic were shadowed and attacked by German long-range aircraft. To meet the emergency, the RN used the few ships available to it for conversion to launch fighters. Only a few naval catapults were available and some warships landed them for use on ships that could accompany convoys. These carried a worn-out aircraft that was considered to be expendable, as it could not be recovered once launched, to intercept a German aircraft and drive it off from the vital convoys. *Maplin* was such a ship. She could carry one or two Fulmars or Sea Hurricanes. Having been converted from an Ocean Boarding Vessel, she retains a 6in gun aft but the forward one has been replaced by a catapult. There is a 12pdr AA aft, four single 20mm AA and quad MGs amidships. The ship carries a Type 286P fully-rotating radar to enable her to detect approaching aircraft. Her scheme is an unofficial disruptive that uses black on 507c.

AUXILIARY AA SHIPS

HMS PATIA F89
Fighter Catapult Ship 1941

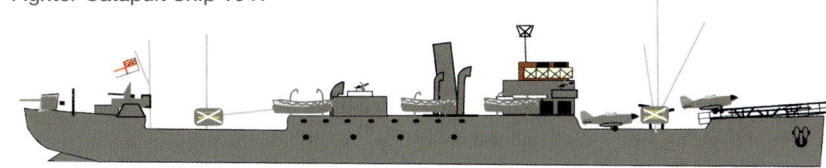

Rapidly converted from an Ocean Boarding Vessel to an FCS at the start of 1941, *Patia* was sunk late in April of the same year. She appears to have been left in the same dark grey overall worn previously. Paint shortages often meant that ships were forced to use whatever was available. Black and white being in reasonable supply meant that grey was the easiest shade to attain. She has a 6in gun aft, with a superfiring 12pdr AA, as well as four 20mm Oerlikon guns. There is a Type 286 fixed radar over the bridge giving coverage 45° either side of the bow. The original varnished wood bridge has not been overpainted. However, her most valuable asset in this form was the catapult from which aircraft could be launched on a one-way mission to drive off enemy aircraft. As a navy vessel, those carried were usually worn-out Fulmars or Sea Hurricanes. The pilot was to bail out and be picked up by one of the escorts after completing his mission. Note that, unlike CAM ships, which were merchant-manned, the naval FCS often carried more than one aircraft.

HMS ULSTER QUEEN F118
Auxiliary AA Ship 1940

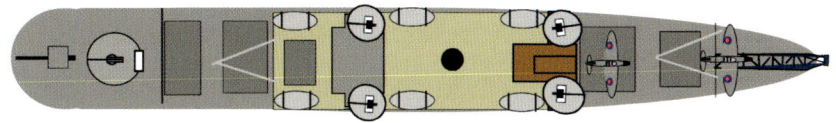

This ship had a good turn of speed and was ten years old when WWII broke out. She was immediately earmarked for use by the Admiralty. It was the realisation of German air power that resulted in her conversion to an AA ship that could accompany fast merchantmen or have a sufficient turn of speed to be able to escort convoys through the danger zone as they approached or left UK waters. However, when allied forces had sufficient strength to be considering landings in Europe, this ship and others were altered to the fighter-control role. She is shown here in an Admiralty intermediate scheme just prior to conversion, when her very powerful AA armament was replaced by three single 6in guns in case she was needed to provide gunnery support when close inshore directing fighter cover over invasion beaches. The colours in use are WS white, PB10 and WA blue.

HMS PEGASUS I35, later D35
Seaplane Carrier / Fighter Catapult Ship 1941

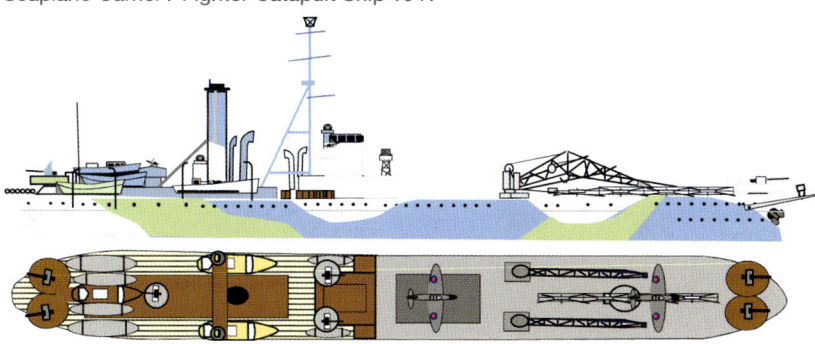

Pegasus was originally the WWI seaplane carrier *Ark Royal*, but was renamed when the newer ship was built. The armament was poor but three 20mm were added. Note the Type 271 radar lantern in front of the bridge and Type 286 at the mast head. Brown areas were Corticene. Wood decks may have been painted grey. She carried two Fulmar fighters but had no means of recovering them. She was worn out and soon relegated to harbour duty. The overall colour was white, with areas of 1941 blue and 1940 green, lightened.

HMS ARIGUANI F105
Escort and Fighter Catapult Ship 1941

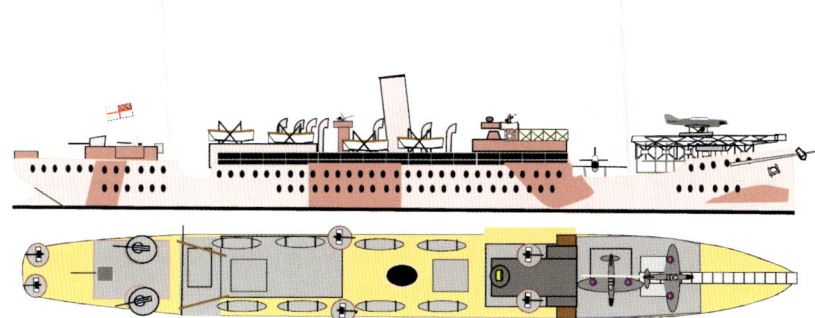

Originally a small liner, this ship was used by the RN as an Ocean Boarding Vessel. These ships stopped neutrals headed for Europe and examined them to see if they were carrying war contraband or enemy reservists returning home to Germany. By early 1941, there were very few such ships to stop and examine, which released some for other duties. *Ariguani* became a mid-ocean convoy escort for a time before taking on the role of FCS. Being naval-armed, she carried Fulmars for that role and could ship a spare as well. She is shown in a two-tone Mountbatten pink style. Popular with crews who thought it had a near-magical ability to hide a ship, Admiralty tests proved that at dawn or dusk it was actually easier to see and the scheme was dropped. She has a 6in gun on the aft deckhouse as well as two 12pdr AA. There are a total of six 20mm carried. Due to a desperate shortage of refrigerated ships, the *Ariguani* was released from naval service in 1943 and returned to her owners.

HMCS PRINCE ROBERT F56
1942

Prince Robert is shown here as ready for Atlantic escort duty. Apart from the PB10 dark patches, her scheme was a typical style suited to Atlantic operations. She had Canadian SW2 radar at the foretop but that would soon be replaced. There was a Type 285 radar on the director, as well as a tall tower for the Type 271 lantern. Her 1943 scheme on the right is typical of many ships where a previous style was changed in colour but retained basically the same pattern. She had previously worn a scheme in mid- to dark blue. The AA armament is formidable for that era. Five twin 4in AA mounts arranged 'A', 'B', 'X', 'Y' and 'Z' and two quad 2pdr mounts amidships. In addition, there are twelve single 20mm Oerlikons.

HMCS PRINCE ROBERT F56
1943

The ex-Canadian National Railways Line *Prince Robert* served in several different guises during WWII. Here, she is a powerful and fast AA ship with an armament that was better than most regular AA cruisers. She wears an Admiralty disruptive scheme using three colours; MS4a, 1941 blue and a washed-out medium blue. Note she has ten 4in AA in five twin mounts, quad 2pdrs and no less than twelve 20mm AA. She later became a Landing Ship Infantry. The Canadian radar has been removed by the time of this illustration and was probably replaced by Type 291 at the masthead. The other equipment remains the same except for the addition of a HF/DF mast on the aft deckhouse.

HMS TYNWALD D69
1941

Tynwald was a fast fruit ship converted to an AA escort for convoys. This sort of ship did not go all the way across the Atlantic with a convoy, but did accompany it in areas where German aircraft could reach to attack in strength. The scheme is a pale version suitable for her operational area in the Irish Sea. It seems to comprise MS4a and WA blue. Incoming convoys were glad of the extra AA protection these ships could provide when they entered the range of German bombers based in France. They were as well-equipped as an AA cruiser. *Tynwald* was the only one to have two directors with Type 285 radar fitted, enabling her to engage two main targets at a time. The masthead radar was initially Type 286 fixed, then Type 286P and eventually Type 291. A tower was provided amidships to carry a Type 271 radar lantern.

HMS GOATFELL 4.36
Auxiliary Paddle AA Ship 1942

Built as the *Caledonian* in 1934 for the tourist trade, she started the war as a minesweeper and became an AA ship in 1940. She wears a paint scheme based around 1940 green on 507c which was probably suitable for her local duties and sorties in support of vital coal convoys passing around the coast. Note single 2pdr fore and aft and on the paddle boxes. Four single 20mm aft and Boulton Paul aircraft-type MG turrets amidships. There are twin Lewis guns forward of the bridge. The masts remained brown.

COASTAL WARFARE CRAFT 12

ML 103
Fairmile 'A' Class 1940

The third WWII ML built, *103* is shown in original form. The hull is B6 grey and all the upperworks are 507c grey. The vessel is armed with a 3pdr aft, twin Lewis guns at the bow and more twin Lewis guns either side at the rear of the bridge. There are also five DCs per side. There are no throwers and the charges are dropped over the side during an attack. There are smoke canisters carried at the stern.

ML 106
Fairmile 'A' Class 1942

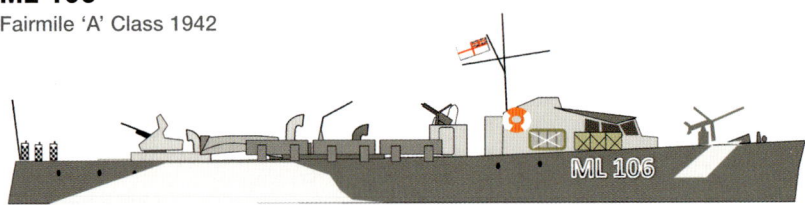

ML 106 became a minelayer and is shown here carrying six ground mines amidships. She is shown painted in 507b dark and 507c light grey. Mining operations mostly took place at night and this could have been quite effective in the light of a flare or a SL. The 3pdr has been moved forward, there is a twin 20mm aft and a twin 0.5in MG amidships. These vessels had three propellers for their Hall Scott petrol motors and could make 25 knots.

ML 111
Fairmile 'A' Class 1940

ML 111 is shown in 507b dark grey and 507c while operating as a rescue vessel for crashed air crew. The structure amidships is a cabin for rescued men. Armament is a single 3pdr and three twin Lewis guns. This vessel was lost in 1940 during the Battle of Britain. Note the top of the bridge was painted black.

ML 108
Fairmile 'B' Class 1943

New Zealand operated twelve Fairmile 'B' class during WWII. Most saw action in and around the Solomon Islands. The armament comprised single 20mm Oerlikons fore and aft as well as single 0.5in MGs each side of the bridge rear. They had been intended as submarine chasers but instead operated in the typical ML role of patrol and general duties. The hull is 1941 blue or a USN colour. The upper areas are 507c or US haze grey.

ML 065
Fairmile 'B' Class 1942

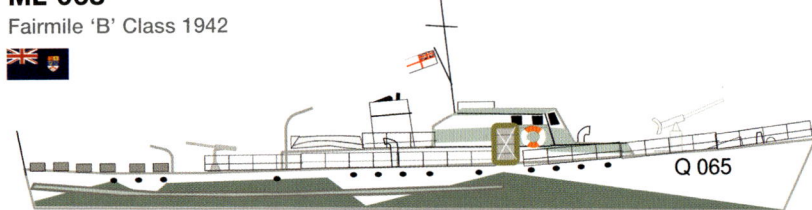

The Fairmile 'B' group were much larger and better sea boats than the earlier 'A' type. This one is shown armed with a 3pdr forward and a single 0.5in MG aft. The ship's boat is carried behind the funnel and handled by a davit. The penalty for size was that, with only two shafts, they were five knots slower than the 'A' boats. The scheme is white overall, broken with areas of MS3.

ML 084
Fairmile 'B' Class 1942

This Fairmile 'B' has a 1941 blue hull and MS4a grey upper common to many larger ships. Her armament comprised a 3pdr forward and a twin 0.5in MG aft. The ship's small dingy was carried on its side amidships and handled by a derrick. There are six single DCs carried on each side aft. These did not have throwers and were simply released to fall over the side when used.

ML 303
Fairmile 'B' Class 1944

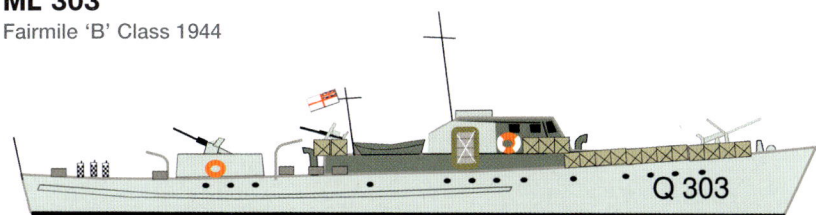

Although slower than the original Fairmile 'A', the 'B' type could carry more weight and were better at sea. This drawing shows *ML 303* off Normandy in 1944; numerous splinter mats were fitted, suggesting that this boat was one of those expected to get very close inshore to land troops or provide fire support. The 3pdr was moved forward, there is a 20mm amidships and a 40mm Bofors gun aft. Only a few DCs are carried. The scheme is one of MS4 on a very washed-out MS3. The single funnel has been removed. There are smoke canisters aft.

ML 579
Fairmile 'B' Class 1944

ML 579 is shown in a scheme using 1940 green and a pale version of MS3 just prior to her loss. The armament has been changed to a single 6pdr gun aft and two single 20mm on the centreline. Type 291Q radar for coastal craft is carried at the masthead.

ML 343
Fairmile 'B' Class 1944

Similar but not the same, *ML 343* wears a blue-on-white scheme generally the same as *ML 344* but with variations that distinguish the two. Gun armament is similar except that amidships the single 20mm has been replaced by a twin 0.303in MG mount. Note the scheme has been carried over the splinter mats and the Carley rafts.

ML 121
Fairmile 'B' Class 1942

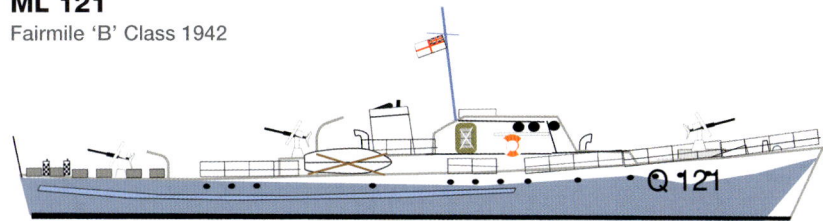

ML 121 has a very simple camouflage scheme comprising a B5 panel that does not go all the way to the bow and pale 507c above it. She is well-armed with three single 20mm on the centreline. There are six DCs per side on droppers. The ship's boat is carried on its side amidships.

ML 344
Fairmile 'B' Class 1944

ML 344 is depicted in a scheme similar in many ways to the WA scheme usually found on larger warships, but with a darker blue. There is a row of seven DCs per side. The 3pdr gun has been moved forward and a single 20mm AA amidships, but aft there is a single Rolls-Royce 2pdr protected by splinter mats. These Mk XIV guns were mostly issued to MLs and were originally less than satisfactory, but experience with them and modifications made them a much more effective weapon.

ML 814
Fairmile 'B' Class 1944

This Australian ML has a complex camouflage in three shades of blue, none of which appear official. As well as DC droppers, it has two throwers to make it a more effective ASW craft. These vessels operated close inshore around various Pacific islands. They were maids of all work, ferrying troops and supplies, providing support, and normal patrol duties.

ML 823
Fairmile 'B' Class 1944

ML 823 was built for the RAN in 1943. These craft spent a lot of time operating in New Guinean waters and, being completed later, they were better armed than the original plans had specified. *ML 823* is shown in blue overall, as was common when working with the USN. Her forward gun is a single 40mm Bofors. There are single 20mm amidships and aft. There are also single 0.5in MGs at the rear of the bridge. These ships had ASDIC for hunting Japanese supply submarines, but also spent a lot of time hunting down supply barges etc.

ML 177
Fairmile 'B' Class 1942

ML 177 wore a complicated camouflage of MS2, PB10 and white. In general, this type of camouflage could be very effective but was difficult for a small crew to maintain. There is a single 3pdr forward and a 2pdr aft. There were twin stripped Lewis guns each side of the bridge rear.

ML 288
Fairmile 'B' Class 1942

ML 288 was sunk in 1942. The vessel is shown here in a typical mid-war camouflage style. The principle was to have colours that were only a few shades apart with the intent that at a distance they would blend together and make the ship nearly invisible. The exact shades are unknown and could be unofficial. The boat is shown armed with a 3pdr forward, twin MGs both side of the bridge and a twin 0.5in MG aft.

ML 120
Fairmile 'B' Class 1940

In 1940, some 'B' type MLs were armed with two 21in torpedo tubes, that had been removed from some of the ex-US destroyers, to act as MTBs. These were removed from most in 1941 when the danger of invasion by Germany had passed. In addition to the torpedo tubes; this unit has a 3pdr forward and a single MG aft. See drawing below. Six DCs are still carried on droppers each side of the vessel. Colours were B6 and 507c.

ML 120
Fairmile 'B' Class 1943

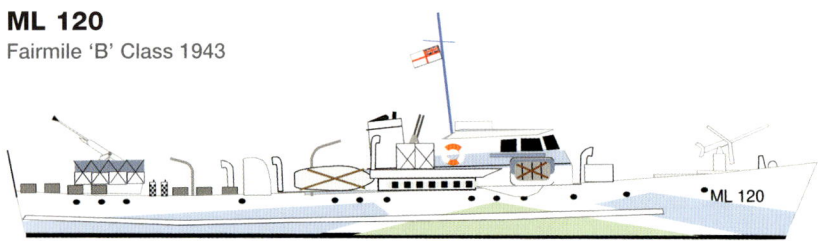

Although most MLs fitted with torpedo tubes landed them within a short time, this does not seem to have applied to all of them. Here is a drawing of *ML 120* in 1943, still carrying torpedo tubes. The gun armament has been modified. There is now a Rolls-Royce 2pdr aft and twin MGs port and starboard aft of the bridge. The 3pdr is still forward. This ML has adopted a distinctly WA scheme of WA green and WA blue on white.

ML 251
Fairmile 'B' Class 1942

ML 251 is shown wearing all-over dark B507 grey while operating in the minelayer role. Four ground mines per side are carried and all DCs landed. There are single 20mm Oerlikon guns fore and aft. No other weapons carried to save weight for the mines. There are plenty of smoke canisters carried on the stern.

RML 529
Fairmile 'B' Class 1943

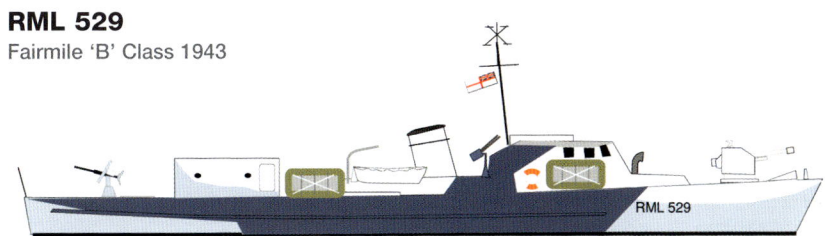

Around fifty MLs were converted to rescue launches particularly for use in the English Channel and North Sea where the rescue of downed aircrew was a daily task. There is a large cabin aft for treatment and transport of rescued fliers. However, these craft often had to work right into waters very close to enemy-held coasts and, as such, they needed to be well-armed. *RML 529* is shown here with a 6pdr gun forward, a single 20mm aft and twin MGs each side at the rear of the bridge. The boat is carried in easy launch position and there are four Carley rafts. The PB10 blue area makes the vessel look shorter against WA blue and WS white.

AAL HAMPTON
Fairmile 'B' Class 1943

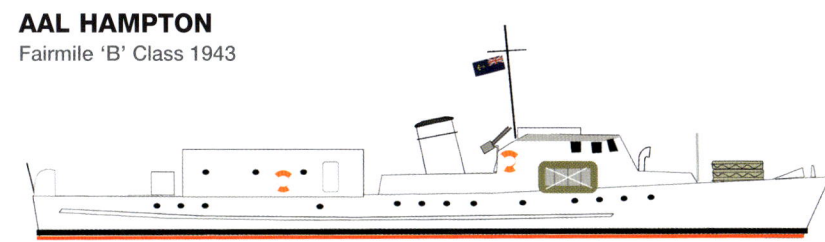

The Admiralty had some Fairmile 'B' class converted into Ambulance Tenders. These were used to transport casualties from incoming ships to shore establishments for treatment. As these were not commissioned ships, they were manned and run by the Admiralty as Fleet Auxiliaries and carried that flag. They were not protected by international law or recognised as Hospital Ships and some carried twin MGs for AA protection. Later, when German air attacks became unlikely, these guns were removed. The vessels were white overall, with a red waterline highlighted with a black boot topping.

MGB 328
Fairmile 'C' Class 1942

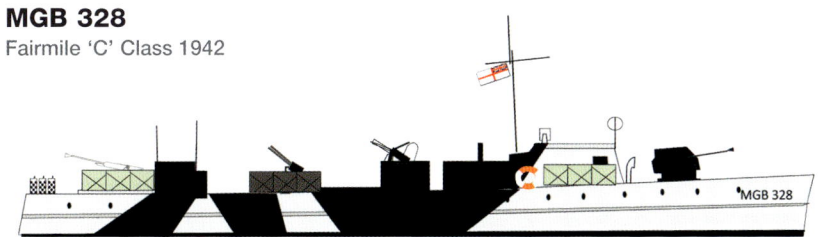

The Fairmile 'C' class were Motor Gunboats intended to provide some back-up support for the MTBs, which in the early part of WWII were very lightly armed and vulnerable to E-boats and other patrol craft. The vessel is shown in a simple black on MS4a grey. There is a powered single 2pdr gun forward and a single Rolls-Royce type at the stern. Twin 0.5in MGs are mounted aft of the bridge, twin 0.303in MGs amidships. There are no DCs, but smoke canisters are carried aft.

MGB 312
Fairmile 'C' Class 1942

MGBs were being out-gunned by their German opposition and were given a heavier armament. Here, *MGB 328* still has the usual 2pdrs but now also has two twin powered 20mm mountings amidships as well. The vessel is MS4a overall with B6 forward and black paint amidships. There is 507a aft. These vessels had no funnel and discharged their exhaust fumes out of the side of the engine room amidships.

HMS LEVANDOU
French CH 41 Class 1941

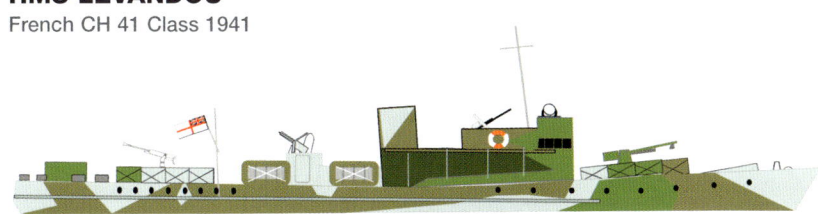

The French *CH 43* was taken over by the RN in 1940 and was used as a large gunboat in support of MTBs. The single French WWI model 75mm field gun forward is the only original weapon remaining. There are single 20mm Oerlikons either side of the bridge, twin 0.5in MGs on the centreline amidships and a single Rolls-Royce type 2pdr aft. There are some DCs carried aft on droppers. The early-war paint scheme is MS4 and 1940 green on 507c grey; well suited to coastal operations.

MGB 43
BPB Type 1940

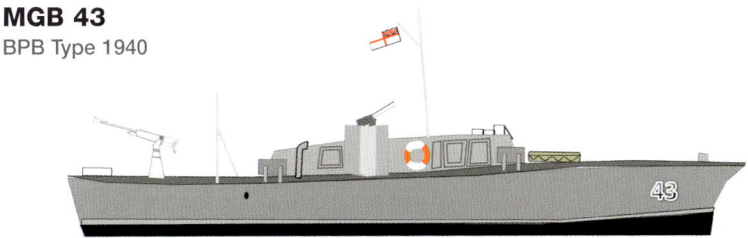

Numerous small anti-submarine craft were built in 1939–40 but it was quickly realised that they were of little value in the ASW role and they were converted to MGBs to support other coastal forces. *MGB 43* shown here has completed in plain MS4a grey but with dark grey decks. The 2pdr aft is in light grey and all masts were white. There were twin MGs in tubs either side of the bridge. Four DCs were carried but there were intended for the mining effect against enemy craft, not submarines.

MGB 13
BPB Type 1941

1941 blue on lighter blue-grey with white at the bow was a scheme adopted in various forms by British coastal craft. The patterns often varied in shape and sometimes green was substituted if available. The white at the bow is an obvious shortening effect or an attempt to give the impression of speed. Dark areas at the stern were necessary to enable following ships to keep station when moving at high speed in low visibility. *MGB 13* has been given a single 20mm aft, single 0.303in MGs on either side amidships and twin 0.5in MGs on either side of the bridge front.

MGB 79
BPB Type 1942

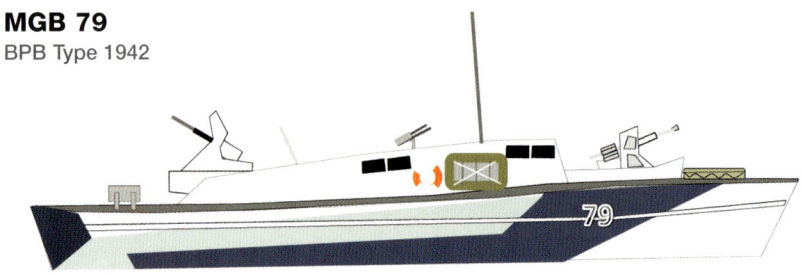

MGB 79 was built in 1942 and, in view of the previous boats being too lightly armed, they were up-gunned. She is shown with twin 20mm aft, a single 2pdr forward and twin 0.303in MGs on each side of the bridge. The scheme involves white overall with 1941 blue and WA blue. There is a large white area at the bow to confuse length and speed.

MGB 100
Higgins Type 1941

MGB 100 is depicted in a style utilising WA blue on white with only a medium blue curved panel. There is a 20mm Oerlikon aft and twin MGs in each bridge wing. Some sister boats were converted to MTBs while still being completed. This group were received under Lend-Lease, having originally been under construction in the USA for Finland.

MGB 64
BPB Type 1942

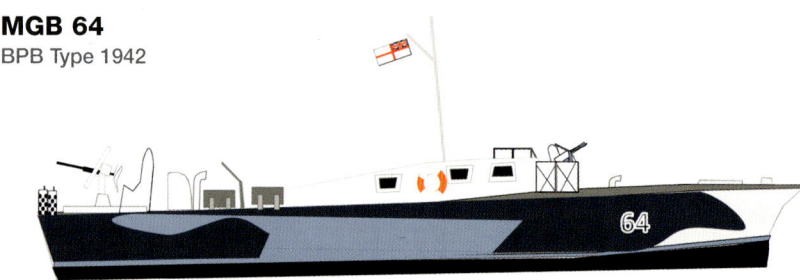

MGB 64 is shown with a variation of the scheme worn by *MGB 13*. There is white at the bow but, in this case, on the superstructure as well. The blue is darker and probably PB10. There are twin 0.5in MGs forward either side of the bridge where they have a very wide arc of fire. There is a 20mm aft and the vessel carries two DCs per side. Intended to provide support for MTBs, these vessels, though very fast, were found to be far too lightly armed when fighting German coastal warfare craft.

MGB 53
BPB Type 1941

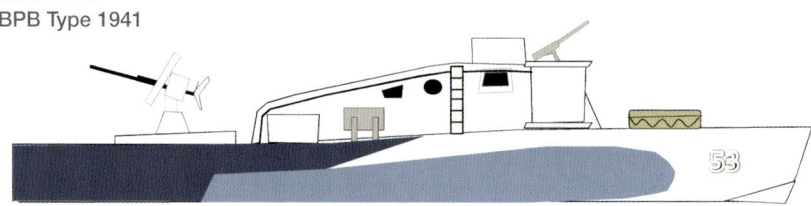

1941 blue with lighter blue-grey then white makes for an effective shortening effect. Dark colours at the stern helped with station-keeping, especially at high speed. Mid shades amidships and white forward were intended to give a false impression of speed while conferring a certain amount of concealment at a distance. This boat is armed with a single 20mm aft and twin MGs in tubs at the front of the bridge. A DC is also shown either side of the bridge.

MGB 123
BPB Type 1942

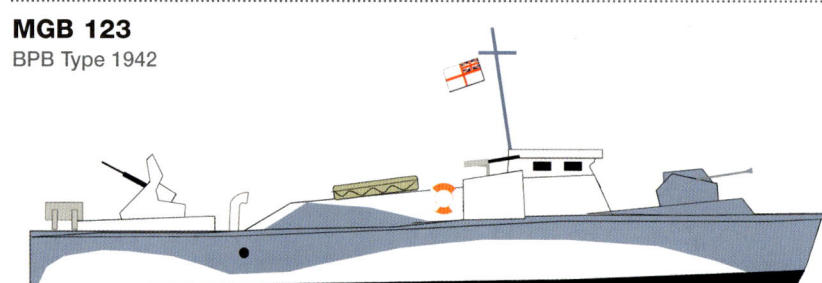

The blue and white theme is used here to produce a false bow impression of speed. There is a power-operated 2pdr single forward and a twin power-operated 20mm AA aft with twin 0.303in MGs in the bridge wings. The gradual upgrading of armament was an acknowledgement that enemy coastal craft were powerful opponents.

COASTAL WARFARE CRAFT

MTB 33
Vosper Type 1941

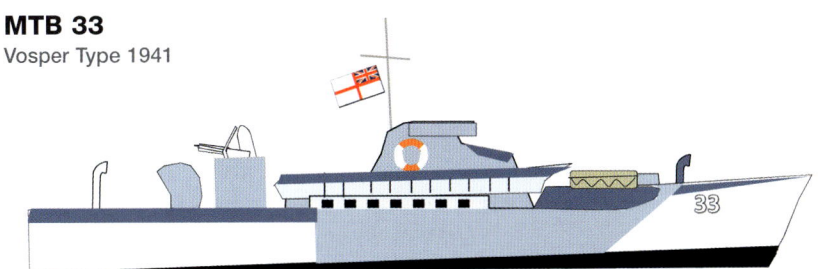

This blue panel on white scheme became a standard in British home waters for some time. The decks were dark grey. The only gun armament comprises a pair of twin 0.5in MGs aft of the bridge. Two torpedo tubes are carried but they were frail in comparison to their opponents. Larger units could have been built quite early but it was considered larger numbers were important.

MTB 66
Vosper Type 1941

MTB 66 is shown wearing the official 'light' version of the scheme shown on MTB 33. It was a simple WA pale blue on white. Decks were dark grey.

MTB 424
White Type 1944

A green-on-white Admiralty design was introduced late in WWII. The forward section is white with much washed-out areas of MS3 followed by G45. This MTB is heavily armed with a 6pdr forward and a single 20mm Oerlikon aft. There are two torpedo tubes, smoke floats and a pair of DCs. Type 291 radar at the masthead, plus there is IFF on the mast.

MTB 363
Vosper Type 1944

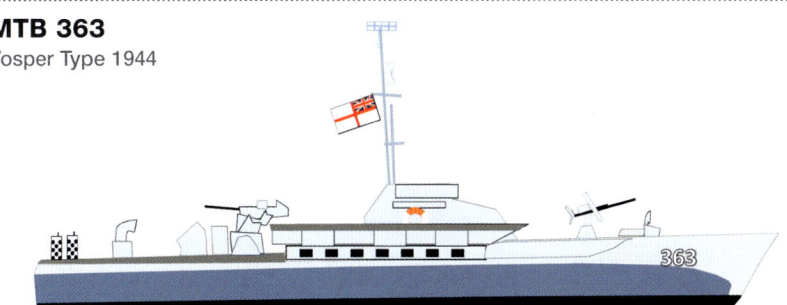

Mid-blue on pale blue forms the basis of this scheme. Although a small vessel, the idea of a blue panel to give a shortening effect seems to have been as popular with coastal craft as it was for larger ships. Deck colour, as usual, was dark grey. There is a single 20mm forward and a twin power-operated 0.5in MG mounting aft. Type 293 radar is carried as well as hourglass-style Type 253 IFF.

MTB 520
BPB Type 1944

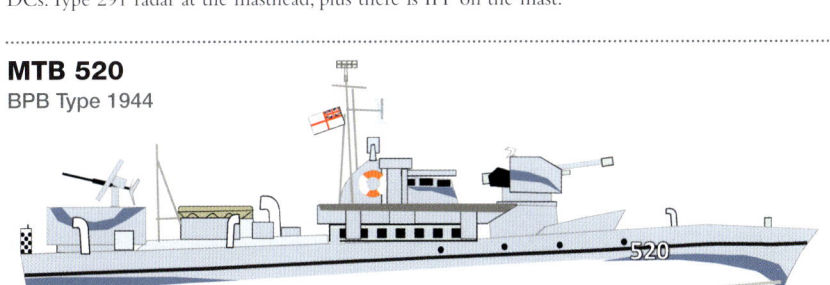

MTB 520 shows an interesting design which uses the common curved coloured panel but in white with a fore and aft edging of mid-blue. The rest of the vessel is pale, possibly WA blue, but with some sections of mid-blue. The vessel is very heavily armed and shown with a 6pdr forward, a 20mm aft and two torpedo tubes. There were also twin light MGs.

MTB 509
BPB Type 1944

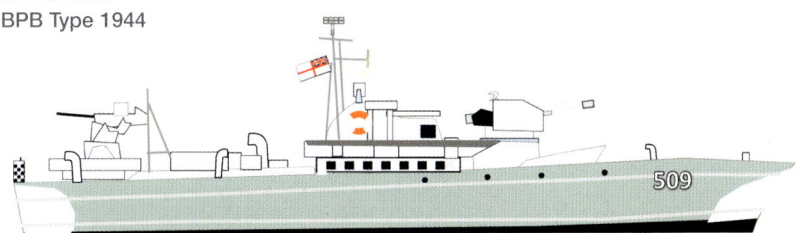

MTB 509 displays a hull panel in pale green-grey with the front and aft sections scalloped to show white to falsify her hull size. The upper works and armament are all white. There is a 6pdr forward, and a powered twin 0.5in MG mounting aft. Note Type 293 radar and Type 253 IFF carried as well. At high speed, the stern sat down and the bow lifted, which is why the deck forward tilts down when stationary or moving slowly.

MTB 378
Vosper Type 1944

On an overall white boat, this Vosper MTB has a 1941 blue panel amidships which curves down at the stern and is rounded at the bow. It was a common form of camouflage for coastal craft, but often not quite so nicely rounded. There is a single 20mm forward and a power-operated twin 0.5in MG aft. Type 291 radar is carried.

MTB 311
Elco 80 Type 1944

This boat shows the usual curved panel at the bow, but it becomes darker near the stern. The front of the hull is pale WA blue rather than white and goes through a pale blue then mid-blue to give the effect of the vessel getting darker near the stern. There are single 20mm fore and aft plus staggered twin 0.5in MGs port and starboard.

MTB 660
Fairmile 'D' 1943

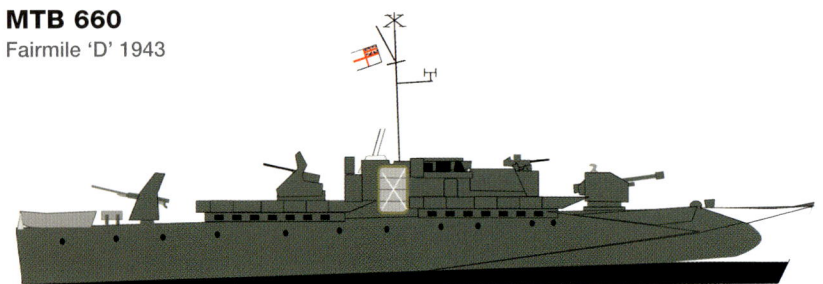

Cooperation between the Admiralty and Fairmile resulted in a large and powerful type of boat that could take on an E-boat and other German coastal craft and outgun most. *MTB 660* is shown here with four 21in torpedo tubes. There is a 6pdr gun forward, a powered twin 20mm mounting amidships and a single Rolls-Royce 2pdr aft. There are twin 0.5in MGs on either side of the bridge front and twin light MGs in each bridge wing. A formidable volume of fire! There is Type 291U radar at the masthead and a Type 244 IFF projecting from the mast. The vessel is depicted wearing MS2 with a small patch of white, a standard scheme devised for this class.

MTB 267
Elco 70 Type 1944

This Elco boat has white at the bow and on the superstructure, light grey-green amidships and MS2 aft. All of the guns and torpedo tubes are WS white. Although the gun armament is weak, the boat has four torpedo tubes. She carries US-type radar.

MTB 607
Fairmile 'D' 1943

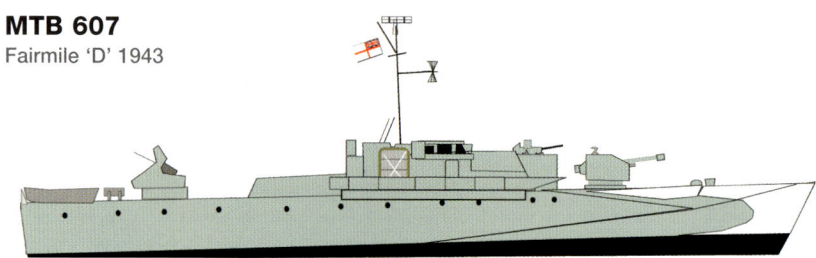

MTB 607 is depicted with the light version of the scheme worn by *MTB 660*. The general pattern is the same but the shade is MS3 or G45. The boat only carries two torpedo tubes. There is a powered twin 20mm aft, twin light MGs in each bridge wing, twin 0.5in MGs on each forward side of the bridge and a 6pdr forward. The armament of the 'D' type varied considerably and it is hard to find a standard boat in photographs.

MGB 673
Fairmile 'D' 1943

As there are no torpedo tubes, this 'D' type was given an MGB designation. In this form, they could make 32 knots as opposed to the MTBs where the weight slowed them to 27.5 knots. The camouflage is a simplified variation on the official Admiralty design, but in dark grey G10. Some were in B15. Instead of the curved area at the bow, the white panel follows the undercut. There is a power-operated 2pdr forward, twin power-operated 0.5in MGs on each side of the bridge front, a twin 20mm powered mount on the coach and a power-operated 6pdr aft. There are twin light MGs in the bridge wings. Type 291 radar is at the masthead, Type 253 hourglass IFF on the mast projection.

HMS GREY OWL SGB305
Steam Gunboat 1944

HMS GREY SHARK SGB306
Steam Gunboat 1944

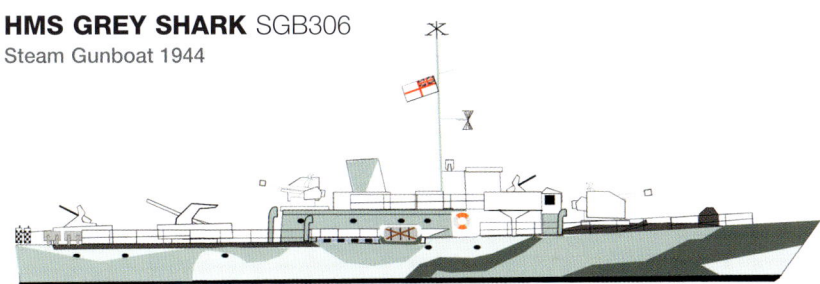

Steam gunboats were developed as the heavy backup for coastal forces where large support ships could not penetrate due to shallow waters. Although originally only numbered, all but *SGB 7* (lost 1942) were later given names with 'Grey' in them, *Grey Wolf*, *Grey Owl*, *Grey Goose* etc. Because of their size, they had a camouflage scheme designed for them and most used something fairly close to it. Here, *Grey Owl* is shown with MS2 or B30 and washed-out MS3 on an overall white hull. The armament shown is heavy – a 20mm bow chaser and a 6pdr forward of the bridge. There are single 20mm on the bridge wings and 6pdr aft of the funnel. A 3in gun is carried on the quarter-deck with a Rolls-Royce 2pdr right aft. However, the actual armament of the class varied considerably and changed from time to time as improvements were made.

Grey Shark is shown in a somewhat more elaborate scheme involving three shades of green with white upper works and guns. The pattern is different to *Grey Owl* but concentrates on much the same colours and style. There are two single 6pdrs and a single 3in aft. There are twin 20mm power mountings in each bridge wing and another right aft. Single torpedo tubes were also carried. As armament increased, the speed of these vessels dropped, but they were formidable coastal warfare craft.

HDML 1322
1944

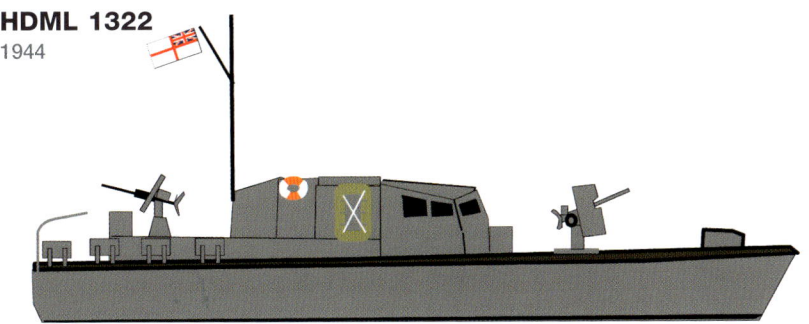

Harbour Defence Motor Launches naturally operated in, around or on the outskirts of harbours. As such, they were rarely camouflaged but were mostly painted in dark grey such as 507b. This is a US-built one supplied to Australia. It has a 2pdr forward and a 20mm aft. The deck is a darker grey again. These boats were intended to operate in groups, forming defensive lines line abreast or in a successive chain. Eight DCs could be carried.

13 SUBMARINES

H 31
'H' Class 1939

'H' class submarines were built in large numbers during WWI and were still in service for training when WWII broke out. Nonetheless, *H 31* and *H 39* were lost in action 1940-1. The paint scheme in use for the boats was MS4a grey with dark 507a grey decks. The rear section was painted black to hide exhaust fumes. The periscope standards were white. The great value of this group was in the training role where they helped new ASW ships get ready to detect U-boats when on convoy duty. They were referred to as 'Clockwork Mice' when they followed a set course while new escort crews tried to detect them. On a dummy attack being made, a hand grenade was dropped and, if the submarine conceded it was on target, it acknowledged the hit.

L 23
'L' Class 1939

Only three 'L' class submarines remained in service at the outbreak of WWII. Only a few operational patrols were carried out in the very darkest days of the war. Their duties mostly comprised training new crews to take over more modern submarines being built. All went to Canada in 1944 to assist ASW training for new escorts. *L 23* is depicted in MS4a but with the upper half of the conning tower painted white, and with a white area at the bow. The stern was painted black even in peacetime to hide diesel fume stains. The deck was 507a as were the saddle tanks.

HMS ODIN N84
'O' Class 1939

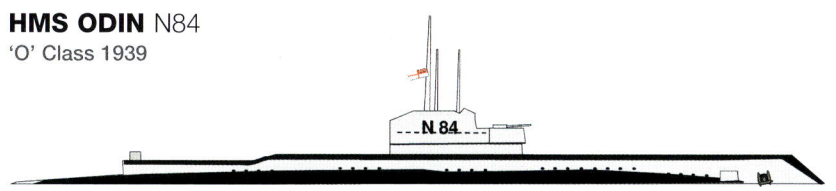

Odin and others of her class were in the East Indies at the outbreak of war and were transferred to the Mediterranean in 1940 where she and most of her class were sunk. The boat is shown in 507c grey with black decks and saddle tanks. Note that the black deck extended down the broad sloped bow to the waterline. These boats were not considered very successful and it was intended to replace them rather quickly had war not broken out. Instead, when sent to the Mediterranean, they were relatively easy kills for the Italian Navy, which was very proficient in ASW.

HMS OTUS N92
'O' Class 1941

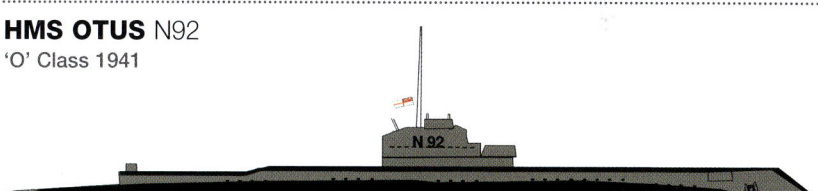

Otus, of the second group of 'O' class boats, was used on supply runs to Malta during the Axis blockade. She is shown here in 507b dark grey but the areas previously black remain so. The deck gun has been removed to save weight for cargo and there are twin light MGs at the rear of the bridge. The main periscopes are protected in a cover and the position of the diving planes was different on the second batch of boats. It was not realised for some time that very dark submarines could be seen from the air while submerged in the clear waters of the Mediterranean.

HMS PERSEUS N36
'P' Class 1940

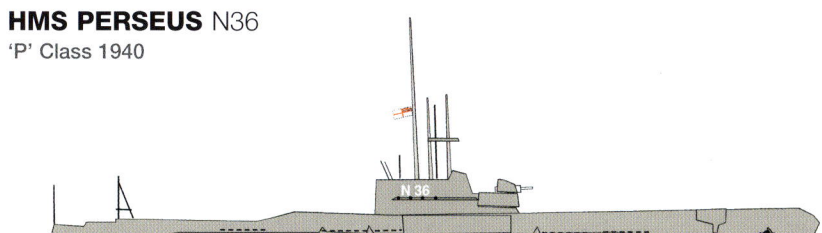

Perseus is shown in the Mediterranean where, to overcome the danger of being sighted underwater by aircraft flying directly overhead, she has been painted in a mid-grey all over, including horizontal surfaces. Dark objects could be seen underwater from a low-flying aircraft. The pennant is in white.

HMS REGENT N41
'R' Class 1941

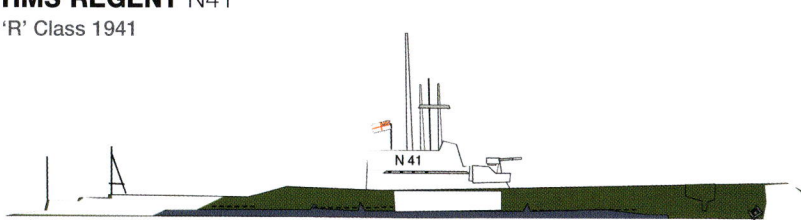

Regent is shown in white and 1940 green with 1941 blue saddle tanks in the period before standard submarine schemes were adopted. The decks may also have been 1941 blue. The general style is similar to an official pattern later used. Various measures were tried to make boats less visible from the air, but the toll of submarine losses to the Italian navy and air force remained high.

HMS CLYDE N12
'River' Class 1943

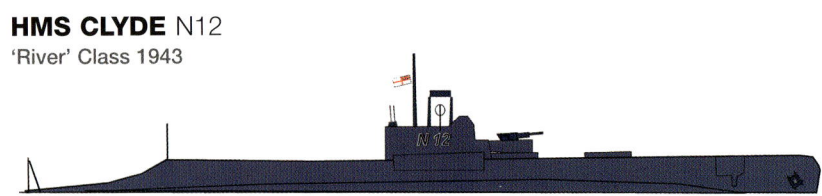

1941 blue was a colour tried by submarines for concealment in the Mediterranean and *Clyde* is shown here in that scheme. It was an all-over style covering vertical and horizontal surfaces. Despite the all-over scheme, the pennant number has been left still clearly visible on the conning tower because there was an ever-present danger of being torpedoed by friendly submarines, as happened several times.

HMS SATYR P214
'S' Class 1943

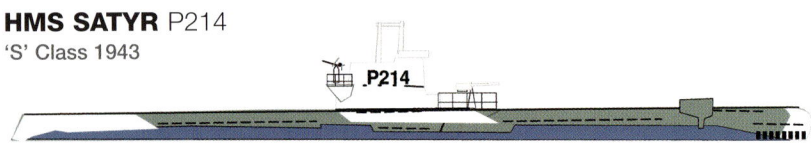

The official Admiralty scheme allowed for a dark and a light version of the same style. This depicts the light version which comprised G45 and B20. It was designated as being for Foreign Service including the Mediterranean. The deck was black. Periscope standards were white as was the conning tower and panels at bow and stern.

HMS SEAWOLF N47
'S' Class 1941

Pale 507c grey but with black saddle tanks and horizontal surfaces was worn by *Seawolf* in 1942. The 'S' class boats were said to be some of the most reliable and safest operational units in the RN submarine service. *Seawolf* is shown here in her as-built state. A 20mm AA was added to the rear of the conning tower later.

HMS TANTIVY P319
'T' Class 1943

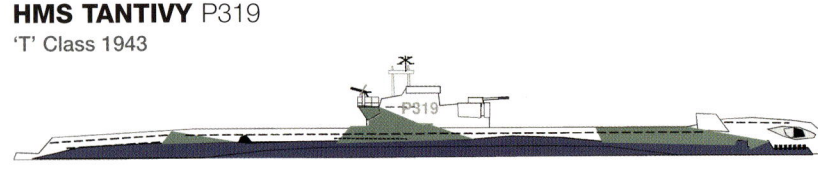

Only a few 'T' class submarines adopted this style of camouflage. The colours are the same as the Admiralty dark type shown on HMS *Safari*. These boats were considered very reliable and saw worldwide service. Radar was fitted to the later boats on completion.

HMS PORPOISE N14
Porpoise Class Minelayer 1941

Porpoise was a minelaying submarine and is depicted in all-over MS2. She operated in home waters for much of the war but did some supply runs to Malta in 1941 before going to the Eastern Fleet. The clarity of the water in the Mediterranean resulted in several experiments with colour to avoid being seen by patrolling aircraft even when submerged. Her sister ship HMS *Seal* was captured by the Kriegsmarine after heavy damage from gas leaking from her batteries.

HMS SAFARI P211
'S' Class 1942

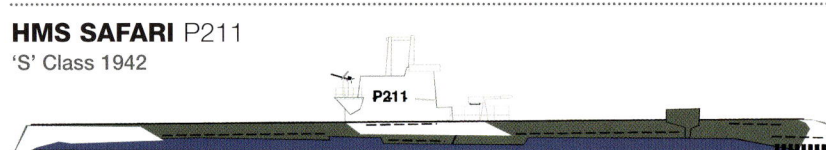

Safari is depicted in the dark official submarine scheme designed by the Admiralty, B30 with white for the vertical surfaces and PB10 blue for all horizontal surfaces. Camouflage was extremely important for submarines working in the closer waters they operated in. Time on the surface was often in waters heavily patrolled and they were unable to lose themselves in the vastness of the Atlantic while charging batteries as U-boats could.

HMS STORM P233
'S' Class 1942

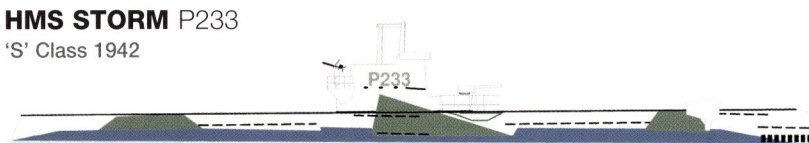

This boat is shown in a variant of the official light scheme which carries part of the G45 up onto the conning tower. It also has more of the casing in white than the Admiralty design. Similarly, this design was used in the darker colours on some units. Decks were black or very dark grey.

HMS TRIBUNE N76
'T' Class 1940

Tribune is depicted here in overall B30, except for decks and saddle tanks which were black. The RN seems to have experienced difficulty in settling on a colour suited for where most submarines were to see service. What suited one region did not necessarily suit another. *Tribune* was a boat of the first group of 'T' class submarines and completed for service only a few months before WWII broke out.

HMS TALLY HO P317
'T' Class 1944

By late WWII, PB10 dark blue was the most common scheme for British submarines operating with the Eastern Fleet and the few still working the Mediterranean. This 'T' class boat has eight bow tubes and three facing the stern. Two of these and two of the bow tubes were carried externally under the casing and could not be reloaded at sea. Type 291W radar was able to give a warning of single enemy aircraft at five nautical miles and twenty-five miles for a formation, which greatly reduced the risk of attack by ASW aircraft. Note pennant number not worn.

HMS UNITY N66
'U' Class 1939–40

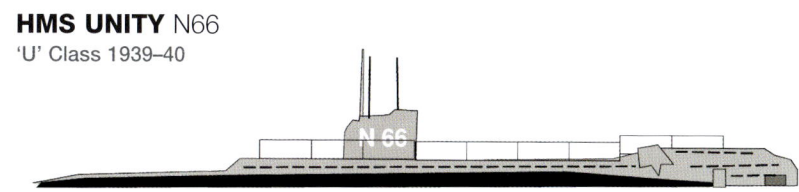

Unity is shown in overall MS4a grey vertical surfaces, black saddle tanks and decks. Note that in the early part of WWII it was common for British submarines to wear large pennant identification numbers on the conning tower to avoid inexperienced airmen mistaking them for German U-boats.

HMS UNRIVALLED P45
'U' Class 1943

Unrivalled was a later unit of the 'U' class and was fitted with a deck gun. There is also Type 291W radar on the conning tower. Her scheme is based on that of Admiralty instructions, using B30 with white, but only a few of this class ever wore camouflage. Most were plain grey with black decks.

B 3
'U' Class 1943

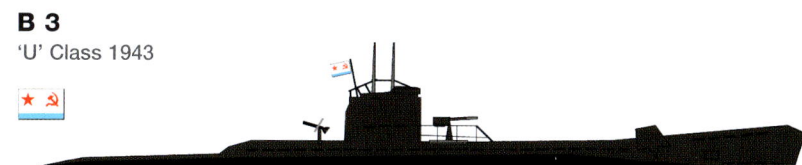

HMS *Unison* was transferred to the Soviet Northern Fleet in 1944 and returned in 1949. She is shown in typical Soviet submarine-style grey with black saddle tanks. Decks black.

HMS VAGABOND P18
'V' Class 1943

Vagabond is shown wearing the official Admiralty dark scheme for submarines but only a few of her class were painted to this standard. Most were dark G10 grey or dark B30 grey-green. A few were very dark B20 blue. The 'V' class were an improvement over the 'U' class, being easier and less expensive to build. After the Italian Armistice, the construction of these boats was cut back as they were of limited range and really only of use in European waters.

HMS GRAPH N46
Type VIIC 1943

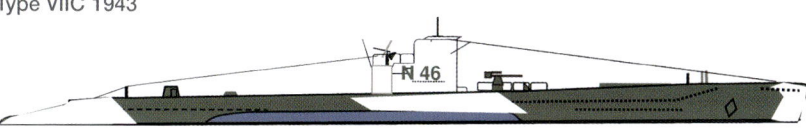

Graph, formerly *U 570*, was a captured Type VIIC U-boat, taken in 1941 and entered into service with the RN. She is shown in a British-style scheme and carrying a prominent pennant number. The boat was put through extensive trials to discover the good and bad points of the design. While operating in that role, it was necessary to make her easily distinguishable as 'British' because she had to operate in UK home waters, always in danger of being sunk by defensive forces. Keeping her capture secret was another reason for making her look as British as possible. As soon as trials and as much intelligence as possible had been obtained, *Graph* was occasionally returned to looking German and used on special operations, including some that were clandestine in nature.

14 MISCELLANEOUS VESSELS

MISCELLANEOUS VESSELS

HMS LADYBIRD
'Insect' Class Gunboat 1939

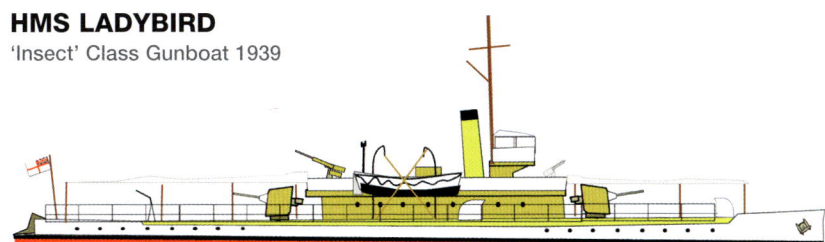

Ladybird and her sister ships spent most of their service on the China Station and various other colonial locations where a river gunboat was needed. The ship is shown here dressed to impress the locals in buff and white. The funnel is pre-war primrose. Canvas awnings are spread and the waterline in red and black. The main armament was made up of two 6in guns and a single 3in AA. There is also a Vickers MG mounted in front of the bridge. It is just as well nearly all the colonial era gunboats were withdrawn before Japan entered the war, as the few that remained were quickly wiped out. These ships had two funnels side by side.

HMS ASSISTANCE
Repair Ship 1944

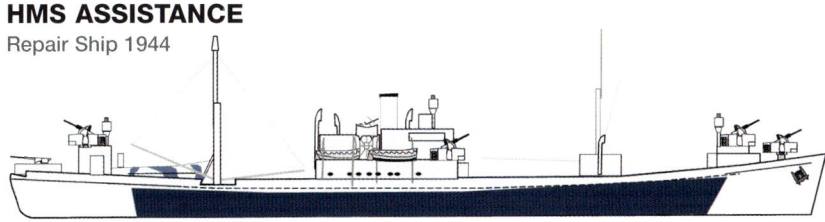

Assistance was one of five Liberty Ships offered to the RN under Lend-Lease converted to repair ships. In the event, three were retained by the USN with only this ship and *Diligence* serving the Royal Navy. As they were intended for use with the Pacific Fleet, they were heavily armed with a single 5in aft, ten 40mm Bofors in twin mounts and two single 20mm Oerlikons. These ships were not as extensively fitted for repair work as *Artifex* or *Wayland* (page 150), but nonetheless were well-fitted out. The paint scheme is US haze grey with a dark blue panel.

RFA WAVE KING X73
Tanker 1943

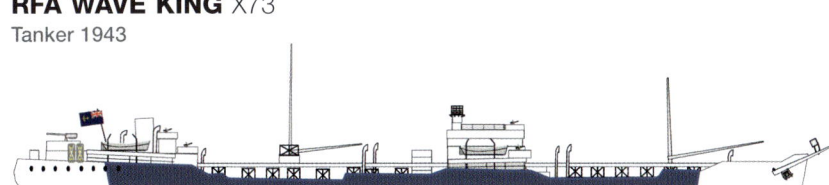

British naval tankers were manned by the Royal Fleet Auxiliary (RFA) and flew that flag rather than the White Ensign. Many were painted with a simple black hull and pale grey upper works, but those that travelled long distances as part of the fleet train were often camouflaged. *Ennerdale* is shown with simple blue area on the hull that gives a false impression of the length of the hull. Unlike the standard blue-panel style, this one follows the shape of the hull. The rest of the ship is 507c with G20 decks.

HMS LADYBIRD
'Insect' Class Gunboat 1941

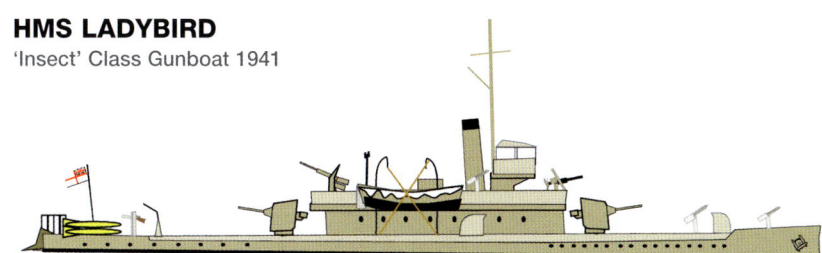

Ladybird and others had most of their weapons and fittings stripped when towed to India where they refitted and then went to join the Red Sea and Mediterranean forces. Although initially grey, *Ladybird* was sent to Tobruk after its capture and became a vital part of the defence during the siege. Almost a daily target of German and Italian aircraft, she was painted all over with MS4 and hid in a small inlet during daylight hours. Then, at night, she emerged to bombard enemy positions. Her AA armament was added to and she is shown with two Vickers MGs forward and another abreast the funnel, a single 20mm Oerlikon in front of the bridge and twin Lewis guns at the stern. Even after being sunk in shallow water, the upper works were used as an AA platform for the defence of the harbour.

RFA PETROBUS X7
Petroleum Carrier 1940

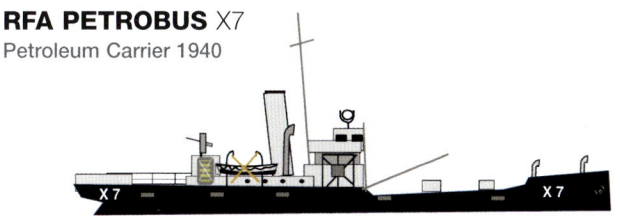

The 'Petro' class were petroleum carriers built for the RN in a period when requirements for petrol were modest. *Petrobus* is shown as she appeared in 1940 with a black hull and MS4a grey upper works. Her only armament is a twin Lewis gun aft of the funnel.

HMS DODMAN POINT
Landing Craft Depot Ship 1945

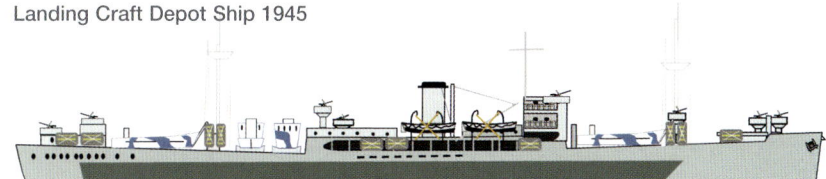

By 1943, there were many hundreds of small landing craft in service and the ships that carried them were not necessarily able to provide for their necessary maintenance and repair needs. Thus the demand for vessels able to act as depot and minor repair ships resulted in a decision to convert some standard Canadian war emergency merchant ships. Most entered service in 1944–5. Their armament was entirely light AA and comprised twenty 20mm Oerlikons. Some ships had singles, or a mix of twins and singles, while the last completed mostly had twin mountings. The paint scheme was MS3 overall with MS2 panel. All the masts and derricks were white.

HMS WAYLAND
Repair Ship 1944

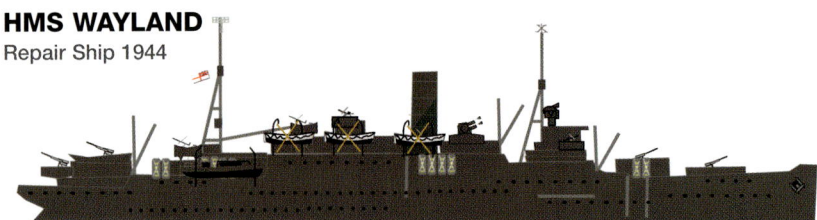

Wayland was the ex-liner *Antonia* which had been called up as an Armed Merchant Cruiser in 1939 but purchased outright in 1942 for an extensive conversion to a repair ship. Her three sister ships, *Aulania*, *Ausonia* and *Artifex*, were similarly converted. *Wayland* was the only one to carry four 4in AA guns; the others just had 20mm. *Wayland* had quad 2pdr mounts port and starboard just before the funnel, as well as eight single 20mm Oerlikons. She is depicted in a very sombre MS1 dark grey all over, which she seems to have worn throughout her service as a repair ship.

HMS STUART PRINCE
Fighter Direction Ship 1944

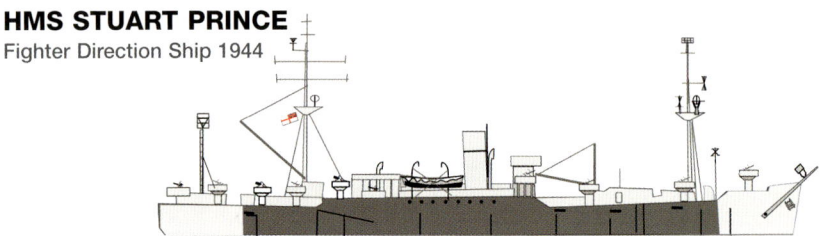

Fighter Direction Ships (FDSs) were vital for the control of aircraft over invasion areas and coordinating the defence of advancing troops near the coast. *Stuart Prince* was converted in 1943 and remained with the RN until sold in 1951. They carried extensive electronic equipment and could not only direct allied aircraft but also pick up enemy controllers and jam them. The Luftwaffe tried to triangulate the position of these vital targets to eliminate them. As a result, they were given a paint scheme rather similar to an ordinary merchant ship so they did not stand out. The ship is depicted with twenty-four 20mm Oerlikons, of which four are in twin mounts and the rest singles.

HMS BOXER
Fighter Direction Ship 1944

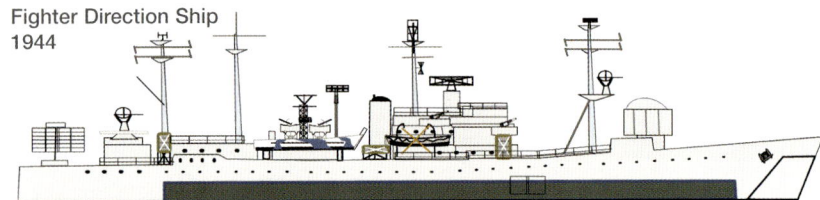

Boxer and her sisters *Bruizer* and *Thruster* were converted to FDSs for the invasion of Europe because their roomy tank decks could be divided into the many offices and compartments required for their complicated role. The camouflage has been kept simple with 507c and the usual later-war central panel but in MS2. As well as lifeboats, they also carried landing craft for resupply and general movement of personnel. Armament was two quad 2pdr AA and eight single 20mm. Built as RN pattern Tank Landing Ships, the doors were welded shut when converted to FDSs.

HMS ARTIFEX
Repair Ship 1944

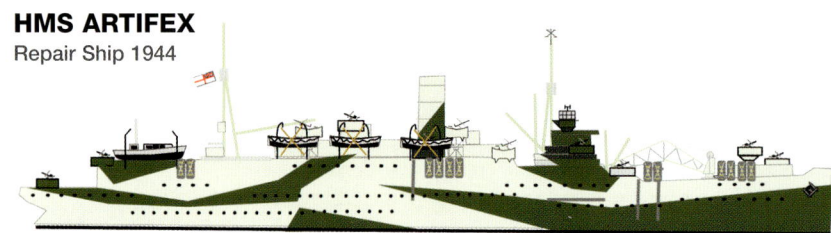

Artifex went to the Far East in 1943 as a heavy repair ship. She is shown carrying an Admiralty-designed scheme with duck egg green and 1940 green. Note this ship carried a large crane forward. Her AA armament comprised twenty 20mm Oerlikons in single mounts. *Artifex* was retained post-war and not scrapped until 1961. The conversion was so complete that even accommodation became limited and there was usually another ship, such as an old liner, present to provide extra accommodation. Compare the large repair workshop in the aft superstructure with *Wayland*, where the 4in guns prevented that.

HMS FDT 13
Fighter Direction Ship 1944

Three US-built LSTs were converted into FDSs. The bow doors were welded shut and a certain amount of armour was added with pig-iron ballast to compensate. These ships had extremely comprehensive electronics and radar. They had IFF and homing beacons to enable fighters to rendezvous for allocation to targets. The AA comprised a single 12pdr aft and twelve 20mm in a mix of twin and single mounts. Most of the offices were established in the tank deck. Crew were a mix of RN and RAF. The camouflage scheme was a common type for landing craft. It comprises overall duck egg blue, MS3 and 1940 blue. These vessels were also referred to as Fighter Direction Tenders. German detectors could find the approximate location of such ships and it was important that they looked much the same as any others that they might be in company with.

RFA BOXOL X10
Low Tank Deck Ship 1940

A series of low tank deck ships were built for the RN at the end of WWI. Most carried petrol or aviation fuel. Despite being small they were found in many locations where British ships were stationed. *Boxol* is shown here painted in a very serviceable black and khaki. The practice of having ships, whose names ended in 'Ol' for oiler, was extensive in the Royal Fleet Auxiliary (RFA) service. She is shown with a single 20mm aft.

MISCELLANEOUS VESSELS

RFA WAR HINDOO X87
Tanker 1942

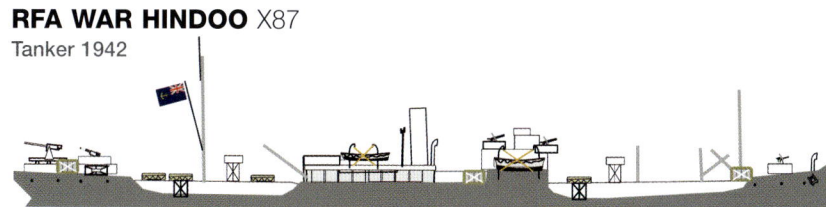

Ten of the 'War' class tankers built in WWI were still in service during WWII. They had been built to resemble standard freighters as oil tankers were a priority target for U-boats. The same applied in WWII. *War Hindoo* spent a lot of time serving the Eastern Fleet and is shown here with a B55 grey hull and washed-out 507c upper works so pale as to be almost white. Her armament comprises a single 4in gun aft with two 2pdrs, four single 20mm on the bridge and two more at the bow.

HMS GUARDIAN T89
Netlayer 1941

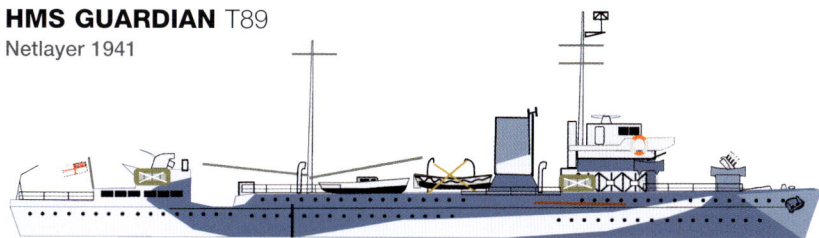

Guardian and her near sister *Protector* were built before WWII for the specific task of laying nets to protect defended harbours against submarines. In wartime, they proved very useful units and were used for more roles than just that which had been intended. *Guardian* could lay enough nets to render an open harbour safe within a few hours. Armament changed during the war but is illustrated here as a twin 4in AA aft, single 20mm in each bridge wing and a quad 0.5in MG mount forward in the place of a 4in gun previously carried there. On transfer to the Far East, the MGs were removed and eight more 20mm added. The scheme worn was designed for her and used washed-out 1940 blue, duck egg blue and a pale grey with a slight purple tinge.

HMS ADAMANT F64
Submarine Depot Ship 1942

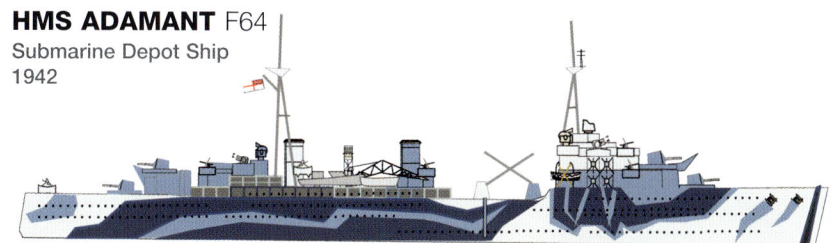

This is an unusual camouflage pattern indeed, using a variety of blue on grey shades to cause a confusion effect. The colours appear to have been MS4a, PB 10 and a dark duck egg blue. This class of submarine depot ships were expected to operate in forward areas, hence they were heavily armed. There are four twin 4.5in AA, four quad 2pdrs and sixteen 20mm Oerlikon. These vessels were not only well-equipped for the repair and support of submarines, but obviously a boon to the AA defence of any harbour.

RFA OLNA X47
Fleet Oiler 1940

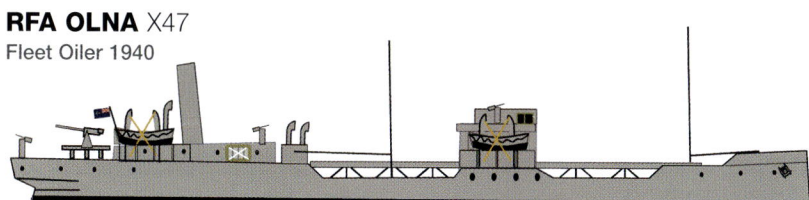

Olna was built in 1921 as a fleet oiler intended to be attached to various commands as required to provide refuelling facilities. However, she was not fitted for refuelling at sea. The ship gave extensive service but was beached and scuttled during the Crete operation in 1941 and another tanker bore the same name from 1944. Although many fleet auxiliaries had a black hull, the *Olna* was painted an overall darkened MS4a grey during her service in the Mediterranean. There was a LA 4in gun aft. The only AA comprises two twin Lewis Gun mounts in the bridge wings, another forward of the funnel and one right aft.

HMS FORTH
Submarine Depot Ship 1943

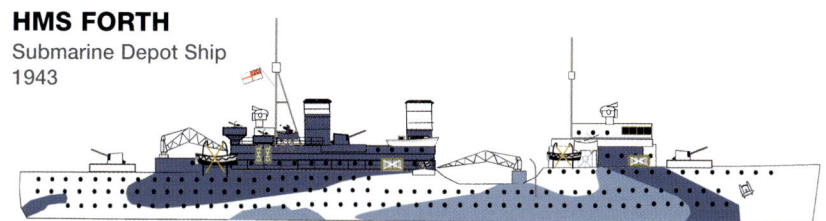

Forth was one of two sister ships built just prior to WWII. Her service was with the 3rd and 4th Submarine Flotillas in home waters, unlike her sister ship *Maidstone* which served in a wide range of war zones. *Forth* is depicted wearing an Admiralty-designed scheme in three colours utilising duck egg blue, 1941 dark blue and an overall 507c hull. Upper decks were G20 or similar. She was heavily armed with eight 4.5in AA in twin mounts, two quad 2pdr, two single 2pdr and at least five 20mm Oerlikons. Her support facilities were extensive.

HMS SPRINGDALE FY51
Mine Destructor Vessel 1942

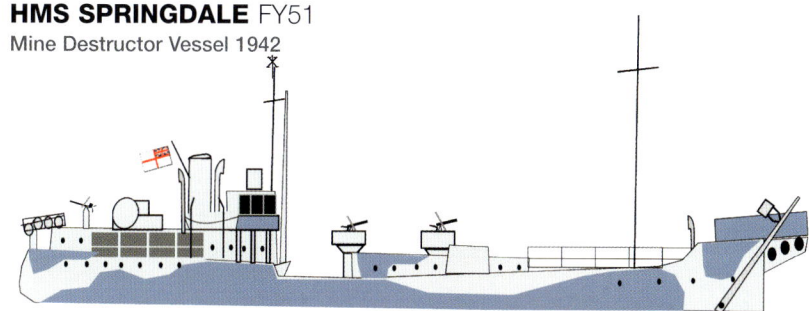

When magnetic mines first appeared, a group of colliers were taken into service and fitted with the means of detonating them. The problem was that the ships were slow and the mines often detonated too close, which damaged them. Eventually, other means of defeating influence mines were found and this ship, along with most of the others, became a support ship for minesweepers and minesweeping trawlers. Her scheme is 507c with a pale, possibly duck egg, blue.

HMS ATHENE D25
Aircraft Transport 1942

On the outbreak of WWII, the Admiralty realised there would be a need to transfer a variety of naval aircraft to various bases and to aircraft carriers. There were several Clan Line vessels under construction and two were converted for the task. *Athene* is shown here in a rather unusual camouflage that uses light blue and dark PB10 blue, on pale 507c grey, with some areas of white.

HMS PLOVER
Coastal Minelayer 1941

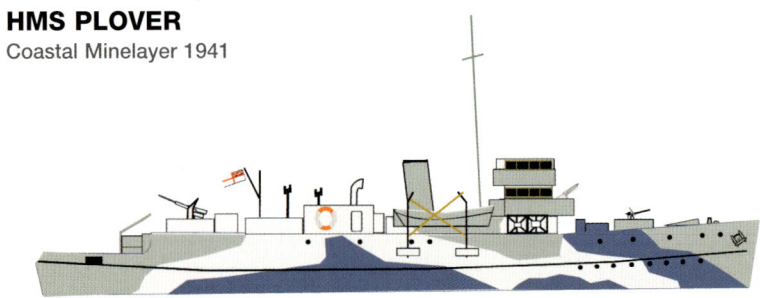

Plover served mostly in the English Channel and laid over 15,000 mines, mostly in defensive minefields. The little ship survived numerous dangerous situations despite her small size limiting the number of AA guns that could be carried without reducing her minelaying capacity. Her scheme is an Admiralty light type and typical of many ships serving in Home Waters and comprises 507c with MS3 and washed-out 1941 blue.

LST 3009
LST (3) 1944

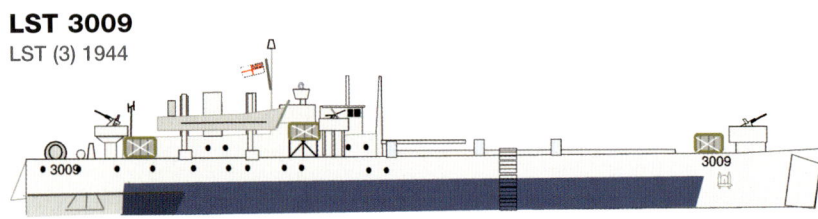

LST 3023
LST (3) 1944

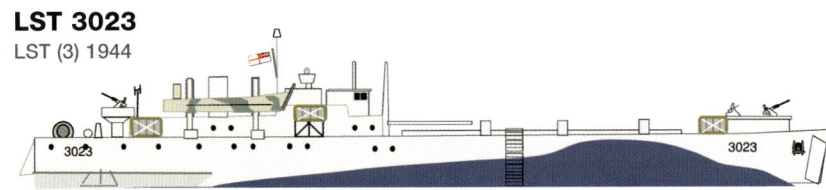

Type 3 LSTs were UK-built and, although mass-produced, were somewhat stronger than their US equivalents. Although intended to have a 12pdr AA aft, this unit has a 40mm Bofors instead. There are two more singles at the bow and single 20mm AA either side of the bridge. With 13kts top speed, the class were three knots faster than the US type. The vessel has a dark PB10 blue panel on the hull and MS4a grey elsewhere. There was a heavy undercut at the stern which created a shadow making that area look darker. Up to seven LCMs could be carried.

This LST (3) also has single 40mm as well as twin 20mm either side of the bow. There are single 20mm AA either side of the bridge. The short funnel was necessary as the class were powered by reciprocating steam engines. There is a LCP carried on davits either side of the superstructure. They could carry fifteen to twenty-five tanks depending on the size; up to fourteen lorries or 170 troops could be carried instead. They were also used for general duties carrying stores of all kinds to beachheads. Her colour scheme is the same as *LST 3009* but arranged in a different manner.

LST 61
LST (2) 1944

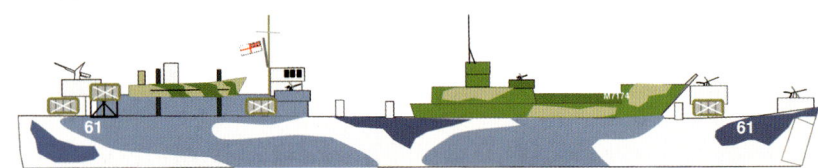

LST 305
LCT (2) 1944

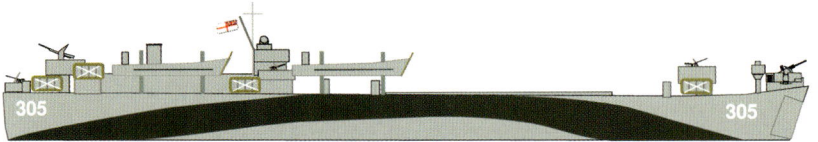

US-built Type 2 LSTs were used by the RN. They were fitted with a British 12pdr AA aft and the light AA comprised six 20mm. This vessel carries an LCT (5) on deck, which were launched by listing the ship and pushing them overboard with an accompanying large splash! Rough and ready but it worked. This LST is camouflaged in the British fashion with two shades of blue-grey on MS4a. The LCT and LCP carried are, however, in MS4 and 1940 green.

LST 305 is shown in MS3 overall, with MS2 in a simple curving wave along the side. The vessel has had a modification to its armament and carries a twin 40mm at the bow and three single 20mm as well as a 12pdr AA. Sailors of both the RN and USN claimed that LST stood for 'Large Slow Target'. Their top speed of 10 knots was, however, only a knot slower than Liberty Ships.

LCT 299
LCT (2) 1944

The British realised that the war could not be won without an eventual return to mainland Europe and the defeat of Nazi Germany. However, unlike the Pacific, where the USN had to carry amphibious forces huge distances, the European theatre involved shorter distances. Much of this was in relatively coastal regions. Starting with the LCT (1) group, the RN steadily built up its invasion craft. Like all ships of the period, camouflage varied considerably and no doubt these vessels would have not had as a high priority as those that went to sea frequently. This unit is in duck egg blue overall with mid-blue contrast. The type could carry seven light or three to four medium tanks. Canvas could be spread over the tank deck for protection from the elements.

LCT 131
LCT (2) 1944

Many LCTs adopted WS white or very pale grey with a second colour added. In this case, it is WA green. The vessel is armed with two single 2pdr aft. They could carry seven 20-ton tanks, or three larger ones. The open tank deck usually had a canvas cover spread over it to provide cover for the cargo being carried. It was never intended that large numbers of personnel would be carried for long periods of time and the facilities were therefore limited. It was always intended that they would be scrapped when the war ended and thus they were not built to last. As a result, some were flimsy and had to undergo refits to strengthen them.

LCT 395
LCT (3) 1944

This class were slightly larger than the previous groups, but at first they had strength problems and had to be given extra strengthening. Over 600 were built and they served in most theatres where the RN was present. The armament remained the same and there are two single 2pdr side by side aft. The scheme adopted is a simple MS4a grey and MS3. The canvas spread over the tank decks and all upper surfaces were painted mid- or dark grey which could vary from ship to ship.

LCT 491
LCT (3) 1944

Landing craft of this type served in many areas including the Mediterranean. This vessel is shown in a camouflage of MS4 and 1940 green. They could carry eleven medium tanks and up to ten 30cwt lorries. They were developed from the previous group of LCTs but had an extra 32ft section added amidships. The tank deck could be covered with canvas to provide protection from the weather. Canvas and all upper surfaces were painted dark grey.

LCF 6
Ex-LCT (3) 1944

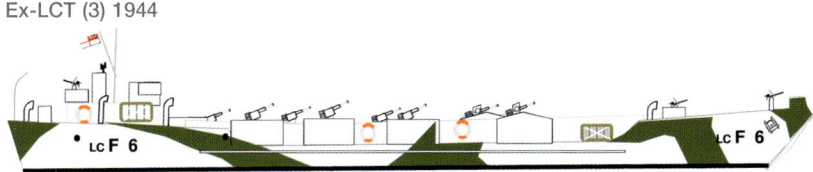

It was expected the Luftwaffe would strongly oppose any landings in Europe. To help provide protection all the way into the beachhead, some LCTs were converted to AA vessels. They were designated Landing Craft Flak (LCF). The armament is formidable for a small ship. There are powered 2pdr AA port and starboard, with manual single 2pdrs aft of them. Forward, there were two single 20mm on the centreline, with the forward one able to engage enemy coastal craft. At the stern they had one or two single 20mm. Part of the tank deck was converted to accommodate the extra crew and to expand support facilities, ammunition stowage etc. Although rarely engaged against the Luftwaffe, these vessels could deliver a lot of firepower onto a beach target and proved valuable in close support. The overall shade is MS4a with darkened 1940 green patches.

LCF 17
Ex-LCT (3) 1944

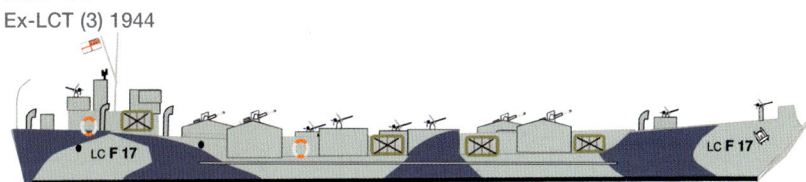

LCF 17 was a later unit and had an armament of four single powered 2pdr mountings and eight single 20mm AA. This vessel is in B6 and B5. Upper surfaces were dark grey. The 'F' and '17' of her identification are bold to enable easy recognition from other craft. They did not spend as much time at sea as larger warships. The original tank deck was given light plating so the AA crews could move about more easily. Ballast was carried to compensate for all the AA weapons. LCFs were quite successful in service and proved very versatile.

LCG (L) 17
Ex-LCT (3) 1944

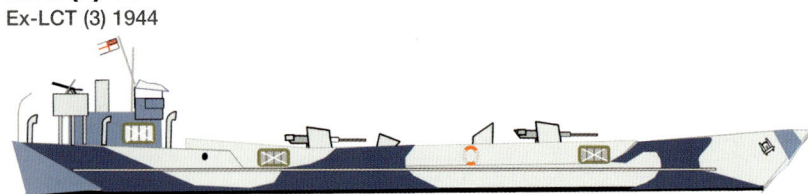

It was foreseen that landing craft would require heavy gun support closer inshore than most warships could provide. To achieve that, guns removed from destroyers refitted as escorts were made available. Two 4.7in were mounted and the craft strengthened to take the weight and shock of recoil. The previous tank deck was mostly plated over and ballast added to compensate for the extra weight carried up higher than the design intended. This vessel has a three-colour camouflage scheme of 1941 blue, duck egg blue and an overall MS4a. Upper surfaces would, of course, be dark grey. The bow doors were usually welded shut but nonetheless they could still beach to provide gunnery support right from the shoreline.

LCT 1022
LCT (4) 1944

This class returned to smaller dimensions and was criticised for flimsy construction. They therefore had additional strength added to the hull and, if to be sent to the Far East, were strengthened even further. Two single 20mm were carried aft. This vessel is shown in a white and blue-grey scheme that covers the mid-section of the hull. These craft could make 10 kts and their range was adequate for European waters. They could carry six to twelve tanks or a dozen three-ton lorries.

LCT 4008
LCT (8) 1944

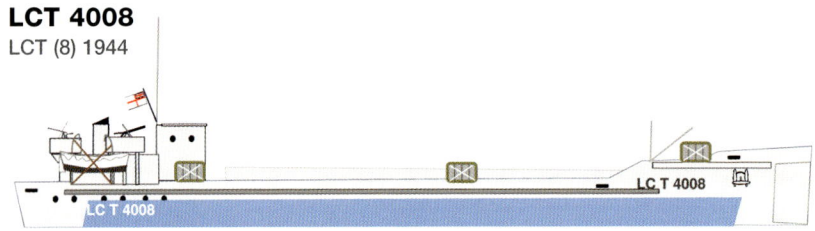

It was apparent by 1943 that the war had turned against Germany and there would be a need for tank landing craft that could travel much further distances such as experienced in Asia and the Pacific. These vessels had a ship bow and door similar to the large LST types. They were of a very blocky design and intended to be easily built by small shipyards with little experience of naval work. They were strongly built and retained in service for some years after the war. This unit has the typical Far East blue panel on a pale 507c grey hull.

LCG(M) 103
Ex-LCT(3) 1944

Some craft were built with a ship bow and were not intended to be beached. Internal arrangements were planned from the start rather than converted from existing types. The main armament was enclosed in two specially-designed turrets which could mount either 25pdr field guns or 17pdr anti-tank guns. These were Army guns manned by Army gunners. Light AA was two single 20mm port and starboard. Two twin Lewis guns or BESA MGs were mounted on the bridge. The round objects aft of the 20mm mounting are not DCs but water tanks. There are smoke floats and a smoke generator aft. Note the way the number is presented with the 'G' and '103' prominent. There were so many variations of landing craft and so many operating in the same area that it could get confusing. Hence 'G 103' was kept the most prominent. The scheme uses white to make the craft look shorter or further away, which would be important if German gunners were trying to range in on her.

LCT 1233
LCT (4) 1944

This LCT has a central blue panel to provide a shortening effect and it includes a false bow. There are areas of green on the superstructure, but the main part of the hull is a very pale duck egg blue. This type of scheme was worn by units sent to the Far East.

LCT 4095
LCT (8) 1944

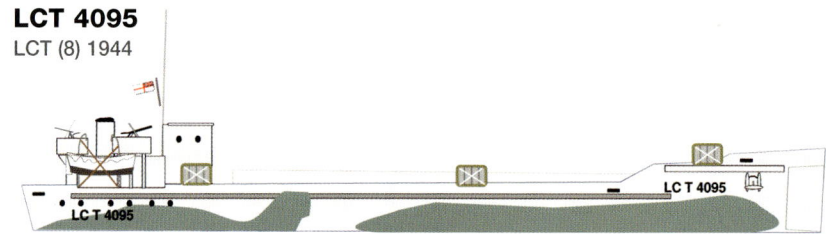

Extra strength and size allowed these vessels to carry up to eight medium tanks or thirteen three-ton lorries for much greater distances. The armament was increased to four single 20mm Oerlikon guns giving them two guns that could cover any bearing. This craft is wearing MS3 on MS4a grey camouflage, suited for European operations.

MISCELLANEOUS VESSELS

HMS BACHAQUERO
LST 1942

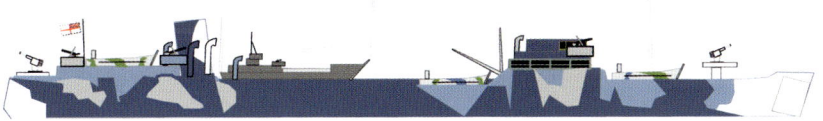

At the outbreak of WWII, the British started to consider ways of delivering tanks onto a beach but the idea did not receive much priority until the fall of France because, until then, ports were always available. This ship and her sister ship were oil tankers with low draught used for delivery of fuel to shallow ports. The entire tank area was stripped out to create a large open vehicle deck. Bow doors were added and the hull forward somewhat flattened. There was a landing ramp which could be extended onto the beach to enable vehicles to disembark. Each ship was equipped with smoke mortars to cover their approach to a beach. AA armament comprised four single 2pdr and six 20mm Oerlikons. LCMs could be carried on deck. Between twenty-two and thirty tanks could be carried depending on their size or up to thirty-three three-ton lorries and 217 troops. The scheme has white at the bow, then mid-blue and 1941 blue with some patches of MS4.

HMS DAFFODIL F101
LSS 1942

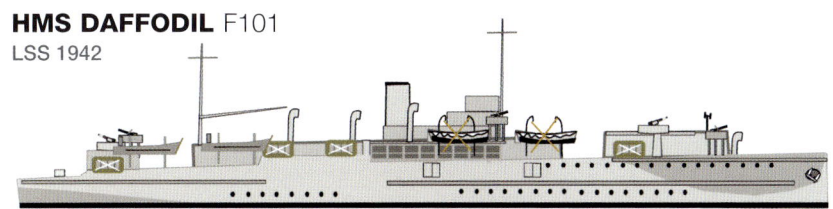

This ship was a pre-war train ferry converted as a landing craft carrier. These were discharged via the stern ramp. Troops could exit via side doors. The vessel was roomy, if not the most attractive ship ever built. It was armed with four single 2pdr AA and five 20mm. It could carry thirteen LCM (1) or nine LCM (3) and 105 troops. There are numerous photographs of this ship and it appears to have been painted B55 grey throughout the war.

SS LLANGIBBY CASTLE 4.196
LSI 1941

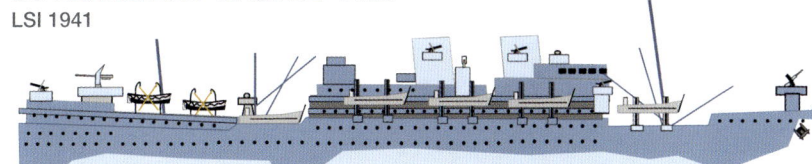

Llangibby Castle was one of many liners employed for amphibious operations but not commissioned as RN ships. This ship was called to service for several operations but, in between, operated as a troopship. The scheme is a three-colour Admiralty type with white at the bow, mid-blue and duck egg blue. Merchant-manned ships performed valuable service and were able to save the RN finding crews for them as manpower problems became acute in 1944. The ship is well armed with two 4in AA and eight 20mm AA, which were Army-manned.

Z346
LLV 1940

Because of the limited capacity of some Mediterranean ports, especially North African, the British built a large number of craft based on the LCT (1) and known as Z Lighters. These numerous craft were used to transport tanks, vehicles and soldiers from ships directly onto beaches. They had a large, strong ramp forward which was controlled by a powerful winch system on a lattice tower. This unit is shown painted in dark and light British Army stone which probably suited the area where it was in use.

HMS GLENGYLE 4.196
LSI 1941

Three 'Glen' class ships were requisitioned for conversion as troop transports and then Landing Ships Infantry (LSI). During operations in the Mediterranean in the darkest period of the war, *Glengyle* wore a camouflage scheme which was almost an elaborate WWI style. These ships were commissioned into the RN rather than operated as mercantile vessels. They were engaged in some dangerous operations, especially in the Mediterranean theatre. On an overall white ship, there are panels and triangles of black, 1941 blue and mid-blue. As she was a valuable target, the camouflage was obviously intended to hide what she actually was from attacking aircraft. Normally, only fully-fledged warships carried such schemes.

HMCS PRINCE DAVID 4.196
LSI 1941

The Canadian Armed Merchant Cruiser *Prince David* was converted to an LSI in 1943. In her new state, she could carry 444 troops. There were two LCMs and six LCPs. The director was retained and controlled the forward twin 4in AA. There was a single 40mm in front of the bridge and six single 20mm AA as well. The scheme is a typical mid-war Admiralty light type normally of three colours, MS4a, B20 and mid-blue, but in this instance the forward mount was white, as was the bridge. Types 285 and 271 radar are carried.

HMT BUSTLER W72
Bustler Class Rescue Tug 1942

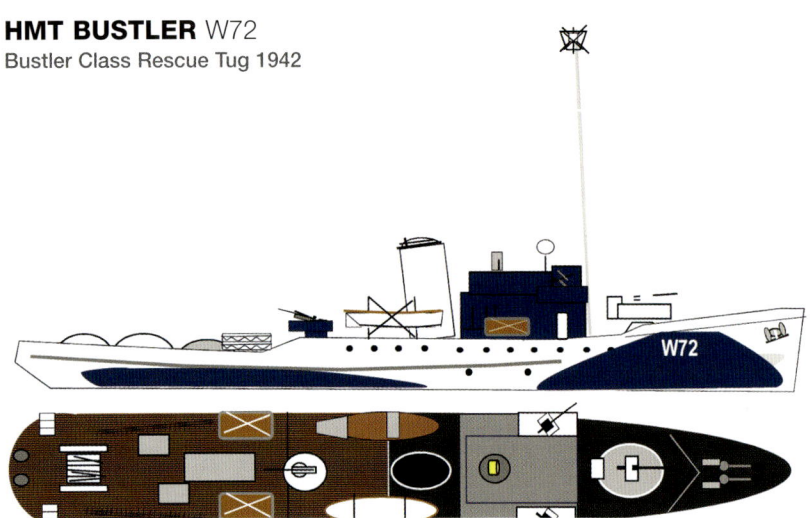

HMT ATTENTIF W68
(Ex-French) Naval Rescue Tug 1942

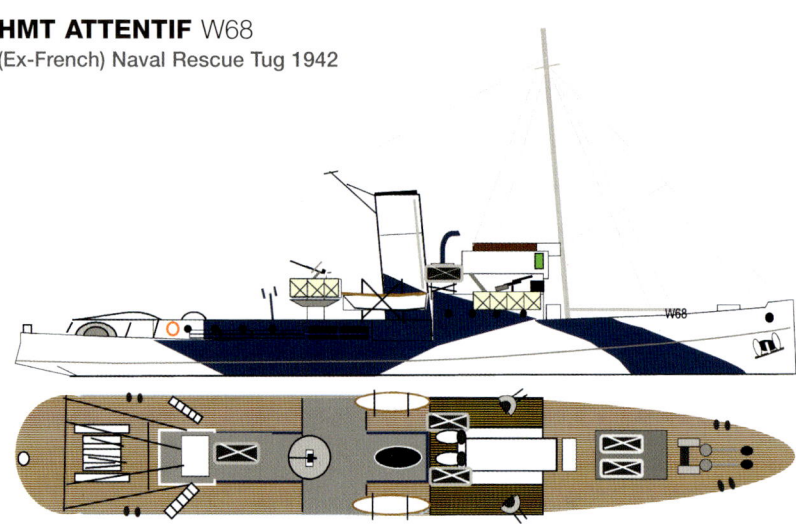

Rescue tugs were vital and had to be well armed as they often went way out into the North Atlantic to rescue damaged or distressed merchant ships. *Bustler* had a 3in forward, 2pdr aft and single Oerlikons in each bridge wing. The tug is shown with Type 286 radar to help find ships in need of aid. This would be changed to Type 291 later. Depth charges aft were defensive or to scuttle ships too damaged to tow home. Rescue tugs had to capable of fighting fires and help merchant crews with damage control during the recovery.

Attentif wears an overall white scheme with PB10 blue areas to break up her outline. She has only one 20mm Oerlikon aft and Lewis guns in the bridge wings. Ships of this kind took many risks to bring home battle-damaged merchantmen and warships. She carries DCs purely to drive U-boats off. The decks are planked as they were more comfortable when crew had to stand on them for long periods of time.

HMT TENACITY W18
Assurance Class Rescue Tug 1943

HMT GROWLER W105
Bustler Class Rescue Tug 1942

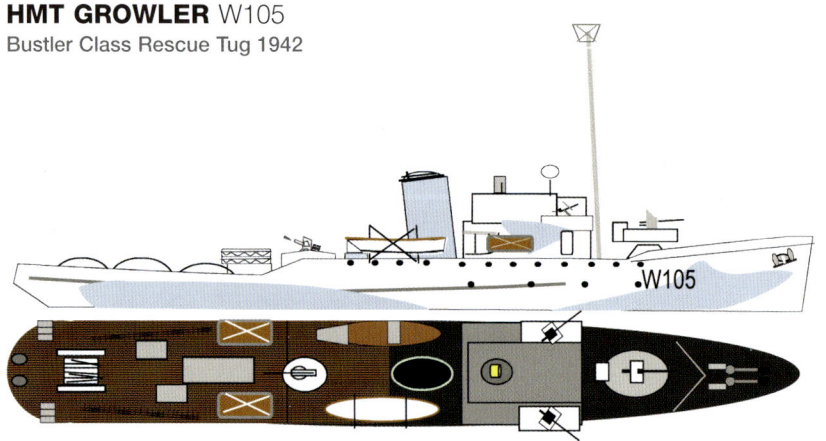

Tenacity was a large high seas rescue tug and is shown with an Admiralty light camouflage scheme utilising pale MS4a grey and pale WA blue offset with a patch of B5 dark blue grey. She has a 12pdr aft of the funnel and two single 20mm forward. This class were built by the RN specifically for the role, rather than being requisitioned commercial tugs.

Growler is shown in a typical WA scheme of blue and white. A Type 286 radar is carried at the masthead, 3in gun forward, 2pdr amidships and two 20mm AA. Depth charges were defensive and could be dropped to make U-boats think the vessel had ASW capability. However, they could also be used to help scuttle ships too damaged to tow home as the 3in gun would have had difficulty achieving that.

MISCELLANEOUS VESSELS

HMS HILARY F22
LSH 1943

Hilary was a small liner taken up as an ocean boarding vessel in the examination service, initially, and then converted to a headquarters ship for landing operations. The ship served in that role until the end of WWII. Armament comprised a single 6in gun forward, a 12pdr AA aft, three single and six twin 20mm Oerlikon AA plus four quad 2pdr AA. She could carry a mixture of smaller-type landing craft and, when operating as a HQ, often carried only four. Troop capacity was 378 men with full equipment for reasonably short distances. Note the array of electronics carried for her HQ role. Types 271, 291 and 293 radar with an egg-timer Type 253 IFF.

HMS ULSTER MONARCH F22
LSI 1943

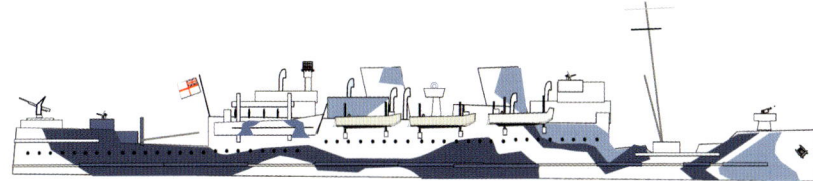

Many small liners were converted to landing ships after service in other roles. They were particularly useful for commando operations as well as major landings. *Ulster Monarch* is shown with an Admiralty-designed light disruptive scheme of 507c overall, PB10 and pale blue. The lines of colour would add confusion if the ship was being estimated for size. There is a 12pdr AA aft, two 2pdrs side by side forward and four single 20mm as well.

HMS KING SALVOR W191
Ocean Salvage Vessel 1942

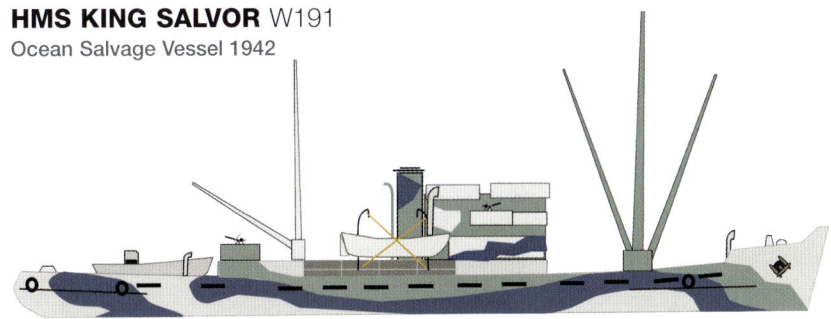

Salvage vessels were very important for clearing wrecks that were sunk in shallow waters where they blocked shipping routes as well as in recovering vessels that could be salvaged. *King Salvor* is shown in an Admiralty dark disruptive scheme of three colours; MS3, PB10 and MS4a. Her armament was quite light and comprised four single 20mm AA.

HMS BARSOUND Z89
Boom Defence Vessel 1943

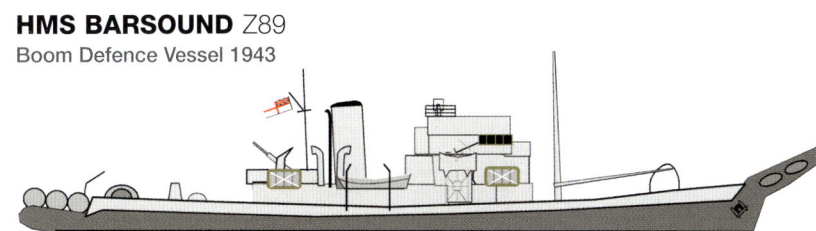

Many vessels were required to lay and open and close the boom defence nets protecting harbours. These ships also had to be large enough to travel to wherever they were needed, and armed to deal with the occasional intruder. *Barsound* had a 3in AA gun aft and two single 20mm in the bridge wings. There were also various MGs that could be mounted as required. The rounded stern was to facilitate the easy laying of buoys and nets. The ship is shown in a simple dark 507b grey lower hull and MS4a grey above that. There was no requirement for these vessels to be heavily camouflaged, not least because incoming ships needed to be able to spot them and locate harbour entrances.

SHIP INDEX

A

Abelia	100
Aberdeen	80
Aberdare	109
Adamant	151
Albury	109
Achates	33
Action	106
Acute	114
Adrias	72
Agassiz	101
Aire	90
Alarm	115
Albrighton	71
Algerine	115
Algoma	103
Algonquin	62
Alisma	102
Alynbank	131
Aylsse	101
Amazon	32
Amethyst	85
Ambuscade	32
Anguilla	93
Annapolis	30
Antigonish	91
Anthony	33
Apostolis	103
Arbutus	105
Arcady	125
Ardrossan	112
Ariguani	133
Arran	124
Arrowhead	101
Artifex	150
Arunta	41
Ascension	93
Ashanti	40, 41
Assistance	149
Assiniboine	34
Athabaskan	42
Atherstone	68
Athene	152
Attentif	156
Aubrietia	99
Auckland	83
Avon	89
Avon Vale	68
Azalea	100

B

B 3	147
Bachaquero	155
Badsworth	71
Ballinderry	90
Bankcert	56
Bamborough Castle	106
Bangor	112
Barcoo	92
Barfleur	65
Barsound	157
Bataan	42
Bazley	96
Beagle	34
Beaumaris	112
Belleview	105
Bengal	118
Bentick	96
Berkeley	67
Betony	105
Bicester	70
Bickerton	96
Bideford	79
Bingera	128
Bittern	83
Blaauwberg	128
Blackmore	69
Blackswan	86
Blankley	68, 69
Blean	71
Boadicea	35
Bowmanville	107
Boxer	150
Boxol	150
Bramble	110
Bramble (ii)	115
Brave	116
Brecon	73
Bridgewater	77
Bridport	111
Brighton	29
Brissenden	73
Brittomart	111
Broke	26
Bulldog	35
Burnie	117
Burra	123
Bustler	156
Butser	122
Buxton	29
BYMS 2022	119
BYMS 2070	119
BYMS 3244	120

C

Cadmus	116
Caesar	65
Caicos	93
Caistor Castle	107
Calvay	124
Cambrian	65
Campanula	103
Campbell	26, 27
Caprice	64
Cardigan Bay	94
Carisbrooke Castle	107
Carron	64
Cassandra	65
Catherine	118
Cattistock	68
Cauvery	87
Cavalier	64
Chameleon	115
Charlock	105
Chesterfield	28
Chiddingfold	70
Clare	28
Clayoquot	114
Cleveland	67
Clive	76
Clyde	146
Coldstreamer	125
Comet	65
Convolvulus	102
Cornwallis	75
Cossack	40
Cotillion	126
Crane	85
Croome	69
Cygnet	86

D

Daffodil	155
Dart	89
Decoy	35
Defender	35
Deiatelnyi	30
Delphinus	128
Diamantina	92
Dodman Point	149
Doomba	110
Duncan	36
Dundee	79

E

Eastbourne	111
Easton	72
Eclipse	36
Echo	36
Eggesford	72
Egret	83
Elkins	96
Ellesmere	126
Emperor of India	132
Enchantress	82
Erne	86
Escapade	37
Esk	36
Eskimo	40
Ettrick	90
Exe	89
Exmoor	69

F

Falmouth	79
Fame	37
Faulknor	37
FDT 13	150
Fleetwood	80
Folkestone	78
Forest Hill	105
Forth	151
Fowey	78
Foxglove	75
Foxtrot	124
Friendship	116
Frisio	103

G

Gardenia	99
Garland	38
Gascoyne	92
Guardian	151
Gentian	102
Georgetown	30
Gild Edge	128
Gleaner	110
Glengyle	155
Gloxinia	101
Goatfell	134
Godavari	84
Goodall	96
Goonambee	129
Goreleston	82
Graph	147
Grey Owl	143
Grey Shark	143
Grecian	118
Grenade	38
Grenadier	125
Grenville (i)	38
Grenville (ii)	60
Griffin	38
Grimsby	79
Grove	70
Growler	156
Gurkha (i)	40
Gurkha (ii)	50
Guysborough	113

H

H41	145
Hadley Castle	106
Haida	42
Halcyon	111

SHIP INDEX

Hampton	139	Kenilworth Castle	106	Loch Alvie	95	ML 121	137	Northern Foam	122
Hardy (ii)	61	Keppel	25	Loch Dunvegan	95	ML 177	138	Northern Gem	122
Harrier	110	Kerrera	125	Loch Eck	94	ML 251	138	Northern Pride	122
Hastings	77	Khartoum	43	Loch Fyne	95	ML 288	138	Notts County	126
Havoc	39	Kilbride	94	Loch Glendhu	95	ML 303	137	Nubian	43
Haydon	72	Kilchrenan	94	Loch Killen	95	ML 343	137		
HDML 1322	143	Killegray	127	Loch Morlich	95	ML 344	137	**O**	
Heiyo	76	Kilmarnock	94	Longbranch	105	ML 579	137	Oakley (ii)	71
Hepactica	101	Kimberly	46	Lookout	49	ML 814	137	Obdurate	53
Herald	76	Kingfisher	98	Lotus	104	ML 823	138	Obedient	53
Hesperus	39	King Salvor	157	Lowestoft	80	MMS 12	118	Odin	145
Hibiscus	99, 100	Kingston Olivine	127	LST 61	152	MMS 16	119	Offa	53
Hilary	157	Kipling	45	LST 305	152	MMS 248	119	Olna	151
Hind	86	Kittiwake	98, 99	LST 3009	152	MMS 1022	119	Onslaught	52
Hindustan	79	Kiwi	120	LST 3023	152	MMS 1044	119	Onslow	52
Hogue	65	Kujawiak	70	Lupin	75	Moa	120	Opportune	53
Hotspur	38					Monnow	89	Oribi	53
Hound	116	**L**		**M**		Montgomery	30	Orillia	102, 103
Huron	42	L23	145	Malcolm	26	Montrose	26, 27	Orissa	113
Hurricane	39	La Combattante	72	Mahratta	51	Moresby	76	Orkan	51
Hurworth	70	La De'Couverte	92	Mallard	98	Morris Dance	126	Orwell	53
		Ladybird	149	Maori	41	MTB 33	141	Othello	129
I		Laforey	50	Maplin	132	MTB 66	141	Otis	145
Ibis	85	La Melpomène	73	Matchless	50	MTB 267	142		
Icarus	39	Lance	50	Martin	50	MTB 311	142	**P**	
Indus	81	Lapwing	87	Mary Cam	125	MTB 363	141	PA 2	104
Inglefield	39	Lawford	96	Medicine Hat	114	MTB 378	142	Palomares	131
Ingonish	113	Lawrence	76	Melbreak	72	MTB 424	141	Pangbourne	109
Intensity	106	LCF 6	153	Mermaid	87	MTB 509	141	Patia	133
Iroquois	42	LCF 17	153	MGB 13	140	MTB 520	141	Panther	54
Islay	124	LCG (L) 17	154	MGB 53	140	MTB 607	142	PB 101	18
		LCG (M) 103	154	MGB 64	140	MTB 660	142	Parramatta	81
J		LCT 131	153	MGB 79	140	MTB 673	143	Pathan	75
Jackal	44	LCT 299	153	MGB 100	140	Musketeer	51	Pegasus	133
Janus	43	LCT 395	153	MGB 123	140	Myngs	63	Pelican	84
Jason	111	LCT 491	153	MGB 312	139			Peony	101
Javelin	44	LCT 1022	154	MGB 328	139	**N**		Perseus	145
Jeanne Deans	132	LCT 1233	154	Middlesborough	113	Nada	103	Petard	54
Jed	90	LCT 4008	154	Mildura	117	Napier	45	Petrobus	149
Johan Maurits van Nassau	92	LCT 4095	154	Milford	80	Narbada	84	Petrolia	106
Jupiter	43, 44	Legion	49	Milne	51, 52	Navarinon	36	Piorun	46
		Leith	80	Miscou	125	Nestor	47	Pirie	117
K		Levandou	139	Mistral	73	Nepal	45	Plover	152
Kandahar	45	Levis	91	ML 065	136	Newmarket	29	Porcupine	54
Kapuskasing	116	Lewes	29	ML 084	136	New Waterford	91	Porpoise	146
Kashmir	45	Liberia	128	ML 103	136	Nith	90	Pozarica	131
Keith	35	Lightning	49	ML 106	136	Nizam	47	Prince David	155
Kellet	109	Lismore	117	ML 108	136	Nordkyn	102	Prince Robert	134
Kelly	44	Lively	49	ML 111	136	Norman	45	Primula	100
Kelvin	45	Llangibby Castle	155	ML 120	138	Northern Duke	129	Puckeridge	71

SHIP INDEX

Puffin	98
Punjabi	40

Q

Quadrant	55
Quail	54
Quality	55
Quantock	67
Queen of Thanet	120
Quentin	55
Quiberon	56
Quilliam	54
Quorn	67

R

Racehorse	58
Raider	58
Rajputana	113
Ramsey	29
Rapid	58
Recruit	115
Red Deer	114
Regent	145
Regulus	116
Restigouche	34
Ripley	29
RML 529	139
Roebuck	58
Rosemary	75
Rother	89
Rotherham	58
Rowena	115
Royal Eagle	132
Royal Mount	90

S

Sabre	16
Safari	146
Saladin	16
Salamander	110
Salisbury	30
Saltash	109
Sandwich	77
Sarawak	93
Sardonyx	15
Satyr	146
Saumarez	59
Savage	59
Scarborough	78
Scimitar	15

Scout	16
Seaham	112
Seawolf	146
Sharpshooter	111
Shearwater	99
Sheldrake	98
Shoreham	78
Sikh	41
Silvio	76
Sir Geraint	123
Sir Tristam	123
Skate	14
Skeena	33, 34
Shawinigan	102
Shikari	15
Somaliland	93
Soroy	104
Sioux	62
South Sea	127
Springbank	131
Springdale	151
Spry	100
Starling	87
St. Albans	30
Stanley	28
Steadfast	118
Stoke City	128
Stord	59
Stork	83
Storm	146
Stronghold	17
Stuart	27
Stuart Prince	150
Sturdy	15
Sutlej	84
Sutton	109
Svenner	59
Swan	81
Swansea	91

T

Tallyho	147
Tantivy	146
Tartar	41
Tawhai	127
Teazer	60
Temptress	104
Tenacity	156
Tenedos	16
Toronto	91

Townsville	117, 118
Thanet	17
Thermistocles	70
Thunder	114
Tribune	146
Troubridge	60
Tui	120
Tunsberg Castle	107
Tuscan	60
Tynedale	67
Tynwald	134

U

Ulster Queen	133
Ulster Monarch	157
Ulysses	61
Undine	60
Unison (B3)	147
Unity	147
Unrivalled	147
Urania	61
Urchin	61
Ursa	61

V

Vagabond	147
Vampire	21
Valorous	22
Van Galen	46
Vanity	22
Vansittart	24
Vanquisher	24
Vega	23
Vendetta	22
Venetia	19
Verulam	62
Veteran	18
Verity	25
Veronica	104
Viceroy	22
Vimy	25
Violet	104
Virago	62
Viscount	24
Vizalma	129
Volage	61
Vortigern	18
Voyager	21
Vivacious	19

W

W101	114
Walker	24
Wallace	23, 24
Walney	82
Walpole	21
Watchman	25
War Hindoo	151
Warramunga	42
Warrego	81
Waterhen	21
Wave King	149
Wayland	150
Wellington	80
Wentworth	91
Wessex (i)	20
Wessex (ii)	63
Weston	79
Whaddon	67
Whimbrel	85
Whirlwind	63
Whitehall	25
Whitehaven	113
Wild Goose	86
Wild Swan	20
Winchester	21
Windsor	19
Witherington	20
Wizard	62
Wolfhound	23
Wolverine	21
Woodcock	85
Woodpecker	85
Woolston	23
Worthing	112
Wivern	19
Wrangler	62
Wye	89

Y

Yarra	81
Yestor	123

Z

Zambesi	64
Zealous	64
Zebra	63
Zest	63
Zodiac	63
Z 346	155